P9-CFC-111

Cherish

Cultivating Relationships with Parents, Friends, Guys, and More

Vicki Courtney

JESSAMINE COUNTY PUBLIC LIBRARY
600 South Main Street
Nicholasville, KY 40356
(859)885-3523

B&H
PUBLISHING GROUP
Nashville, Tennessee

Copyright © 2016 by Vicki Courtney

All rights reserved.

Published in association with the literary agency D.C. Jacobson & Associates, LLC, an Author Management Company, www.dcjacobson.com, and Alive Communications, Inc., an Author Management Company, www.alivecommunications.com.

ISBN 978-1-4336-8784-6

Published by B&H Publishing Group
Nashville, Tennessee

Dewey Decimal Classification: 302
INTERPERSONAL RELATIONS / GIRLS /TEENAGERS

Unless otherwise noted, all Scripture is taken from the Holman Christian Standard Bible (HCSB), Copyright © 1999, 2000, 2002, 2003, 2009 by Holman Bible Publishers, Nashville Tennessee. All rights reserved.

Those Scriptures marked CEV are from the Contemporary English Version. © 1991 by the American Bible Society. Used by permission. Those Scriptures marked ESV are from the English Standard Version. © 2001 by Crossway Bibles, a division of Good News Publishers. Those marked NIV are from the Holy Bible, New International Version®, NIV® Copyright ©1973, 1978, 1984, 2011 by Biblica, Inc.® Used by permission. All rights reserved worldwide. Those marked NKJV are from THE NEW KING JAMES VERSION. © 1982 by Thomas Nelson, Inc. Used by permission. All rights reserved. Those marked NLT are from the Holy Bible. New Living Translation copyright© 1996, 2004, 2007, 2013 by Tyndale House Foundation. Used by permission of Tyndale House Publishers Inc., Carol Stream, Illinois 60188. All rights reserved.

Printed in October 2015 in LongGang District, Shenzhen, China

1 2 3 4 5 6   20 19 18 17 16

Introduction

If you saw it, you wouldn't think much of it. It's an old painted glass Christmas ornament that's probably around sixty to seventy years old. The red paint is faded and chipping off in some places, revealing a splotchy silver undertone. Because it's old and extremely fragile, I keep it wrapped in tissue paper and pack it away in a box to protect it. The ornament is not particularly pretty, and it's certainly not valuable, but I cherish it. Why? Because the ornament belonged to my grandparents, and they used to hang it on their Christmas tree each year.

My grandparents are gone now, and every year at Christmastime, I look forward to unpacking the old, dingy ornament and hanging it on my Christmas tree because it reminds me of them and the Christmas Eve celebrations in their home. What I would give to go back and celebrate just one more night before Christmas in my grandparents' home! I cherish the memories of my big, loud family gathered together in their cramped living room with our plates piled high with food (including my grandmother's famous green Jell-O salad). We would sing Christmas carols (out of tune) and read the Christmas story (Luke 2:1–20) before tearing into a pile of Christmas presents.

As a child, I was far more focused on what was in the presents *under* the tree than the old red ornament hanging *on* the tree in the backdrop of our family scene. Today, I couldn't tell you what was in any of those packages because nothing I received had lasting value. But I cherish the ornament because it is a reminder of a gift that matters more than material things—the gift of relationships. If you look up the word *cherish* in the dictionary, you might find this definition: "to hold or treat as dear; feel love for." We might love a lot of things, but we don't necessarily cherish everything we love.

The ornament reminds me of some of the relationships I "hold or treat as dear" in my life. It reminds me of the relationship I had with my grandparents, but more importantly, it reminds me of the relationship my grandparents had with Christ. Their faith was a huge factor in my decision to become a Christian and follow Jesus Christ when I was twenty-one, the relationship I cherish most in this life.

What do you cherish?

On your list, you might include your smart phone, Blue Bell ice cream, summer vacation, your very own bedroom, or maybe an assortment of other material items. Can I tell you something? These things won't matter as much to you in fifty to sixty years (except for maybe the Blue Bell!), but you know what will? Your relationships and the memories you make in them.

Cherish was written as a guide to help you navigate the relationships that matter most in your life—your relationships with family, friends, guys, and God. Whether you read *Cherish* on your own or grab a few friends and read it together, it is my prayer that your relationships will be richer as you learn to cherish what truly matters most in this life.

Vicki Courtney

As you read, you'll find several QR codes with questions next to them. Using any QR reader app, scan the codes to connect to videos of teen girls giving their answers to the questions. How do their answers compare to yours?

When you see a QR code like this, scan it!

Scan for Video Answers!

About the Writers . . .

Vicki Courtney is a speaker and best-selling author of numerous books and Bible studies. She began writing about the culture's influence on tween and teen girls in 2003 and has a passion to see girls and women of all ages find their worth in Christ. Vicki is married to Keith, and they live in Austin, Texas. They are parents to three grown children, who are all married and live nearby. Vicki enjoys spending time at the lake, hanging out with her family, and spoiling her grandchildren rotten. More information about Vicki can be found at VickiCourtney.com.

Pam Gibbs (project editor) is a writer, editor, speaker, youth minister, and amateur archer, but her favorite titles are wife and mom. She is a graduate of Southwestern Baptist Theological Seminary and leads teens at her church. When she's not hanging out with her tween daughter and teacher/coach husband, you'll find her curled up with a good mystery book and some dark chocolate.

Susie Davis is the author of *Unafraid: Trusting God in an Unsafe World*. She and her husband, Will, cofounded Austin Christian Fellowship, where they pastor some of the most fabulous people in town. Susie loves McDonald's coffee, pink geraniums, and the yellow finches that flood her backyard every morning. For more info, visit her website at susiedavis.org.

Whitney Prosperi has a heart for girls and girls' ministry. She is the author of *Life Style: Real Perspectives from Radical Women in the Bible*, a twelve-week Bible study for middle and high school girls, as well as *Girls' Ministry 101*, published by Youth Specialties. She lives in Tyler, Texas, with her husband, Randy, and daughters, Annabelle and Libby.

Contents

Friends

4 Must-Have's in a Real Friend

by Whitney Prosperi

A friend loves at all times.

—Proverbs 17:17

One afternoon when I was in college, my friend Tammy and I went to the grocery store. Before we even began our shopping trip, we started goofing around, and soon we were speeding the length of the store with our shopping cart (not a good idea, by the way).

When Tammy got some speed going, she jumped up on the metal rail under the front of the cart and started to coast. Well, here's a tip for free: make sure the cart can hold your weight. The end of the cart tipped up, and Tammy fell headfirst into the basket. The shopping cart (with her inside) turned upside down and flew toward the deli counter.

Honestly, it was one of the funniest things I have seen. Ever. And also the scariest. But she and the deli meat survived. Her hands were cut and bruised from the shopping cart. Her ego hurt worse.

After Tammy and her racing cart came to a halt, and while I was helping her climb out and stand up, we noticed one of our other friends a few aisles away staring at us. We waved at her. And then it happened: she literally acted like she didn't see us. She turned around and walked the other way. She was too ashamed to talk to us.

Ever had a similar experience? Have you ever thought someone was your friend, but when you did something that embarrassed her, she dumped you and turned the other way? We've all been there. It's much worse than bruised hands and a stiff back from a shopping cart.

Real friends are sometimes hard to find, but when you discover one, you have received one of God's best gifts. How do you know if you've got an authentic, stick-with-you-through-it-all kind of friend?

The one who walks with the wise will become wise. —Proverbs 13:20

Iron sharpens iron, and one man sharpens another. —Proverbs 27:17

Whoever conceals an offense promotes love, but whoever gossips about it separates friends. —Proverbs 17:9

A good friend:

1. Doesn't ditch you.

Everyone wants to be your friend when you're throwing a big party or have an extra ticket to the concert headlined by your favorite band. But what if you trip in the lunchroom? Or when you stand up for the right thing even though it's unpopular? Will your friend support you, or will she act like you're uncool? A true friend sticks with you on your best days and your worst days.

2. Keeps a secret.

Ever had a friend who can't keep her mouth shut? You share something personal and then find out later that she texted some of your other friends. Trust is a must in real, I-can-count-on-you friendships. Ask God to bring you a friend who can—and will—keep things to herself.

3. Chooses what's right.

A true friend won't ask you to bail on what you believe. She will help you make a wise choice rather than pressure you to make a stupid one. She will choose what's right rather than what's popular. This kind of friend is crucial because you become like the people you spend time with.

4. Points you toward God.

The best kind of friend challenges you to follow Christ. She knows that you'll be happiest and most fulfilled when you pursue God. She will pray for you and remind you to put Him first. This kind of friend will help you stay on track and urge you on in your own walk with Christ.

WHAT ABOUT YOU?

Take a second to think about the kind of friend you are. Do you stand with your friends, even when it's not easy? Do you pull them down? Can you be trusted? Remember what your mom always tells you: you have to be a friend to have a friend. Becoming the kind of friend you want to find is a good place to start.

5 FRIENDSHIP FIXERS

by Susie Davis

Your friendships are a huge part of your life. You spend endless hours a week with them. You laugh together, you tell them secrets, and you share that pint of ice cream together. But even the best of friendships can get a little rocky sometimes. Sometimes you feel really close, but other times . . . If your friendship needs a little work, check out the fixers on the next page. See which ones would help right now, and keep the others in mind. You'll probably need to use those later.

Everyone should look out not only for his own interests, but also for the interests of others.

—Philippians 2:4

1. Take Second Place

Most people think of themselves first—especially teenagers. At school or on the ball field, you've learned from culture to look out for yourself first. This seems right, but what happens when you both want to be on center stage? Danger ahead.

A good friend gave me an idea to fight selfishness. It's called the "second cookie" concept: Imagine that you and your friend are at your house and your mom has just made homemade cookies. Your mom hands you the plate. What do you do? If you want to be selfless, you let your friend choose first, and you take the "second cookie." But what if your friend asks you to take one first? Chose the smallest cookie—the second choice.

2. Join the Cheer Squad

Cheer on your friend whenever you can. Support your friend when she hits a homerun or gets a good grade—even when it's better than yours. Comment when she opens the door for a senior adult. You can even help her do chores at home. Think of ways to cheer her on as she tries new things—let her show you the jewelry she's made or watch her play at the next volleyball game.

3. Give Her Space

Give your friend the freedom to enjoy other people. Don't be possessive. Don't make her feel bad about going with other friends to the mall. Instead, tell her to have a good time. You can take the opportunity to make plans with another too. Nothing will kill a friendship like possessiveness. Don't smother your friends.

4. Hang Out in the Garden

Did you know that Jesus needed supportive friends? When Jesus was grappling with his impending crucifixion, he called out a few of his best friends and took them to the Garden of Gethsemane. He asked them to remain with Him and stay awake while He poured out his heart to God. We all need "garden" friends," people who are just "there" when the world turns upside down. Go to the hospital. Sit beside her. Go to the funeral. Don't bolt when you feel uncomfortable and don't know what to do. Just *be* there.

5. Forgive First

Even your best friend will let you down. She will hurt your feelings. And sometimes you will hurt each other at the same time. The cure? Be the first to forgive. More than once, I've heard girls say, "I'll forgive her, but she has to make the first move. She has to say she's sorry first." Is that *really* forgiveness? I don't think so. Forgiving first means you care more about the friendship than you care about being right. You're willing to let go of pride for the sake of the relationship. Being the first to forgive doesn't mean that she was right or that you are more at fault than she is. It just means you are willing to let go of your hurt so you can hang on to your friend.

Just as the Lord has forgiven you, so you also must forgive.

—Colossians 3:13

When To Say Goodbye

Signs It's Time to Part Ways with a Friend

When you were young, the two of you were inseparable. You rode bikes together. Traded stuffed animals. Ate snow cones on the sidewalk. Spent the night at each other's houses—all summer long.

Now? Things are different. Strained. Awkward. Uncomfortable.

In the past, planning a trip to the mall together gave your day a lift. Now it just leaves you with a pit in your stomach.

Not every person is intended to be a lifelong friend—that lifelong friend that you'll enjoy even after college, career, and countless other changes. So how do you know when to let go of a friendship and when to fight for it? Here are signs it's time to say goodbye.

When you give and she takes

Did you ever play on a seesaw when you were a kid? My friends and I would try to balance ourselves on the teeter-totter so that we were equally in the air (we didn't understand the whole different weight thing back then). Eventually, one of us would sink down to the ground and then push back up and the balancing act would start all over again.

Friendship is a lot like that—a balancing act of give-and-take. You talk, she listens. She drives, you pay for snacks. You console her when her crush breaks her heart. She helps you study for your AP chem test. That's how friendships are supposed to work.

Only sometimes they don't. Sometimes a friend will stop giving and keep taking. That's a huge unbalance. And eventually resentment and anger will build. You might be able to talk things out, but that doesn't always work. If that's the case, then say goodbye to your playground friendship.

When you constantly fight

It's normal for best friends to fight. When you spend a lot of time together, you will get on each other's last nerve. You will disagree. You will get tired of being together. You will bicker. (Think about it. She's like a sister, right? And all sisters fight sometimes!) When that happens, spending time apart with other friends usually resets the friendship so you're back on track. Only sometimes it doesn't. When you constantly fight and can no longer respect each other's opinions, it may be time to bid farewell for good.

When the jokes get personal

Best friends joke around. You'll call each other names—as a joke. You will create personal nicknames that nobody else will understand. You'll have inside jokes. These shared experiences build and strengthen your relationship. However, if a friendship turns toxic, the jokes get personal. The side remarks are no longer funny—they are intentionally hurtful. If you hear yourself (or your best friend) constantly saying, "I'm just joking" or "I was only kidding," that's a warning sign. Either talk about what's bugging you both (which is what Jesus tells us to do), or say adios to the friendship. Trying to keep the friendship intact will only cause both of you heartache and hurt feelings.

When there's no room to breathe

When I was younger, I was friends with a girl from church. We'd known each other from events and started talking on the phone (yes, we actually used a *real* phone for a *real* conversation!) We hung out together during the summer and made frequent trips to the shaved ice hut to beat the Texas heat. When school began, though, I started to feel, well, smothered. Like Cling Wrap over my mouth smothered. She always wanted to be at my house. She always met me at my locker. She got insecure when I had plans with other friends. She called me. All. The. Time. If I didn't call back immediately, she'd call even more. I didn't understand it at the time, but she was unhealthy emotionally. She relied on me to make herself feel important. Worthy. Accepted. Luckily for me, I moved the following summer, and the distance made it easier to let the friendship fade.

If you find yourself in a friendship like this, it's time to put some distance between you and your friend. You can do this gradually by texting less, planning time with other friends, and encouraging her to make other friends. If she doesn't understand these social cues, you may be forced to have that uncomfortable conversation about not hanging out anymore. Be patient, though. Time and space often soften the blow of a friendship's end.

Gossip Much?

"Did you hear what she told Jamie?"

"Her parents were gone over the weekend. You know what was going on!"

"I can't believe she thinks she looks good in that!"

by Pam Gibbs

Gossip.

If you're a teenage girl, you can't avoid it. It's in the hallways. It's on your cell phone. It's on every social media app you have. Being a girl should come with an instruction manual on how to handle gossip when it comes your way. Unfortunately, you weren't born with one. And unfortunately, the world doesn't offer the best advice.

So how do you avoid gossip? Here are a few tips for navigating those shark-infested waters.

Avoid the Feeding Frenzy

If you've ever watched a show about sharks on TV, you know that they can engage a feeding frenzy. When this occurs, get out of the water. They smell the blood of fish in the water, and their hunting instincts kick in. First, it's just a couple of sharks. Then more arrive. Before you know it, the waters are teeming with a bunch of bloodthirsty predators who are ready to chomp down on the nearest wounded prey they can find.[1]

Girls who are prone to gossip are a lot like those sharks. They are just looking for their next victim—the girl who dresses unfashionably, the teacher with bad breath, the popular girl who gets attention from the guys. First a couple of them talk. Then more join in. Before long, an entire group of girls will tear apart the nearest available victim.

The best option for you? Avoid it. Stay away from those girls. Nothing good can come from being a part of their feeding frenzy. You'll only end up with a bad rep and the real possibility of becoming prey yourself. Sharks have been known to turn and devour each other when food is scarce. Translation? If they will gossip *with* you, those girls will gossip *about* you. Get out while you still can.

1. See http://www.redorbit.com/news/science/1112716854/bull-shark-bite-great-white-102112.

Whoever conceals an offense promotes love, but whoever gossips about it separates friends. —Proverbs 17:9

Give the Sharks Something Else to Chew On

If you are with a group of friends and you sniff blood in the water, you can avoid an all-out gossip frenzy by changing the subject. You can't stop someone from starting a rumor or talking about someone, but you can put an end to the conversation by starting another one. The subject doesn't matter—just give them something else to talk about. The upcoming ACT test. How the geometry homework is pure torture. Whether or not you want to go see the new movie over the weekend. Redirecting the conversation is a subtle yet effective way of keeping the discussion from turning into an uncontrollable free-for-all. Somebody will get wounded in the process.

Keep Your Jaws Clinched

A bull shark's bite can register a force of almost five hundred pounds, which is enough to bite a sea turtle. In half. But you won't feel the force of that pressure as long as the shark is just swimming merrily along, not concerned about food. Unless eating, most sharks keep their mouths shut. There's a lesson in that.

If a friend or classmate tells you something personal, keep it to yourself. Part of being a good listener is keeping confidential information private. You don't want your friends sharing your deepest secrets, so don't share theirs. Be known as a person whom others can trust, and you will have no shortage of friends.

When You Become the Prey

Becoming the topic of gossip is an inevitable part of being a teenage girl. At some point, you will become the person at the center of the feeding frenzy. Unfortunately. You can't control whether or not people talk about you, but you *can* control how you respond. Fighting one rumor by starting another rumor only throws more blood in the water and makes the problem worse. Gossiping about the rumor-starter is a bad idea. I know this is hard, but try not to respond at all. Pretend like the rumor is stupid and doesn't bother you at all. The bullies (yes, gossip is a form of bullying) will see you're not in the mood for a gossip war, and they will likely move on to another topic.

However, if the gossip doesn't stop, or if it intensifies into emotional abuse or physical confrontation, you need to tell someone immediately. Talk to a teacher, school counselor, or your parents. You're not a snitch or a loser. You are standing your ground and standing up for yourself. That takes courage. And self-respect.

And the best way to kill gossip is a healthy dose of self-respect.

Quiz: Are You a Gossip Girl?

1. **Your best friend gets dumped by her boyfriend. You . . .**
   a. plan a girls' night out to make her feel better.
   b. tell her you are sorry by commenting publicly on social media where all can see.
   c. quickly text a few friends with the news.

2. **You're wearing a cute new outfit. You . . .**
   a. don't mention it until someone compliments you.
   b. tell everyone—and I mean everyone—how expensive it is.
   c. point it out to your friends when they don't notice it.

3. **Your worst enemy gets caught drinking over the weekend. You . . .**
   a. question whether it's true.
   b. can't wait to tell everyone at school.
   c. text your best friend right away.

4. **You just found out you made the volleyball team. You . . .**
   a. celebrate by having a dinner out with the family.
   b. post it online for the world to see.
   c. send a group text to let your close friends know.

5. **You got your ACT score in the mail, and it's AWESOME! You . . .**
   a. tell your parents when they get home from work.
   b. take a pic of it and put it on your social media apps.
   c. text your best friend.

6. **You just found out that your parents are getting a divorce. You . . .**
   a. tell your best friend and ask her to pray for your family.
   b. use social media to talk bad about your parents.
   c. send a group text to your friends.

Scoring:

Mostly A's—So far, you've avoided being the class gossip. Be careful, though, or you will fall into the trap of talking about others.

Mostly B's—Girl! Get a grip! You are a gossip queen! Remember, nobody wants to be best friends with girls who can't keep secrets. Being a gossip can be awfully lonely.

Mostly C's—You try to avoid gossiping too much, but some things are too good to keep to yourself. You still have some things to work on.

10 *TIPS FOR SURVIVING GIRL DRAMA*

by Vicki Courtney

Let's face it, girls can be mean. If you haven't experienced some level of girl drama by now—jealousy, gossip, cliques, mean girls—then you likely just skipped high school. Girl politics is nothing new. Ask your mom. I bet she can share a story or two from her teen years.

Girls who dole out poison through girl politics are no different than the male schoolyard bully. They just leave bruised hearts instead of black eyes. This speak-your-mind-tell-it-like-it-is generation has taken the definition of *mean* to the next level. Add into the mix technology, and it's no wonder girls find themselves in a battle of alliances.

You can't avoid girl politics, so how can you deal with it while still remaining sane? Below are ten survival tips to help you avoid the landmines ahead.

1. Remember, you are who you hang out with.

If you hang out with girls who gossip, talk ugly about others, and leave girls out on purpose, chances are good that you have been dubbed one of the "mean girls" at your school. Choose your friends wisely. If you want to avoid mean girls, don't hang out with girls who have made it their favorite hobby.

2. If you are on the receiving end of girl politics, don't escalate the situation.

If you are the victim of a mean girl, remember that the instigator is provoking you to get under your skin. If she doesn't succeed, chances are she will move on. Don't even give her a minute of your time and energy. If the problem doesn't resolve itself, then consider how to respond. Talk to an adult. Talking to your friends will probably make the situation worse.

3. I realize that I may lose you on this next one, but the Bible tells us to "pray for those who mistreat you."

It's a radical concept, and few Christians will succeed in loving their enemies, much less praying for them. God knew that the best remedy for healing our own hurt feelings is to take the focus off ourselves. When we pray for others who hurt us, it keeps bitterness from taking root in our hearts and sometimes gives us compassion for the wounds of the girl who hurt you.

4. Know the difference between a clique and a peer group.

A clique is any group that purposely excludes others and acts as if they are better than everyone else. The average clique usually includes one to two strong-willed girls who are the ringleader(s) and a number of other girls who are the followers. Many sweet girls are lured into cliques because they have falsely defined their worth and base their worth on the superficial acceptance of the group. Of course, no clique is complete without one or more targeted victims.

The best way to protect yourself is to avoid cliques at all costs. On the other hand, a peer group is safe. Most girls will gravitate toward girls they have things in common with. This is normal, and there is nothing wrong with having a preference for some friends over others. When you were younger, Mom probably made you include all the girls in your class to avoid hurt feelings. As you get older, this becomes more unrealistic. The key is to be kind to everyone. Never close the door to new friendships. You may discover you have common interests with someone who is not in your peer group.

5. If you often find yourself on the receiving end of gossip, don't be flattered.

It means that they think you are a willing party and a fellow gossiper. If you make it clear you are not comfortable participating in gossip, it won't take long for your friends to figure it out. No one wants to share tasty tidbits with someone who won't play the gossip game. If you don't want to gossip but can't figure out a way to tell your friend without sounding preachy, try telling them,

"I always feel bad after I gossip, so I'm trying to do better." That way you put the problem on yourself while making it clear that you don't want to take part in gossip any longer.

6. Remember that anyone who readily shares gossip with you will readily share it about you with others.

I have witnessed gossip separate friends when one person trusted the other with their secrets. Never trust a gossip girl to keep secret things you don't want others to know, no matter how close a friend she is. If you are not getting along one day, what's to keep her from spilling the beans?

7. A true sign that a person feels good about herself is her ability to take joy in the successes of others.

The next time someone achieves something that you desperately wanted or gets asked out by the guy you like (ouch!) or gets an award and you didn't, make an effort to celebrate with her. The more you practice joy in others' successes, the easier it will become.

8. Remember this general rule: People who make fun of others are extremely insecure.

Somehow if they point out the flaws of others, they think they will feel better about their own flaws. Unfortunately, making fun of others doesn't make you feel better—it makes you feel worse. So don't fall into that trap.

9. *Avoid groupthink.*

Groupthink is when you conform to the group's point of view in order to stay in the group's favor. Many girls will go against their morals and gang up on others because the whole group is doing it. Conforming shows that you are too insecure to stand up for what's right.

10. *Consider finding a friend who also seeks to honor God in the area of girl politics, and agree to hold each other accountable.*

It's as simple as trading texts once a week to check in on each other. You should both agree in advance what you want the other person to ask you on text. For example, if you struggle with participating in gossip, ask your friend to ask you each week if you have gossiped about someone or listened to gossip. When you know that someone is going to lovingly checking in on you, you will be more likely to hold your tongue. Most importantly, agree to pray for each other.

Three-Word (or more) Gossip Starters

- Did you hear . . .
- She told me . . .
- I can't believe . . .
- She's such a . . .
- Did you know . . .
- Can you imagine . . .
- Bless her heart . . .
- Heard the news?
- Let me tell you . . .
- I'm dying to tell you . . .

THE BALANCING ACT:
Spending Time with Christian and Non-Christian Friends

You've read the Scriptures that talk about being holy and separate from the world. You've heard sermons about not being conformed to this world and have been warned about spending too much time with people who don't share your faith beliefs.

At the same time, your youth minister and Bible class teachers have encouraged you to tell your friends about Jesus. They've challenged you to break out of your Christian huddle so that other people can hear about God. Only, you can't talk about God without spending time with your non-Christian friends and classmates.

So which is it? Do you spend your spare time with Christians? Or do you take time to invest in friendships with people who don't know Christ?

The answer is yes. Both. Scripture tells believers to support and love one another, but it also tells believers to share the gospel with others. The key is finding balance between the two.

Daniel and His Friends

Perhaps you've heard of the Old Testament character named Daniel. A book in the Old Testament is named after him and chronicles his experiences. Remember Daniel in the lions' den? That's him. Early on in the book of Daniel, before his encounter with the lions, Daniel faced a different sort of dilemma.

As just a teenager, he was shipped off to Babylon because its king, Nebuchadnezzar, had overthrown Daniel's homeland. While there, he and some friends were chosen to serve in Nebuchadnezzar's court. They would undergo training for three years and then go to work. Daniel and his friends submitted themselves to the training except for one aspect—the food. To eat some of the offered food would have been a sin against God. (Long story, but it relates to clean and unclean food.)

For you and me, eating food wouldn't be a big deal. For Daniel, though, eating that food would be like following the practices of the non-Christian world (like getting drunk or gossip would be today). The Scripture says that

Daniel "resolved not to defile himself" by following these rules. Instead, he offered a solution. He asked to eat a different diet. In the end, he was healthier than everybody else, and the rest of the men adopted Daniel's dietary plan.

Daniel Walked the Line

The meat of this story isn't really about food. It's really about how Daniel walked a careful line between being in the world but not being worldly. His choices provide a great example for you and me as we try to lead our lost friends to Christ without being sucked into the world's way of thinking and acting. What can we learn from him?

1. Daniel was humble.

If you get a chance, read Daniel 1. You'll discover that Daniel didn't make a big show of his disapproval of the foreign food. He didn't yell at the Babylonians for their eating habits or pronounce judgment on them as a pagan nation. He humbly went along with the king's program as long as he could in good conscience.

When you're with friends who don't know Jesus, be careful about your attitude. Don't get judgmental with them. Don't get in their faces and confront them about their horrible sins and their fate in hell if they don't repent immediately. Nobody likes to hang around someone who thinks she's superior or better than others. Just be yourself and hang with your friends as long as you don't go against what God says.

2. Daniel spoke up when necessary.

Notice that Daniel didn't object to everything he experienced. He didn't object to the training. He was a willing participant, until the training crossed a line and would mean compromising his faith. At that point, he raised his hand in objection, so to speak.

Like Daniel, you can participate in things with your non-Christian friends—to a point. You can go to the movies. You can spend the night. You can be on the dance team. Those things are not necessarily sinful. But like Daniel, if those things will lead to sinning, you need to offer options. Offer suggestions for a different movie, like one without as much violence or language. Change the direction of a conversation. Suggest a different song or different dance moves if they are becoming too sexually suggestive. You don't have to act like a diva. Just humbly ask for an alternative.

3. Daniel didn't go it alone.

In Daniel 1, we learn that Daniel had some friends. The four of them stuck together when it mattered. Given the size of Babylon and the training they underwent (including language and literature classes), they probably didn't sit together all the time or do homework together. But when it mattered, they leaned on each other. No doubt their friendships were close. Imagine being in a foreign land away from family and away from others who shared their values.

The same applies for you. Don't try to go it alone. It's okay to spend time with non-Christian friends, but you need to have strong, deep relationships with Christian friends who share the same biblical values and who can hold you accountable if it looks like you're in too deep. Lean on each other. Pray for each other. You don't have to do everything together. (If you did, you'd never be salt and light in the world.) Just make sure that your closest friends are seeking the Lord as much as you are.

Jesus' Example—Circles of Friendship

If you look at the life of Jesus, you'll notice that He had relationships with all sorts of people—prostitutes, religious leaders, tax collectors, fishermen. However, His relationships were not all the same. Some relationships were deeper than others. Think about it this way:

The inner circle of Jesus' friends was small. Scripture shows us that on some occasions, He spent time with only Peter, James, and John. Other times, He hung out with all of the disciples—the next smallest circle. Then, He spent time with other friends, like Mary and Martha and Lazarus. As the circle gets wider, the more people are included and the relationships become less intimate, but those relationships included people who didn't yet believe in Him. The way He spent His time and energy is a model for us.

At the innermost circle should be your relationship with Christ. The next outer circle should be your closest friends, and those friends need to be growing Christians who are seeking to follow Jesus like you are. You'll want to spend a lot (but not all!) of your time with them. In the next circle are other Christian friends who aren't as close as your best friends. Then, as you move outward in your relationships, you'll include more and more non-Christian friends. You'll spend time with those people, but the friendships will not be as deep as those in your inner circle.

Here's a blank graphic for you to use.

Who belongs in the center? Yep, Jesus. Who is in the inner circle of closest friends? Write their names down. Then keep writing down names of friends and where they are in relationship to you. Hopefully, you'll discover if you have a balance of Christians and non-Christians in your life, and hopefully, you'll balance your time with them so that you can influence others who need Jesus without being wrongly influenced by them.

HOW TO BE A REAL FRIEND IN A DIGITAL WORLD

by Pam Gibbs

Acronymns. Abbreviations. Emoticons. You and your friends can carry on a complete conversation using a handful of symbols. And chances are, you've probably made fun of your mom or dad for failing miserably when they try to use the same symbols! While you may be able to carry on a dozen digital dialogues at one time, you may struggle with being able to talk to others face-to-face. Your generation is the most connected in history—gadgets, gizmos, and technology, oh my. However, your generation is also the most disconnected generation in history. You may have thousands of "friends" on different social media sites, but you may not have many in real life. Because you have grown up with a device in your hand (that many of us parents put there), your native language is not English. It's acronyms, emoticons, and incomplete sentences. As a result, developing deep, lasting friendships can be a challenge.

As I have been typing this article, I have been watching two girls sitting near me in the coffee shop. They have been sitting across from each other for at least twenty minutes now. In that time, I've heard them speak to each other twice. Yes. No. Yea. Okay. What are they doing? Both are typing into their tablets. Intensely. I don't know if they're visiting from outer Bangladesh and don't have Internet service there, but I haven't seen them look directly at each other—or anybody else for that matter—even one time. Not once.

10 Ways to Be a Real Friend

If those girls were to walk over to my table and ask my advice about developing friendships, here's what I would tell them.

1. Be in the moment.

When you are with a person, be with that person. Sounds like Eastern mystic garbage, but it's not. Be fully present. Put your phone away (or turn it completely off if you dare!). Turn off the TV, put away your tablet. Don't check the time, watch other people, daydream about your crush, or worry about your chemistry exam. Give all of your focus to the person you are with.

2. Be loyal.

A good friend doesn't ditch you when a cute guy comes along. A good friend will stand up for you and will side with you, even it isn't comfortable. She doesn't turn on you when you're the victim of a mean girl. She won't abandon you when you get dumped or even when you hurt her feelings. If you want to be a real friend, stick by others even when it's not easy.

3. Be mindful.

A good friend will remember your birthday; she will know that you can't eat chocolate and hate broccoli (doesn't everyone?). A good friend will let you know when your favorite band's newest album is available for download. Being a good friend means remembering the things that make your friend unique, the things she loves and hates, the things that make her sad and mad. Doing this means listening and being attentive (see #1).

4. Be quiet—sometimes.

Being a good friend is about give-and-take. Sometimes you talk, sometimes you listen—that's how friendships work. Don't commandeer the conversation or ramble on endlessly, clueless to the fact that your friend fell asleep ten minutes ago. How can you learn about your friend if you are the only one doing the talking?

5. Be vulnerable.

Let a friend get to know the real you, including those things that scare you, the mistakes you've made, your dreams, and your goals. A friendship cannot develop if all you talk about is superficial stuff.

6. Be honest.

Friendships cannot survive when they are based on lies. Tell her when she hurts your feelings (but be respectful when you do). Tell her when you're having a lousy day. Don't make promises you aren't willing to keep. If she is making a bad decision, gently share with her your concerns. If you don't, then who will?

7. Be respectful.

Allow her to have different opinions, likes, political views, religious ideas, and passions. Don't degrade her or make fun of her when she makes mistakes. Don't take her stuff without asking. Ask before reading her texts. Don't tell others her secrets. Agree that you will disagree sometimes.

8. Be intentional.

When she talks to you, look her in the eyes. Give her feedback so she knows you understand. Ask questions when you need clarification. Nod your head when you agree (but only when you agree). Don't start talking about a new subject when she's still talking about the other.

9. Be approachable.

If you constantly have a scowl on your face, or if you always look like your dog just died, others will hesitate to get to know you. When you walk down the hall, look others in the eye. Say hey. Don't be negative all the time. Sit with people at lunch. Be willing to meet new people.

10. Be yourself.

A friend can't get to know you on a deeper level if she doesn't really know who you are. Don't try to impress her. Laugh when you want to (and it's appropriate). Cry when you're sad. Don't put on a mask and try to be what she wants you to be. You'll be miserable, and so will she. God gave you unique gifts and abilities and a personality different than anybody else's. Let her see that, and you can't go wrong.

Q. Does social media put pressure on girls to compare themselves to others? How have you struggled with this?

Scan for Video Answers!

WHEN NOT
TO TEXT YOUR FRIENDS

WHEN YOU ARE TICKED OFF.

When you are angry with a friend, stay away from your phone. Don't rattle off an angry rant on your phone and send it. You'll only create a worse situation. Instead, cool off first. Then, evaluate the situation. Do you still need to talk? If the answer is yes, then call her. Or better yet, go see her face-to-face.

WHEN YOU NEED TO APOLOGIZE.

A text apology is lame. And lazy. And insincere. And your friends know it. When you make a big-time mistake, admit it—in person. If you can't meet up, then call her. Better a phone apology than no apology at all.

WHEN A FRIEND IS HURTING.

If a friend just broke up with her boyfriend, her feelings merit more than a text. Call her or go see her. Let her unload. Let her cry. Let her rant and rave. She will appreciate the time and energy you took to listen to her.

WHEN YOU HAVE BAD NEWS.

When my dad was first learning how to text, he actually sent me this message: "Tigger died last night." Tigger was the dog my parents had raised from a pup. He was like another member of the family. Hearing that he'd died was sad, but getting a text about it made it even worse! Keep bad news out of cyberspace and reserve it for real-world conversations.

WHEN YOU ARE REALLY, REALLY TIRED.

Two things are likely to happen: You will misunderstand your friend, or your friend will misunderstand you. When you're tired, your texts are more likely to be snarky and emotionally driven. Unfortunately, emotions can be easily misunderstood over texting. Just sign off with a quick "gnstdltbbb" (good night, sleep tight, don't let the bed bugs bite), and talk in the morning. You'll be glad you did.

ARE YOU THE JEALOUS TYPE?

by Pam Gibbs

Have you ever wanted something? I mean, really longed for it? Spent time thinking about it. Dreamed about it. Told your friends you wanted it. Maybe even prayed for it? Perhaps you wanted a boyfriend. Or to make the team. Maybe you wanted a special pair of boots. Or a car. Or to make that particular SAT score.

What happens when you don't get it? Could you live without it?

Here's a more difficult question: What if your best friend got "it"—that thing you really, really wanted?

Or what if your worst enemy got it instead?

Fury is cruel, and anger is a flood, but who can withstand jealousy?

—Proverbs 27:1

What do I do with jealous feelings?

Jealous thoughts and feelings tempt everyone, especially in an American culture that says that you should have everything you want—when you want it. However, when that temptation pops up, how do you respond? Do you give into it?

Here's a scenario: You and your best friend both like the same guy. You promised each other that if he started talking to one of you, then the other would be not get all jealous. Only he asked your best friend to hang out and not you. You feel the jealousy creep in, ever so quietly, until you secretly wished that they would have a horrible time.

Obviously, you could give in to those feelings of jealousy. You could let them take root and grow in your heart like a cancer as it eats away at the joy and gratefulness inside you. You could act on those feelings and gossip about your friend, stop talking to her, or just drop her altogether. But what's the benefit of that? In the end, you're still jealous, you lost a friend, and you got a reputation for being a gossip. Not exactly a storybook ending.

So what other choice do you have? Perspective.

What is perspective?

Perspective is the way you look at things. It's an attitude toward some-thing, a point of view. An outlook.

Before you let jealousy dictate your attitude and actions, stop and get perspective.

For example, is that guy (whom you'll probably never see again after you graduate from high school) really important enough to destroy a lifelong friendship? Probably not.

Perspective means that you re-frame the situation to see the alter-natives, to perhaps see the reality rather than being lost in the fantasy you've created.

Here's another example, one from my own life. When I was a junior in high school and got my driver's license, my parents got me a car. Or rather, a tank. A very uncool, grandmother-looking, image-killing tank on four tires. I was mortified. Horrified. And angry because I didn't get to pick out my own car. I cried.

Yes, I cried because I got a car.

I had zero perspective that day. It didn't matter that most of my friends—including my best friend—were carless. It didn't matter that my parents paid for the car. And the insurance. And the gas (which was significant, because tanks hold a lot of gas!). It didn't matter to me that they managed to provide a car for me even though they had two older children, and a mortgage, and car payments. And bills. On blue-collar salaries. Zero perspective.

The right perspective would have produced gratitude for the gift my parents had given me.

What's the right perspective?

Perspective simply turns jealousy into gratitude. When you change your perspective, you can see how God has already blessed you in innumerable ways that you probably take for granted. Your family. Your talents. Your home. Your school. Your sense of humor. Your intelligence.

Perspective means you don't get jealous when a friend gets that new pair of shoes because you know you already have a dozen pair in your closet that you never wear.

Perspective means you're not so worried about popularity because you know your worth isn't determined by the crowd.

Perspective means that you may get angry at your parents, but you're also grateful for them because they actually care about you.

Perspective means that it's okay that you don't have the newest phone. Or the best car. Or the highest GPA. Or that new pair of jeans. Why? Because you already have more than you need.

In the end . . .

Someone will always be prettier than you. Someone will be more popular.

Someone else will have a boyfriend. Or great basketball skills. Or more expensive clothes. Or . . . you get the picture. The temptation to be jealous doesn't go away—even as an adult. (That's why so many people are in debt up to their eyeballs!) The next time those feelings of jealousy creep in, try looking at the situation from a different perspective. You might find that your life is pretty sweet after all.

We must not become conceited, provoking one another, envying one another.

—Galatians 5:26

Do You Jump to Jealousy?

You tried out for the soccer team with your best friend. She made the team, but you didn't. You . . .

_____ are bummed, but you go to her games to cheer her on.

_____ avoid her for a while. It's not fair! You're a better player than she is.

A friend just got a sweet new pair of jeans. You . . .

_____ ask to borrow them ASAP!

_____ suddenly need a new pair of jeans ASAP.

Your friend just got chosen for a special school trip for a few select students. You . . .

_____ worry that she'll get close to the others on the trip and forget you exist.

_____ ask her to bring you back a T-shirt.

You studied all week for a beastly midterm, but a friend got a better grade. You . . .

_____ will ask her for help on the final. She's got some mad study skills.

_____ just know the teacher plays faves.

Your best friend gets asked to prom, but you're stuck at home because nobody asked you. You . . .

_____ put on your PJs, grab a gallon of mint chocolate chip, and watch reruns.

_____ hang out at her house, helping her get ready.

The guy you like is paying more attention to one of your friends than you. You . . .

_____ blame your friend and avoid her later.

_____ don't worry about it. You trust your friend not to betray you.

You and your friend both compete on the track team. She won two second-place medals, but you don't place at all. You . . .

_____ congratulate her and ask to see her medals.

_____ ignore her all the way home.

What did you learn about yourself? Nobody is immune from the jealous trap. While you might not get jealous about everything, you might need to be on guard for those things that tend to spark envy—a guy, killer clothes, or a higher grade. The antidote for jealousy is gratefulness. The next time you feel the envy start to rise, look for something to be thankful for. Over time, you'll learn to be content with the accomplishments and blessings that come your way instead of grouching about what you don't have.

WHEN A FRIEND NEEDS HELP

by Pam Gibbs

One night, a friend comes over to spend the night at your house. You're having a great time, watching movies, goofing off, when you notice it. A long, red cut peeking up over her sock. At first, you don't think much about it. Then, later in the evening when you're grabbing a snack, you see another cut—this time, on her arm. Your stomach turns in knots. Maybe you are mistaken? You finally muster up the courage and ask.

"Um, Kelsey? I . . . noticed . . . well, I saw your cuts. Are you okay?" you ask in a quiet, mousy voice.

That's when she tells you. She has been cutting herself. She just can't handle the pressure of her parents' constant fighting, so it's the only way she can deal with the stress. You talk a little bit more, but your thoughts keep flying back to the bombshell she just unleashed.

You're worried sick about her, and you don't know what to do. Do you stay quiet and risk your friend seriously hurting herself more? Do you tell someone and risk losing her friendship forever? Do you talk to her parents? Your parents? Your youth pastor? What do you do?

This is probably one of the most difficult situations friends can find themselves in. You're torn between feelings of helplessness, loyalty, confusion, and frustration. There are no easy answers, and it feels like every choice you have could be the wrong one. You want to help, but in many ways, your friend's problems are much bigger than you can handle. You don't really know what advice to give, but you're not sure she would listen even if you did.

Research tells us that many high school students cut themselves to relieve stress and deal with inner turmoil. Others hurt themselves by burning or bruising parts of their bodies. Some students drink and use drugs. Other students are being abused physically or sexually. Situations like these all have one thing in common—the students feel like they have to keep everything a secret.

That's where you come in. If your friend has confided in you about behavior that is potentially dangerous or life threatening, or if she tells you she's being abused, chances are that she has asked you to keep it secret. So what should you do? Keep the promise at the risk of her health—or her life? Just rat on her? Do you ask other friends in hopes that someone will know what to do? No. First, pray for God's wisdom, and then move forward cautiously. Use the following suggestions to help.

Talk to an adult. Before you take any action, talk with someone older (an adult!), possibly someone who has dealt with these situations before. You may talk to your youth minister or a parent. Or perhaps a volunteer at your church or a teacher at your school. Tell him or her your dilemma. He or she will give you advice in what the next step needs to be to help your friend. Depending on the seriousness of the situation, that adult may intervene and take action for you. Trust that he or she will do whatever is necessary to make sure your friend is safe.

Although you may be afraid that your friend will get mad because you talked with an adult, keep in mind that remaining silent does not guarantee that you'll stay friends. People involved in drugs and alcohol often ditch their non-using friends. Or something dangerous could happen to her, and you might lose her anyway. You don't want to live with the regret if something happens to her. There's no upside to keeping silent.

Talk to your friend. You need to tell your friend that you have confided in a trusted adult. She will most likely be mad, so prepare yourself. But eventually, she will be relieved when she realizes that she doesn't have to bear this painful secret alone anymore. Obviously if your friend becomes so angry that she threatens suicide or behavior that would hurt someone else, you'll need to get help immediately. Many times these threats are just threats, but you never know if your friend is being serious, and you can't take the threats lightly.

Support your friend. Once you tell an adult about your friend's dilemma, the adult can help her find a way out from the dangerous situation she's in. She may need to enter a rehabilitation program. She might need to talk to a professional Christian counselor about her problems. The police may get involved. Whatever happens, she still needs your friendship. Text her. Find out how she's doing. Ask her to do things. When you're together, you don't always have to bring up her problem. Just treat her like you would any other friend. She may bring up her situation, or she may not, and that's okay.

You alone cannot help your friend deal with her problem adequately. You are not a counselor, and when you stay quiet when your friend is in danger, you risk her life. The longer she remains in that situation, the more she is at risk. Don't stay silent. Doing so could mean dramatic consequences for your friend.

Recognizing a Friend in Trouble

Everybody struggles from time to time. Your friend can get depressed. Maybe she broke up with a boyfriend. Or her parents are fighting. When that happens, you're likely to see a few of these signs show up in your friend for a few days. However, if you see some of these warning signals in your friend, and they last longer than a couple of weeks, then you need to talk to an adult about getting your friend some help.

- Becoming withdrawn (avoiding friends, social events, even skipping school)
- Changes in sleep patterns (sleeping too much or not sleeping at all)
- Dramatic behavior change, like a shy person acting wildly
- Use of drugs or alcohol
- Unexpected spurts of anger or crying
- Change in eating patterns (eating too much or not eating at all)
- Giving away valuable possessions
- Excessive guilt or shame
- Low self-esteem
- Talks about feeling hopeless or worthless
- Acts tired or exhausted all the time
- Can't seem to concentrate or make decisions
- Grades drop
- Stops caring about her appearance or hygiene
- Writing a will or farewell letters (this one might require immediate help!)

The wounds of a friend are trustworthy.

—Proverbs 27:6

WHEN YOUR BEST FRIEND GETS A BOYFRIEND

by Vicki Courtney

When you were in fifth grade, you made a pinkie swear with your best friend: no boy would ever separate you. You'd already seen some of your friends start to act all weird and drop their friends to go hang out with a guy. No way would that EVER happen to you. Guys were annoying. And anyway, friends are way more important.

But then it happened. Gradually, almost sinister-like, a guy creeps in. First it's the attention he gets in class. Then, he invades your locker space between classes. And then, in an ultimate act of betrayal, your soon-to-be "ex-best friend" starts spending time with him. You're alone.

If you're in high school now, you've probably experienced the frustration of a best friend getting a boyfriend. Instead of spending all of your time together, you have to share that time with him. If the relationship gets really serious, you may find yourself looking for a new best friend. This was my case when I got to high school and my closest friend from middle school discovered the world of dating. Within weeks of our freshman year, she went from one serious boyfriend to another for the next four years. Sometimes she switched boyfriends so fast, I wondered if she was working her way through a waiting list. Sure, I had a few boyfriends in high school, but I didn't really have a serious boyfriend until my junior year.

We're Not in Middle School Anymore

Most girls enter high school assuming that the social situation will be similar to middle school. Most girls don't consider the possibility that some of their friends—even a best friend—will bail on their girlfriends when the first cute guy looks her way. Once girls are officially allowed to date—go out in a car with a guy— you may feel like you get to see your best friend about as much as you see that distant great aunt who stops in every few years to visit and bring you cheesy Christmas sweaters.

Here's the truth, as painful as it is: You can't change your friend's mind and make your friendship go back to what it used to be like before guys entered the picture. However, you do have the choice of being a supportive friend even while your friend is in the Twilight Zone and forgets all about reality. Let her talk about "him." Keep texting and talking, even though you may not feel as close. Be creative about time together (at practice, doing homework, school projects, clubs, etc.). And be patient. Eventually, your friend will come out of the clouds, and she will recognize that she still needs friends.

Don't Ditch Your Friends

If your friend has traded her time with you for a guy, the best thing you can do is to make sure you have other friends to hang out with. And remember, if you meet a guy and the relationship gets "serious," don't drop your girlfriends for the guy. No guy is worth losing your best friend, especially in high school. One of my biggest regrets in high school was giving up my girlfriends for a serious boyfriend in my junior and senior year. I wasted two years of high school in a joined-at-the-hip relationship that practically emulated marriage. The relationship ended when we went to two separate colleges, and we haven't seen each other since. What a waste.

Girls Who Can't Be Alone

Girls who invest the majority of their time in serious dating relationships are revealing a deeper problem. They do not feel significant unless they "belong" to a guy. They dread being without a boyfriend because deep down inside, being boyfriendless means they are undesirable (at least that's what they think). It doesn't matter how many girlfriends they have. They have falsely defined their worth by having a boyfriend. Unfortunately, many of these teenage girls move into college and adulthood with that same wound and end up in unhealthy (and sometimes abusive) relationships. If this describes you, talk with your parents or another adult. Don't ignore this problem.

What I'd Do Differently

If I had it to do over again, I would value and nurture my friendships, knowing those relationships were more likely to last over the years than a relationship with a high school boyfriend. I envy some of my friends today who valued and nurtured their friendships in high school. They still get together twenty or thirty years later. (Yeah, I am old.) I forfeited my close, lifelong friendships for a guy I haven't seen since high school. Take a lesson from me, and don't let that happen to you.

WHAT *NOT* TO DO

WHEN ONE OF YOUR FRIENDS GETS A BOYFRIEND

1.
Don't criticize the guy.

That's one way to create a wall between you and your friend.

2. Don't gossip about her or the relationship. Eventually, the rumor will get back to your friend and you'll lose her for good.

3. Don't make her choose between you and her boyfriend. You'll probably lose that battle. And your friend.

4. Don't isolate yourself. Make new friends. Hang out with ones you already have. You'll discover that you have more friends than you thought.

5. Don't get a boyfriend just to have one too. You're more likely to date the wrong guy and end up miserable in the end.

6. Don't try to compete for her time. When it comes to matters of the heart, infatuation wins out. Be grateful for the time you do have together, and make the most of it.

7.
Don't ignore your friend so she will pay attention to you.

She will likely get frustrated, and the friendship will be even more strained. Or, she won't notice you're giving her the cold shoulder, which would make you feel even worse.

8. Don't try to make her feel guilty. You don't want a friendship based on guilt. Both of you will end up miserable.

9. Don't try to steal him away. That's a deathblow to any friendship.

10.
Don't get discouraged about your-self.

Just because your friend has a boyfriend doesn't mean something is wrong with you. A boyfriend isn't a measure of your value or worth.

Help!

I have a serious problem. I am shy. Like my face gets ready any time I try to speak up. My palms get sweaty, and my voice cracks, and I just know everybody thinks I'm weird and awkward. Some people think I'm a snob because I don't talk. That's really not true. I'm just too petrified to talk to them. What do I do?

Signed,

Scared Just Thinking About It

Dear Scared,

I can understand that being shy is hard, especially when you're a teenager. The teen years are all about breaking away from your family, being with your friends, and gaining your independence. That's easy for the extroverts. But for people who'd rather be behind the stage instead of on it, making friends can feel like leaping from an airplane.

Here are a few ideas to help ease your anxiety and help you take the risk of reaching out to others. Hopefully, you'll discover that it wasn't so difficult after all.

- Get comfortable with the people around you. In each class, pay attention to the people who sit near you. Listen to what they say. When they make a joke, try to laugh a little. When the girl next to you asks you what page she's supposed to be on, answer nicely.
- If you're too shy to talk to people, try taking a few deep breaths before you walk in the room. This may be a little weird, but it actually works! And when you feel the nervousness kick up a notch, take another deep breath and exhale slowly (and quietly).
- Be nice to people. Share your dessert with the others at the table. Hold the door open for others. Being nice is a cue that you're approachable and want to be friends with people.
- Say hi to people you know as they walk by you. That means you'll need to hold your head up when you walk down the hall. You can't memorize the pattern of the floor tiles.
- Look for someone who might want to be friends with you. If you get along with your lab partner, take the next step and try to talk to her. Ask about her interests or her family. She may ask you the same question in return. Presto! You're having a conversation!
- Accept invites. When a girl invites you to hang out, accept the invitation! If a group is going to the game, go! There will be lots of stuff to talk about if you run out of things to say.

My best advice is to keep trying and never give up. You may never want to be a public speaker, but eventually, you might be able to answer a question in class without fainting!

Question: What qualities do you look for in a friend?

WE ASKED—YOU ANSWERED!

Someone who makes me laugh until my abs hurt and a Christian who can help me be accountable.—*Brittany, 16*

Honesty, loyalty, a good sense of humor, and someone who will always have my back.—*Lauren, 15*

Trustworthy—I can tell them secrets, and they won't tell the whole world. —*Natasha, 13*

Someone who I know loves the Lord so that when I ask her for advice she will look to God and not just give me her opinion.—*Samantha, 16*

Someone who has the same values I do. It's nice if she's funny and a good shopper as well!—*Lindsay, 15*

Someone who is there for you no matter what.—*Hannah, 14*

I think a friend should be someone who not only loves you but is completely devoted to Jesus Christ. I want my friend to be someone I can lean on when temptation, trials, and worldly things become overwhelming.—*Jessie, 14*

A true friend never puts you down.—*Vanessa, 17*

I don't like it when a friend flip-flops to other girls who are more popular. —*Kaitlyn, 13*

I like a friend who doesn't care what other people think.—*Emily, 14*

A good friend will never let a guy come between us.—*Taylor, 15*

I look for someone who looks beyond stereotypes.—*Kendra, 16*

Q. What qualities do you look for in a friend?

Scan for Video Answers!

Are You an Attention Junkie?

Hi. My name is_____.
And I'm an attention junkie.

Do you crave attention? Take this quiz to find out.

1. **A friend calls you and excitedly tells you she is going snow skiing over spring break. You went to the same place a few years ago. You . . .**
   a. let her finish and, when the time is right, tell her that you have been to the same place.
   b. immediately interrupt her and scream, "I've been there!" and start talking about your trip.

2. **You are at cheer practice, and everyone on your team is going on and on about the new girl who can do a back with a full. You just did the same thing last week, but they didn't see it. You . . .**
   a. join in and agree that her full is incredible, knowing they will see yours in due time.
   b. tell them that you successfully completed a back full last week at open gym.

3. **When you are in a group of friends, you . . .**
   a. usually take part in the conversation by allowing others fair time to speak.
   b. usually dominate the conversation and often interrupt others with your viewpoint or comments.

4. **You are shopping for new school clothes. When you are trying on an outfit, you . . .**
   a. wonder if the ensemble looks like "you."
   b. worry about whether others will be impressed.

5. **You are with a couple of your friends, and they mention a party coming up. You didn't get invited. You . . .**
   a. express your disappointment but don't dwell on it.
   b. go on and on to your friends about how no one likes you, hoping they will tell you how awesome you really are.

If you answered "b" two or more times, it's time take a serious look at your need for attention.

WHAT IS AN ATTENTION JUNKIE?

An attention junkie (AJ) craves the spotlight, a lot like an addict craves a drug. She wants to be the focus of attention from everyone in the room, all the time. To make sure that happens, AJs will employ a number of tactics:

1. **Attention junkies over share.** They give personal details that nobody really wants to know. Unfortunately, they also give out personal details of their friends, earning the title of Gossip Queen.
2. **Attention junkies underdress.** These girls get the attention of guys by their lack of modest clothing. Unfortunately, it's the wrong kind of attention. And, in the process, girls write AJs off as potential friends. Nobody wants to hang around them.
3. **Attention junkies can be bullies.** When you've somehow offended them, they will get all up in your face to make sure you (and the rest of the room) know who is important.
4. **Attention junkies pose seductively.** You see dozens of selfies per day on social media. AJs take those pictures to a whole new low, often simulating seductive or sexual poses, mostly for the shock value.
5. **Attention junkies exaggerate.** You never know what the truth is because they lie all the time about stuff.
6. **Attention junkies cry.** For no apparent reason. Except for one—their need for attention.

Why AJs Need Attention

Some people are extroverts. They like big groups of people and love to get together as often as possible. Extroverts can be the class clown or the best storyteller in the group. They make friends quickly and have lots of them. But extroverts are not attention junkies. They love crowds because they derive pleasure and energy and joy from being with people. That's why you'll always see them having a blast in a crowd. On the other hand, an attention junkie acts out because she inwardly lacks worth, value, and confidence. Her fear of not being accepted and liked fuels her unwanted behavior, which in turn makes people not like her. It's a horrible cycle.

Overcoming Attention-Seeking Habits

Just like any other area in life that needs growth, it takes time to move from insecurity to confidence, from craving the spotlight to sharing it willingly. Here are a few skills you can practice that will jumpstart the change:

- **Wait to talk.** Don't interrupt. Let others finish their thoughts and stories. Then express yours.

- **Take turns.** Don't dominate the conversation. Everyone in the group should have equal stage time. Ask yourself if others have had a chance to talk. If not, be quiet for a while (I know, it's hard!) so others can take part in the discussion.

- **Wait for compliments.** Rather than fishing for empathy, a pat on the back, or reassurances of your worth, allow them to come naturally. People will compliment you in due time, but they might not if they know you just want attention.

- **Don't always try to one-up everyone.** Even if someone shares an experience you have also had, wait to share yours, if at all. It's not a competition—it's a conversation.

- **Give to others.** By giving others your time and attention, you remember that the world doesn't revolve around you. Also, when you give of yourself in service and ministry to others, you feel good about yourself. But make sure you don't serve just so others will think you're awesome.

- **Get in the Word.** Spending time in Scripture will help you refocus your attention on the One who created you. He will give you confidence if you ask. He will give you His undivided attention, which is what you need the most.

The Last Word on Friends

Two are better than one because they have a good reward for their efforts. For if either falls, his companion can lift him up; but pity the one who falls without another to lift him up.
—Ecclesiastes 4:9–10

Family

Help! My Parents Don't Trust Me!

by Pam Gibbs

"My parents just don't trust me."

I've heard that statement dozens of times. You think you're old enough to start exercising your independence, but you feel like your parents are super strict. As a result, you argue with them. And fuss. And fume. And roll your eyes (not a good idea, by the way). Have these tactics earned you more freedom? Probably not. However, you can do some things to give your parents greater confidence in giving you a little more independence.

1. ***When your parents ask you to do something, do it.*** Not later. Not in two days. The first time they ask. Don't whine, complain, offer a snide comment, or give them that heavy sigh. Just do what you've been asked to do. (That's a sign of maturity.)

2. ***When you ask to go somewhere, give them details—who will be there, what you will be doing, what time it will be over, whether or not adults will be there.*** When you withhold that information, that secrecy looks like you're trying to deceive them. They just want to know you are going to be safe. They're not trying to make you miserable or get all up in your business. I promise.

3. ***Don't throw a temper tantrum if your parents say no.*** Tantrums are for three-year-olds, and they confirm your parents' suspicions about your maturity level. You say you're old enough to have more freedom. Then act like it when you don't get your way. Whining about it does nothing but annoy them. That sound is like a thousand fingernails on a chalkboard.

4. ***Always follow curfew rules.*** Even if the party is "just getting started," go home when you're supposed to. Even better, be home before you are asked to be home. Ask yourself: Is one trivial party going to be worth the consequences?

5. ***Associate with people of good character.*** Your parents want to know you have good decision-making skills about choosing "good" friends or people to hang out with. If your friends spend more time in detention than in the classroom, you might want to reconsider those friendships. Remember, you will become like whomever you spend the most time with.

6. *Don't get defensive and angry if your parents want to give you advice (even if you know it already).* From their perspective, they feel like the clock is ticking and they only have a few more years to cram you with wisdom and knowledge before you head out the door for college. Simply sit there and listen. Look in their eyes. Say thanks, and tell them you will think about what they said.

7. *If your parents accuse you of doing something you didn't do, relax and calmly tell your side of the story.* Don't raise your voice ten octaves and start bawling about how they don't trust you. Take a deep breath, and explain the situation with as many details as possible. (Remember, giving no information feels like secrecy.)

8. *If you made a mistake, big or small, admit that you were wrong.* Just be honest and say, "I messed up" (or something like that). Don't add a "but" at the end of your apology because anything you say will sound like an excuse, a reason not to take responsibility for your actions.

9. *Don't lie.* Ever. That is the FASTEST way to lose your parents' trust. Remember that old parable about the boy who cried wolf? Although you likely don't guard sheep for a village, the principle still

stands. If you keep lying and deceiving your parents, they won't know when you're telling the truth. And they won't trust you with anything.

Think of your parents' trust like a bank account. Every time you do what you promise, you deposit a little bit of trust into that account.

Clean your room without being forced? Ka-ching.

Come home from a date fifteen minutes before your curfew? Ka-ching, ka-ching!

Help out with your sister's homework? Triple ka-ching! You get the idea.

Likewise, when you fail to do what you promise, you withdraw a little bit of trust. Did you promise to do the dishes, only they're still in the sink three days later? Trust withdrawal.

Did you promise to babysit your little brother and then back out the day before? Withdrawal of trust.

Did you come home from a date fifteen minutes after your curfew? Withdrawal of trust.

Did you lie about spending the night at a friend's house? Serious withdrawals of trust.

Trust is hard to earn, but it is easily broken. Every time you break a promise, lie, deceive, withhold information, or demonstrate the maturity of a six-year-old, you lose even more of your parents' trust. And you'll have to work that much harder to earn it back again.

25 *things that will make your parents smile*

1. Shut doors gently.
2. Put your clothes away.
3. Cook dinner.
4. Compliment Mom's outfit.
5. Thank Dad for fixing things.
6. Come home from your date early.
7. Do the laundry.
8. Call/text when you'll be late.
9. Avoid rolling your eyes.
10. Say please.
11. Mow the lawn.
12. Ask for advice.
13. Speak to them in a respectful tone.
14. Put your towels on the rack, not on the floor.
15. Clean up around the sink.
16. Put gas in the car.
17. Study.
18. Go along with family trips without pouting.
19. Offer to help put groceries away.
20. Help out at church.
21. Don't sigh.
22. Don't leave an empty carton in the fridge.
23. Don't break promises.
24. Don't answer their questions with the following: *Yes, no, yeah, I dunno, whatever, duh, fine*, or any other one- or two-word answer.
25. Give them a hug when you walk out the door.

Bonus: *If you use your mom or dad's stuff, put it back where you found it!*

E IS FOR "EMBARRASSING"

by Vicki Courtney

When I was a teenager, my mom was the taxi in charge of carting my friends and me to the mall. I was nervous, wondering if she could make it the full five miles without embarrassing me (I seriously doubted it). As we reached the front of the mall, I breathed a huge sigh of relief. I was actually going to escape the car embarrassment free!

Or so I thought.

As we were pulling up, a car in front of us slammed on the brakes, and my mom reacted by honking her horn loudly and screaming, "Great balls of fire!" Fortunately, she didn't hit the car in front of her! My friends were hysterically laughing as we got out of the car, and for the rest of the day, they found any excuse to say, "Great balls of fire!" Arrrrgh! Like, what does that even mean?!

Not on Purpose

Moms don't set out to embarrass you on purpose. We may joke that our mission in life is to make your life miserable, but it's just a cover-up. The truth is, we just can't help it. We don't want to embarrass you. The problem is that sometimes we are out of touch with your world. We don't get your funny jokes; we don't understand references to TV shows and movies. And your language? Totally foreign. But if you think about it, being out of touch with your world is probably a good thing.

You don't really want that mom who dresses like you and your friends, talks like you and your friends, and wants to hang out with you and your friends. If given a choice, you probably want a mom who acts like a mom.

I realize that some of you have legitimate complaints about your mom's most embarrassing moments. I remember moms who would scream at their daughters in front of others, tease them about liking a certain guy, and criticize their daughter's outfits. Those problems go way beyond temporary embarrassment. That stuff needs to be addressed.

It's Okay to Speak Up

Some embarrassing moments happen because your mom just doesn't have a clue. But if your mom embarrasses you more often than not, sit down with her and calmly (!) tell her about the times she has embarrassed you. Most definitely talk about times when her words were hurtful. Most moms are reasonable people who can remember back to their own growing-up years when they had an embarrassing mom.

Leviticus 19:3 says, "Each of you is to respect his mother and father." Even when your mom makes your face turn ninety shades of red, resist the temptation to lash out at her in front of your friends. Don't treat her with disrespect or make fun of her behind her back. Never yell at her. Instead, wait for the right time to talk (alone!) and let her know how her comments or actions made you feel. If you treat her with respect, she will likely treat you the same way.

Now, does this guarantee she'll stop parading around the house in those goofy brown loafers and white crew socks? Not a chance. You're stuck with that. The good news is that if you have kids someday, you get to continue the legacy and become an embarrassing mom!

WHEN YOUR PARENTS DIVORCE

by Pam Gibbs

That morning was just like any other. You woke up (probably late), got ready, grabbed your books and a breakfast bar, and headed out the door to catch the bus. You were bored in English (again), confused in algebra (again), and couldn't wait for lunch so you could talk with your friends (always). After conditioning at softball practice (you hate doing squats), you grab a ride home from a friend. A routine day in your routine life.

Until you walk through the door. Your mom is home. Your mom is never home this early. Something is wrong; you just know it.

You find her in the living room, almost as if she is waiting for you.

"Honey, I need to talk to you. This is difficult to say, but your dad and I are getting a divorce."

She says a bunch of stuff after that, it all sounds like muffled garble. All you can hear is that word, over and over and over in your head—*divorce*.

Then, out of nowhere, a flood of questions comes crashing in like water spilling over a dam:

Who will I live with?

What about my dog? Do I get to keep him?

Why didn't my parents try harder?

Where will I live?

Will I have to move?

Is it my fault?

Who else knows?

Will I still be able to go to college?

Did my parents ever love each other?

Isn't divorce wrong?

Why is this happening to me?

How can I fix this?

Who do I blame?

Unfortunately, many of your peers have already asked those questions—or they will. About half of your classmates will experience the bombshell of divorce before they graduate from high school. Some of their parents will divorce more than once. The fact that your classmates understand your situation doesn't take away the barrage of feelings and questions you are facing, but it can bring you some reassurance that you're not alone. Your friends might also tell you that it really, really stinks, but you can make it through. Perhaps these following truths and principles will help you.

It's Not Your Fault

The most important thing for you to know up front is this: the divorce is not your fault. Your behavior didn't cause your parents to break up. And, you can't do anything to fix it. They won't get back together if your grades get better, if you clean your room, or if you make their lives easier by doing the dishes or fixing dinner. You can't guilt them into getting back together. Nothing you did caused this to happen, and nothing you could do will fix it.

Get Ready for the Flood

When you first hear that your parents are divorcing, you may become numb emotionally, but that numbness won't last forever. You will experience a gazillion different emotions. Some of them may look like this:

- **Shock:** Maybe you weren't expecting the divorce.
- **Sadness:** Sometimes you can't even pinpoint why you're sad.
- **Worry:** Maybe you will get divorced when you're an adult.
- **Fear:** You fear losing a parent or that your parents don't care about you anymore.
- **Guilt:** You wonder if the divorce is your fault
- **Anger:** Sometimes the anger is at your parents, other times for no particular reason.
- **Anxiety:** What will your future look like? Who will take care of you?
- **Embarrassed:** Your parents have become a statistic.
- **Loneliness:** No one understands what you're feeling.
- **Relieved:** At least the tension and arguing will end.

You have every right to feel what you feel. And it's okay to be completely confused about what you feel. You are not weird or different from other teens who have gone through this experience. You are grieving, and with grief comes emotions that don't always make sense, and those emotions usually leak out (or flood out!) when you least expect it. You may struggle with concentrating. You may feel responsible for younger siblings. Reactions like that are normal, and healing from the experience will take time.

Ask Questions

One of the ways to alleviate some of the worry and anxiety is to ask questions. Talk to both of your parents. Focus on what you need to know in order to feel more secure, such as:

When will the divorce happen?
Who will be moving out?
How will we pay for stuff?
What will visitation arrangements be like?
Do I get to choose which parent I will live with?

Keep in mind that your parents may not know the answers to all of your questions. And if you're just too emotional or confused to ask the questions aloud, try writing them in an e-mail, text message, or even in a notebook. They can either come talk to you, or they can write you back.

Don't Choose Sides—Even When Asked

You may be tempted to choose sides with a parent, especially if the divorce wasn't a mutual decision or if the divorce is the result of an affair. However, creating alliances with one parent is a bad, bad idea. In fact, your mom or dad may unconsciously (or intentionally) try to get you to side with one or the other. They may criticize each other; one of them may act needy so you'll come to their side; they may "forget" appointments or "slip" and call the other parent a name. Most of the time, these tactics are designed to hurt the other parent and to avoid their own pain and anguish. However, caring for your parents is NOT your responsibility! You are not an adult and should not be asked to play an adult role in your parents' lives. You are not the peacemaker or referee between them. Just as you did when they were married, love them both. Continue relationships with both (unless, of course, you are at risk for some kind of abuse).

Find Some Allies

Teenagers are proud of being independent. However, this is not one of those times to go it alone. You need friends and family members to support you, love you, listen to you, and care for you. There's no benefit in trying to "be strong." In fact, isolating yourself from other people only adds to your feelings of loneliness and abandonment. Even Jesus relied on His closest friends when He was struggling the most (remember the Garden of Gethsemane?). Admit that you are human and need help in figuring out what your life will be like now. You can turn to friends, your church group, group therapy, or even a professional counselor. Relying on others is not a sign of weakness. It takes a lot of courage and wisdom to know you can't walk through this alone.

Take Care of Yourself

Adjusting to your parents divorce will take its toll on you. You will be physically, emotionally, and spiritually drained. Take time to rest. Try to exercise. Play. Find a way to release your tension. Run. Go to the batting cages. Find time to be quiet and still. Journal. Read. Above all, make spending time with God a priority. He is strong and mighty and can take care of you. He says that He will renew your strength so that you can run and not get weary, walk and not faint (see Isaiah 40:31).

Give Your Parents a Break

Your parents have feelings too. Even though they are divorcing, they are confused and scared and unsure. And they are worried about you. Even though they may not show their emotions the way you do, they are struggling too. You have a right to be angry with them, but in the midst of that anger and the cauldron of other emotions brewing underneath, don't do something you'll regret later. Give your parents a little grace too.

Your life is changing. The future may feel incredibly scary. You may wonder whom to trust. Although everything else in your life may feel upside down and out of control, remember that there is One on whom you can rely. God says to you: "I am your rock, your fortress and your deliverer; I am your rock, in whom you can take refuge, your shield and the horn of your salvation, your stronghold" (Psalm 18:2).

And that's a promise He will never break.

The LORD is my rock, my fortress, and my deliverer, my God, my mountain where I seek refuge, my shield and the horn of my salvation, my stronghold. —Psalm 18:2

When Home Isn't Safe

by Pam Gibbs

Family secrets. Every family has them. Grandpa snores like a lion. Aunt Edna isn't really a blonde. Your dad got lost on the way to take your sister to college. Some family secrets are more opportunities to joke around at family reunions. For others, though, family secrets are painful realities covered under layers of lies and shame. Maybe you know what I'm talking about. You have held a secret so horrible and shameful that you feel like you could never tell anyone. Nobody in the family will talk about "it," much less admit that "it" has happened. "It" is abuse.

Abuse comes in all forms, and it takes place in all kinds of families. It affects all races, all neighborhoods, and all religions, even in Christian homes. And it's more common than you might think.

Physical Abuse

Some teenagers suffer physical abuse from parents, siblings, or other relatives who find it hard to control their tempers. If you are physically abused, you might cover the injuries so nobody will see them or ask you a question you are afraid of answering. You'll make excuses for the marks if someone sees them, saying that you fell or tripped, or you got in the way of a fight or . . . And you have lots of ways to explain away your hurts so nobody knows the anguish you're hiding. Inside you want to tell others the truth, but shame holds you back. You desperately want out, but you are afraid of what will happen to you (or another family member) if you talk about what's happened.

Emotional Abuse

Emotional abuse is a little harder to recognize because the abuse doesn't leave physical scars. If you've been abused this way, you've been ignored or rejected; you've been verbally shamed, ridiculed, or bullied. You may think being treated this way is normal. A friend of mine grew up in an emotionally abusive environment but thought all families functioned that way. When she went to college and got some distance from the situation, she realized that what she had experienced was actually a form of abuse.

Sexual Abuse

One out of every three girls will experience some form of sexual abuse before she turns eighteen. This may mean you were touched inappropriately or were forced to touch someone. You may have been forced to have sex (been raped)—even by a peer. Some girls are exposed to pornography. Teens who suffer from this abuse often carry a heavy burden of shame, guilt, and fear. You've been told you're bad and told that if you told anyone else, you'd be in trouble.

Hear this clearly: What has happened to you was not your fault, no matter what you've been told.

If home has become an unsafe place, you are not alone. And you don't have to suffer silently. There are people in your life who care about you, people who want to help you, and people who want to make sure the abuse stops—for good.

Speak Up

Maybe as you read this article, you thought of a youth leader, teacher, or friend's parent who is safe to talk to. Call, text, message, or e-mail him or her and ask if the two of you can talk—as soon as possible (so you don't talk yourself out of it!). I'm not saying that speaking up will be easy or simple or painless. You've been taught to keep the abuse a secret. You've been taught that you're at fault. You may have been threatened with even worse violence if you tell. Even though it's hard, you can do it. You have the strength and courage to speak up, even though you don't think you can. You have endured the abuse, and that has taken great strength and resilience.

Telling your story will be difficult—but it will also start the healing process and the process of setting you free from the silent prison you've been living in. Once the secret has been exposed, authorities may get involved to ensure your physical and emotional safety. That may seem scary, but these people are trained and experienced in making you feel at ease, and they can protect you from your abuser. You will also need to talk with a professional Christian counselor who will walk with you through the process of healing. She can be a safe person to tell parts of your story that you couldn't share with others.

Rob the Secrets of Their Power

Secrets lose their power when exposed with the truth. When you share them with someone else, you are robbing the shame of its ability to paralyze and control you. You are taking the power back from the person abusing you. You are taking the first steps in recovering the life you deserve and finding the healing your heart craves. You will learn that you're not alone in the journey to healing. Others will join you along that journey, some who have experienced the same pain you have; many others want to offer tangible hope and assistance.

Although healing is a process and it won't happen overnight, remember that God can and will bring healing to you. In fact, He's the only one who is able. Healing the brokenhearted is His specialty. Restoring hope is right up His alley. He is your loving Savior, full of compassion and mercy. God cares about your situation and loves you very much. He will use caring and compassionate people to support and love you. He will heal your wounds no matter how deep they go.

He heals the brokenhearted and binds up their wounds. He counts the number of the stars; He gives names to all of them. Our Lord is great, vast in power; His understanding is infinite. —Psalm 147:3–5

But You Yourself have seen trouble and grief, observing it in order to take the matter into Your hands. The helpless entrusts himself to You; You are a helper of the fatherless. —Psalm 10:14

Signs of Abuse in a Friend

You may suspect that a friend or classmate is being abused in some form. You can't put your finger on it, but a tiny feeling in the back of your brain tells you something is very wrong. The symptoms below often characterize someone who has been abused, either now or in the past. If a friend shows many of these signs, talk about your suspicion with an adult immediately so you can help your friend.

- Being excessively withdrawn or very clingy
- Becoming secretive
- Low self-esteem or insecurity
- Outbursts of anger
- Sudden weight loss or weight gain
- Self-harm (cutting, scratching, or burning)
- Running away
- Skipping school
- Avoiding going home
- Drug and/or alcohol use or abuse
- Poor social skills
- Suicidal behavior
- Criminal behavior (stealing, vandalism, etc.)
- Being highly anxious or scared
- Emotional numbness
- Feelings of guilt and worthlessness
- Sexual promiscuity
- Change in grades from good to poor
- Seems distracted or distant at odd times
- Thinks of self or body as repulsive, dirty, or bad

We Are Family

Getting Along with Your Siblings

by Pam Gibbs

When I was growing up, I got stuck with the hump seat. If you have brothers and sisters, you know exactly what I'm talking about. That spot in the middle of the back seat. Yeah, the one with the least amount of room because there's no place to put your legs. You know it. I hated that seat.

Even though it made logical sense because my brother was ten years older and two feet taller and my sister was older and taller too, I still resented always being stuck in that seat. Always. Try talking logic to an aggravated kid who hated being the youngest one. I was miserable in that seat. My brother was always sticking his elbows in my ribs, or my sister was touching her legs against mine. I hated that seat. So I decided to make everybody else unhappy too. I poked my sister with my finger over and over and over, and I pulled my brother's headphones. I was a brat.

But so were my brother and sister. It's a miracle that my parents didn't ship us all off to boarding school in Mongolia.

Siblings. Can't live with them. Can't live without them.

Why is it sometimes so stinkin' hard to get along with our siblings?

Why Siblings Fight

Brothers and sisters fight for lots of different reasons. Here are a few. Which ones apply to you?

1. ***Close quarters.*** When you live with someone else, you will get on each other's nerves. This happens in every living situation, whether it's your brother or sister, your roommate in college, or your husband. Your brothers and sisters have quirks, just like you do. Your brother only eats one food on his plate at a time. Your sister brushes her teeth ad nauseam. The youngest can't sleep without a nightlight. This is especially true in the winter months when the days are shorter, the nights are longer, and nobody gets enough time outside.

2. *Jealousy.* Sometimes a brother or sister (or you!) will pick a fight because he or she feels jealous. Or you feel like a parent is showing favoritism toward another sibling. Unconsciously, you or your siblings may be trying to get your parents' attention by acting out and misbehaving. Your brother or sister may take out his or her frustration on you instead of talking to your parents about feeling left out or marginalized.

3. *Misdirected feelings.* Your teammate left you out today at practice. You can't yell at her, so you go home and yell at your sister. Unfortunately, family members are prone to do this to each other. Your brother lost the football game, so the next day he picks and picks and picks at you until you blow up. Then he gets to yell back. See the pattern? A lot of sibling arguments take place because you're really ticked off about something else, but your family members are the closest targets. So they get the brunt of the anger instead of where the anger should be directed.

4. *Selfishness.* You want stuff; and you want what a sibling has, so you take it. Your brother's iPad. Your sister's sweater. You'll swear you were only borrowing it and you would have asked her, but she was out with her friends while you were stuck at home babysitting your little brother. You were going to put the iPad back when you were done, and your brother wasn't using it anyway, so what's the big deal? You wanted the last cookie, the TV, the video game. Your brother drank the last coke. Your sister changed the channel while you went to the bathroom. The root of a lot of arguments can be traced back to this one problem—selfishness.

5. *Competition.* Good or bad, intentional or not, siblings compete with each other. Who gets the better grades, who plays a sport better, who won the last game of Monopoly. Anything and everything can become a competition. Even the race to see who can capture the attention and affection of mom and dad. This is especially true if you have a sibling with special needs or if one of your siblings gets sick. You'll fight with your siblings for the any remaining attention your parents have.

6. *Different temperaments.* Your brother is an extrovert. You are an introvert. Your sister is a morning person. You're a night owl. Your sister is a rational thinker. You're not. Mix together all of the different aspects of your personalities, and chaos will eventually erupt. Because all of you bring to the dinner table different perspectives, viewpoints, preferences, opinions, and dislikes, you will disagree. Guaranteed. And because it's more fun to argue than to carry on a civil debate, the neighbor three doors down can hear you shout at each other.

Sibling Sanity

Believe it or not, it is possible to get along with your brothers and sisters. You might even begin to—gasp—like each other. All it takes is a little effort on everyone's part to make life a little easier for each other.

Try out these tips for bringing a little serenity and peace to your home.

1. *Be patient.* Ouch. Of all of the ways to improve your relationships with your siblings, this is probably the most difficult. However, Scripture is clear about the need for patience (Romans 12:12; 1 Corinthians 13:4; Proverbs 16:32; 1 Thessalonians 5:14). When you are tempted to lash out at your sister, stop. Take a deep breath or two. Or three or ten or a hundred. Try not to respond in the height of your frustration. Walk away. Think before you speak. And sometimes that means not speaking at all.

2. *Don't compare yourself.* I have a sign on my wall that reads, "Be yourself. Everyone else is taken." Don't measure yourself against your brothers and sisters. God created each of you uniquely different, with different strengths and weaknesses, different skills and talents. Find that one thing you like that nobody else does, and you won't be so prone to play the competition game.

3. *Learn to share.* Would it really hurt that much to let your sister borrow your iPod? You don't play with that video game system much, so don't fuss so much about your brother using it without your permission. Stuff is just stuff (profound statement, huh?). Hurting your relationship with your sister over a pair of earrings is a bad choice. Love people. Like your stuff. And don't get those mixed up.

4. *Give each other space.* I am an introvert by nature, which means that if I've been around a lot of people during the day, I need some space to chill when I get home. Otherwise I'm snarky and cranky and no fun to be around. Sound like a family member you know? If you know your sister doesn't like to talk in the morning, don't sing to her in the bathroom. If you know your brother gets grumpy if he loses a basketball game, don't tell him he did a great job even though his team lost. Space. Give each other space. You'll be glad you did.

5. *Apologize.* I know what you're thinking: *But it was her fault! She started it!* Yeah, I know. But very rarely is any argument, fight, squabble, or war the fault of only one person. Take responsibility for the part you played in the disagreement. And when you do hurt your siblings' feelings, apologize. When you take something without permission, apologize. When you lock your sister out the bathroom, apologize. See the pattern? Apologizing doesn't come naturally because it stems from humility. Part of growing up, though, is recognizing that you are sinful too. You make mistakes too. Everyone does. But I would rather hang out with the person who will admit it than the person who won't.

Q. *What's your best advice for getting along with your family members?*

Scan for Video Answers!

What do I do?

When I was a little girl, my dad and I had a great relationship. We played games together. We went on hikes and rode bikes. But now, things seem really different. He doesn't come into my room as much. And he doesn't hug me as often. When I look at him, he has this weird look. What's the deal? I know some girls who are glad their dad is in another world, but I'm not.

Signed,
Missing the old times

Dear Missing,

I know it seems like your dad is in another world, but in all actually, YOU are in another world. It's called the teenage years. And dads have absolutely no clue how to be a part of that world.

You're no longer a little girl anymore. As you go through the teen years, you are going through a lot of changes inside and out. Your hormones are going haywire, parts of your body are developing in new and (sometimes) scary ways, and you are becoming more independent. You look more like a woman than a little girl. You are developing your own ideas and opinions. You are solving problems on your own. And your mood swings are enough to give him whiplash. Where does a dad fit into this new world?

When you were little, he knew his role. He was protector and provider. He was wisdom giver, boo-boo kisser, frog catcher, ice cream buyer, and wrestling partner. But now . . . What is his role now? Besides protecting you from all the guys, of course . . .

If he seems distant, he is trying to figure out what this new relationship with his little (grown) girl will look like. At the same time, he is trying to give you space. Remember, that's what you asked for. Your relationship will seem awkward for a while, but as both of you figure out how to relate to each other, you'll soon discover that comfortable familiarity.

In the meantime, you could help your dad out. Don't leave him to read your mind (guys are horrible at that!). Sit on the arm of his chair and lean in for a hug. Break out a game you used to play together. Put in a movie and huddle up to him on the couch. Those are unspoken reassurances that you still need your daddy, and that will give him more comfortable in being a part of your new world.

In the Mixer

MYTHS, FACTS, AND TIPS ON BEING A BLENDED FAMILY

by Pam Gibbs

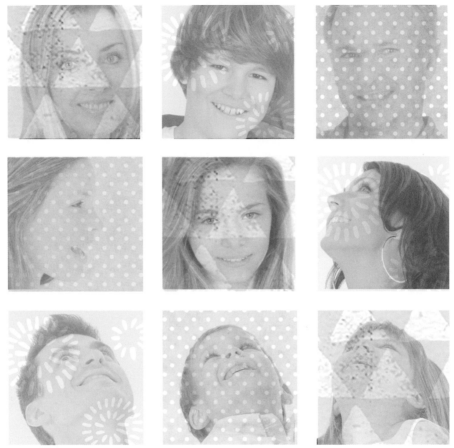

Start with two siblings, a mom, and a dad. Add two more siblings, take out one dad, and add another. Add a cupful of personalities, two sets of rules, umpteen schedules, and add three bowls of stress. Then mix together continually.

The result? A blended family.

Back in the days when *The Brady Bunch* was on TV, blended families were the exception rather than the norm. Today, however, the reverse is true. If you take an informal poll of your classmates, chances are a good percentage of them live in some sort of blended family situation. Maybe you do too. Unfortunately, there's not that much information out there for teens who find their lives dramatically changed by remarriage. Hopefully, these truths and tips can help you (or a friend) make the transition a little less rocky.

Myths (and Truths) about Blended Families

Hollywood has made blended family living seem, well, dramatic. TV shows and movies present the most extreme and outrageous situations possible. Other shows depict family conflict resolving in thirty minutes or less. The bad news is that a lot of myths about blended families have developed in the media and have begun to seep into our thinking. Let's look at a few of those myths and the truths they hide.

Myth #1—Members of blended families get along with each other instantly.

Truth: Developing any relationship takes time, regardless of the living situation.

Your parent and the new stepparent took time to build their relationship, so it makes sense that the rest of the family members need time to get to know and respect each other. Don't expect to become instant best friends with your new siblings or other relatives. And it's okay if it takes you time to feel really comfortable with a new adult in the house. Just move forward at your own pace and don't feel pressured to make instant connections. Some families will fall into place faster than others. And some may never "click."

Myth #2—Blended families function just like non-blended families.

Truth: Every family, regardless of origin or makeup, functions differently.

A blended family doesn't share a similar history; it hasn't yet developed its own traditions. Even inside jokes need to be developed. The upside is that blended families can bring together a rich diversity of traditions, milestones, birthdays, holidays, and even family worship. Although adjusting to these requires openness and a willingness to change, the benefit of different ideas and histories can make for great shared experiences.

In addition, blended families are just different than any other family dynamic. Combining all those unique personalities, schedules, backgrounds, and preferences can make for a chaotic and even bumpy transition. However, you can ease the stress of your new situation by living in the present and accepting your stepfamily for what it is—unique and changing and evolving and growing.

Myth #3—Being in a blended family means choosing the new family members over the old ones.

Truth: You don't have to choose between your biological family and your blended family.

You get to have relationships with everyone —biological parents, step-siblings, and even extended family of your new stepparent. Your mom or dad may struggle with you having new family relationships, but this is not your fault. Nor is it your responsibility to make sure your parents don't feel bad. Your job is to learn how to be a supportive and productive family member in the new family while still maintaining a relationship with the noncustodial parent.

Myth #4—Blended families work like a sitcom.

Truth: Bringing two families together takes time, hard work, and patience.

The Brady Bunch was a blended family. But it was not real. That show, along with the newer ones on TV and in the movies, don't tell the full story. There's no storyline about what happens when two step siblings are on opposite baseball teams. No episode revolved around how to plan Christmas, fall breaks, birthdays, or religious rites. Because you only see the fairy-tale ideal, you may think that blended families should live in bliss, solve their problems instantly, and never face serious conflict. Just like any other family, successful blended families result from a lot of hard work. Don't feel guilty when your new family doesn't live up to a fairy tale.

Tips For Adjusting to a Blended Family

As a teenager, you may not have a choice about your new living situation. However, you do have a choice about how you handle the change. Here are a few tips to survive—and even thrive—in your new family.

1. Be patient. Be patient with yourself. And your biological parents. And your stepparent. And your new siblings. Giving yourself and everybody else space and grace to adjust, process their emotions, make mistakes, and learn along the way will make the transition of blended families a much less stressful experience.

2. Talk about everything. Nobody can read your mind, so pouting, sulking, giving others the silent treatment, and being quietly resentful won't do anybody any good—especially yourself. Talk about how you feel. Ask questions. Give your opinion. Tell others what you want and need.

3. Search for an ally. Find someone outside of your family who has been in the same situation as you are in now. Ask how she adjusted. Find out what she would do differently if she had to do it all over again. Talk to her about what drives you nuts, what scares you, and what you're worried about. Having been through this, she will give you insight that no one else can.

4. Pray. Maybe that sounds strange, but talking to God helps. He knows your situation and your new family members. He created them, remember? Ask Him to guide your new family. Ask Him to give you patience and grace and wisdom (see tip #1). He cares about your situation and wants to help if you will let Him.

5. Give it a chance. You may hate the situation. You may think this remarriage is the worst idea ever. You may have concluded that this whole blended family thing will end in a disaster of epic proportions. And you could be completely wrong. This blended family could turn out to be one of the biggest blessings in your life. You may discover that your new stepdad is really cool and that having a younger sister is actually a lot of fun. To learn that, though, means giving this new family a chance. Go into it with a positive attitude (as much as you can). Be open to doing new things—different foods, a new store, a different church. You may just find that you actually like this new family.

5 Good Things About a Blended Family

Can anything good come from being in a blended family? Yes! Look for these and other benefits as you adjust to a new way of life.

1. ***Extended family.*** You'll have a new stepparent, new grandparents, aunts, uncles, cousins, and siblings. These adults can give you advice, wisdom, and examples to live by. They can also be great friends if you give them the chance.

2. ***Conflict resolution skills.*** When you live in a blended family, you must learn how to negotiate, how to resolve problems, and how your actions can affect others. Although this may not seem important now, you will definitely need those skills later on at work and in your own marriage.

3. ***A happy parent.*** You want your mom and dad to be happy. You want them to find a person with whom they can spend the rest of their lives. Marrying again and creating a new family can provide that for them. As a bonus, if your parents are happy, your family environment is more likely to be happy as well.

4. ***Ability to change.*** When you live in a blended family, you must learn the art of flexibility. You must incorporate new traditions. You may go to a new school or a new church. You may even move across the state or across the country. You'll need to learn how to compromise and give and take. These skills will benefit you both as a teenager and into adulthood. Have you ever enjoyed being around someone who just couldn't go with the flow? Me neither.

5. ***More love.*** Believe it or not, your blended family may be a great place for support, encouragement, love, and the occasional kick in the backside. These new family members may be your best cheerleaders, allies, tutors, defenders—and maybe even your best friends.

25 *Activities You Can Do with Your Family*

1. Family movie night
2. Cookie baking night
3. Eating dinner together—at the dinner table, not in front of the TV
4. Game night
5. Bicycling around the neighborhood
6. Technology-free night (all phones and other electronic devices are off!)

7. Cookout
8. Campout
9. Go-karts
10. Volunteer day at a 5K or other benefit
11. Miniature golf
12. Plan a vacation together
13. Picnic at the park
14. Hiking
15. Video game night

16. Geocaching
17. Rock climbing
18. Go to a museum
19. Go feed the ducks
20. Play basketball together (horse, of course)

21. Serve at a soup kitchen
22. Laser tag
23. Bowling
24. Make a home movie with your phone
25. Eat at an ethnic restaurant (Thai, Koran, Indian, Caribbean, Cuban, etc.)

Scan for Video Answers!

Fill in the blank. The best way for a teenager to have fun with her family is to

_____.

WHEN YOUR MOM IS THE MEAN GIRL

by Pam Gibbs

She makes fun of the way I wear my hair.
She criticizes my clothes.
She calls me fat.
She says no guy would ever want me.

And she's my mom.

If this describes your life, you are not alone. A quick search online shows about nine million Web pages that talk about teens and kids whose moms are bullies. You deserve to grow up in a healthy family, with a mom and a dad and siblings who are committed to provide for, encourage, challenge, disciple, and above all, love you unconditionally. The home should be a safe place where you can run from the bullies and mean girls at school.

Except sometimes the mean girl wakes you up every morning.

Why Some Moms Are Mean

Every mom is different, so there are lots of reasons why a mom may be a bully. However, most mean mom behavior stems from similar situations:

1. Generational patterns. Most of the time, moms act like mean girls because their moms were mean girls. Unhealthy behavior like bullying is often a generational cycle. It begins with one parent and then is passed on to the child, who then becomes the bully instead of the victim. If your mom lived in an abusive home (and bullying is abuse!), she may not know anything else. She never heard words of affirmation from her parents. She didn't have any positive role models who invested in her and told her how precious and valuable she was. She never had the chance to heal from her own hurts.

If you notice that your mom doesn't talk to her mother (your grandmother), or if you have never met your maternal grandmother, this might be a hint. As an adult, your mom has cut off contact with her mom. Or, you may notice that your grandmother criticizes your mom a lot. She complains about your mom behind her back. She criticizes her parenting. Or the way she dresses. If your grandmother is constantly on your mom's case, then you know why your mom treats you that way too.

2. Insecurity. Some moms only feel good about themselves when they tear down those around them, including friends and family. Highlighting the flaws and mistakes of others allows a mom to hide her own imperfections.

By putting you down, your mom feels like she is elevating her own worth. However, what she doesn't realize is that her attempts at feeling better by hurting you only make her feel worse too. Deep inside, she feels guilty and angry and ashamed that she has treated you this way.

3. *Poor parenting skills.* A friend told me about her mom, who had gotten pregnant at age seventeen and moved out on her own as a young parent:

My mom always yelled. Always. She always sounded so angry. When I didn't clean my room, she yelled. If I left the fridge door open, she yelled. I was so tired of constantly being yelled out that I left. I could never do anything right. Anything was better than the constant screaming.

My friend's mom was too young to have a baby. She lacked any sort of parenting skills. She was too young to mature and plan a pregnancy and accept the responsibilities that go with it. Rather, she was thrown in the deep end and had to learn how to swim (parent) on her own. When that happens, many moms become defeated and resigned, and their children become the magnet for those negative feelings and behaviors.

4. *Jealousy.* Some moms were bullied as girls because they didn't fit in. Or because they weren't cute enough, thin enough, or liked enough. Then their daughters experience just the opposite in middle school and high school. They are popular. Successful. Pretty. Fashionable. Watching their daughters thrive and flourish sparks jealousy in some moms. All of those old emotions of shame and embarrassment come flooding back in, and rather than deal with their own pain, they just perpetuate the pain.

What To Do When Your Mom Is Mean

Knowing why your mom is so mean gives you insight into her world, but it doesn't really change your situation. How do you respond when your mom bullies you? Can you prevent it from happening again?

Recognize who is at fault. You are not responsible for your mom's mean-girl behavior. She may even say something like, "If you wouldn't be so stupid, I wouldn't . . ." You didn't make her treat you poorly. You didn't force her to be mean. She is making her own choices. What is happening is not your fault.

Talk to your mom if possible. She may not even be aware of how her words and actions come across to you. When the atmosphere is calm, and your mom seems to be in a good mood, approach her calmly and maturely. Share that you feel belittled and hurt when she criticizes you and makes fun of you. If talking to her is impossible, write a letter. Tell her that you love her, but some of the things she says are hurtful. Give her specific examples. Explain that you need her unconditional love and support. Allow her to write you back or talk to you in person so she can share her thoughts. Then wait to see if her attitude or her actions change.

Talk to another family member. First, try to talk with your dad. If that is not an option, you can also talk to an older aunt or cousin, or even a grandparent (if she's safe and not a part of the problem). Explain how your mom's mean girl approach hurts you. Ask for wisdom and insight. A relative may be able to see things from a different perspective, or she may be able to speak to your mom. If nothing else, having someone else understand what you're going through can help you feel less isolated and alone.

Talk to a counselor. Some schools have counselors on staff who are trained and experienced at helping teens work through their problems. They might be aware of resources you can use and actions you can take to counter the bullying. As an alternative, your church might have a counselor on staff. You may even be able to talk with a therapist that is covered under your parents' insurance. (You can ask your dad for help with this.)

Find an "adoptive" mom. Think about who could provide the nurture and care you need and deserve. She may be that relative you talked to. It could also be your youth minister (if she's female), the youth minister's wife, or someone else in the church. Spending time in her home with her family will give you a glimpse into what healthy family interaction looks like (although no family is perfect). Watching how she interacts with her children could provide a good model for you to remember in the future when you have your own children.

As a last resort, involve the law. If your mom continues to bully you and the torment becomes unbearable, talk with a police officer. He or she can tell you what options you have. The police will also be aware of community service that could help you. You may even need to go to court to ask a judge to allow you to move and live somewhere else. (Note: Of course, if you are being physically abused, contact the police right away.)

Remind yourself continually of your value. Being bullied over and over can leave you thinking that you are not worth anything, that no one really loves you, and that you are a mistake and a failure. None of these things is true. God created you uniquely and wonderfully (Psalm 139:14), and He loves you very much. Other family members love you. Your church family loves you. So do your friends. Your life matters, and you have a purpose and a calling given by God. To remind yourself, memorize Scripture, put verses and inspirational quotes around your room or on your bathroom mirror. Find phone apps that will send daily reminders. Do whatever necessary to counter the garbage thrown at you and replace it with the truth.

Whatever you do, don't allow despair to creep in. Your life can get better. You can overcome this battle and become a dynamic, confident young woman. And you can break the cycle of bullying. You can be the one to change your family forever.

5 Ways to Improve Your Relationship with Your Parents

Have you ever seen those cheesy blue ribbons with "World's Best Mom" or "World's Best Dad" on them? You might have even given your parents one when you were a kid. Being a parent is a hard, thankless job. However, you have the opportunity to make your parents' lives a little easier and more rewarding. Check out the five tips below. Put a few into practice, and maybe you'll get one nifty "World's Best Daughter" ribbon to hang proudly in your locker (yeah, right!).

Tip #1: Show Respect

Your parents deserve your respect. Even when you disagree with them. Even when they embarrass you in public. Even when they try to talk to you. Try not to zone out when your parents want to talk with you about something. Make an effort to listen carefully to their point If you don't agree, don't get defensive. It only makes matters worse. Think about their perspective—their actions are rooted in love. Your parents make the final decision, and you must respect their rules and boundaries. Rather than argue until you are all mad and frustrated at each other, accept your parents' decision. And a simple "yes ma'am" or "no sir" can do wonders.

Tip #2: Talk to Them

"How was your day?" "Fine." "Do you have a lot of homework?" "No." "Are you ready for your biology test tomorrow?" "Sort of." Is that really a conversation? I know it's hard when your parents start drilling you with questions, but look at the positive side: at least they care enough to ask! Try answering with three words or more. Believe it or not, their questions are not an attempt to annoy you—they just want to maintain a relationship with you. They care about what's going on in your life. Try sharing something small about your day, even if they don't initiate the conversation. You don't have to share your deepest secret. Just open a little bit so they can peek inside. Trust me—a little communication goes a long way.

Tip #3: Say Thanks

Your parents do a lot for you. Shuttling you to practice, club teams, and summer camp, driving on field trips, paying for braces, baking cookies for church, making emergency runs to the store for poster board for your project. A parent's job is never done. Sometimes it's easy to take your parents for granted. A lot of kids around the world lack the essentials—a roof over their heads and three meals a day. Yet most parents wear themselves out taking kids to countless activities, watching their games (even when it's minus four degrees outside), and working extra hours so you can get that smartphone you've been wanting for Christmas. Take some time to say thanks. E-mail your parents. Text them. Make them a cheesy homemade card. And say, "Thanks!" when they go the extra mile.

Tip #4: Give Them a Break

I know parents can be, well, embarrassing. Dad mows the lawn in old jean cut-off shorts. Mom can't make it ten minutes without embarrassing you when you have a sleepover. And bless her heart, the waistband on her jeans comes up to her armpits. And she tucks her shirts in and wears a belt. Yikes! Most parents are not cool, and so don't expect them to be. Remember, someday you will have kids who think you are uncool and who laugh when they see your old pictures. And you might even want those mom jeans someday. For a costume, of course.

Tip #5: Say "I love you"

A few months ago, I woke up at 5 a.m. to catch an early flight for a speaking engagement. As I was heading down the stairs, I found the greatest surprise from my daughter. She had taped about ten pieces of notebook paper together and written me a sweet note and draped it across the top of the stairs. I cried. I folded up the sign, put it in my bag, and showed it to all my friends. Other times she will leave me a Post-it note on my desk or sneak a note into my bag. I have saved every one of them. I would rather have her homemade notes than a store-bought gift any day. Consider leaving your mom or dad a reminder that they are loved—"I love you" on a Post-it note; an e-mail; a text. It's guaranteed to make your mom cry—or at least put her in a better mood.

Honor your father and mother, which is the first commandment with a promise, so that it may go well with you and that you may have a long life in the land. —Ephesians 6:2–3

HONOR
your Father
and Mother

My Parents Don't Believe In Jesus

by Pam Gibbs

You're at lunch one day, sitting with two friends who go to church with you. As usual, the topic of parents comes up in the conversation.

"I can't believe this. My mom is a sponsor for the lock-in."

Your other friend replies, "Oh, no. That stinks. Mine was at the cookout. I was so embarrassed."

You listen to them go back and forth about all the horror they must endure because their parents go to church. You smile and laugh with them, but inwardly you're thinking, *You don't know how lucky you are.*

Being the only person in your family who goes to church can be tough, especially if your parents don't believe in Jesus. While other families pile out of the car and file into the church, your mom or dad drops you off at the door. And oh, please, please don't let either of them still be in their jammies.

I understand. I've been there. When I was a tween and teen (and even in my adult years), I was the only one in my family who went to church. Back then (you know, way back then), the church van actually came by and picked me up. And dropped me off afterwards. Luckily, I wasn't the only one my age in that predicament. Some of my friends were in the same boat, and we hung together. Otherwise, I might not have stayed faithful.

I deeply longed for my parents to believe as I did, to want to go to church with me, to want to go on trips with my youth group.

I was also confused. *How do I tell them about Jesus so they'll listen? How can I be a witness? Do I stand up to them when their opinions defy Scripture? Or do I respect my parents and keep my mouth shut?*

Below are some lessons I learned, some of which came from doing the exact opposite. Hopefully they'll give you a little reassurance, encouragement, and wisdom to take into your relationship with your parents.

Live It Out, Don't Talk It Up

You can talk about how much you love Jesus every day, but if you backtalk your mom when she tells you no, your words are meaningless. Living your faith out in front of your family is just hard. Very hard. Your mom and your dad, your siblings, and your other relatives see you at your very best—and at your very worst. They see your excitement when you come home from camp, but they also know what it's like to be on the receiving end of your smart mouth and critical spirit. The most important thing for you to do as a believer is to live so that your family is drawn toward God, not turned off to Him because of your actions.

I wish I done a better job of that when I was younger. I tried some cheesy tactics to talk about God. I'd give them a religious birthday card. Or a faith-based book for Christmas (like Golfers for God or Prayers for Stressed-Out Moms). I'd even leave them stupid notes when I came in late. I found one recently while going through some papers my mom had kept. It said, "I got home about midnight and I'm wiped out. Please

don't wake me up—unless Jesus is coming back." Yeah. I know. You get the point.

Expect To Be Misunderstood

Opening presents from my family on my birthday and at Christmastime is always, well, a little disappointing. And sometimes amusing if I have the right attitude. Because I am a believer, and my parents and family know that I am, they assume that I would want religious gifts. And oh, my. There have been some doozies. I have to give them some credit. I did get one beautiful cross necklace and a Bible that still sits on my shelf to this day. But the other gifts? Um, not so much. One year I got this Bible on a stick. That's really the only way I know how to describe it. An artist (?) had opened a hardcover Bible to the middle-ish, placed that obligatory silky bookmark in the middle, and then petrified the whole thing with a substance that would keep the space shuttle together if it landed on the sun. The artist then drilled a hole in the bottom, and attached a thick, four-inch dowel rod that was then hammered into a wood base. The result? Bible on a stick. Really? It. was. u.g.l.y. What teenage girl wants THAT in her room?

All kidding aside, that Bible is just one example of how my parents didn't understand my faith. Oh, they allowed me to develop spiritually on my own, but they just couldn't identify with my choices. I would rather go hang out with the group at my youth minister's house than hang out with my non-Christian friends. I worked at the church without getting paid. And I tithed.

Even as a teenager. That was hard for my parents to understand, especially when I got into college and was broke.

You may feel misunderstood because of your faith. I get it. That's why being at the church and being around other Christians was so important to me. They reassured me, mentored me, showed patience toward me, and loved me to Jesus. And I am forever grateful for it. Hopefully your church will engulf you in its arms too.

Respect Your Parents—Always

Like any typical teenager, I argued with my parents. Mostly, I just griped about doing dishes or cleaning my room, but sometimes the discussion was more controversial. In high school, I decided to write a persuasive speech on why abortion is wrong. I did all of my research (back when you had to look in actual books, not on the Internet!), compiled my data, and outlined my speech. My mom came up to me, a half-filled glass of water in her hand. She asked me, "Is this glass half full or half empty?" I understood her point. From her unredeemed, worldly way of looking at life, abortion wasn't necessarily wrong. Now in that moment, I could have started into a heated argument with all my facts and rebuttals. For some reason (God's Spirit), I refrained. I simply said, "Depends on how you look at it." If I had responded with a snarky response in a disrespectful tone, I wouldn't have been drawing her toward Jesus. I would have given her even more reasons not to believe.

Scripture commands children to both honor and obey their parents (Exodus 20:12; Ephesians 6:1–2). Nowhere in those verses is there an exception clause. It doesn't say, "Respect your parents and obey them unless they aren't Christians." Regardless of your parents' spiritual history or practices, you are commanded to respect and obey them. Ouch.

You Make a Difference

I'm my family's chaplain. The token religious person. That means I'll be asked to give the prayer at every family meal, especially at Christmas and Thanksgiving when you traditionally give thanks. Being the chaplain also means I'm the go-to person when life turns upside down. In a crisis, my family asked me to pray for them. They wanted Bibles. They came to me for advice. That came later, in college and beyond, but I know the seeds of that trust were sown when I was a teenager. And being the chaplain meant preparing my mom's funeral service, where my old youth minister preached and his wife sang. My journey had come full circle.

Living out your faith in front of your family matters. Your mom and dad (and other members of the family) are watching you. You don't need to be perfect. Just be real and honest about your faith. As you do, God's Spirit works, even when you can't see any evidence.

The truth is, you won't know how much your life mattered on this side of heaven until you arrive on the other side. Then you'll see. Your family needed your faith.

Me?
A Role Model?

by Pam Gibbs

Do you remember being in the fifth grade? You probably idolized the sixth graders. You wanted to talk like, dress like, look like and act like the girls who seemed so much more mature, confident, and independent. And when you moved to the sixth and seventh grades, you likely idolized the high school girls. Whether or not you realize it, you're always looking for role models in your life. In fact, you could probably name three or four you have watched and wanted to be and act like.

But here's a question: Have you ever thought of *yourself* as a role model?

If you have a younger sister, brother, or cousin, you are an example, whether you like it or not. And even if you don't have any younger relatives, you can bet someone is watching you. It may be a neighbor or a girl at your church. It could be the younger sister of a friend. It could even be a girl in a grade below you. She wants to act just like you. She listens as you talk to your friends and notices the choices you make.

Today's culture encourages teenagers and young adults to use these early years to do whatever you want. Drink. Party. Be reckless. Embrace danger. Do whatever you want now, because when you "grow up," you'll have to be responsible and mature. However, God's perspective on your life is very different. First Timothy 4:12 urges us, "Don't let anyone look down on you because you are young, but set an example for the believers in speech, in conduct, in love, in faith and in purity" (NIV). God wants you to be an example to others, even though you are young. Rather than waste the gift of these teenage years, why not use it as a powerful influence? Consider the possibility that your example may change someone else's life or influence a whole nation.

Think back over the last forty-eight hours. How would your actions measure up against the verse above? If someone was watching you, what kind of example did you set by your words? Were you mean or critical? Did you pass along a juicy piece of gossip? Think about your conduct. If a parent or youth leader were to "grade" your conduct and actions, would you be happy with that grade? Have you shown love to others even though they are different than you? Have you shown mercy and forgiveness, even in your own family? This may be the hardest place of all to

set an example. If you have younger brothers and sisters, your patience may be pushed to the limit. It's much easier to act mean, to get back at them, and to make them as mad as they've made you. But think about the example you are setting when you demonstrate kindness, grace, and forgiveness. What you do and what you say matters.

A friend of mine became a Christian when she was about ten years old. She tells the story of how she constantly left Bible verses in her little sister's room and told her about Jesus every day. She taught her songs and Bible stories so that her little sister would understand what it meant to follow Jesus. And one day she had the opportunity to pray with her sister as she committed her life to Christ. Instead of being irritated and frustrated with her sister's immaturity and aggravating quirks, she chose the irreplaceable role of encourager and model.

Will you leave a legacy of purity to the girls who are younger than you? If you don't want your younger sister pushing the limits with her boyfriend when she's older, then make sure you model a life of purity now. If you don't want a younger girl to use foul language, then make sure you don't. Guard the messages you put in your mind through TV, movies, music, and the Internet, and you'll be sending a message to those who look up to you.

Remember the warning of Jesus to those who would tempt someone younger or weaker to sin. "But whoever causes the downfall of one of these little ones who believe in Me—it would be better for him if a heavy millstone were hung around his neck and he were thrown into the sea" (Mark 9:42). Do you take your position of role model as seriously as God takes it? If not, stop right now and say a prayer asking Him to help you as you set a Christlike example for others to follow.

You have the opportunity to lead the way for a younger generation. Will you take the role of a mentor, living out a lifestyle of love and purity? Will you set a positive example in the choices you make? In your speech? In your faith? You may not believe it, but younger girls watch everything you do, and they will copy you someday. Make sure that as they are following you, you are following Jesus.

Don't let anyone look down on you because you are young, but set an example for the believers in speech, in conduct, in love, in faith and in purity."—1 Timothy 4:12 NIV

Quiz: What Kind of Role Model Are You?

1. You tell others about God's blessings

a. _____ every chance you get.

b. _____ only when they sneeze.

2. Your sister or brother would say you are nice

a. _____ most of the time.

b. _____ sometimes.

3. Your motto is

a. _____ "Others first."

b. _____ "It's all about me."

4. When it comes to purity, you think of

a. _____ honoring God.

b. _____ a brand of bottled water.

5. Your friends would describe you as

a. _____ loyal.

b. _____ flaky.

6. When you overhear some juicy gossip, you

a. _____ keep your mouth shut.

b. _____ pass it on to your best friend as soon a possible.

7. Your boyfriend wants to go too far, so you

a. _____ dump him.

b. _____ consider it.

8. When it comes to your curfew, you

a. _____ make it home with time to spare.

b. _____ make up a good excuse (even if it's not true).

9. When others find out you are a Christian, they

a. _____ are not surprised.

b. _____ cannot believe it.

Which of these three descriptions characterizes you, based on your answers?

If you had 1-3 A's . . .

Your character is going up in flames. If you want to redeem your reputation, refocus your attention on pursuing God rather than doing whatever makes you happiest. "Happy are those who keep His decrees and seek Him with all their heart" (Psalm 119:2).

If you had 4-6 A's . . .

You have some work to do, but it's worth the effort. People are watching, so don't miss opportunities to reflect your faith positively on others. "Live your life in a manner worthy of the gospel of Christ" (Philippians 1:27).

If you had 7-9 A's . . .

You're on the right path. Keep your focus on God, and let your life be an example for others to follow. "In the same way, let your light shine before men, so that they may see your good works and give glory to your Father in heaven" (Matthew 5:16).

The Last Word on Family

Two are better than one because they have a good reward for their efforts. For if either falls, his companion can lift him up; but pity the one who falls without another to lift him up.
—Ecclesiastes 4:9–10

Me &
My World

Making Peace with Your Body

by Vicki Courtney

Have you ever stood in front of your mirror and grumbled, "I hate my body"?

Have you ever wished you had longer legs, a flatter stomach, or bigger boobs?

Do you wish you were fatter, thinner, taller, or shorter?

Do you look at the images in magazines and instantly get depressed and discouraged because you could never be that beautiful?

Have you figured out by now that Barbie's shape is totally messed up?

In fact, if Barbie were life-size, her measurements would be 38-18-34, which is not natural. Even if you never played with Barbie dolls, chances are you are like the rest of us when it comes to how you feel about your body.

I will praise You because I have been remarkably and wonderfully made. Your works are wonderful, and I know this very well. —Psalm 139:14

As someone who struggled off and on with an eating disorder, I can attest to the power of the message to be thin coming from media, magazines, and the culture. I wanted desperately to look in the mirror and approve of the image staring back at me. Unfortunately, acceptance eluded me until I hit my thirties and decided that life is too short to obsess about the unattainable perfect body. After almost two decades, with God's help, I made friends with the shape I saw in the mirror. I decided that my contentment would no longer be based on the readout on the scale or how I looked in a swimsuit. I was going to like me, imperfection and all.

Now, I'm not recommending that we just let ourselves go, eat five boxes of Twinkies, veg in our rooms, and blow off exercising. I'm talking about accepting our shape for what it is—whether it's pear shaped, apple shaped, hourglass, short, tall, big-boned, or petite. Even if you are currently overweight or underweight, you can still aspire to reach a healthy weight range and accept yourself at the same time. What I am encouraging you (and me) to do is to grow to the point where we can look at ourselves in a full-length mirror and honestly say to God, "I will praise You because I have been remarkably and wonderfully made. Your works are wonderful, and I know this very well (Psalm 139:14).

But how, exactly, do we get there? How do we make peace with the way God made us—to the point that we can actually praise God for the way He made us? Unfortunately, we can't just take a pill or say a mantra. Even surgery won't solve the problem, be-cause the underlying condition isn't physical. It's emotional. However, you and I can take some steps to move us in the right direction. If we can put into practice these tips and keep doing them as we grow older, we can protect our hearts and live knowing our worth comes from God, not our looks.

Focus on the things you like. Do you like your smile? Your hair color? Your eyes or your nose? Every girl can find at least one thing they like. Thank God for it. Then, thank God for one more thing, maybe even your soccer skills or singing voice. You'll discover that you like yourself more than you think—and for more reasons than what shows on the outside.

Get moving. Scientists tell us that exercise boosts metabolism and releases chemicals that help us feel better. Play golf. Jog. Walk the dog. Jump rope. Dance. Join a self-defense class. Do something that works out your muscles and puts your heart into action.

Choose your role models wisely. Think about your role model, that person you look up to and want to emulate. Do you want to be like her only because she's skinny and wears cool clothes? Or do you admire her because she's smart and tenacious? Admiring people for their character and accomplishments shifts your focus from outward appearance to what ultimately matters—what's on the inside.

Turn off the TV. If you're like me, you have to flip through a gazillion channels to find what you want to watch. In the process,

you're subjected to hundreds of ads and info-mercials that remind women they are not skinny enough, tall enough, fit enough, or pretty enough. Instead of surveying TV shows, record the ones you like. Then find something else to do. Then when you're ready to watch, you can bypass the channel flipping and can fast-forward through the commercials.

Eat right. Good nutrition means you're giving your body healthy foods. Switch to foods like veggies, fruit, whole grains, low-fat dairy foods, lean meats, legumes, and nuts, and limit sweets and unhealthy fats. Try to slow down or stop eating processed foods and stick to whole natural foods, which are nutrient-dense and provide more energy for fewer calories.

Listen to the truth. Rather than listening to what the world says about your body, listen to the truth from God's Word. Memorize Scriptures like the following:

But the LORD said to Samuel, "Do not consider his appearance or his height, for I have rejected him. The LORD does not look at the things people look at. People look at the outward appearance, but the LORD looks at the heart."—1 Samuel 16:7 NIV

I praise you because I am fearfully and wonderfully made; your works are wonderful, I know that full well.—Psalm 139:14 NIV

Charm is deceptive and beauty is fleeting, but a woman who fears the LORD will be praised.—Proverbs 31:30

For we are God's handiwork, created in Christ Jesus to do good works, which God prepared in advance for us to do.—Ephesians 2:10 NIV

Do you not know that your bodies are temples of the Holy Spirit, who is in you, whom you have received from God? You are not your own; you were bought at a price. Therefore honor God with your bodies.—1 Corinthians 6:19–20 NIV

You have a choice. You can listen to the lies of the enemy who wants to steal, kill, and destroy you (John 10:10). Or you can listen to the voice of your Creator who made you uniquely and for a purpose.

Q. **What is your favorite thing about yourself?**

Scan for Video Answers!

Did You Know?

- If clothing store mannequins were real women, they would be too skinny to have a period or have children.

- If Barbie were a real woman, she'd have to walk on all fours. Because of her unrealistic proportions, she would not be able to balance on her long legs and tiptoes.

- The average American woman weighs 144 pounds and wears a size 12 to 14.

- One out of every four college-age girls uses unhealthy methods of weight control, including fasting, skipping meals, excessive exercise, laxative abuse, and self-induced vomiting.

- Models in fashion magazines are airbrushed and retouched.

- Twenty years ago, models weighed 8 percent less than the average woman. Today, they weigh 23 percent less, and many of them fall into the weight range for anorexia.

Source: See wetzel.psych.rhodes.edu/223webproj/bodyimage/food.html

Anorexia Nervosa and Related Eating Disorders, Inc. © 1999. All rights reserved.

THE ROLLER COASTER OF MOOD SWINGS

by Vicki Courtney

When my family was in the market to buy our first puppy, I researched breed after breed to find the perfect dog. I wanted a small dog that wouldn't shed and had loads of personality. I chose the Yorkshire terrier breed because it seemed to match my preferences. I found a breeder, and within months my little Lexie was born. When we brought her home when she was six weeks old, she only weighted eleven ounces

Now Lexie is full grown. She is small, she doesn't shed, and she has loads of personality. In fact she has loads of personalities. I believe there is a medical term for this—multiple personality disorder. She goes by a variety of names in our home: Psycho Pup, Devil Dog, and Lucy (short for Lucifer). One minute she can be the sweetest, most charming puppy on earth; and the next minute, she can turn into a snappy, feisty, growling pit Yorkie. In fact, I often joke that we didn't get a Yorkshire terrier—we got a Yorkshire terror.

Talk about mood swings!

I'm willing to bet you have experienced fluctuating moods in your teen years. One minute you can be laughing, full of life; and the next minute you can be in tears, worn out, and really wanting to be alone. Up and down, like riding a roller coaster. Can you relate? If so, take a deep breath and relax. Mood swings are normal. Although there is not a whole lot you can do to avoid them, you can learn to manage them. Here is some advice from someone who's been there:

1. ***Avoid making sudden spontaneous decisions during this time.*** When you are emotional, you can easily blow things out of proportion and overreact. Don't respond to texts or other social media when you feel snarky. Wait until your emotions settle down a bit.

2. ***Find an adult who will listen to you.*** Make sure she understands what you are going through and will be empathetic and remind you that it is temporary. The best choice is your mom (don't roll your eyes!), but I realize that not all girls have the luxury of a close mother-daughter relationship. Avoid leaning on someone your age when you experience mood swings, because she may be in a mood of her own. And don't dump on guys. They're not prepared for it!

3. ***Write out your thoughts.*** Using a journal allows you to say whatever you want without censoring yourself. Once you've vented, you might discover that those intense emotions are not as overwhelming.

4. ***Lean on Christ.*** Make it a discipline to pour out your heart to Christ when you are feeling low. The sooner you learn to lean on the Source of all comfort, the better. Don't worry about making Him mad. He can handle it.

5. ***Don't self-medicate.*** Whatever you do, don't try to alleviate your pain with drugs, alcohol, overeating, undereating, depressing music, or promiscuity. Those choices can have serious repercussions later. Run to Jesus, and let Him fill your heart with a settled peace.

This out-of-control roller coaster of mood swings rarely continues in your adult years. However, if your moods seem more severe and more frequent than those of your friends (girls your age), let your parents know. You could have a chemical imbalance that can cause emotional upheaval. A simple trip to the doctor could make a huge difference. If you are like most girls, though, the frequency of your mood swings will die down as you progress through high school. Some girls will continue to experience PMS (a term for intense mood swings that occur about the time of your period). That's normal too. Hopefully your mood swings won't be as vicious as Lexie's!

Trust in the LORD with all your heart, and do not rely on your own understanding; think about Him in all your ways, and He will guide you on the right paths. —Proverbs 3:5–6

Help!

Q: *I don't look anything like the girls in the magazines, on television, or in the movies. Why would anybody want me the way I am?*

A: Let me tell you a story about my friend Elizabeth. She always asked herself that same question when she was a teenager. It usually surfaced after flipping through a fashion magazine and seeing the seemingly perfect models with sparkling white teeth, slender legs, flawless skin, and the cutest outfits imaginable. And there she was—short with stubby muscular legs, less-than-perfect skin, rather boring hair, and to top it all off, a set of shiny braces. She looked nothing like the gorgeous girls in the magazine. The more she thought about it, the more her physical appearance depressed her. She wanted to be a popular girl, surrounded by people who loved her and wanted to be her friends. She thought the only way to be loved was to be attractive.

That same year, Elizabeth tried out for the school dance team, a group of girls known for being popular and beautiful. After making the team, she thought she had it made. Working hard every day in practice, she became one of the better dancers, which caused the others to pay more attention to her. In the locker room every day, the girls would help her straighten her hair, fix her eye shadow, or give her a spray of their designer perfume. Soon she knew how to act like a popular, pretty girl, and she took pride in being on the team. There was nothing better than strutting through the halls on the day of a pep rally, decked out in her uniform and dolled up with makeup. She thought she was one of the coolest girls in the school.

The happiness was short-lived. Later in her sophomore year, Elizabeth realized that most of the girls had nothing more than skin-deep beauty. They knew how to apply mascara and wore fashionable clothes, but most of them were empty on the inside. Although Elizabeth was a Christian, most of the girls weren't believers, a fact that became more apparent as she saw their behavior. Every morning she was surrounded by girls who did things she knew didn't make God happy—drinking, smoking, cussing, and gossiping. And even though they appeared to have it all, she began to realize just how consumed they were with their appearance rather than what was in their hearts.

Over a year's time, Elizabeth's desire to fit in with these girls had hurt her relationship with God. She eventually ended up quitting the team and working on redefining her definition of *beauty*. As she developed friendships with other people, she focused more on their internal beauty than their outward appearance. In doing so, she found genuine friends who loved her for the beautiful person she was on the inside. More importantly, she asked God to help her develop qualities the Spirit produces: love, joy, peace, patience, kindness, goodness, faithfulness, gentleness, and self-control (Galatians 5:22–23).

Next time you see girls who look "perfect" on the outside, remember that lots of girls are empty on the inside. True beauty begins in the heart. Proverbs 31:30 says, "Charm is deceptive and beauty is fleeting, but a woman who fears the Lord will be praised." To fear the Lord is to love Him with all your heart, soul, mind, and strength. And when you see the models on the pages of the fashion magazines, remember the word *fleeting*. Twenty years from now, those models will be well past their physical prime. If they've staked their worth on outer beauty, their self-worth will plummet and they will be left with an empty hole in their hearts.

But the fruit of the Spirit is love, joy, peace, patience, kindness, goodness, faith, gentleness, self-control. Against such things there is no law. —Galatians 5:22–23

Encountering Different Faiths: What Other Religions Believe

What do Muslims believe?
Which religion believes in reincarnation?
Can you be a Christian and still be a Mormon?

Which group believes that everyone will go to heaven?
What's the difference between Wicca and Satanism?

Religion	Origins	God	Human situation
Christianity	God is eternal. He created the universe, including all of humanity.	One God known in a Trinity, consisting of God the Father, God the Son, and God the Holy Spirit	All people have sinned against God and are separated from Him.
Atheism	Evidence of atheism appears in ancient history, but especially after the Age of Enlightenment (the nineteenth century).	There is no evidence of God or a divine being. Beliefs about the universe are based on science.	Humans have great potential. No deity intervenes to help humans in need.
Bahá'í Faith	Founded by Bahaullah in 1863	There is one God who has revealed himself throughout time through the founders of the major world religions.	The soul is essentially good. In life, a person should develop spiritually and draw closer to God. Sin is excused because God is benevolent.
Buddhism	Founded by Siddharta Gautama (the Buddha) around 520 BC	None, but there are enlightened individuals who become Buddhas.	Purpose in life is to avoid suffering, and release from the cycle of rebirth (reincarnation) to ultimate enlightenment.
Hinduism	No founder	One Reality (Brahman) who is manifested in limitless gods and goddesses	Humans are enslaved to ignorance.
Islam	Muhammad, 622 BC	One God known as Allah	Sin goes against the teachings of Allah. All human beings sin because no one is perfect. Allah, who created us and all of our imperfections, knows this and is merciful, compassionate, and forgiving.
Judaism	God is eternal. He created the universe, including all of humanity.	One God known as Yahweh (YHVH)	Violation of Ten Commandments; sin is an act, not a state of being
Jehovah's Witnesses (not recognized as a religion)	Charles Taze Russell, 1879	One God named Jehovah; Christ is God's first creation; the Holy Spirit is a force.	Disobeying Jehovah
Mormonism (not recognized as a religion)	Joseph Smith, 1830	God the Father, the Son Jesus, and the Holy Ghost are three individual beings	Humans existed as gods and goddesses, spirit children of God who have entered into mortality in order to gain a physical body. To be saved is to return to God.
Satanism	Anton LaVey, 1966	Atheistic; God is an invention of man; they see themselves as their own gods.	Encourages gratification of desires; there are nine Satanic sins, which include stupidity, self-deception, conforming, lack of perspective, counterproductive pride, not appreciating beauty
Wicca	Based on ancient pagan practies; modern form founded in the 1900s by Gerald Gardner	Belief in many gods, centered on the Goddess and God; also believe in a Supreme Being over all	"If it harms none, do what you will."

These are just a few of the questions students ask me from time to time. When your mom and dad were young, they probably shared the religious views of their classmates, but your classmates may hold completely different opinions and beliefs than you do. In talking with your friends, knowing what they believe can be helpful in starting faith conversations. We've provided a chart with many of the religions, cults, and belief systems compared to Christianity. Hopefully it will give you a basic understanding of your friends' beliefs.

Salvation	Afterlife	Practices	Sacred Texts
Salvation is through faith in Jesus Christ, God incarnate, who was the acceptable sacrifice for sin.	Eternal heaven or eternal hell, based on one's acceptance of Christ as Savior	Prayer, Bible study, communion, worship, service	The Bible
Because no deity exists, there is no need for salvation.	none	none	None. But secular writings include those of Sigmund Freud, Carl Marx, and Voltaire; modern authors Carl Sagan and Richard Dawkins
A collaboration between God and humans; good works counter evil deeds to show a person worth of heaven.	The soul separates from the body and journeys toward or away from God. Heaven and hell are states of being.	Prayer, scripture reading, hard work, work to bring about social justice and equality	Writings of Bahaullah and other Bahá'í leaders
Nonattachment to the world; following the eightfold path; reincarnation until reaching enlightenment	Nirvana as the highest destiny of a human spirit. This is a state of indescribable bliss.	Meditation, mantras, detachment from the world, mandalas, devotion to Buddhas	Tripitaka, the Mahayana Sutras, Tantra, and Zen texts
Leaving behind material possessions, physical pleasures, and emotional attachments; commitment to Atman Brahman (ultimate reality); growth toward perfection by reincarnation	Nirvana; extinction of selfhood into Brahman; a state of indescribable bliss	Yoga, meditation, devotion to a god or goddess, pigrimage to holy cities, living according to your dharma (purpose and role in life)	The Vedas, Upanishads, Bhagavad Gita, Ramayana
Submission to the will of Allah; living by the Five Pillars: belief, prayer, alms giving, fasting, and pilgrimage to Mecca.	Judgment: paradise and hell. Paradise obtained by following the will of God	Living by the Five Pillars; specific rules of conduct as set forth in the Qur'an, including no alcohol or eating of pork; holidays related to pilgrimage; fast of Ramadan	Qur'an (Koran)
Early: animal sacrifice; Post-temple period: faith and righteous living; messianic deliverance.	Judgment resulting in heaven and hell	Circumcision; bar/bat mitzvah; synagogue participation; no pork or nonkosher food; Jewish holidays; pursuing justice, righteousness, and truth	The Hebrew Bible known as the Tanakh, which includes the Torah, the Prophets, and the Writings
Salvation is through faith in Christ and through obeying Jehovah's laws.	Heaven for 144,000 chosen JW; eternity on new earth for all other JW; all others are annihilated; there is no hell.	Baptism; meetings at the Kingdom Hall (church); strong emphasis on evangelism; no blood transfusions; no celebration of holidays, no use of religious symbols (like crosses)	Russell's Study in Scriptures
Salvation by faith in Christ, plus good works, following the ordinances, and evangelism; baptism required for forgiveness of sins. You must repent of every sin.	Three levels of heaven based on earthly works; hell for those who reject God after death	Abstinence from alcohol, tobacco, and caffeine; baptism for the dead; eternal marriage; wearing temple garments (under daily clothes); active evangelsim	The Book of Mormon; Doctrine and Covenants; Pearl of Great Price; the Bible
Since there is no God, there is no sin.	None	Rituals, meetings, questioning authority	No sacred texts, just self rule
There is no sin, so there is no need for forgiveness; whatever you do will come back to you (karma).	Reincarnation until you reach the Summerland, the "land of eternal summer"	Prayer; casting a circle; drawning down the moon; dancing; singing; reciting spells	No sacred texts

SHAME ON ME, AGAIN

by Vicki Courtney

It happened suddenly and without warning.

One minute I was sitting in a booth, laughing over a cup of coffee with my youngest son on his college campus (which just so happens to be my alma mater). The next minute, I'm driving away from my old college stomping grounds, and the mere sight of a corner drugstore triggers a painful reminder of my past.

It just so happened to be the same corner drugstore that one of my roommates and I ducked into late one night under a cloak of darkness to purchase a pregnancy test. She was late and had assumed the worst. It turned out it was negative, but it just as easily could have been me purchasing the test.

In fact, it had been me, which is what triggered my sudden feelings of shame that day. At the age of seventeen, I had been the one taking a pregnancy test; and unfortunately, I got a positive result. This in turn led to my decision to terminate the pregnancy. I've spoken openly about this part of my past and have been walking in victory for many years,

but every so often, the feelings of shame will still come.

And that's what shame does. It shows up uninvited to steal your joy and accuse your soul.

The dictionary defines shame as "the painful feeling arising from the consciousness of something dishonorable, improper, ridiculous, etc., done by oneself or another."

We avoid talking about shame because it is messy.

The earliest account of shame was felt in the immediate aftermath of Adam and Eve's sin in the garden. Prior to their sin, Genesis 2:25 tells us they were both naked and unashamed. One chapter later they are sewing fig leaves together and playing a game of hide and-seek with God. With that one forbidden bite came man's first bitter taste of shame.

Like Adam and Eve, our instinct is to hide our shame. We attempt to cover it with modern-day fig leaves ranging from addictions to breakneck busyness. We bury our shame beneath perfectionism, good deeds, and yes, even ministry service. Been there, done that.

There is therefore now no condemnation for those who are in Christ Jesus. —Romans 8:1 ESV

Some people are more prone to experiencing feelings of shame, while others seem better equipped to avoid its sting a with a healthy understanding of guilt and grace. Those who grew up in households where shame was a mainstay of the family diet will often turn around and serve it in their own families, passing it down from generation to generation.

Shame is not the same as guilt. Guilt says, "What you did was bad." Shame says, "What you did was bad, so therefore, you are a bad person."

Shame is not the same as regret. Regret says, "If I could go back and do things differently, I'd do this . . . or that." Shame says, "I'll never get it right. I'm a failure."

Shame is not the same as embarrassment. Embarrassment says, "Everyone experiences embarrassing moments." Shame says, "Yet another reminder that I'm a loser and nothing will change that fact."

Guilt is always connected to *behavior*, while shame is always connected to *identity*. Guilt draws us toward God, but shame sends us away from God.

Although we can't completely abolish painful reminders of shame that show up uninvited from time to time on the doorsteps of our souls, we can refuse to answer the door.

And that's exactly what I did that day when I drove past the drugstore and the old shame tapes began to play. I hit the eject button and boldly declared out loud,

There is therefore now no condemnation for those who are in Christ Jesus.

Over and over, I proclaimed it until, once again, I believed it. I showed shame the door. And you can too.

Let us draw near to God with a sincere heart and with the full assurance that faith brings, having our hearts sprinkled to cleanse us from a guilty conscience and having our bodies washed with pure water. —Hebrews 10:22 NIV

Reflect

When was the last time you experienced a painful encounter with shame? Did you allow the shame tapes to play, or did you immediately turn to Christ, hit eject, and show shame the door?

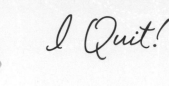

I Quit!

by Pam Gibbs

For as long as she could remember, Grace loved playing softball.

She started playing T-ball when she was just three. Even then, the coaches saw something special in her. The way she held the bat. The hand-eye coordination that was well beyond her developmental capabilities. The attention she gave to the game when the rest of her peers were tossing dirt into the air or picking weeds in the outfield.

Grace's love of the game grew with age. She played on a boy's baseball team when not enough girls signed up for softball, and she was better than most of the boys. Fielded better. Threw faster. Hit harder. She. Was. Good.

Finally, finally, Grace graduated to middle school. A softball team. A real girls' team with girl players. Fast-pitch didn't bother her because she'd been playing baseball and was used to the speed. She only got better with time. And in middle school, Grace could sign up for "travel ball" with teams that competed outside of school. She was in softball heaven.

Tournaments. Dirt under her nails. Traveling on the weekend and eating in fast-food restaurants. Watching other teams play as hers waited in line. She lived softball.

High school was no different, only better. The competition got fierce, which suited Grace just fine. As the game got more difficult, her skills improved even more. She started as a freshman, a feat accomplished by few girls in school history. Team ball. And travel ball. Year-round she got to play. Except for those stupid rules about dead periods and giving players rest. She hated those times.

Until her junior year.

Something shifted in Grace's heart. Something unsettled. At first, she couldn't quite put her finger on what she was feeling. The game didn't excite her as much as it had before. Even on the field, she found herself daydreaming about school, guys, lunch, and everything else—except softball. She stopped recording college ball on TV. She didn't want to watch other teams play in the tournaments. She'd rather just veg with her friends.

She'd traveled thousands and thousands of miles on teams, visiting fifteen states (she counted them) over the years. She never had a summer off. Vacation time was spent at tournaments and camps. Her parents had spent thousands and thousands of dollars on equipment, fees, trips, lessons, gas money, and food.

How could she just let it all go? Did she want to let it all go?

Can you relate? Maybe that was you a few years ago. Or perhaps you feel like Grace right now. You've invested your whole life up to this point doing something, but now you want out. Or you think you do. Honestly, you're just not sure.

Your love may not be softball. It could be debate team, drama, or tennis. Academic decathlon, art lessons, or horses. Writing or 4H. Whatever your passion was, it's not so much a passion anymore. It feels more like . . . work.

What do you do? How do you get out? Do you walk away after all those years invested and all that money spent? What will your parents say? Your coach? Your teammates? Your friends?

To Walk or Not to Walk

When you feel the urge to hang up your cleats or put away your paints, remember that you don't have to decide immediately. You can take a few intermediate steps to gauge whether or not you really want to pursue something else.

1. Ask yourself a difficult question. Why do you want to stop? Sometimes, as girls and guys get older, their interests change. And that's perfectly normal. However, you need to evaluate if that describes you. If it doesn't, then why do you want to quit? Here are some things to think about:

Do you want to quit:
- *because you're not as good as you'd like to be?*
- *because you're bored?*
- *because you are tired of the pressure that comes with competition?*
- *because you don't like your teammates? Teacher? Leader?*
- *because the training is just too tough?*
- *because you want to spend your time doing other things?*
- *because your passion just isn't fun any more?*

2. Take a break. You don't have to give up your passion for good. Just get a little space. Take some time off. Skip a tournament. Put aside your racquet for a week. Read a book just for fun. Giving yourself some time and space to pull back from your passion can give you a better perspective. Compare your situation to being at an art museum. If you get too close to the painting, you won't be able to see the whole picture—its mood, meaning, message. All you'll see is brushstrokes and lines. Step back and, ah! The big picture comes into view.

Taking a step back from that thing you've loved for so long can give you the bigger picture of your situation. You can see if you're ready to quit or if you are just tired. You can see if you like spending time doing other things. You can watch to see if your stress level goes down. You can tell if you've made this passion an idol, taking the place of God. You can decide if you're ready to move on—or not.

3. Talk with your parents. Explain to them how you've been feeling and how long you've been feeling it. Your parents know you (more than you think!) and they can offer a different perspective on what's going on. They may confirm your feelings because they've been seeing a shift in your emotions and desire. Just be honest with them. Keeping your thoughts to yourself won't do you any good.

4. Try something completely different. Try skeet shooting. Go rock climbing. Volunteer at Special Olympics. Take a painting class. Explore other interests that you've had in the past but couldn't pursue because of the time you didn't have. If you like what you've tried, keep at it. You may be developing new interests, which is totally cool. If you find yourself missing your old activity and would rather be doing that, then you know the passion isn't gone.

Change Is Scary

Letting go of an activity you once loved can feel a little scary. For all those years, you've been known as Grace the Softball Player or Hannah the Painter. What happens now? Who are you now?

You're still you. The same girl you've always been. Your identity isn't determined by your ability to run fast or your chocolate mousse recipe. Your friends and family love you because of who you are, not because of your skills. Your identity has already been determined. You are God's child. You are His creation. That doesn't change, no matter what you do (or don't do anymore).

With that identity intact, you can explore all your options. Chase a different dream. Walk down a new road.

Try it all. And have a blast doing it.

Act Your Age:

DON'T GROW UP SO FAST

by Vicki Courtney

Teen girls today face the constant pressure to grow up way too fast.

I was struck by this truth one day when flipping through a vintage copy of *Seventeen* magazine from the early 1980s, which just so happens to be when I was a teenager (don't laugh!). I chuckled when I saw an ad for sleepwear. It featured a cheesy picture of teen girls at a sleepover with a bowl of popcorn and a big behemoth-sized record player in the center of the room. The girls were dancing in their flannel floor-length nightgowns trimmed in white lace. I remember begging my mom for a nightgown just like the ones in the ad.

Fast forward to today. Girls your age are wearing pjs more suitable for your honeymoon than a slumber party. Several years back, my then sixteen-year-old daughter's cheerleading squad had a Christmas party where they drew names and exchanged gifts. I couldn't believe how many girls received intimate underwear from Victoria's Secret. Really?

When I got engaged, I could hardly wait to go to Victoria's Secret and register for lingerie for my upcoming lingerie shower. In those days, the unwritten rule was that you didn't set foot into the store until you had an engagement ring on. Now, when you step into a Victoria's Secret store, you are greeted with display after display of colorful thong underwear and sexy boy-cut shorts geared to girls your age. In fact, you don't even have to go to a lingerie store to get sexy lingerie. It's in all the trendy teen retail stores, many times in the coed stores, right by the checkout where it's no big deal for guys to see the display.

While lingerie retailers are trying to entice you to buy grown-up lingerie, clothing retailers plaster ads and window fronts with immodest clothes that encourage girls to cultivate sensualities that were meant to be saved for the wedding night. Add to those pressures the message in many pop songs that your body is meant to be nothing more than a tool for the gratification of men. That's probably why your mom and dad "overreact" when they hear you humming along to some of the songs on the radio. And don't forget the TV shows with adult themes—all of which are popular among teen girls. Is it any wonder that many girls your age say that they "miss being little"?

You jumped straight from little girl to adult woman. One day you had Barbies and the next day you're asking your mom for thong underwear.

Is it even possible to "act your age" in a culture that demands you to grow up too fast?

Yes.

Some teen girls in my church (and other churches) are choosing to act their age instead of acting like full-grown adult women. They hang out with friends instead of being attached to a boy all the time. They don't dress immodestly because they understand that many guys read more into a revealing outfit than just a simple fashion statement. They aren't interested in shows that feature hooking up as a norm. They are beautiful both inside and out. Now, does this mean they are perfect and never listen to pop music or shop at Victoria's Secret? Nope. Do they get along with their parents? Not always. They are just teens who aren't so worried about becoming adults.

Are you in a hurry to grow up? Hang on to your girlhood. Trust me, one day you will look back and wish you had enjoyed every possible moment of this no-longer-a-child-but-not-yet-a-woman season of life. Don't be ashamed to be young.

You who are young, be happy while you are young, and let your heart give you joy in the days of your youth. Follow the ways of your heart and whatever your eyes see, but know that for all these things God will bring you into judgment.—Ecclesiastes 11:9 NIV

15 **THINGS YOU CAN DO JUST FOR FUN**

1. Play with bubbles.
2. Get out some chalk and scribble on your driveway.
3. Jump on your trampoline in the yard. It misses you.
4. Swing at the playground.
5. Make a fort, and read a book inside it.
6. Bake cupcakes.

7. Play a board game with your family.
8. Use fingerpaints to create a picture.
9. Grab a camera and take pictures of everything that catches your eye.
10. Pull out that recipe that you and your mom once used together.

11. Watch a movie you loved when you were a kid.
12. Write a letter to a grandparent, and put it in the mail.
13. Take a bubble bath.
14. Eat an ice-cream cone.
15. Play with Play-Doh.

Q. Do you like being your age, or are you eager to be older?

Scan for Video Answers!

WHEN YOUR TEACHER IS WICKED MEAN

by Pam Gibbs

No one wants to get stuck with her. Classmates avoid her in the halls. Students she has taught shiver when she walks by. Rumors about her have been circulating for decades.

The Warden. Medusa. Snake Tooth. The Enforcer. Evil Eyes.

Every school has "that" teacher—the strict teacher who hasn't smiled since Ronald Reagan was in office. It's absolutely impossible to get along with her. She would make even Hello Kitty cry.

And you have her this semester.

You walk into the first day of class with an open mind. Surely, the rumors are just that—rumors. Maybe she really loves students and the nicknames come around every year just to scare incoming freshman. Or maybe the nickname got started by a bunch of troublemakers who made her life miserable every day.

After five minutes in class, you know the answer—the rumors aren't true—she's WORSE than anyone's description. You're almost in tears as you race to the door when the bell rings. Those looks. That tone of voice. Her attitude. Really, she could overthrow a dictator of a small nation.

How to Make Things Better

Unfortunately, you can't avoid her. And you can't change teachers. She's the only one who teaches this class, and you need it to graduate. So, the only option left? Yep. You must learn how to get along with Snake Eyes.

Hopefully, these tips will give you a slight edge in the "teacher's pet" department, which for her, means a not-so-scary stare.

1. Do your homework with excellence. My husband has been a high school teacher for more than twenty years, and I see my fair share of homework come home with him. Some of the papers come in late. Some are only half completed. Some teens don't even write legibly. Nothing is more frustrating than to see laziness and apathy. One of the best ways to get on your teacher's good side is to do your homework and turn it in on time. Completed. And neat. Oh, and don't forget to put your name on it.

2. Answer questions in class. I know, you think you'll be labeled a part of the geek squad. From a teacher's perspective, participation matters. When you talk (not to your best friend!) in class, you are communicating that you're listening and that you care about the subject (even if you really don't). In truth, nobody likes to hear the teacher's voice, so hearing somebody else talk may be a welcome change for everyone.

3. *Act respectful.* Use the words *yes, ma'am* and *no, sir.* Use *please* and *thank you.* Don't talk while the teacher is talking. Pick up trash. Bring supplies to class, and be ready to go when she starts lecturing. And don't do the things that normally get you in trouble with your parents— eye rolling, sighing, and slamming things (like your book).

4. *Don't cheat.* Let me tell you a secret: teachers know when you cheat. Even when you don't leave any evidence behind and she can't prove it, your teacher knows when you've cheated. Do you know why? It's impossible to turn in half-completed homework, sleep while she's talking, and still get an A on the test. If all of your homework is in the 90s and you make 70s consistently on tests? You've been cheating on homework. (Remember, my husband is a teacher, and he's seen everything). Cheating will earn you disfavor with a teacher before you can say *pencil.*

When You Can't Make Things Better

Sometimes, though, despite being respectful and doing your work, you may just get a bad teacher. Then what? First, give it time. The first few days and weeks can sometimes be rough, especially if you have a large class. If the situation doesn't improve, talk to your parents. Don't exaggerate. Be honest—even if that means admitting any fault on your part. From there, keep practicing the principles above, and let your parents handle the matter from there. They may set up a meeting with the teacher and you. Or, they may just meet without you.

You will face your unfair share of difficult people in your lifetime. Although you can't change how they treat you, you can always control how you act. Remember the Golden Rule? It's actually from the Bible—"Do to others what you would have them do to you" (Matthew 7:12 NIV).

Make that your guiding principle, and you won't go wrong—at least in God's eyes.

Do to others what you would have them do to you. —Matthew 7:12 NIV

What the Bible Says About *You*

You are the light of the world.—Matthew 5:14

But to all who did receive Him, He gave them the right to be children of God, to those who believe in His name.—John 1:12

I [Jesus] have called you friends, because I have made known to you everything I have heard from My Father.—John 15:15

Don't you yourselves know that you are God's sanctuary and that the Spirit of God lives in you?—1 Corinthians 3:16

Therefore if anyone is in Christ, there is a new creation; old things have passed away, and look, new things have come.—2 Corinthians 5:17

I no longer live, but Christ lives in me. The life I now live in the body, I live by faith in the Son of God, who loved me and gave Himself for me.—Galatians 2:19–20

Because you are sons, God has sent the Spirit of His Son into our hearts, crying, "Abba, Father!" So you are no longer a slave, but a son, and if a son, then an heir through God.—Galatians 4:6–7

For He chose us in Him, before the foundation of the world, to be holy and blameless in His sight. In love He predestined us to be adopted through Jesus Christ for Himself, according to His favor and will.—Ephesians 1:4–5

For we are His creation, created in Christ Jesus for good works, which God prepared ahead of time so that we should walk in them.—Ephesians 2:10

Therefore, God's chosen ones, holy and loved, put on heartfelt compassion, kindness, humility, gentleness, and patience.—Colossians 3:12

For you are all sons of the light and sons of the day. We do not belong to the night or the darkness.—1 Thessalonians 5:5

But you are a chosen race, a royal priesthood, a holy nation, a people for His possession, so that you may proclaim the praises of the One who called you out of darkness into His marvelous light.—1 Peter 2:9

Look at how great a love the Father has given us that we should be called God's children. And we are! The reason the world does not know us is that it didn't know Him.—1 John 3:1

SMART TIPS FOR LIVING IN THE DIGITAL WORLD

Being online is a part of teen culture. Social media sites and apps for your phone connect you with others across the street and across the globe. Living in this age of digital communication is great—if you are careful. Even if your parents restrict you to looking online only for research purposes, you still need to be careful about what you search for—and who might be searching for you. Review this checklist below to make sure you've done the basics to protect yourself in a world where nothing is ever secret.

Get the green light from Mom and Dad. I know, you probably use social media apps all the time, and you're connected to your friends 24/7 However, some types of social media are no good. Anything that degrades a person by grading their physical appearance should never be in your app arsenal. Neither should anything that asks if you want to hook up. And some kinds of social media have downsides (some of which can be dangerous) that you might not even be aware of. Talking with your parents just puts another layer of protection between you and the bad guys.

Use the privacy controls. Using those privacy options adds an extra level of protection. It sends a clear message to predators that you are not interested in meeting strangers. You can invite friends to join your social media circles so you won't miss out on being in the know. Remember, this only adds a level of protection and is not 100 percent foolproof.

Never share personal information. Ever. This includes your school name, church name, city, phone numbers, screen name, e-mail address, or other identifying information that makes it easy for strangers to find you in real life. You may think that listing a few things like your church or your school is okay, but predators are pros at using small bits of information to seek out their prey. You can never assume that only "good people" are viewing your profile.

Make sure your pictures are appropriate. Never upload pictures in swimsuits, pjs, or undergarments. Do not pose suggestively or seductively. You may think those poses are funny, but people may misinterpret them. And it only takes a second for other people to screenshot and save that selfie you posted, so they'll have the shot even if you have second thoughts and delete it the next day. (Hence the privacy settings!)

Limit your friends to "real friends." Who needs online strangers as friends? Your time could be better spent with real friends in the real world doing good things. If you want to meet new people, join a club at school. Volunteer. Sign up to be an exchange student. There are safer ways to meet people in real life than taking the risk of online "friendships."

Report suspicious activity. By suspicious, I mean anything that makes you feel uncomfortable. If you get that feeling that something is not quite right, that might be the Holy Spirit warning you of danger. Show your parents what you've received (text, e-mail, personal message, etc.), and they can help you report it to the authorities. Also, take a screen shot of the page and send it to the administrators of the website or app. They will investigate from their angle as well. Don't worry that you may be wrong. You may be the one to catch a predator.

Remember that information you delete never really goes away. Every time you post something online or in an app, it is like leaving a trail of bread crumbs for anyone who might want to trace your journey back to its starting point— even though you are long gone! Colleges, employers, and other organizations are searching Google for information about potential students or employees— it's cheaper than doing a background check!

If the thought of Mom, Dad, Grandma, teachers, a youth minister, a boyfriend's mom, neighbors, school officials, potential employers, and a slew of strangers seeing what you post (including pictures of you in a bikini!) makes you a little squeamish (or A LOT!), you might reconsider. Once it's on the internet, it's out there—forever—and completely beyond your control.

ARE YOU ADDICTED TO YOUR PHONE?

Have you ever (check all that apply):

_____ Been accused of being addicted to your cell phone?

_____ Argued with your parents about how much you use your cell phone?

_____ Left your phone face up on the dinner table or right beside you?

_____ Secretly tried to check your phone under the table?

_____ Been on the way to school and begged your mom to go back home because you left your phone in your room?

_____ Asked your mom to bring your phone to you from home?

_____ Slept with your cell phone under your pillow (this is a fire hazard, by the way!)?

_____ Read a text or texted while you were having a real-life conversation?

_____ Interrupted a conversation by laughing at a text?

_____ Texted while walking?

_____ Texted while driving? (Please don't do this!)

_____ Checked social media sites multiple times an hour?

_____ Gotten really mad when your phone didn't get service?

_____ Had your phone taken away because your parents knew that was the best way to discipline you?

_____ Fallen asleep while texting a friend?

_____ Kept your cell phone charger with you at all times?

_____ Panicked when your battery ran out and you didn't have a charger?

_____ Downloaded so many apps on your phone that you no longer have storage space?

_____ Taken so many pictures on your phone that you no longer have storage space?

_____ Gotten mad at your youth minister for taking away phones during a retreat?

If you just made a lot of checks, that's a pretty good indication that you are developing an addiction to your phone. Remember, anything that becomes more important than God is an idol, so even your cell phone can be your focus of worship. Perhaps it's time to make some changes.

TAMING THE MONSTER INSIDE

by Pam Gibbs

You would have thought I had asked them to give up a kidney.

This summer, I took the students in my church on a youth camp/mission trip. We participated in worship and Bible study in the morning and then participated in mission work in the afternoon. When I met with the parents, students, and chaperones, I informed all of them that I would be taking up cell phones at breakfast each morning and would be returning them after evening worship.

The look on each student's face was one of shock and horror.

How could I?

Reluctantly, the students dropped their cell phones in the designated backpack where they were all stored until the evening. I had not made any new friends.

At the end of the week, the whole group met together for church devotion time, and I asked my students what God had done in their lives, what they'd learned, or what had surprised them.

One girl raised her hand. "I was really angry that you took away our cell phones during the day. But I'm really glad you did. If you hadn't, we wouldn't have gotten as close to each other as we have."

Score! (Cue the youth minister doing a happy dance inside.)

Even one of the chaperones, a parent of two teens, commented about her hesitancy. The idea of not having instant access to her children at all times was a bit disconcerting. Her comments at the end of the week, "I learned that they could survive without me. And I could trust them more than I thought I could."

Score!

The Blessings of Technology

Sociologists and other important lab-coat-wearing people call you and your friends "technology natives." That means that technology has always been a part of your life. You've grown up around computers, laptops, GPS systems, tablets, cell phones, and smart phones. You can speak emojis and LOL as easily as you can speak English. Your brains are wired for gadgets and apps and shortcuts and

Easter eggs (ask a gaming friend if you don't know what those are.)

Being a technology native has its advantages. You can access information 24/7. You know how to find out anything you want, any time. You can connect with a friend who lives on another continent. You can text your mom to let her know why you're late. You can do research about a lab in Greenland and actually tap into their live webcam feed. The world is at your fingertips—literally.

But is there a downside to technology? Is there a price to pay for instant access to everything?

The Downside of Technology

Here's the problem with technology. Rather than you controlling it, it can actually control you. I'm not talking about artificial intelligence or robots taking over the world or implants in your brain connecting you to the Collective.

I'm talking about addiction.

When you think of addiction, you probably think of alcohol and drugs. Or pornography or gambling or even shopping. But addiction to technology?

Absolutely.

According to Merriam-Webster, addiction is "a strong and harmful need to regularly have something (such as a drug) or do something (such as gamble); persistent compulsive use of a substance known by the

111

user to be physically, psychologically, or socially harmful."[9]

Here are just a few questions to ask[10] to evaluate your use of technology:

- Have you ever manipulated or lied to obtain screen time?
- Do you regularly use screens when you wake up or when you go to bed?
- Do you avoid people or places that do not approve of you using screens?
- Has your job or school performance ever suffered from the effects of your screen use? Have you ever lied about how much you use?
- Have you ever tried to stop or control your using?
- Does using tech interfere with your sleeping or eating?
- Does the thought of being away from technology scare you?
- Do you feel it is impossible for you to live without screens?
- Is your screen use making life at home unhappy?
- Have you ever felt defensive, guilty, or ashamed about how much time you spend on technology?
- Have you ever used screens because of emotional pain or stress?

Busted? Me too.

What's the harm, though? Really. What's so wrong with being on the grid continually? The fact is, over time, technology controls you. Being connected to a device dictates your time, controls your money, derails relationships. Here is what a few kids from five different continents said about going without technology and the media for just one day[11]:

"I feel like a slave to media."
"I began to feel distress and despair."
"I felt so lonely."
"I felt incomplete."
"Media is my drug. Without it I was lost."
"The silence was killing me."
"It felt as though I was being tortured."

The Solution

Obviously, you cannot avoid technology altogether. You'd be living in a monastery in rural France. However, you can take some steps to tame the technology monster within.

Try these ideas:

1. Don't text while driving. This is not up for debate. This is not only for your own benefit, but also for the benefit and safety of others. If you need to text, do it before or after you drive. Risking your life just to text a friend (or even your parents!) is beyond foolish.

2. *Don't pull out your cell phone in the bathroom.* Seriously? You can't be away from your phone long enough to take a potty break? Think about it from a health perspective: now you've got those nasty bathroom germs all over your phone. You can't wash those off in the sink.

3. *Put your phone away at counters.* When you are ordering food or paying for something at the register, put your phone away. You will save everyone around you time and frustration.

4. *Put your device away at meals.* There's no need to text, watch videos, play games, send pictures, or mess with apps while you are eating, especially when you are eating with friends and family. That's just rude.

5. *Don't use devices while watching TV.* Your attention is divided. If you want to be on your digital device, turn off the excess noise (the TV).

6. *Set hours for your technology.* Turn on your phone or tablet after breakfast and turn it off at 9 p.m. If you use your phone to wake you up in the morning, ask your parents to buy you an alarm clock. If you explain why, they'll fork over the dough on the spot.

7. *Turn off the alert signals and notifications from your apps.* This will keep you from jumping to your device every time you hear it beep, ding, sing, or honk. Who wants to be a slave to the sound of a gong?

8. *Use real-life communication.* If your best friend just broke up with her boyfriend, texting back and forth just won't do. Go to her house. Let her talk as long as she needs. Send your grandmother a real birthday card instead of putting a note on social media. Walk into the other room and tell your dad "thank you" personally.

One Last Thought

When you spend so much time and energy on technology that you have no room for God, that's idolatry. And that's a big problem. Nothing is more important than your relationship with Him. He deserves the first place in your life, not your cell phone, your social media updates, or a game you're trying to beat.

Ask yourself this question: Do you spend as much time with God each day as you spend on your cell phone?

Be careful—you may not like the answer.

9. See http://www.merriam-webster.com/dictionary/addiction.
10. See http://www.inhabitots.com/technology-and-kids-startling-statistics-about-addiction-to-iphones-screens-that-every-parent-should-know.
11. See http://theworldunplugged.files.wordpress.com/2010/12/addiction-grid-new.pdf.

TALK ABOUT EMBARRASSING!
What's Your Worst Embarrassing Moment?

In the fifth grade, we had "the talk" (if you know what I mean). That day at lunch, we had hamburgers, and I spilled ketchup all over the front of my khaki pants. Oh yeah. I had to walk around for the rest of the day with a coat zipped up around my waist.—Jennifer, age 13

My most embarrassing moment was when I was in seventh grade. I was at junior-high church camp and I had a huge crush on this guy. Some of my friends decided to write him a love note from me and gave it to him without me knowing. He came up to me and was like, "I only like you as a friend." I had no idea what he was talking about!—Amberly, age 16

One time my friend was joking around with her mom and threw her bra at her. Her mom picked it up and threw it back at her, but it ended up hitting me in the head, and the hooks got caught in my hair!—Amy, age 14

One Saturday night, my youth group went to play miniature golf. I was sitting in the van behind the cutest guy in. the. world. On the way home, I started feeling queasy. Before I knew it, I threw up all over the guy—and everyone sitting in that row. It was pretty hard to live that one down.—Pam, age 17

One embarrassing moment was when I thought that Sonic did home deliveries. I saw a sign on their back door that said, "No deliveries between 11:30 a.m. to 1:30 p.m." I didn't catch on that the sign was for vendors delivering the food to them!—Amber, age 19

I am captain of our school's flag corps for marching band, and we practice during first period. We had just started a rifle routine and I was tossing my rifle up in a horizontal toss, and the rifle came back and hit me in the nose. Everyone rushed over to see what had happened. I was fine until someone pointed out that my face had started to swell. It stayed that way the rest of the day.—Christine, age 18

DEATH:
Seeing It Up Close for the First Time

by Pam Gibbs

My friend Sara died this week.

You would have loved her. Really. Even though she was forty-two, she acted like she was twenty. She loved children, Legos, and the E! Network. She drank sweet tea (always) and ate donuts from Krispy Kreme. She never married, never had kids, never even went dancing. Sara suffered from a rare condition called osteogenesis imperfecta (OI), a rare genetic disorder that caused her bones to break easily. She was confined to a motorized wheelchair (named Heidi) because she could not bear the full weight of her child-sized body. But that didn't stop her. She went to the beach. Learned how to fly a kite. Taught preschoolers in Sunday school. She adored Mexican food and all things Vanderbilt University (her alma mater). And she laughed. Oh my, she laughed.

Why do I tell you about her? Because when she died, many of the children and teens she impacted experienced grief up close for the first time. When you lose someone you care about, it's a big deal.

What Grief Is Like

If you've never experienced a deep loss, feeling the pangs of grief can be scary and overwhelming, so knowing what they can be like may alleviate a little anxiety when they wash over you. Going through the process of grieving feels a lot like being in the ocean during high tide. Without warning, a huge wave of grief knocks you over, and you feel like you can't get your footing. You feel like you are tumbling over and over in the undertow of emotions— anger, sadness, disappointment, regret, and everything in between—and the weight of them feels like a huge elephant is sitting on your chest (sorry to mix metaphors, but that's the best way to describe it). Gradually, your emotions settle down a little, like a wave settling down at the water's edge. Only, just when you get your footing, another wave crashes in, knocking you over again.

That feeling of being at the mercy of your emotions (like being caught in an undertow) doesn't last forever.

Fortunately, as time passes, the waves of grief won't crash in as often, and the waves won't be as strong. As you adjust to life without that loved one, the aching doesn't threaten to overwhelm you. Little by little, even without your recognizing it, the pain and anguish lessen until one day you laugh about something and realize you can actually feel good again.

I'm not saying that you'll never be sad again. You will experience low points, especially in the first year, when you live through "the firsts"— the first birthday without her, the first Christmas, the first anniversary of her death. You are likely to feel grief at other times too, like when her favorite song comes on the radio or you see someone who looks just like her. And when you experience another loss (and you will), you are likely to hurt over both losses, not just the most recent one.

Helpful Hints for Handling Your Grief

Believe it or not, you can choose *how* to grieve. Although you can't choose to avoid loss (it's a part of living in an imperfect world), you can take steps to keep you from being derailed by it.

Don't ignore your feelings. Some people think that if they ignore their pain and grief, they can overcome the loss more quickly. The opposite is true. Ignoring what you feel only lengthens and complicates the grief process. Face what you feel—even if you feel numb. Allow yourself to experience it fully. In doing so, you'll learn that you *can* handle what you feel.

Tell God how you feel. The Bible tells us that God comforts us (2 Corinthians 1:3–4) when we are hurting and that we can cast our cares on Him because He cares for us (1 Peter 5:7). God can handle your emotions, no matter how strong or scary they feel to you. He can even handle your anger toward Him. Just be honest with Him. He can take it.

Don't censor your feelings. No emotion is off-limits when you are grieving. It's okay to feel mad, angry, hurt, disappointed, confused . . . No one gets to tell you how you *should* feel. You just feel what you feel. What matters is what you do with what you feel.

Don't rush your feelings. There is no timetable for grief. Everyone processes their feelings differently, so you may work through grief quickly while others don't. Or vice versa. Don't assume something is wrong with you if you're at a different place and stage of the grieving process.

Take care of yourself. Your body can be affected by grief, so take steps to care for it. Eat on a regular basis—even when you don't feel like it—and strive for healthy foods. Junk food will make you feel sluggish. Get enough rest. Sleep deprivation only makes grief worse. Keep up your personal hygiene. Regularly showering and brushing your teeth can improve your mood.

Find ways to celebrate your loved one's life. When my sister and my mother died (separate events), I planted a tree in my yard for each of them. When they bloom every year, I think of my mom and my sister in fondness. They would have liked the colors. During football season, I fix a batch of queso dip and watch football as a way to remember my mom, who was a big Dallas Cowboys fan.

Talk about your loved one. It's okay to talk about the person who died. In fact, it's a healthy and positive way to grieve. Sharing memories and even laughing together about funny stories helps you keep your loved one's legacy alive.

Don't go it alone. God never intended for you to go through grief alone. In Scripture, He encourages us to bear each other's burdens (Galatians 6:2) and to weep with those who weep (Romans 12:15). You are not the only one to suffer loss, and you will not be the last. Lean on others who have walked this same journey. Talk to them. Share your story. Pain is lessened a little when it's shared.

COMMON SYMPTOMS OF GRIEVING

Although everybody grieves differently, many people experience common symptoms when they are grieving. Here are a few:

- Feeling physically drained all the time
- Can't sleep
- Forgetful
- Unable to think clearly
- Changes in appetite, liking eating a lot less or a lot more
- Staying overly busy to avoid the grief
- Participating in harmful activities (drugs, alcohol, etc.)
- Sensing a loved one's presence or dreaming about the deceased
- Becoming withdrawn, lonely, and apathetic
- Sighing and crying a lot

The Last Word on Me & My World

Do not be conformed to this age, but be
transformed by the renewing of your mind,
so that you may discern what is the good,
pleasing, and perfect will of God.
—Romans 12:2

Guys

GUYS:
You Asked, They Answered

Describe the perfect girl.

Christian, confident, talkative, good cook, amazing video game skills, strange obsession with all the sports teams I like.—Ryan, 18

Well, I guess the perfect girl is someone who laughs at my jokes, even the dumb ones. She is comfortable with who she is. She wants a relationship with God and sticks to her convictions.—Chris, 17

There has to be physical attraction as well as personality attraction, if that makes sense. She needs to be well-mannered and nice.
—Tom, 16

She has to have a great personality. She has to be able to carry on the most intellectual conversations and the absolute dumbest ones as well. She would have to be in love with sports like me because that's basically all I think about.
—Jared, 16

Nice, somebody you can have fun with but still bring home to mom. It would be nice if she cares about herself and is in shape.—Spencer, 14

Smart, not overly needy or high maintenance, active, funny but able to have serious conversations, generally happy, and able to help me through anything.—Travis, 17

What are some things about girls that send you running in the opposite direction?

DRAMA, shy, insecure, gossipers, forwardness, too flirty.—Ryan, 18

Smoking, drinking, swearing constantly, overly competitive, rude to people, immodest, blows things out of proportion.—Trav, 16

A ditz. Guys don't buy that front. We know girls are smarter than that, and the fact that they choose to act stupid or unintelligent is a total turn off.—Ben, 17

Bad attitude. If a girl is real snobby and thinks she's better than everyone else, it's really annoying. Also, if she has no manners and acts just like one of the guys.—Todd, 16

If they always need to be in the limelight—the ones who talk about themselves all the time. Riley, 15

When they wear so much makeup! They are beautiful no matter what.—Holden, 15

When girls are really flashy in a sexual way. I know they're just trying to get attention, and that's not what I'm looking for.—Nicholas, 14

Bad manners, bad teeth, bad hygiene, not modest, whiny, two-faced, treats grown-ups bad.—Cabe, 14

Why do some guys act like they like you one day and then completely ignore you the next?

I think you are overanalyzing this—we are really very simple.—Ryan, 18

We're probably having a bad day or stressed about something.—Noah, 14

Here's what I think: most commonly, they don't know they are "acting like they like you" and more than likely, they're just good friends with you and have no further intentions. Less commonly, they like you and are too embarrassed or don't know how to go about tell you or asking you out; they like you, but around certain people, it's more important that they be "cool" than to like you.—Matt, 18

Maybe he's decided he doesn't have a chance.—Joe, 15

Guys don't even know they're doing it. In all honesty, we have no clue that you like us, and we have no clue that we are tearing up your heart by the way we act.—Jake, 16

Probably because guys are always trying to impress others.—Colton, 15

Depends on the guy. Some like you but don't think you like them, and they don't want to be vulnerable. Some are just so shallow that they change every other day to the girl they think is the easiest or hottest or whatever.—Jared, 18

The world may never know . . .—Tom, 16

Q. When it comes to guys, what are some common struggles teen girls face?

Scan for Video Answers!

Do You *Really* Need a Guy?

by Vicki Courtney

I was *definitely* boy crazy when I was in school. My first official "boyfriend" came rather unexpectedly on the first day of fifth grade. A classmate sitting in the desk behind me tapped me on the shoulder and handed me a folded-up note. Before I mistakenly assumed that he was the sender, he quickly pointed to a cute boy with a shaggy haircut sitting a couple of desks behind him and whispered, "It's from him." I unfolded the note and read the following words: "I like you. Will you go with me? Circle YES or NO. From, Dorwin." (I know, that's some name!)

I didn't know a thing about this guy except that he held the school record for the hundred-yard dash. Sounded like good creds to me, so with little thought, I circled YES and passed back the note. My heart skipped a beat when I glanced back and saw him open the note and flash that cool guy smile. We were officially "going steady." Don't laugh—that's what we called it back then. And back in the day, sometimes a guy would even give you a clunky silver ID bracelet with his name on it, a token of honor and admiration. I was awarded the ID bracelet on the second day of school, and voilà! I had a boyfriend.

And thus began my string of boyfriends. Throughout middle school and high school, I almost always had a boyfriend. I never stopped to think that going from boyfriend to boyfriend was a problem. Lots of girls did. At the time, I didn't understand that I had allowed a boyfriend to determine my worth. Having a boyfriend meant that I was desirable. Not having a boyfriend meant that I was a loser. Or so I thought.

Funny thing though, even when I had a boyfriend, my heart never felt at peace. The initial flutter in my heart always wore off over time. That's because a guy can bring satisfaction temporarily, but he can never fulfill you or make you whole. Only God can do that.

I understand why being in a relationship never quite did the trick. Exodus 34:14 says, "Do not worship any other god, for the LORD, whose name is Jealous, is a jealous God" (NIV). Did that sink in? God—the one who flung the stars in the sky and knows them each by name—is jealous about His relationship with you! You were created to love Him above all else; and until you do, your heart will never be fully satisfied. Not by money, power, success in school, popularity, good looks, or even having a boyfriend. Having a boyfriend in God's will and timing can bring satisfaction, but he is never supposed to give—or take away—your worth.

Fortunately, God stuck with me over the years. He patiently waited for me to let Him take the rightful place in my heart, a place that I had attempted to fill with a steady stream of boyfriends. When I was twenty-one, I finally gave my heart to Him, and my life has never been the same. I felt worth, value, and purpose in life. Who needs a silver ID bracelet when the God of this universe wants to inscribe His name on your heart?

Do not worship any other god, for the LORD, whose name is Jealous, is a jealous God.—Exodus 34:14 NIV

Guy Crazy

10 SIGNS YOU ARE OUT OF CONTROL

1. Your friends roll their eyes when you start talking about guys—again.

2. You dress to get attention from him (you know the one!).

3. You have multiple crushes—at the same time.

4. You "stalk" your crush(es) on social media.

5. You believe your life would be complete if you had a guy.

6. You replace one crush with another as soon as guy number one falls off the list.

7. Your journal is full of ramblings about your steady stream of crushes.

8. Guys are ALWAYS the number one topic of conversation among your friends.

9. When you're driving, you take a detour to see if the guy you like is working.

10. Your jealousy is out of control when someone else gets a boyfriend.

ARE YOU *TOO* INTO GUYS?

Are you a rational, intelligent, mostly mature gal—until a guy enters the room? It's normal to like guys, but sometimes desire for a guy can get out of control. Check out these five signs to find out if you need to get a grip.

1. **Your friends say you talk about guys too much.** This is the first and biggest sign you may be going overboard. In general, teen girls talk about guys. They are a part of your subculture, and you see them every day (maybe not during the summer). It only makes sense that guys would come up in conversation. However, if even your friends—the ones who talk to you about guys—say you talk about guys too much, then you've got a problem. Ask yourself: *Why am I talking about guys so much? Am I just trying to talk so that people will pay attention to me? Do I think I'll fit in more if I talk a lot about my current crush?* Whatever the reason, you may want to filter what comes out of your mouth, lest your friends become frustrated with you. Let others guide the conversation, and chime in when you can offer a relevant idea.

2. **You hop from boyfriend to boyfriend with little time in between.** Have you been in more dating relationships in one semester than most teen girls have in a year? When you cannot bear to be without a guy, ask yourself: *Why can't I be without a guy at my side?* You may be surprised at your answer. Lots of girls date so they will feel good about themselves. In their eyes, having a boyfriend means they're accepted and loved. When you allow a guy to validate your worth, you are determining your value based on another person's opinion. And that can be really, really, dangerous. What happens when you break up? Does that mean you are no longer important or valued? Absolutely not. Beware the trap of guy-derived worth.

3. **You change your plans or your routine so you can hang out with the guy you like— or even just run into him.** Maybe you stalk his posts on social media looking for clues to where he is and arrange to coincidentally make an appearance. This is a bad sign, but it's not as bad as changing plans with your friends—or ditching them altogether—so you can be available in case your crush decides he wants to do something. That tells your friends they are not important, and it tells everyone you are obsessed. That could lead to a bad rep.

4. **You've lost a friendship over a guy.** If you live in a smaller town, the "pool" of available, desirable, date-able guys can be small. And when you're committed to dating only Christian guys (which is a good idea, by the way), that number may drop significantly. As a result, you may find yourself at odds with one of your friends who happens to like the same guy you do. If you're not careful, that situation could deteriorate into World War III. If this has happened to you, then your priorities are out of order. If this has happened on more than one occasion, then it's time for some serious changes. I know the present moment feels like forever, but the chances of a guy-girl relationship lasting forever are a gazillion to one. Losing a friendship that could last into adulthood because of a guy you'll forget in a couple of years isn't good math.

5. *You get jealous when other girls get guys' attention.* How do you respond when another girl wears a cute outfit and the guy you like notices her? Do you immediately hate the girl, call her names in your head, and tell everyone what a horrible person she is? Hopefully your obsession with guys won't go that far. However, I have seen girls pout and get depressed when a guy just happens to look at someone else. I've also seen lots of girls ignore, gossip about, prank, and even bully the "competition." Really? Do you really want your character to sink that low? Is that guy really worth treating someone so poorly? Remember, as a Christian, you show others what it's like to follow Jesus. When classmates and friends see you acting in such an unloving way, they may second-guess this whole Christianity thing.

Questions to Ask Yourself

Here are a few questions to ponder to see if you might be too into guys:

___ Are guys the main topic of most of the conversations you initiate with your friends?

___ Do you send flirty texts to multiple guys in one day?

___ Have you ever taken the long way to class, just so you could spot your crush in between classes?

___ Do you get scared or anxious when the guy you like pays attention to another girl?

___ When you're shopping for clothes, do you choose things based on what the guys will think or whether or not you personally like it?

___ Have you become defensive about any of these questions?

Was it painful to read those questions? Were these questions just confirming what you already knew about yourself but were unwilling to admit? The good news is that the first step in creating change is realizing you have a problem. Now that you know, you can look for a little balance in your life. It's okay to like guys—and it's even okay to date them (as long as mom and dad approve), but don't let your emotions turn you into psycho woman!

Happily Ever After in the Hookup Culture

by Vicki Courtney

Some couples should last forever.

Fred and Wilma.

Mickey and Minnie.

Marge and Homer.

Barbie and Ken.

Whoops, strike that last one. Several years ago, media outlets reported that Barbie and Ken had broken up. (Can you say publicity stunt?!)

For those of us who played with Ken and Barbie when we were small, the shock of their breakup is still painful. We (and perhaps you) spent countless hours planning Barbie's day, which always included a date with Ken at some point. And every weekend was homecoming weekend in Barbieland. Barbie and her clones would gather together at my best friend's Barbie mansion (I only had the pop-up camper) and spend the entire day getting ready for their dates. The troop of Kens would arrive in a convoy of sports cars and jeeps (on time!). They would walk to the door, ring the doorbell, and gasp in awe when our girls descended the staircase. After an evening of dancing in each other's arms (no twerking or grinding allowed—we didn't even know such a thing existed), Ken escorted Barbie home, walked her to the door; and sometimes, but not always, gave her a light kiss on the cheek. Eventually, Ken would propose in the most romantic way possible, and we would all join in on a chorus of "dum, dum, da dum" as the lucky doll made her way down the aisle to meet her groom.

Even though we didn't understand why, we all knew we were each waiting for a turn to walk down that aisle—not just in Barbieland, but in real life.

In the end, Barbie and Ken defined love as a feeling rather than a commitment. Not that they hadn't survived their share of tough times. They stuck it out through her career changes—nurse, astronaut, paleontologist, Olympic athlete, fashion model, and rock star. Ken endured Barbie's forty-three pets, including twenty-one dogs, twelve horses, a parrot, a panda, a giraffe, and a zebra (just to name a few). When it was all said and done, the power couple would join the ranks of the rest of the "wonder couples" of the world—when the going got tough, the couple would just split because that's what couples do today.

I can't help but wonder if you and your friends, deep down inside, would choose to return to the simpler days of innocence and purity of your childhood. You know, the days when you dreamed about meeting that one special guy who would sweep you off your feet, ask you out on dates, pay for the date, court you, pursue you, and eventually, get on one knee and propose with a ring and a dozen red roses. Ah, but who am I fooling? Such dreams are silly when you can instead hook up for the night with no strings attached and then move on to another Ken.

Funny, but the culture you live in never highlights the moments *after* a hookup. Nobody talk about the emptiness that most girls feel after exercising their freedom and independence by giving their bodies and hearts over to a guy, only to have him ignore you the next day because those are the new ground rules. There *are* no rules. Anything goes. Except your heart doesn't really understand those rules.

I bet a good many girls would give anything to go back to more innocent days, back to the days when Barbie's biggest worry was her pet zebra—not what she had to do to get Ken to pay attention to her, pursue her, and then love her. If you ask me, that's a badly warped version of "happily ever after." In fact, it makes me want to head up to the attic, brush the dust off my daughter's trunk of Barbie dolls, and beg her to play just one more time.

And I pray that you, being rooted and established in love, may have power, together with all the Lord's holy people, to grasp how wide and long and high and deep is the love of Christ, and to know this love that surpasses knowledge. —Ephesians 3:17–19 NIV

Help!

I can't believe I'm asking you this question. A guy from my youth group texted me and asked for a picture of me—topless. What do I do? I mean, a lot of other girls are okay with it, but it feels wrong.
  Signed, Confused

Dear Confused:

You don't have to be confused about one thing: A guy who respected you would never ask you to compromise yourself by sending him a picture of yourself without being fully clothed. Unfortunately, even Christian guys struggle with lust. My advice? Say no. Say something like, "I don't go there," and leave it at that. Then, put some distance between the two of you. If he's asked other girls for the same thing, he's developing a reputation as a player, and you definitely don't want to be a part of that scene.

The mom in me would advise you to keep a copy of that message (take a screen shot of it) in case you have problems with this guy later. Keeping that message (and any others) creates a history that shows his pattern. You or someone else may need it later.

One other thing: Please remember that your body is too valuable to throw away on some stupid text or picture you send to a guy. Scripture tells us your body is God's temple. You should treat it with respect and honor. If you do, so will a guy.

Help!

Why do guys always go for the girls who are more developed?
Signed, Still Waiting

Dear Still Waiting,

I wondered the same thing when it seemed like all my friends were upping their bra sizes and I was still wearing the same size I had in middle school! However, I have since realized that the parts of me I view as imperfect, God sees as absolutely perfect, because I am "fearfully and wonderfully made" (Psalm 139:14).

It's true that some guys will only go for the more developed girls, but I can tell you from experience that those guys are shallow, and they are not the kind of guys you want to go out with anyway. Just avoid them. They are basing their decisions from a worldly viewpoint that devalues a girl and equates her with her body size and type.

Also, think about the dilemma the more developed girls face—they will always have to wonder if a guy likes them for who they are on the inside or for their bra size. Although it may *seem* like most guys are drawn to the girls who are more developed, not all guys act like that. A godly, Christian guy will be drawn to the inner beauty of a girl.

Dressed to Lure?

by Vicki Courtney

When my sons still lived at home, they were obsessed with fishing in a wooded area behind our house. Because this pond can only be accessed by a few homes in our neighborhood, it is well stocked with fish of every kind. My boys never got tired of hiking to the pond with their nets, poles, and tackle boxes. Their quest: big-mouth bass. These teasers would occasionally swim near the surface of the water. Trust me, these fish were smart, which is why they were so big. Fortunately, my boys were only interested in the challenge of the catch, and once they got one out of the pond, they pulled out the hook and threw their prize catch right back in the pond. Both my boys insisted that the key to snagging these fish was the bait. They relied on fancy spinner lures, complete with shimmering pieces of metal and rubber tentacles that dangle from a hook.

What does fishing have to do with the way you dress? Given the fashion trends of the day, many girls are unaware that the clothes they wear can act as bait—the kind of bait that attracts the wrong kind of attention.

Girls and Guys: Wired Differently

Girls and guys are wired differently. (Duh, you know that.) Girls tend to be initially attracted to a guy based on an emotional attraction, but guys tend to be initially attracted to a girl based on a physical attraction. An article in my local paper proves this point.

A sampling of guys were interviewed and asked what they thought of some of the girls who walked by wearing revealing clothes. One guy suggested that girls dress that way because they want attention. Another guy said their clothes were an "invitation." He said, "When girls dress like that, it tells guys they're easy."[1]

The truth hurts. Many girls wear the latest fashions because they're in style. Unfortunately, guys read more into an outfit than a fashion statement. Just like the lures my sons used to attract fish, your clothes may be sending out an invitation to guys—an invitation that you never intended to send.

On the other hand, some girls are *fully* aware of the power they can have over the opposite gender when it comes to clothes. They know they are attracting attention with that cleavage-baring top, those short shorts, a bare midriff, or tight-fitting clothes altogether. For these girls, negative attention is better than no attention at all.

Despite the motives, the results are the same. Like the bass drawn to the bait, guys will be drawn to you, but for all the wrong reasons. Do you want to send that kind of message to the guys?

What Scripture Says About Clothes

The Bible actually addresses what you should wear. First Timothy 2:9 says, "I also want women to dress modestly, with decency and propriety" (NIV). The actual word for "propriety" is a Greek word, *sophrosunes*, which means "sanity or soundness of mind."[2]

Translation: do your clothes show that you've lost your mind?

I am shocked at how many Christian girls who show up at church are dressed inappropriately. During one Sunday morning service, one of the girls in the youth group took part in a skit. She wore a skirt that was small enough for my five-pound Yorkie. Clearly she hadn't thought this through, and when she went to sit down during the skit, her skirt was eye level of the audience, and she ended up flashing everyone in the congregation, including the pastor on the front row! There's nothing cool about that!

The Bottom Line

Here's the bottom line when it comes to clothes: Don't dress in such a way that it would make *you* the focus, rather than *God*. I am not advising you to dress like a nun. It *is* possible to dress *both* fashionably *and* in good taste, but it may take some effort and extra time to find the clothes that would pass the test. What is the ultimate test? Take God shopping with you next time you go. When you look in the mirror, ask Him what He thinks. His opinion is the only one that matters. Remember, if you are a Christian, your body is the temple (or living space) of his Holy Spirit, so He has an interest in how you adorn your body.

You also want to wear clothes that reflect who you are on the inside. That way, when a guy is drawn to you, it will be for the right reasons. Dressing discreetly and tactfully not only demands respect from the guys, but also demonstrates self-respect. You want to feel good about yourself without dressing to attract the wrong kind of attention.*

Each day, do a mirror check before you head out the door. Ask yourself, *Is this outfit screaming "lure" or "pure"?*

Note: I think it's important to clarify that each guy is personally responsible for how he responds when he sees a girl who is dressed inappropriately. Girls who dress inappropriately do not cause guys to "stumble." Girls may send a wrong message with the things they wear, but they are not to blame for another person's wrong choices.

3 Simple Fixes to Your Wardrobe

If you realize you've been dressing inappropriately, you don't have to chuck your entire wardrobe. Three simple tricks can move your wardrobe from skanky to socially acceptable.

Layers: If you're showing too much bare skin, layer your shirts, or throw on a jacket.

Longer: Some clothes are inappropriate because they're just too short. Consider wearing leggings underneath so you don't show off too much. Or pass it down to your little sister.

Larger: Purchase larger sizes. Every clothing company sets its own criteria for sizes. In any given store, a size 7 can be a size 3 or 5. Don't trust the sizing label. Find clothes that fit well but aren't too tight. Try them on before you buy them. You should be able to move around easily and sit comfortably. If you can't breathe, of if the zipper looks like it could break apart, it's too small.

1. "What Girls Wear, and What Boys Think." *Austin American Statesman*, April 2001.
2. *Strong's Greek & Hebrew Dictionary*, © 1993. Used by permission of Online Bible, Winerbourne, ONT. All rights reserved.

HOW FAR IS TOO FAR?
The Wrong Question to Ask About Sexual Purity

Have you ever watched a person rescued from an icy lake?

I was flipping channels recently and landed on a random show. What caught my eye was the rescue taking place on the screen. Somehow, a woman had walked onto some thin ice and fell through the surface. In a matter of seconds, she found herself frantically treading water that was quickly causing hypothermia. When the rescue team arrived, they assembled away from the hole, tethered themselves together with a rope, and created a chain from the safe ice onto the thinner ice. Then, the person on the end of the chain threw a lassoed rope out to the woman, who was still conscious enough to put the rope around her body so the team could then pull her out.

The rescuers didn't get close to the woman because to do so would put all of them in jeopardy. They didn't push the limits of what the ice shelf could hold. Rather, they created an escape plan that didn't involve the risk of falling in. The task of that rescue team was to save the woman, not to get as close to danger as they could.

How does that relate to physical intimacy when you are dating?

When people ask the question, "How far is too far?" they are trying to push the limits of their self-control and purity. Metaphorically, they are walking out as far as they can on the ice, trying to be as physically intimate as possible without actually having sex.

"How far is too far?" is the wrong question to ask.

The question to ask yourself (and your boyfriend) is this: *How much respect do I want to show this person?*

What Scripture Says

The New Testament doesn't record a conversation with the disciples in which Jesus outlined the parameters for physical intimacy before marriage (the guys were probably already married anyway). He didn't provide a checklist of things you can explore without sinning. However, He did provide a general guideline.

In Matthew 22:37–40, Jesus said, "Love the Lord your God with all your heart, with all your soul, and with all your mind. This is the greatest and most important command. The second is like it: Love your neighbor as yourself. All the Law and the Prophets depend on these two commands."

Love God. Love other people like you love yourself. Those are pretty simple instructions that apply even to dating relationships.

When you ask the question, "How much respect do I want to show?" or "How best can I demonstrate Christlike love?" a shift takes place. The focus is no longer how much you can get from a person's body (or how much he can get from you). Rather, the focus shifts from yourself to the other person. You are more concerned with loving that guy enough to protect his purity rather than focusing on yourself.

All the time I hear the justification that if you both love each other, then it's okay to have sex before marriage. This idea totally warps the biblical concept of love. If you really love each other—love as described in 1 Corinthians 13—then you will protect each other's purity by refraining from sexual activities. You will want the very best for your boyfriend, and the very best is physical purity before marriage.

Today's Culture of Technicalities

At stake is not just your reputation or your virginity. At stake is your purity—and the purity of your boyfriend. To do everything but have vaginal intercourse is not fulfilling a pledge of purity. Too many Christian teen girls get involved with sexual activities that are reserved for marriage (like oral sex), but because they didn't "do IT", they consider themselves virgins. That's technical virginity. And that's far from what God designed for you.

Scripture doesn't advocate technical virginity. Rather, the Bible challenges us over and over again to seek purity:

Flee from youthful passions, and pursue righteousness, faith, love, and peace, along with those who call on the Lord from a pure heart. —2 Timothy 2:22

Flee from sexual immorality. Every other sin a person commits is outside the body, but the sexually immoral person sins against his own body. Or do you not know that your body is a temple of the Holy Spirit within you, whom you have from God? You are not your own, for you were bought with a price. So glorify God in your body. —1 Corinthians 6:18–20 ESV

For this is God's will, your sanctification: that you abstain from sexual immorality, so that each of you knows how to control his own body in sanctification and honor, not with lustful desires, like the Gentiles who don't know God. . . . For God has not called us to impurity but to sanctification. Therefore, the person who rejects this does not reject man, but God, who also gives you His Holy Spirit. —1 Thessalonians 4:3–5, 7–8

Do these passages tell you not to hold hands? Do they say you can't kiss a guy? No. The principle is much broader than that. The principle centers around what would be the most loving and God-honoring thing to do.

Different Questions to Ask

Instead of asking how far you should go, perhaps you should ask the questions, *Do my actions honor God? Is God glorified by what we do together? Is my boyfriend treated with honor and respect? Am I being treated with respect and honor? How can I show love in a way that respects him and honors God at the same time?* If you use those questions as guidelines, you'll stay far away from the icy edges of impurity.

Setting Physical Boundaries

1. Be up front. Before you date a guy seriously, he needs to know about your commitment to purity. Talk about it early on, or you'll likely forget or cave in when the first temptations surface.

2. Be specific. A guy can't read your mind to know what you mean by "pure." You'll need to say something like, "I will hold hands, and I will kiss, but I don't want to do anything else."

3. Be accountable. That means someone else needs to know about your boundaries. She (preferably an older woman) has the right to ask you from time to time if you are keeping them.

4. Be careful. Some places and situations will lend themselves to compromising your purity. Don't hang out with a guy in the house by yourself. You're just asking for temptation to walk right on in. Plan your dates so that you won't have a lot of free time (i.e., boredom). When teens get bored, they tend to get into trouble.

GOOD GIRLS AND BAD GUYS

By Susie Davis

At sixteen I made up my mind. I just *had* to go out with Jeff.

He was gorgeous . . . and dangerous. I knew Jeff had a "bad boy" reputation. And I knew all the negative gossip I heard about him was probably true, but I was obsessed with going out with him. In my teenage mind he was *unbelievable*. As just a sophomore, he was the starting quarterback of the varsity football team. He was great looking and quite charming. Every girl in school (it seemed) had a crush on him.

Forget the fact that I was a Christian girl trying to hold on to a good reputation. Forget the fact that my friends warned me that Jeff was not my type. Forget the fact that my youth minister always advised, "Never date a guy you wouldn't marry."

I wanted to go out with Jeff.

It took months before I got exactly what I wanted—a date with Jeff. He finally asked me out, and I have to tell you—it was one of the *worst* dates of my life. He was after one thing (my body) that I wasn't willing to give, so the evening was rather uncomfortable. So awful that he brought me home from the date early. Real early.

Why are "good girls" attracted to "bad boys"?

Is it all about the challenge? Is it about trying to "fix" them? Is it about the popularity? Maybe you are just curious about what it's like to be a little wild. Or maybe you just want to look a little less like "church girl."

Although we may never answer that question, one thing is sure: it is dangerous to date a "bad boy."

Why?

Because it is dangerous to entrust yourself to a guy who does not value what matters to you. For example, let's say you are a virgin, something you value based on what God's Word says. (The Bible says God designed sexual intimacy to be shared between a married man and woman.) If your bad boy is sexually active and everyone knows it, don't fool yourself into thinking you are going to save him and change his values about sexual activity. If you date a guy who is just out for sex, you might end up losing everything you have worked so hard to reserve for your future husband.

If you don't party, but your bad boy drinks and uses drugs, don't think you can pull him out. You will likely be the one pulled into that black hole.

If you are trying to attract attention by dating guys like that, I have some news: You will. You'll get lots of attention from other guys just like the bad boy—not the kind of attention you were hoping for.

I don't know all the reasons nice girls are attracted to not-so-nice guys, but I can promise a ton of heartache if you insist on going out with bad boys.

Every guy you date is a potential mate. That guy you are just dying to go out with could well become your husband. You might be thinking *Oh, come on. I'm just having fun. It's not that big of a deal if I go out with the bad boys I know I would never marry. It's not like I'm going to fall in love.*

Do you really want to take the risk? Is being popular that important? What will you lose if you choose to hold out for God's best? The possible pay off of dating Mr. Wrong just isn't worth what it could cost you.

The bad boy/good girl scene might make a good TV drama, but it's dangerous business in real life. The good news is that you *can* hold out for God's best for your life. You can survive and even thrive without dating the bad boy. Who knows? Maybe Mr. Right is watching to see what you will do.

Do not be deceived: "Bad company corrupts good morals."
—1 Corinthians 15:33

HOW TO KNOW HE'S WRONG FOR YOU

He's the wrong guy for you if . . .

- he makes fun of your faith.
- your friends warn you he's bad news.
- he treats his mom with disrespect.
- he has dated your close friends.
- he wants you to change how you look or dress.
- he asks you to lie to your parents.
- it's all about him.
- he makes you feel bad about yourself.
- you can't trust him.
- he talks over you and interrupts you.
- he doesn't show up when he says he will.
- he lies to his parents.

Q. What qualities should teen girls look for in a guy?

Scan for Video Answers!

Quiz: Are You a Flirt?

You are dying to get the attention of a guy you like who sits behind you in geometry. You . . .

a. accidentally drop your pencil to see if he'll pick it up for you.

b. offer to be his tutor after you hear him talk about his grade. Who cares if you're barely passing yourself?

c. smile at him but don't break a sweat trying to get him to notice you.

The new guy in school is the most gorgeous creature you've ever seen. All the girls are dying to meet him, and his locker is right next to your best friend's. You . . .

a. ask your friend to share her locker for a few days.

b. show up at your friend's locker dressed to kill, introduce yourself to him, track down his cell number through social media and send him a text: "If you need anything, give me a call." As an added bonus, you throw in a smiley-face-kiss-blowing emoticon. Mission accomplished.

c. What? He has a locker beside your best friend's? Oh well, only time will tell if he's as gorgeous on the inside as he is on the outside.

It's one week before homecoming, and you still don't have a date. You've already bought a dress, so you . . .

a. enlist your best friend to hint to a few guys that you're available.

b. turn on the charm, baby. It's time for Operation "Ask-Every-Available-Cute-Guy-Until-One-Says-Yes."

c. make plans to go with your friends.

You and your friends are at the football game together, and you really want to sit next to the guy you like. You . . .

a. buy a large tub of popcorn so you can offer to share it with him.

b. wait until your friends are at the concession stand. Then you sprint into the stadium and grab the seat next to him. Friends? What friends?

c. remind yourself that if he's interested in you he will make the effort to sit next to you. Or he might get in touch later.

You have been called a flirt . . .

a. once or twice. No harm in having a little fun, right?

b. often. But hey, they're just jealous.

c. never. It's just not who you are.

MOSTLY B's: Ding, ding, ding! Bells sounding, lights flashing—we have a winner! Unfortunately, that's not a good thing. Instead of attracting guys, you are probably scaring them off with your aggressive behavior. Don't act so desperate for guys to like you. Instead, just be yourself. Relax.

MOSTLY A's:—There are no bells sounding yet, but be careful. You're on the verge of becoming a full-time player in the flirting game. View this as a wake-up call. Check your heart and your motives. Is this the kind of person you really want to be?

MOSTLY C's:—Okay, so you're not into the flirting game, but trust me, that's a good thing. You're confident in who you are and don't need a guy to make you feel better about yourself. You don't play games, and character is more important in your book. Keep trusting God for your future, and He will take care of it!

SOLVING THE MALE MYSTERY
What Guys Say and Do When Girls Aren't Around

by Vicki Courtney

When my friends and I were your age, we would sit around for hours and analyze what some guy meant when he said such and such. Was he flirting? Did he like me? Is he going to ask me out? Should I call him? (No such thing as texting back then!) In these girl-talk sessions, every syllable the guy had uttered was dissected for further research and study. We almost always cracked the code of what the guy actually meant by what he'd said—or so we thought. If worse came to worse and we still didn't have a clue, we resorted to the reliable "get-your-friend-to-ask-him-if-he-likes-you" method.

My friends and I had no idea that on the flip side, the guys were totally and completely clueless about what we were doing. We had imagined that they also sat around and tried to crack the code of the female mind. In reality, nothing could be further from the truth. Imagine a guy calling one of his friends and saying, "After class she said, 'maybe I'll see you later.' Do you think she said that because she *wants* to see me later, or did she mean that *maybe* she wants to see

me later?" I can guarantee you this: They don't. Ever. Not at all.

So, what do guys talk about? What do they do when they're hanging out together? Let me give you an idea.

One day I was returning home after running a few errands. I pulled up in front of my house just in time to witness my oldest son who was about sixteen at the time, sailing down the hill of our driveway on a rolling office chair. Now let me point out that this is not your average driveway. My driveway is about 125 feet long and has a steep downhill slope from the top to the bottom. My son was picking up speed while grabbing the bottom of the chair and screaming for his life. His intended target was a skateboard ramp at the bottom of the driveway, and beyond the ramp was a pile of cardboard boxes, no doubt intended to cushion his fall. His friends stood by cheering him on as they waited for their turn. (You would think they would change their mind after watching him.) As I watched my son travel down that driveway at rocket speed, launch off the ramp, and crash into the boxes,

I sat in my car dumbfounded. I was relieved to see him finally get up and limp back up the hill so he could, no doubt, get in line to try it again. It was at that moment it hit me: all those years when my friends and I sat around talking about guys, this was the kind of stupid stuff the guys were doing.

Now don't get me wrong—they talk about girls, but it's usually short and sweet. Just like their texts—no drama, just the facts. One day, I made a comment to my son about one of his friends going out with a girl. I had found out about the "new couple" from his friend's mother when we went out for coffee. My son was totally clueless when I brought it up. He said something like, "Yeah, I guess that's why I've been seeing them together at school a lot." Amazed and confused, I said, "This is one of your best friends. Don't you guys talk about anything?" His answer? "Mom, we're guys, and guys don't talk about stuff like that."

So there you have it. While you and your friends are sitting around trying to solve the latest cryptic guy puzzle, they are busy rolling down steep driveways on office chairs.

Maybe that's why girls seem more mature than guys.

The brains of guys and girls are built differently, with different strengths. Girls typically have nearly ten times the amount of white matter, which aids language skills.[3]

When males are stressed, they tend to either move toward the danger (fight), or run away from the danger (flight)—the fight-or-flight response. When females are stressed, they are more likely to turn to other females for support and to defend each other—the "tend-and-befriend" response.[4]

3. See http://www.livescience.com/3808-men-women-differently.html.
4. See http://www.education.com/facts/quick-facts-gender-differences/boys-girls-brains-different.

WHY ARE YOU DATING?

by Vicki Courtney

Daughter: *"Mommy, I have a boyfriend."*

Me: *"Really? What's his name?"*

Daughter: *"Jacob."*

Me: *"When are you going out on a date?"*

Daughter: *"We won't ever go out. That's just gross."*

That's a nine-year-old for you.

Even early on, girls prepare for the day when they will begin dating. They will practice their dating skills by "liking" that boy in third grade. They'll dress up and put on makeup. They will go on pretend dates with their daddy. They will talk about boys with their friends (although they won't talk to an actual boy!).

As girls get older, though, the dating scene becomes a reality rather than just fantasy. Girls and guys start to pair up. First one gets a boyfriend. Then another. Before long, it seems like *everybody* else has a boyfriend (not true).

Before you start dating—or even if you already have a boyfriend—it's important to ask yourself one question:

Why are you dating?

If you starting going out for the wrong reasons, you could find yourself in a heap of trouble. Here are four different kinds of dating that you should avoid:

1. Dating by physical attraction

You know that guy—the crush of every girl in your school. Chances are, he's cute.

Really cute. That smile. Oh, and those beautiful blue eyes. And he's a football player too. Fit. Muscular. Every girl's dream. So what's the harm in going out with him?

Because your hormones are in overdrive, and you're likely to make poor decisions in that situation. Many guy-girl relationships are based on nothing more than an initial physical attraction. What happens when that attraction wears off? When he turns out to be a royal jerk and asks for inappropriate pictures? Physical attraction is a lousy foundation for a relationship. Build friendships and spend time in group settings where you are free to be yourself and get to know each other over time. Once you know his character, you'll know whether or not you can trust him.

2. Dating by emotion

Most teen girls enter into dating relationships based on how they feel. They rationalize that if it feels good, it must be right. Proverbs 4:23 provides a word of caution: "Guard your heart above all else, for it is the source of life." Too many girls proclaim their undying love to every guy they date because their emotions drove their decisions. And they will experience heartache after heartache because they gave their hearts away too quickly. And often, when girls give guys their hearts, they'll give away their bodies as well.

Girls who follow their emotions in dating are more likely to give into sexual temptation. Hormones send a message he must be "the one," and many will give in sexually because they believe it is the next step in the relationship. You may *feel* ready to have sex, but that doesn't change the fact that sex outside of marriage is wrong.

Part of guarding your heart will be learning to trust God more than your emotions. God would not want you to give your heart away prematurely by swapping casual proclamations of "I love you" in a relationship that years later will most likely be nothing more than a faded memory with "what's his name."

3. "Joined-at-the-hip" dating

Many dating relationships evolve into serious, long-term relationships that look like marriage. Often a couple will give up time previously spent with friends in order to spend more time together. Girls especially are attracted to dating relationships that emulate marriage because of their natural desire for romance and love. This type of "joined-at-the-hip" relationship almost always leads to physical intimacy due to the amount of time spent together.

Some Christian dating relationships between two students remain innocent and sexually pure, but they are the exception, not the rule. I have openly shared with others my regret of having been involved in a "joined-at-the-hip" dating relationship that lasted over two years in high school. We spent almost every waking moment together, swapped proclamations of love and eventually gave up our virginity for each other. Even though I was not a Christian, I knew in my heart that sex outside of marriage was wrong. Nevertheless, I justified my behavior

because having sex seemed the next step in a marriagelike relationship. Of course, like so many high school romances, the relationship ended within months of going our separate ways in college.

4. "Mission-field" dating

Many girls compromise their faith when they date a non-Christian guy. Second Corinthians 6:14 cautions against Christians being "yoked together" with unbelievers (NIV). Although this Scripture is talking about marriage, most marriages begin with dating. I am amazed at how many Christian girls (and guys) ignore this verse because it would prohibit them from going out with someone who makes their heart beat faster.

Am I suggesting that it is wrong to have guy friends who are not Christians? No way. Scripture encourages us to be salt and light in the world—to influence others with our faith. However, being friends is one thing, but dating is quite another. You will be a more effective light for Christ if you are not tangled up in a relationship with someone who does not know Christ.

When it comes to dating, go before God in prayer well in advance of the "going out" stage and ask Him for the wisdom needed to determine if and when to date. In addition, ask God to help you determine your standards for dating: Whom will you date? What will you do on dates? Where will you go? Or not go? What will you do if a guy treats you poorly?

Determining why you want to date and who you would be willing to date will save you a lot of time—and a lot of heartache.

Questions to ask before you go out with a guy:

1. Is he a Christian?

2. Why do I like him?

3. Why do I want to go out with him?

4. What is his reputation at school?

5. How does he treat other girls?

6. What would my parents say about him?

7. How long have I known him?

8. Am I going out with him to make someone jealous?

9. Am I going out with him because everyone else has a boyfriend?

10. What do I really know about him?

11. Are my friends warning me not to go out with him?

12. Have I asked God about dating him?

SURVIVING A BREAKUP

by Vicki Courtney

I hate to be the bearer of bad news, but if you date during high school, you're likely to experience a breakup. Even if you end up marrying your high school sweetheart (which is rare!), you'll know firsthand the anguish of saying goodbye to a guy. Although you can't keep a breakup from happening, you can do some things to make sure you don't end up on the couch with a pint of mint chocolate chip ice cream, watching reruns of *The Gilmore Girls*.

1. *Don't fall for the "let's just be friends" speech.* Many times, guys promise to be friends just to lessen the blow of a full-fledged, cold-turkey breakup. It may seem a reasonable solution at the time, but going back to being casual friends rarely works. This is especially true if you've been sexually active. Sex creates an emotional bond that is not easily broken when the relationship ends. The odds of being friends after a breakup with someone you have been intimate with are slim to none.

2. *Limit your contact.* Resist the urge to call him, text him, or track him on social media. Don't checkup on him through mutual friends or purposely show up where you know he'll be (class, work, etc.). It will take longer for your heart to heal when you purposely place yourself in his path in an attempt to prolong the inevitable.

3. *Find things to take your mind off the breakup.* Hang out with family and friends. Watch a movie, go shopping, or read a good book. The more you engage your mind with other interests, the less you will think about him. You'll realize that you can live without him and your life will go on. On the other hand, avoid watching sappy chick flicks and listening to your love songs playlist. Delete any old messages. Those will only keep you in Heartbreak Hotel.

4. *Resist the urge to get back together.* When I was in college, I had one relationship where breaking up and getting back together became a weekly routine. What a waste of valuable time! Why do girls cave in so easily? (Because we want to be loved, not rejected!)

If you are tempted to get back together, remind yourself of all the reasons you broke up in the first place. If it helps, make a list and keep it handy. Getting back together doesn't solve the previous problems, it only creates new ones. When the breakup occurs again, you start all over in your healing process. It is emotionally draining to float in and out of a doomed relationship.

5. *Dwell on your one perfect love.* When you find your mind drifting back to the pain of the breakup, pick up your Bible and read the Psalms. Talk to the Lord throughout your day, and tell Him exactly how you feel. Remember, He is no stranger to rejection and heartache. Write down Scriptures that speak of God's perfect and unfailing love, and take them with you wherever you go. God's Word will lift your spirits and give you a peace that endures—even through a breakup.

6. *Give it time.* Breakups take a toll on your emotions. Healing from a lost relationship takes time. Go easy on yourself, and don't expect overnight results. When you date someone, you invest a part of yourself in him. It only makes sense that you would feel a sense of loss when a breakup occurs. Above all, remember that God is the great Comforter. Fortunately, He's only a prayer away.

Ten Things You Can Do With Your Time After a Breakup

1. Clean your room. (It'll make your mom happy too!)

2. Volunteer at an animal shelter. Loving on those little critters is guaranteed to soothe your bruised heart. Just remember: you can't take them all home!

3. Read that book from English class . . . you know, the one you'll have a test over next week? The one you haven't started yet?

4. Go hiking, jogging, swimming, or bungee jumping (okay, maybe not). Physical exercise boosts the natural feel-good chemicals in your brain. It'll give you an extra boost.

5. Research your roots. If your family doesn't have one, create a family tree. Discover who was in WWII, who lost a brother in infancy, and who helped the Underground Railroad.

6. Spend time with a senior adult in your church. She would love the company, and you could learn a lot from her. Maybe you could even make her famous lemon pie together!

7. Give a single mom a break. Offer to babysit her kids for an evening so she can go out with friends. She needs a chance to eat a meal without someone throwing peas across the table.

8. Find a new hobby. Go to any craft store and pick out a new hobby. Maybe you're great at making flower arrangements. Or mosaic tiles. Who knows, you may have a secret talent for origami!

9. Check out your attic. You'd be surprised at what you might find—old pictures of your grandparents or the pogo stick you played with as a child. Maybe you'll even find the makings for next year's Halloween costume!

10. Clang around in the kitchen. Try out some new recipes. Bake some cookies, and deliver them to the police station. The officers will enjoy the sentiment, and you won't be tempted to eat all the cookies.

How Do I Know I'm Really in Love?

When you're together, nothing else matters.

When he walks in the room, your heart rate spikes.

When he looks at your from across the cafeteria, your face turns red.

You must be in love.

Or are you?

When it comes to matters of the heart, our hearts can get confused easily. Sometimes it's not so easy to think logically about a relationship, especially when hormones and emotions get mixed in. Everything feels upside down, and you can't decide what to believe.

You've been dating for a few months, and you just *know* you're in love. Your mom keeps insisting that you're just infatuated. So which is it? And how can you tell the difference?

Love and Infatuation Side by Side

Below are some comparisons between love and infatuation. Hopefully, you can step back long enough to discover whether your relationship is built on infatuation or is growing into love.

Infatuation	Love
Develops quickly	Develops over time
Deepens little with time	Deepens more over time
Unpredictable	Dependable
Based on feelings	Based on meeting each other's needs
Self-centered	Self-controlled
In love with the idea of being in love	In love with a person
Wants sex now	Wants to wait until marriage for sex
Emphasizes outward appearance	Emphasizes internal character
Possessive	Encourages friendships with others
May feel this way with more than one person	Feels this way toward only one person
Up and down emotionally	Consistent
Physically based	Spiritually based
Takes	Gives
Conditional	Unconditional

Love and Infatuation: Two Case Studies

Case #1: Caroline and Blake have been dating about a month, but they already know everything about each other. Caroline texts him first thing in the morning. Then they meet up before school to hang out as much as they can. She watches him during basketball practice. He goes to see her on her breaks at work. They've already talked about possibly going to the same college in the fall, even though Caroline has a scholarship to a different school. So far, they've been careful not to go too far sexually, but both of them can sense the tension of wanting to do more. Neither of them has hung out with friends since they started dating. When Caroline does talk to her friends at school, they casually warn her about going too deep too quickly. She blows them all off. They just don't understand what it's like to be in love. She and Blake may face problems, but she's confident that they can handle whatever comes their way because their love is strong.

Case #2: Courtney and Zack started out as friends in the youth group. They went on a bunch of group trips together and didn't really start dating until their freshman year in college, when they ran into each other on campus. That was six months ago. They see each other a few times a week. Occasionally, they will study together, and more often than not, they'll go to the football game together with a group of friends. Both spend time with other friends, and neither of them is overly concerned about the future. After all, they have four years of college ahead. They aren't dating anyone else, but Zack and Courtney trust each other when they're apart. Both of them were up front about kissing and other forms of physical affection, and they've honored the boundaries they've set up.

These may seem a little cheesy as you read them, but they are accurate representa-

tions of two kinds of dating relationships—one based on infatuation (or lust), and the other based on love.

Infatuation lives in fairy-tale land. The prince and princess fall in love immediately, conquer all foes, overcome their obstacles, get married, and live happily ever after. Birds gather and sing as the couple holds hands and walks into the sunset. Cue sappy music.

Love lives in reality. Two people choose to commit to each other because over time they've developed love for each other. They live in the town of Normal Life. They argue, forgive, compromise, learn, change, grow. And so does their relationship.

Do you see the difference?

The Honest Truth

Can I be honest with you? The majority of teen dating relationships will not last. And an overwhelming percentage of them will never lead to marriage. In my many decades of ministry, I've only seen one godly, love-based teen relationship that resulted in marriage. Most teen relationships are short-lived because they are based on infatuation—emotions and hormones that feel intense and real in the moment. Infatuation fades into boredom, frustration, and irritation.

Before you declare your undying love (again), ask yourself whether you are infatuated or if you really, truly care about the guy. The answer to that question will determine how long the relationship will last.

CAUTION: LOSER ALERT!

by Vicki Courtney

Wouldn't it be great if the guy you liked came with a warning label?

Just like the warning label on cigarettes and other tobacco, a warning label could tell girls that certain guys pose a serious risk to their physical, emotional, or spiritual health. Of course, some girls are so blinded by "love" that they would find a way to justify just about anything from "anger management issues that may lead to mass murder" to "you will never measure up to his ex-girlfriend so don't even try."

Over the years, I have heard many sad stories about the loser these girls are dating, dated, or even married. In most cases, there were warning signs that trouble was ahead. Most women didn't see them (or didn't want to). And before you mistakenly assume that Christian guys can't fall into the loser category, let me assure you they can.

The biggest mistake that the girls and women made was thinking they could somehow change the guy in question. Painfully, they discovered the hard way that only God can change a willing heart.

So what are the warning signs of a loser in the making? They are described below. If you see them in a guy, don't date him! If you are dating a guy with these flaws, break up—quickly!

WARNING! Avoid contact with any guy who displays one or more of the following character flaws. Do not pass go, do not collect $200, scram, flee, run for your life, get outta there!

1. Controlling and manipulative

Run from the guy who seeks to control you through manipulation and mind games. In college, I dated a guy who was overly jealousy of any guy who talked to me. At first I thought it was endearing and cute, but after a few months, it got out of hand. He became suspicious of my actions and made ridiculous accusations, always assuming I was betraying him.

Some girls assume that a guy's infatuation proves the girl has some powerful force over him that leaves him crazy with obsession. In truth, this guy is not infatuated with the girl—he is infatuated with controlling the girl. Jealousy, control, obsession, and manipulation are just forms of emotional abuse.

2. Angry and violent

When I finally broke up with my always-jealous boyfriend, he reacted by putting his fist through the door in my apartment. I was fortunate that he didn't hurt me, but I have no doubts that he would have physically hurt me had I stayed with him. He was so controlling that he stalked me in the months that followed. He called and made threats to hurt any guy he saw me out with. It got so bad that my parents had to move me out of my apartment before the lease was up and move me into a condo complex with a gated entry and high security.

Some girls are not so lucky. One girl made the headlines in Austin, Texas, when her ex-boyfriend murdered her when she broke up with him. They started off as the "cute couple" in high school. But it didn't take long for his true nature to emerge. The warning signs were all there. Her friends and family repeatedly warned her. Unfortunately, his behavior escalated to murder.

3. Cheater, cheater

Many girls who date cheaters justify it and think they will be the *one* girl to capture his heart and end his cheating ways. Yeah, right. You cannot change a person, remember? Do not be fooled for a minute—a guy who cheats on his girlfriend will most likely cheat in marriage, so woe to the poor girl who marries this type of guy and rationalizes his cheating habits away. Do not let this type of guy convince you that you will be the one girl who will make him faithful; he probably said the same thing to his last few girlfriends.

4. Self-centered

A self-centered guy will always find a way to turn the attention or conversation to himself. It is *always* about him. Even when he is clearly wrong, he will not take responsibility. He will find a way to turn it into "poor me for having to put up with all this."

Because they are extremely selfish and self-centered and have determined that life is all about them, narcissists focus on themselves at the expense of others. Often they are charming, handsome, and confident. They are used to getting attention and have come to expect it. Many girls will fall prey to this guy because they are initially attracted to his self-confidence. Unfortunately, self will be the center of his life while the needs of others around him are ignored.

5. Preoccupied with sex

In today's culture, it is nearly impossible to escape inappropriate sexual imagery. Television shows, movies, and music speak openly of sex outside of marriage, homosexuality, and other sinful behaviors. Vulgarity and crudeness have reached a whole new low. As a result, record numbers of teenage boys and men are becoming addicted to online porn. Steer clear of a guy who exhibits a pattern of coarse joking or sexual talk, whether online or in person. He will view girls as objects rather than people and often obsesses over physical features. Do not take any chances on him, even if he is a Christian and acknowledges the problem. With a willing heart that is broken and repentant, change is possible, but it will take time and effort. DO NOT stick around for the healing process. Nothing will ever measure up in his mind to what he has been exposed to through porn. Run fast and far from this type of guy.

An angry man stirs up conflict, and a hot-tempered man increases rebellion. —Proverbs 29:22

But sexual immorality and any impurity or greed should not even be heard of among you, as is proper for saints. And coarse and foolish talking or crude joking are not suitable, but rather giving thanks. —Ephesians 5:3-4

Do nothing out of rivalry or conceit, but in humility consider others as more important than yourselves. —Philippians 2:3

5 LIES *YOU HEAR ABOUT SEX*

When it comes to the topic of sex, you've probably heard every rumor, myth, and lie started from friends, TV, the Internet, and even your boyfriend. Here are the top five lies you're likely to hear, along with the truth to keep you from believing them.

LIE 1: *Everyone is doing it.*

Based on the attention sex gets in media ads, movies, music, television, and magazines, girls could easily assume that everyone is having sex. The truth is that a majority of high school students are not doing it. In fact, just a little more than half of them have had sex.[5] Although this is good news, many high school seniors have had sex by graduation, and huge number will have sex before marriage, so we still have a long way to go.

Why does it seem like everybody is doing it? Part of it is due to the media. Most TV programs with teens as the main characters show them in sexual situations. The media falsely shows sex as a rite of passage, something everyone does as a sign of maturity. In addition, TV and movies use high school as a backdrop to portray girls in bed-hopping flings, losing their virginity to "the one" and fixating on appearance. The result? The more that teens are exposed to sexual content in movies, the earlier they will start having sex.[6] If that wasn't bad enough, the media is also making homosexual relationships the norm rather than the exception. I recently tuned into the premiere of one show geared for teen girls. This first episode featured two girls kissing within the first ten minutes. Seriously.

The other reason you might think everyone's doing it? Lies. Guys admit to lying about their sexual conquests. They lie about their virginity, how many girls they've been with, and how far they've gone.[7] When you hear that, you logically think that girls must be doing it too.

LIE 2: *As long as you love the person, it's okay to have sex.*

In today's "anything-goes" culture, lots of girls think it's okay to have sex as long as you love the guy. This begs the question: how do you know what is "true love"? True love says, "I love and respect you enough to wait until we are married." In 1 Corinthians 13, love is defined as not being "self-seeking" (NIV).

Love is patient, love is kind. It does not envy, it does not boast, it is not proud. It does not dishonor others, it is not self-seeking, it is not easily angered, it keeps no record of wrongs.—1 Corinthians 13:4–5 NIV

True love is demonstrated when two people respect each other enough to resist the temptations to have premarital sex. I cannot imagine a girl out there who doesn't desire to be loved and respected in that way. In a culture that says, "It's all about me," it is rare to find displays of the type of love described in 1 Corinthians 13.

Do you really want to marry a guy who has slept around with a lot of girls? If anything, it's a sign that he can't resist temptation and he gives in easily to sin.

LIE 3: *It's not sex unless you go all the way.*

As unpleasant as this topic is to discuss, it is necessary given the times. Oral sex among teens is on the increase, especially among the younger teens. Surveys show that oral sex is viewed by many teens as no big deal. One girl explained, "It's a sexual thing that keeps us from having sex."[8] Another girl explain, "The consensus in my high school is that oral sex makes girls popular, whereas intercourse would make them outcasts."[9]

I wish teen girls could see the shame and remorse so many adult women carry over from sexual promiscuity in their teen years. We are wired to know when something is wrong. No wonder so many teen girls who have sex (oral and/or intercourse) outside of marriage end up carrying guilt and shame in the years that follow. Of course, we know that God will forgive and forget our sins, but unfortunately we don't have the same luxury of forgetting what we've done.

LIE 4: *Condoms protect against pregnancy and sexually transmitted diseases (STDs).*

Perhaps one of the greatest lies taught in sex education classes is the myth of "safe sex." Sex is only 100 percent safe when an individual abstains from sex until marriage and marries someone who has also done the same. Often, the "safe sex" statistics regarding the ability of condoms to protect against unwanted pregnancies and STDs make the unrealistic assumption that condoms will be used 100 percent of the time with a zero percent failure rate.

Even 100 percent condom use does not eliminate the risk of any STD, including HIV.[10] Also, teens need to be told that even when condoms are used every time, they can at best only provide a 50 percent reduction in the transmission rates of syphilis, gonorrhea, and chlamydia. Condoms do not appear to provide any protection from HPV, which causes 99 percent of all cervical cancer. Apparently, "safe sex" really isn't safe.

When I was a freshman in college, I was asked out by an incredibly handsome, funny, and charming guy. When he asked me out, I felt like the lucky one. A few weeks after we went out, a friend told me that he had herpes and had given it to his ex-girlfriend! Fortunately, I was not the promiscuous type, or I could have contracted an incurable disease. His ex-girlfriend went on to marry someone else after college, and she had to tell the man she was going to marry that she was infected. She was fortunate that he married her anyway. She will forever carry this painful reminder of having sex outside of marriage. Her husband will be forced to wear a condom to protect himself from contracting the disease. She will have to deliver her babies by C-section to prevent them from passing through the birth canal and contracting the disease. She will also forever suffer painful flair-ups from the disease. That's a big price to pay for a few moments of pleasure, if you ask me.

LIE 5: *If you don't have sex, you won't know what to do when you're married.*

This is perhaps the most ridiculous lie of all. Give me a break! Here is something to think about: The first time you are sexually intimate is *always* awkward. Would you rather experience that awkwardness with someone you won't likely marry, or with someone who loves you enough to commit to spend the rest of his life with you?

Some girls claim that they have sex so they'll know what to do on their wedding night. Seriously? People have been having sex for centuries without experimenting before marriage. I have yet to meet one married couple who "couldn't figure it out." Trust me on this one—you will know what to do.

If you have reasoned that sex outside of marriage will make you more experienced on your wedding night, remember this: Any physical pleasure on your wedding night from "experience" will be lessened by the fact that you gained that knowledge from sex with someone else, outside of marriage, and outside of the will of God. Why not follow God's plan and wait until your wedding night and enjoy sex without any regrets? Remember, God created sex to be an emotional, physical, and spiritual experience between a husband and wife in marriage. Don't settle for less.

5. See http://www.cdc.gov/HealthyYouth/sexualbehaviors.

6. See http://www.psychologytoday.com/blog/real-healing/201208/overexposed-and-under-prepared-the-effects-early-exposure-sexual-content.

7. See http://usatoday30.usatoday.com/news/health/2010-01-26-boysandsex_ST_N.htm.

8. Neil Howe and William Strauss, *Millenials Rising: The Next Great Generation* (New York: Vintage Books, 2000), 200.

9. "Sex/Not Sex: For Many Teens, Oral Doesn't Count," *USA Today*, 16 November 2000, front page cover story.

10. "Sex, Condoms, and STDs: What We Now Know," *The Medical Institute for Sexual Health*, Austin, Texas, 2002.

5 REASONS
to Choose Sexual Purity

If you're a Christian, chances are good that the "don't have sex until you are married" speech is ringing in your ears. Yet sometimes parents and youth ministers are so busy telling you to say "I don't" until you say "I do" that we fail to tell you why committing to purity is so important.

The first reason alone is reason enough to wait. However, some Christian girls, for whatever reason, choose to ignore God's guidelines regarding sex. They know God designed sexual intimacy to be shared between a husband and wife, but they have given in to temptation. Even if you are committed to waiting, this list may help you convince a friend who is already sexually active or is considering it. Should you ever find yourself spiritually weak and tempted to yield to the temptation, reasons 2 through 5 should serve as a sober reminder.

1. Your body is not your own; it belongs to God.

When you became a Christian, you surrendered all of you to Christ—including your body. Christ paid much too high a price for you to squander away your purity for some cheap imitation of love in the back seat of a car. One of the highest expressions of devotion to God is your pursuit of purity in all areas of your life so that others will see the love and life of Christ in your own body.

2. You will regret it.

More than 70 percent of teens regret their decision to have sex and wish they had waited.[11] Interestingly, though, girls who have had sex often try to convince their friends to lose their virginity too. Even though most girls regret their decision, they feel less alone if most everyone they know is doing it. The saying rings true—"misery loves company." It makes no sense to have sex outside of marriage if so many girls regret it. Out of the girls who choose to wait until marriage to have sex, 0 percent regret their decision. The question is, Do you want to have no regret?

3. You will likely develop a bad rep.

Ninety-one percent of teens surveyed said a girl can get a bad reputation if she has sex.[12] Girls may think that the boys will like them more if they have sex, but boys respect girls who choose to save physical intimacy for marriage. A whopping 90 percent of teens said it is generally considered a good thing for a girl to be a virgin.[13] Remember that the next time anyone implies that it's uncool to be a virgin.

One teen boy confirms what I'm saying:

"I'm a guy, eighteen, and I have something to say to girls who sleep around. They may think they are 'hot stuff,' but they should hear what is said about them in the locker room. These poor girls think it is flattering to be sought out—that it is a compliment to have sex. Not so! It is cheap and degrading to be used."[14]

Ouch. The truth hurts.

4. You can get a sexually transmitted disease (STD).

Forty percent of sexually active teen girls have had an STD that can cause infertility and even death.[15] Let me put that in perspective for you: If you were to line up ten girls in your math class, four of them would be infected with an STD. Try to imagine the embarrassment of having to explain to your future husband that you have an STD. If you wait for sexual intimacy until marriage, you don't have to worry about any of that.

5. You gamble with becoming pregnant.

The US has the highest teen pregnancy rate in the entire world. Wow. Then let this statistic sink in: more than 33 percent of teen girls become pregnant by age twenty.[16] Therefore, three girls in ten will be faced with the reality of raising a child, placing a child up for adoption, or having an abortion. Regardless of the choice those girls make, the emotional scars will leave their mark for years to come. Unfortunately, a lot of girls make the disastrous decision to have an abortion. Each year, 200,000 teen girls will have an abortion.[17] Those noble enough to give their babies up for adoption will suffer emotional scars of a different kind. Is sex outside of marriage really worth the risk?

If God says to wait, you need to wait. He knows you better than you know yourself. He knows the negative consequences you will face, even if you're lucky enough not to get pregnant or get an STD. Girls who compromise their purity regret their choice. Girls who remain pure have no regrets.

Seems like an obvious choice to me.

11. See http://www.safeteens.org/stds/waiting-abstinence.
12. See http://www.lifeway.com/Article/parenting-sexuality-true-love-waits-Sex-smarts-for-teens.
13. Ibid.
14. Austin American Statesman, no date.
15. See http://www.hhs.gov/ash/oah/adolescent-health-topics/reproductive-health/stds.html#_ftn1.
16. See http://www.livestrong.com/article/12504-teen-pregnancy-rates-usa.
17. See http://www.teenpregnancystatistics.org/content/teenage-abortion-statistics.html.

Flee from sexual immorality. All other sins a person commits are outside the body, but whoever sins sexually, sins against their own body. Do you not know that your bodies are temples of the Holy Spirit, who is in you, whom you have received from God? You are not your own; you were bought at a price. Therefore honor God with your bodies. —1 Corinthians 6:18–20 NIV

What Guys Think About

PUSHY GIRLS

by Vicki Courtney

I collect vintage issues of *Ladies Home Journal* and *Seventeen* magazines. While recently thumbing through a copy from 1950, I stumbled upon an advice column for high school girls. One submission made me laugh out loud, but amazingly, the advice given is still as valid today.

This is what the girl said: "Some days the boy I like is extra sweet to me and the next day he just flips me a casual 'hello.' . . . I have tried to make him jealous, but he says he doesn't care if I go with other boys. I often go to the drugstore where he works to see him, but he never calls me for a date. . . . "

Here is the advice: "And just when would the boy have time to call you when you are chasing him all the time? Too much attention, too many invitations, and the unhappy habit of hanging around the place a boy works are the fastest ways to convince him that he sees enough of you without having you around as a date-mate too. Give him a chance to miss you once in a while!"

Times have changed. We're not in the 50s anymore. No more waiting by the phone for that special guy to call. No more anxiously wondering if every call could be Mr. Dreamy.

Nowadays, if a girl wants to talk to a guy, she sends him a quick text. A guy hardly thinks twice if a girl contacts him first. But is that a *good* thing?

Most girls don't realize that by doing all the hard work (texting, talking, hanging out at his locker, etc.), they let the guys off the hook. The girl who contacts a guy first with invitations to do things and go places doesn't require any special effort. The guy doesn't have to wonder if a girl likes him. Aggressive girls don't require a guy to ask them out, pick them up, and pay their way. No risk, no cost. It's a win-win for a guy.

But at the same time, a pushy girl doesn't feel valued. Pursued. Wanted. And deep down inside, most girls want to be chased and pursued.

I'm sure it's tempting to make the first move. And I'm sure it must feel like agony to watch other girls talking to your crush while you wait patiently (or not) for him to notice you. Trust me: if a guy is interested, he will tell you. He will seek you out. He will find a way.

You are worth being pursued. You are worth being chased. You are worth being asked out on a real date—with a meal and sweaty palms and butterflies in your stomach. You are worth being treated like a lady. But first, you must *act* like a lady. If you want to be pursued and want to

know you're liked, you won't text as many guys, and you won't text them as often. You won't see every guy as a potential boyfriend. You won't flirt with every guy.

I realize that waiting for your crush to act *first* is a radical concept in today's "girls can do the same things boys can" culture. Why not be different than the norm? Sit back. Wait it out. While other girls are knocking themselves out pursuing guys, pursue Jesus instead. The guys worth waiting for will notice. And if they don't, they're not worth your time.

For in this hope we were saved. But hope that is seen is no hope at all. Who hopes for what he already has? But if we hope for what we do not yet have, we wait for it patiently.

—Romans 8:24–25 NIV

DATING VIOLENCE:
Suffering in Silence

by Pam Gibbs

It was an average evening, not different than most others, the first Wednesday night of the fall semester. I was a small group volunteer at our church, and that night, we were doing an opening activity to get to know each other a little better. I had the young teen girls in my group draw the outline of their hands on pieces of construction paper, something they'd probably done as kids. Then, on each of the fingers, girls completed this sentence: *You probably don't know_____.*

In typical small group fashion, they all read their statements aloud. Again, nothing out of the ordinary: You probably don't know I'm afraid of spiders. I wish I could go out with _____ (which was no surprise to any of us). I hate the deep end of the swimming pool. I've been going to this church all my life. Normal stuff.

Then Brittney spoke. She was new to the church. In fact, I'd never met her before. She was a junior, popular in her class (I'd learn later), and got plenty of attention from the guys. She rattled off a few mundane facts. And then she said:

You probably don't know my boyfriend used to hit me and push me around.

The oxygen suddenly evaporated out of the room, and I couldn't breathe. Neither could anyone else. I looked at my coworker and she looked at me, both of us asking each other the same silent question: *Now what do we do?*

I don't remember much after that. I know I asked a lot of questions, making sure she wasn't in any imminent danger. And I know we talked about dating violence. I remember that because in my twenty-plus years of ministry, that was the first time a girl actually admitted to me that her boyfriend beat her.

Toto, I don't think we're in Kansas anymore.

Is Dating Violence Really a Problem?

When you hear the term "dating violence," I'll bet you don't picture it happening in your own backyard. It's not something you think is happening at your school, in your neighborhood, or to your friends. The truth is that dating violence is a problem. A serious problem. Here are just a few statistics to think about.

- One in three girls in the US experiences physical, emotional, or verbal abuse from a dating partner.[18]
- Twenty-five percent of high school girls have been victims of physical or sexual abuse or date rape.[19]

- Teen girls who are physically or sexually abused are six times more likely to become pregnant and twice as likely to get a sexually transmitted disease.[20]
- One in three teens who have been in a relationship say their partner has texted them from ten to thirty times an hour to find out where they are, what they are doing, or who they are with.[21]
- One in four teens in a relationship (25 percent) say they have been called names, harassed, or put down by their partner through cell phones and texting.[22]

What disturbed me most about the research I'd done was this: only one-third of teens in an abusive relationship ever told anyone about the abuse.[23] That means that there are a whole lot of girls (and boys, in some rare cases) who are suffering in silence because they are too afraid or too ashamed to tell anyone. Some girls don't even realize that their boyfriends' behavior is abusive.

What Is Dating Violence?

Simply put, dating violence is a pattern of abusive behavior used to demonstrate control or power over a dating partner, either male or female.[24] If you are hit, punched, bullied, threatened, intimidated, or even stalked online just one time, you are a victim of dating violence. However, in most relationships, the abuse occurs more than once and gets worse over time, which puts the victim in more and more danger. Types of dating violence include:

- Physical abuse. Using physical force to harm, intimidate, or scare you, including hitting, shoving, kicking, strangling, or even holding your arms down.
- Verbal (emotional) abuse: Using words to threaten, intimidate, or humiliate. This can also involve constantly keeping track of our activities and even stalking.
- Sexual abuse: Most commonly rape, but can also include being coerced (talked into), shaming, or guilting you to have sex.

In recent years, dating violence has taken a new form in digital abuse. This is becoming more common because of the accessibility of technology. This kind of abuse occurs when a guy uses cell phones, computers, tablets, or other electronic gadgets to intimidate, harass, or threaten you. This kind of abuse could include cyberbullying, sexting, threatening texts, stalking you on social media sites, or even demanding to know the passwords to all of your digital groups.

18. Davis, Antoinette, MPH. 2008. *Interpersonal and Physical Dating Violence among Teens.* The National Council on Crime and Delinquency Focus. Available at http://nccdglobal.org/sites/default/files/publication_pdf/focus-dating-violence.pdf.
19. See http://www.teendvmonth.org/research# ftnref4.
20. Decker M, Silverman J, Raj A. 2005. *Dating Violence and Sexually Transmitted Disease/HIV Testing and Diagnosis Among Adolescent Females.* Pediatrics. 116: 272-276.
21. See https://www.breakthecycle.org/sites/default/files/pdf/survey-lina-tech-2007.pdf.
22. Ibid.
23. Liz Claiborne Inc., conducted by Teenage Research Unlimited, (February 2005).
24. See http://www.teendvmonth.org/dating-violence.

Signs of Dating Violence

So how do you know if you are a victim of dating violence? Here are some of the most common signs of abuse:

1. He checks your cell phone or texts without permission.

2. He doesn't let you hang out with friends.

3. He tells you what to wear.

4. He is constantly calling or texting to see what you are doing and who you are with.

5. He puts you down or calls you names.

6. He has to be with you all the time.

7. He is extremely jealous or insecure.

8. He threatens to hurt you, your family, or even himself if you don't do what he wants.

9. He has an explosive temper.

10. He makes false accusations.

11. He touches you or kisses you when you don't want him to.

12. He has major mood swings.

13. He physically hurts you in any way.

Why Do Girls Stay with Abusive Guys?

From the outside looking in, staying with a guy who's abusive doesn't make any sense. You've probably heard friends say something like, "I don't know why she stays with that guy." Maybe you've even asked that question—about yourself. Maybe you've stayed with a guy even though he's bad news and has hurt you. Here are a few reasons girls stay in abusive relationships.

- *Fear.* A girl is afraid of the consequences of leaving the guy, especially if the guy has threatened to hurt her family or friends. She may just be trying to protect herself and her family.
- *Abuse is her norm.* Unfortunately, many girls don't know what a healthy dating relationship looks like. Some of them have grown up in an environment where abuse was common and even accepted.
- *Embarrassment.* Lots of girls stay with the guy because they're too embarrassed to tell anyone they've been mistreated. Girls may worry that others will think they are stupid for dating the guy in the first place. Unfortunately, shame plays a big role in dating violence.
- *Love.* Everyone wants to be loved. Unfortunately, a girl in an abusive relationship believes that the guy really does love her. Some girls are so desperate to be "loved" that they will put up with abuse.

Some girls believe that the abuse is their fault (it's NOT—EVER). And some girls believe the lie that the guy won't ever do it again. And again. And again . . .

What to Do?

If you know your boyfriend is abusing you, break it off. Fast. No matter what he says to convince you to stay, hold your ground. Don't give in to his lies (and yes, they are lies). Talk to your parents, and accept their help. You may need to change your cell phone number. Change your passwords on all of your accounts. Change classes if needed. You may even need to involve the police to ensure your safety and peace of mind. Lastly, find a counselor to talk with. You've been through a lot, and you need someone who can help you deal with the trauma and work through your emotions.

As you take the steps to take back control of your life, keep in mind God cares about you. He hurts for you. His heart breaks with yours. He promises to be close by. He promises to heal. And He promises to love you.

And that's a love you can trust.

The LORD is near the brokenhearted; He saves those crushed in spirit.
—Psalm 34:18

He heals the brokenhearted and binds up their wounds. —Psalm 147:3

The Last Word on Guys

Young women . . . . , I charge you:
do not stir up or awaken love until
the appropriate time.

—Song of Solomon 8:4

MORE THAN CLOUDS AND HARPS:
What Heaven Is Like

Streets of gold. Mansions. Worship. Angels. Pearly gates.

Heaven.

What is it like? What will we do? Who will be there? You'll hear lots of different viewpoints on TV and in the media, but don't use those as your source for information. Nobody who has gone to heaven has ever come back (since Lazarus), so the only information we can rely on is what we find in Scripture and what we hear from Jesus Himself.

What Revelation Says

The book of Revelation uses vivid scenes and sights to describe heaven. Keep in mind, though, that brilliant theologians throughout history have tried to dissect this book, but nobody can say definitively what exactly God is trying to communicate about the ultimate destination for those who believe in Christ. If you read Revelation, here are some of the things you can expect in heaven:

- Worship (15:4; 21:24)
- Beauty beyond imagination (21:18–21)
- God wiping away our tears (21:4)
- No more death (21:4)
- No more sorrow or crying (21:4)
- Angels surrounding God on His throne and proclaiming His holiness day and night without ceasing (4:8–11)
- The ability to hear Christ (14:2)

- The glory of God (21:11)
- The Lord Himself as the light (22:5)

In the end, God reigns supreme, and His followers reign with Him. Revelation 3:21 says, "To him who overcomes, I will give the right to sit with me on my throne, just as I overcame and sat down with my Father on his throne" (NIV). Scripture doesn't tell us what this reign will look like, but if it's with God, then it'll be good!

What Jesus Said About Heaven

Just before His crucifixion and death, Jesus talked about heaven. He said:

"Do not let your hearts be troubled. You believe in God; believe also in me. My Father's house has many rooms; if that were not so, would I have told you that I am going there to prepare a place for you? And if I go and prepare a place for you, I will come back and take you to be with me that you also may be where I am. You know the way to the place where I am going." —John 14:1–4 NIV

These verses describe two key facts:

1. *We don't need to worry about heaven.* Jesus said that if we trust God, then we can know with certainty that He prepares a place for us. So you don't have to worry about being left out or forgotten when Jesus is the one saving your spot.

It's just like when you hear your mom calling you into the kitchen for dinner. You don't walk toward the dining room wondering if there's a place setting for you. Instead, you walk into the room with confidence that there is room at the table for you—your place—and no one else will take it. In much the same way, Jesus was reassuring the disciples (and us) that if we've trusted in Him, then we don't have to worry about what lies ahead of us in heaven.

2. *God has a house there.* Now I'm not too sure what God's house is like, except that it has a lot of rooms and I've been invited to be in one of them. I can only imagine what His house would be like. I imagine that I will feel as though I have finally arrived at the place I have been longing for all my life but couldn't quite find. Psalm 90:1 says, "Lord, through all the generations, you have been our home" (NLT). Did you catch that? God Himself is our home.

Think of a time when you were gone a long time, maybe on vacation or away at camp. After a while, you've had enough fun and you begin to get a little homesick. All you really want to do is go home and sleep in your own bed. Cozy up with a favorite book. Take in some silence. Peace. Comfort.

Just like your house reflects your family, heaven itself will mirror God. We will love heaven—whatever it looks like and whatever we do—because we love God. God is that thing we've been craving deep down in our spirit. That thing we've been longing for all of our lives but couldn't quite define.

Surprise!

My husband loves gifts. And he hates them too. He loves the giving and the receiving. He just hates the waiting. He wants hints. And he loves to give hints. On the other hand, I don't mind the waiting. I think part of the fun is in the anticipation. I absolutely love watching the person unwrap the gift and experience that moment of happiness that comes from that special gift given just for them, specifically for them. So I don't give hints. And it drives my hubby nuts.

Sometimes I think God didn't give us many details about heaven for that very reason—He can't wait to watch us experience the joy and excitement and bliss that He knows we will experience when we see heaven for the very first time. What He has prepared for us is beyond our imagination, so He left what clues He could.

Until then, we wait.

Anticipate.

Hope.

Envision.

We dream.

Even then, when we see heaven, we will know that we didn't dream big enough.

WHAT OTHER SCRIPTURES
SAY ABOUT HEAVEN

People will build houses and live in them; they will plant vineyards and eat their fruit. They will not build and others live in them; they will not plant and others eat. —Isaiah 65:21–22

For My people's lives will be like the lifetime of a tree. My chosen ones will fully enjoy the work of their hands. They will not labor without success or bear children destined for disaster, for they will be a people blessed by the Lord along with their descendants. —Isaiah 65:22–23

But as it is written: What eye did not see and ear did not hear, and what never entered the human mind—God prepared this for those who love Him. —1 Corinthians 2:9

For we know that if our temporary, earthly dwelling is destroyed, we have a building from God, an eternal dwelling in the heavens, not made with hands. —2 Corinthians 5:1

Since, then, you have been raised with Christ, set your hearts on things above, where Christ is, seated at the right hand of God. Set your minds on things above, not on earthly things. For you died, and your life is now hidden with Christ in God. When Christ, who is your life, appears, then you also will appear with him in glory. —Colossians 3:1–4 NIV

If we have died with Him, we will also live with Him; if we endure, we will also reign with Him. —2 Timothy 2:11–12

5 Ways to Boost Your Prayer Life

What comes to your mind when you think of prayer? Do you picture long robes and hard wooden pews? Or do you flash back to the last time you really tried to give prayer a shot and woke up an hour later? If you're like most people, prayer doesn't come easily. We often have the best intentions, but it's hard to know how to start and how to stay interested. The following five tips will jump-start your conversation with God.

1. Start small.

If you go to church, you've been told a gazillion times that you should pray. It's not that you don't *want* to pray; you just find it hard to stay consistent. Try this: instead of deciding to pray for an hour, just set aside ten minutes. If that seems like too much, start with five. It's like training for a 5K. The first time, you jog, it's hard and you can't run for very long. But the more you keep at it, you can run longer and without as much effort. The same applies to prayer. Start small and gradually increase your time. Before long, you'll realize that prayer has become natural, just like breathing

2. Minimize distractions.

As soon as I start to pray, my mind whirls with my to-do lists. Or my phone buzzes. Or someone knocks on my door. Can you relate? If so, make a plan to minimize distractions. Turn off your cell phone and your tablet. Put a note on your door. Find a quiet place where no one will interrupt you. When you squelch the distractions, it'll be easier to talk with God.

3. Remember the relationship.

When you were little, did you go see Santa Claus at the mall with your Christmas list in hand? That works for Santa, but it doesn't work with God. He wants more than your fix-it list and demands. He wants your heart. He wants you to focus on Him. Don't get me wrong. God *does* want to hear your needs. In fact, Isaiah 30:18 says, "Therefore the LORD is waiting to show you mercy, and is rising up to show you compassion, for the LORD is a just God. All who wait patiently for Him are happy." God longs to meet our needs, but it's important to remember that prayer isn't simply firing off our requests; it's spending time with God.

The next time you pray, take some time to really listen to Him.

4. Change it up.

One way to keep things fresh in your relationship with God is to break from the norm every now and then. Take a walk and pray. Find a journal and a cool pen to record your prayers. Type and store your prayers on your computer. Write a poem or a song. Be as creative as you want. The point is to use different ways to communicate with God. Just be sure the focus is on time with God, not on doing something cool.

5. Be quiet sometimes.

Have you ever had a friend who talked ten times more than she listened? Trust me, it can be exhausting. Just when you want to say something, even if you need to tell her you have to leave, you can't get a word in edgewise. Sometimes I think that's how God must feel. When we spend time with Him, that's all we do: talk. And talk. And talk. When we do that, we miss out on what God wants to say to us.

The next time you pray, take some time to really listen to Him. Be still. Quiet your mind and your mouth and ask Him to speak to you. He may bring a Bible verse to your mind or point out an area of your life that needs a change. Or He may just assure you of His love for you. One of the biggest ways He speaks to us today is through His Word. Read it and listen for how it applies to you. Don't make the mistake of doing all the talking. If you do, you'll miss out on the coolest part of prayer—the part where the God who created the whole entire universe talks to you. Yes, little, tiny you.

CAN YOU BELIEVE THE BIBLE?
Reasons Why It's Trustworthy

by Vicki Courtney

Sometimes I hear people say they wish life had come with some sort of instruction manual. The good news is that it does! God has given us the Bible as our instruction manual. How sad it is that most everyone in this country owns a Bible but few will recognize its importance. It contains everything we need to know to make it through life. Critics will argue that it is just a book. The real proof is that it changes lives because it tells us the truth about the way the world is, who we are, and who God is.

Why Is the Bible Different?

So what makes the Bible different than any other book? Why is it more valuable than other works of literature, like Homer's epics the *Iliad* and the *Odyssey*? It is different because of its origin. Every other written book has been produced by human beings, but the Bible finds its origins in God:

First of all, you should know this: No prophecy of Scripture comes from one's own interpretation, because no prophecy ever came by the will of man; instead, men spoke from God as they were moved by the Holy Spirit. —2 Peter 1:20–21

The Bible itself tells us why it is different. The Holy Spirit guided the writers to record God's message to humanity. Homer's poetry may be considered classic literature, but only Scripture can claim to come from God Himself. It contains exactly what you and I need to know to live in a right relationship with Him.

One thing that catches many Christian teens off guard when they go to college is the number of outspoken critics who deny the authenticity of the Bible as the inspired Word of God. Many of these critics are college professors. Unfortunately, many Christians do not have a ready defense for those who deny its authority because they have never been taught about the internal and external proof that supports its accuracy. Christians do not need to check their brains at the door when it comes to supporting the validity of the Bible. When the critics speak out against the accuracy of the Bible, will you have a ready defense? What are the factors that support the Bible's credibility and authority?

Archaeology

An overwhelming amount of archaeological evidence supports the validity of the history in the Bible. For example, a recent study of ancient Jericho concluded that the walls did, in fact, tumble down as the Bible indicates and when it said it did. More than twenty-five thousand archeological sites have been discovered that connect to the Old Testament period and writings. These discoveries have provided much evidence to support hundreds of scriptural assertions about the history in the Bible. In fact, not a single archaeological discovery has contradicted or disproved a biblical assertion.

Consistency of Scripture

When I participate in friendly debates concerning Christianity, one of the most common arguments I hear against the Bible is that it could not *possibly* reflect the meaning of the original documents since it has been translated so many times over the years. However, the Bible as you read it today is remarkably similar to the portions that were originally written over a span of 1,400 to 1,800 years. One Bible scholar concluded from a lifetime of studying early documentary evidence, that "not more than one-thousandth part of the New Testament is affected by differences of reading." He added that there were only insignificant variations in grammar or spelling between various documents.[1]

When it comes to the reliability and accuracy of the Old Testament, the year 1947 marked one of the greatest archaeological finds of all time—the Dead Sea Scrolls. The scrolls were contained in ancient jars found in caves in the valley of the Dead Sea, which borders Jordan, Palestine, and Israel. The manuscripts date back to 150 BC to AD 70. Archeologists found the entire book of Isaiah as well as fragments of every book of the Old Testament except Esther. When the scrolls were compared to the text written a thousand years later by Jewish scribes (from which our Old Testament is derived), the Dead Sea Scrolls proved to be remarkably accurate. This fact is not surprising because when copying the original texts, the scribes took great care to make sure their copies were accurate. Scribes were known to wipe the pen clean before writing the name of God; they copied one letter at a time (rather than one letter or one sentence at a time) and they counted the letters of the original and the copy to confirm accurate transmission. In most cases, if even one error was found, the entire copy was destroyed.

Fulfilled Prophecy

Dr. Hugh Ross, a well-known astrophysicist, says that out of approximately 2,500 predictions in the Bible concerning the future, some 2,000 have already been fulfilled. Every one of these predictions has been fulfilled in detail without a single error. Dr. Ross has calculated that the probability of two thousand predictions coming true without error is 1 in 10 to the 2000th power (that's a 1 with 2000 zeros written after it).[2] Science considers any probability greater than 1 in 10^{50} impossible. So how did these predictions come true with such accuracy? God inspired the writers of these predictions to record them. We have those records still today.

If you do a little research, you'll find more reasons to trust the Scriptures as reliable and authoritative for your life. You can't ask for a better or more dependable instruction manual than that. Your life is more likely to function the way God designed it to if you read and follow His directions. Without them, I'd be lost—and you would be too.

1. F. J. A. Hort quoted in *Know Why You Believe*, 4th edition by Paul E. Little (Downer's Grove, IL: InterVarsity Press), 77.
2. Ibid.

Quiz: What Do You Believe?

Did you know that a large percentage of Christian teens turn away from their faith during their college years? Most of them are caught off guard when they go to liberal colleges and sit under professors who are openly opposed to Christianity. In one of my classes, a professor asked the Christians to raise their hands to identify themselves. A few students had the boldness to do so. The professor proceeded to announce that one of his goals would be to expose the stupidity of the Christian faith and tear apart their belief system by the end of the semester. Sure enough, he picked on those Christians when the topic of discussion lent itself to bashing Christians.

Are you ready to stand up for what you believe? First, you have to know *what* you believe. How would you answer the following true-false questions?

True   False   1. All faiths (Buddhism, Christianity, Islam, etc.) worship the same God.

True   False   2. Satan is not a real being but rather a symbol of evil.

True   False   3. As long as you're a good person, you will go to heaven.

True   False   4. The Bible is nothing more than a compilation of stories written by men.

True   False   5. The Bible tells us that God helps those who help themselves.

True   False   6. There is more support for the belief in evolution than the belief in creation.

True   False   7. Homosexuality is not mentioned anywhere in the Bible.

True   False   8. Abortion is acceptable because life doesn't really begin at conception.

True   False   9. Gay marriage is okay because #lovewins.

True   False   10. Truth can only be defined on a person-by-person basis and will vary from situation to situation.

If you answered "True" to any of these statements, you have misunderstood the basic tenets of Christianity. It would be a good idea to do a Bible study that addresses these issues. Your worldview (or view of the world) will determine your beliefs, which in turn will determine your actions. To align your worldview with God's view of the world, read God's Word on a regular basis. The more you learn about the truth as God defines it, the easier it will be to tell fact from fiction.

Q. **What does it look like to be a Christian teen in today's world?**

Scan for Video Answers!

CAN YOU CALL SOMETHING WRONG?
The Dilemma of Today's Teen

Is homosexuality wrong?
Is living together before marriage wrong?
Is cheating wrong?
Is abortion wrong?
Is lying wrong?

Fifty years ago the average American would wonder why someone would bother to ask those questions. They were "no-brainers" back then.

Yet, over the years, our thinking has been skewed. Even Christians struggle to brand certain behaviors as "wrong." That word sounds so judgmental. Many Christians remain silent, not wanting to make waves or risk offending anyone. And where has our silence taken us?

Our silence has resulted in couples living together instead of getting married. Legalized gay marriage. Transgender teens allowed to use the restroom or locker room of their choice even if it offends the majority. Aborted babies who could otherwise live on their own outside the womb.

Can it get any worse than this?

Letting each person define her own standard of right and wrong leads to an "anything goes" mentality. What may be wrong for you may not be wrong for me, so we won't call *anything* wrong. Unfortunately, the logical conclusion to this philosophy is a world with no values and no standards at all.

I cringe at the thought of where we will find ourselves in fifty years.

Terminate a pregnancy because the ultrasound showed that the unborn child was not the desired gender?

Abuse hard drugs in the privacy of our homes?

End an adult's life because she has outlived her usefulness to society?

You may wonder why this topic of absolute truth (some things ARE wrong) is important to Christian girls. How does the issue of right and wrong affect Christian teens? Surprisingly, only one out of ten Christian teenagers believes in absolute moral truth. That statistic is nearly identical to what non-Christian teens believe. Clearly we have a problem.

In one survey teens were asked the question, "When you are faced with a moral or ethical choice, which one of the following best describes how you, yourself, decide what to do?" The most popular answer among teens—both Christian and non-Christian— was this: "Whatever feels right or comfortable in that situation." That is scary.

If the majority of teens make decisions based on what *feels* right versus what God's Word says is right, what will those teenagers do when faced with the temptation to have sex? Teenage hormones will win that battle. When faced with the temptation to drink, cheat, lie, or steal, what will those teenagers do? Only a handful would seek God's Word for the answer. What would happen to those teens when faced with peer pressure? Feeling included sure beats being the outcast. The rest would just go with what feels good. Unfortunately, going by what feels good at the moment leads to dire consequences that don't feel good at all.

God created an absolute standard of right and wrong that is rooted in Scripture. Those standards are not up for editing. It's the Ten Commandments, not the Ten Suggestions. Right is right and wrong is wrong. Nothing will change that fact—even people who base the rules on what feels good to them.

For you were once darkness, but now you are light in the Lord. Walk as children of light—for the fruit of the light results in all goodness, righteousness, and truth—discerning what is pleasing to the Lord. Don't participate in the fruitless works of darkness, but instead expose them. For it is shameful even to mention what is done by them in secret. Everything exposed by the light is made clear, for what makes everything clear is light. Therefore it is said: Get up, sleeper, and rise up from the dead, and the Messiah will shine on you. Pay careful attention, then, to how you walk—not as unwise people but as wise—making the most of the time, because the days are evil. —Ephesians 5:8–16

I've Got the *Joy, Joy, Joy, Joy* Down in My Heart

By Susie Davis

I would love to feel happy all the time. I want to wake up every morning in a good mood, knowing everything is going my way and nothing is wrong. I don't like to feel sad or confused or mad or frustrated. However, the things that make us happy change from moment to moment, and the things that we think will make us happy aren't always the things that are best for us. For example, when I was in high school I was certain that if I could just weigh a certain number (which was not a healthy weight) or get a certain guy (who was not the best choice), I would be happy. I thought I would be happy if I were popular or got chosen as "friendliest" or "most beautiful." Although some of those things did come my way, the happy meter in my life didn't always stay full. For instance, when I got elected cheerleader (which I begged God for) I was happy for a while, but I didn't stay happy. Cheerleading was fun, but it was not enough to make me wake up every morning saying, "Wow! I am the luckiest person alive because I am a cheerleader!"

When you think of what will make you happy, can you determine what things will last? Try something. Write down ten things you believe will make you happy on the list at right. Start each with "I would be happy if . . ."

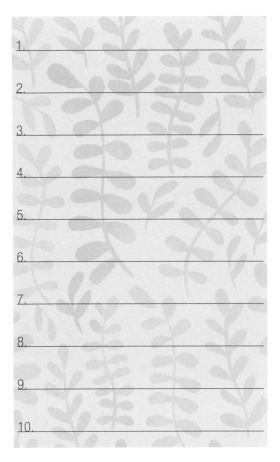

1.

2.

3.

4.

5.

6.

7.

8.

9.

10.

Now look over the list and honestly evaluate whether those things bring lasting happiness. Granted, your list may be genuine and real. Maybe you wrote down, "I would be happy if my grandma weren't sick with cancer." Or maybe, "I would be happy if my parents were back together." Even so, many of our "happy" requests are about getting out from under the discomfort in our lives. God wants something more for your life. He wants you to experience peace and joy despite your circumstances.

What Is the Key to Happiness?

When I was in middle school, I witnessed a crime. I was not happy about it and wanted God to make all the bad feelings from it go away. I didn't want to see the mental pictures, I didn't want to feel afraid, and I didn't want to forgive the person who committed the crime. If I could have prayed for one thing to make my life happy, I would have asked God for a rewind button. I would have asked Him to take me out of the place where the crime took place or, better yet, just erase the crime forever. For many years I felt that would have fixed the problem.

But as I got older, I started to realize I could experience peace and joy despite all other circumstances. I needed joy because the world's alternative—happiness—is short-term. It's based on the circumstances around you. Joy comes from knowing God's presence even in the pain. No person or circumstance can take away your joy. Your grandma's cancer can't take peace and joy away. Your parents' divorce can't take peace and joy away. Romans 15:13 says it this way, "May the God of hope fill you with all joy and peace as *you trust in him*, so that you may overflow with hope by the power of the Holy Spirit" (NIV).

So what is the secret of a happy life? To stop searching for *happy* and start choosing *joy*. When you are able to trust God and believe that He causes all things to work together for good, you will experience peace and joy, which are much deeper than happiness.

Does that mean you will never experience disappointments? Gut-wrenching hardships? Confusing personal relationships? Serious and stunning situations? Of course not. We live in a world wrecked by sin, remember? We all will experience our share of tough stuff in life—it's inevitable. Jesus not only predicted problems in our lives, but He also warned us about them. Look at the words of Jesus in John 16:33: "I have told you these things so that in Me you may have peace. You will have suffering in this world. Be courageous! I have conquered the world."

The truth is that unhappy times will come. Bad stuff will happen and bring discomfort into our lives. We can't control that. However, God has promised to care for us in those situations, and His love can give us peace and joy despite any circumstances.

May the God of hope fill you with all joy and peace as you trust in him, so that you may overflow with hope by the power of the Holy Spirit.

—Romans 15:13 NIV

WHY DO BAD THINGS HAPPEN?
A Small Answer to the Big Question

By Susie Davis

Something happened to me in junior high that changed my life forever. I didn't meet my future husband. I didn't discover a talent for writing that would lead me to become an author. I didn't make the cheer squad, the basketball team, or the honor roll.

Remember the crime I mentioned a few pages ago? Well, that was it. When I was fourteen, I witnessed a murder.

One of my classmates walked in with a rifle and shot and killed our teacher in front of our class. There I was sitting in class, cutting up with my friends and laughing with the teacher, and then out of nowhere a guy walks in and shoots my teacher. I am sure you can imagine how horrific it was. It was extremely frightening.

That event created a load of excruciating doubt about God's goodness and His love. I had already become a Christian, so I knew enough to know that God was in control and that nothing ever happened without His permission. He allowed a troubled teenage boy to take a man's life. God allowed a man's death—a violent, gruesome one at that. He allowed a wife to become a widow and a child to become fatherless.

And He allowed me to be in the room to witness a brutal crime.

This knowledge wreaked havoc in my teenage brain. It created doubt about God, and it created the need to answer a difficult question: Why do bad things happen?

In my struggle to understand, I sought the Bible, and here are some of the hard but real answers I found.

Why, Why, Why?

First, I wrestled with why bad things happen at all. Romans 5:12 says, "Adam sinned, and that sin brought death into the world" (CEV). Romans 5:15 says, "That one sin brought death to many others" (CEV). That was the answer: bad things happen because of sin in the world.

When Adam and Eve sinned, a horrible cauldron of unspeakable ugliness and hurt was unleashed. Sin spilled out all over every single person from the beginning of time forward, and we are exposed to its effects: Divorce, abandonment, and hate. Conceit and bigotry. Terrorism and sex trafficking. And when sin entered human existence, it affected all of creation: tsunamis, earthquakes, hurricanes, and tornadoes. Nothing escaped the influence of sin in the world.

Although we would all like to blame Adam for all the heartache, the Bible clearly states that we all fall short of God's standard and make sin choices. Romans 3:23 puts it this way, "For all have sinned and fall short of the glory of God." Those sin choices create chaos in life, and no one is exempt from the chaos of sin, either by sinning or by experiencing the resulting consequence of sin.

We Create Pain and Suffering

The nasty problem with sin is that your sin not only affects you, but it also affects other people. In my situation, that student's sinful choice to shoot my teacher impacted the teacher's wife, son, family, friends, and all the students in the class. We all felt the blow of that sin. As much we are tempted to point a finger and blame others for all the hurt in the world, we are responsible for creating hurt too. In this way, we all become accomplices to creating pain and suffering around us. If I am tempted to point my finger at my classmate and blame him, I must also accept that I am responsible for hurting people in my life too. When I want to point the finger at God and ask, "Why do You allow all this pain?" I must realize that God never wanted us to experience pain and suffering. However, He gave all of us the freedom of choice, and we as a collective group created that pain and suffering for each other.

Hope, Not Despair

But God didn't create us for hopelessness in life, an unending cycle of sin and pain. Another set of verses in Romans helps us understand God's plan for the problem of sin. Romans 5:15–16 says, "Yet in an even greater way, Jesus Christ alone brought God's gift of kindness to many people. There is a lot of difference between Adam's sin and God's gift. That one sin led to punishment. But

God's gift made it possible for us to be acceptable to him, even though we have sinned many times" (CEV). Romans 5:20 says, "Yet where sin was powerful, God's kindness was even more powerful" (CEV).

What is the final biblical perspective to the problem of sin and death? God's kindness is the most powerful answer. When He sent Jesus to deal with the sin and pain problem, His love and kindness won out. God did not leave us without hope or without a comfort in horrible times. Instead, He provided Jesus as the final answer on any doubts about God's goodness and His love.

When Life Still Hurts

When I was trying to understand why my teacher was murdered, knowing the biblical answer to the question did not help me feel all better. I spent years sorting out the pain and dealing with the consequences of seeing something horrifically violent. I had to deal with fear issues that created anxiety. I questioned God's goodness and love, His provision for me as an individual. I grappled with the question, *Did God step out of the room just when I needed Him most?* I had trouble trusting that He really was able to take care of me and make good decisions for my life. I didn't know if I could trust Him—really trust Him—with my life.

That distrust resulted in lots of soul searching. I felt alone in the world, trying very hard to protect myself from the possibility of future pain. I didn't so much want to know *why* it happened as much as I needed to know *how to deal with what happened.*

It took years of God carefully and tenderly unfolding comfort in my life. It took years to gain hope in God's plan and His goodness over my life. I am telling you this because many times when people feel the effects of tragedy firsthand, they don't care that suffering exists because of sin. That doesn't help them. Instead, they need time and lots of mercy. They need prayer. And sometimes they need a friend who will grieve with them. They need God in the most real way possible. They need God to plant new hope in their lives, just like He did for me. And you can be the one who helps them to hope again.

10 Never Evers about God

Never ever forget God loves you deeply.

Never ever make sin a lifestyle of choice.

Never ever discard God's free gift of eternal life through Jesus Christ.

Never ever assume that your sin is too great to be forgiven.

Never ever think you can outrun God.

Never ever forget that you are wonderfully made.

Never ever think that there is only one way to pray.

Never ever let your love relationship with God become stale.

Never ever lose sight of the fact that the Bible is able to change your thinking.

Never ever let God become second in your life to anyone or anything else.

PICTURE PERFECT:
God as Your Father

By Pam Gibbs

Father.

What comes to mind when you hear that word? Maybe you picture wonderful images of sitting on your dad's lap, listening to him read you a story. Or you remember when your dad helped you learn how to ride a bike or pitch a softball. We all have a mental picture that flashes in our minds when we hear the word *father*.

Maybe when you hear that God is your heavenly Father, you cringe inwardly. Maybe your earthly father left. Or you never knew him. Or you wished you had never met him. Maybe he was abusive and cruel. Does that mean God is the same way? Will God hurt you if you trust Him? Will He make you think you can trust Him and then hurt you in some horrible way?

Perhaps your dad was physically present in your life, but he was emotionally distant and withdrawn. He had so many problems of his own that he didn't pay attention to your needs. You wonder if God will treat you in the same way. You're afraid that if you believe He loves you, you'll end up disappointed and betrayed. Again. If this describes you, don't quit reading. There is good news.

Romans 8:15 says, "For you did not receive a spirit of slavery to fall back into fear, but you received the Spirit of adoption, by whom we cry out, 'Abba Father!'" The word *Abba* may not be familiar to you. It means "daddy." Not "father" or even "dad." It means "daddy." Even though God holds the entire universe in His hands and created that universe out of nothing, He has a daddy's heart. That's the kind of intimate relationship He wants to have with you. He's not just any daddy. He's a *perfect* daddy. He will care for your needs. He is tender, compassionate, forgiving, and strong. Unlike some human fathers, God the Father isn't shackled to past pain that keeps Him from loving you. He loves you freely and unconditionally, all of your life.

How to Develop a Good Father Image

If you've grown up with a less-than-accurate image of God, how can you develop a good one? How do you discover what He's actually like? Start by looking at the life of Jesus. Why? Because in John 14:9, Jesus said, "The one who has seen Me has seen the Father." If you want to know what the heavenly Father is like, look at Jesus.

Was Jesus loving? Yes, and so is the Father.

Was He forgiving and compassionate? Oh, yes.

Was Jesus patient with people who doubted Him? Yep.

If you want to know what God is really like—not how the world portrays Him—look to Jesus. He is God with skin on.

Has your mom ever taken down an old picture of you (maybe the one with the bad haircut) to replace it with the newest photo? In much the same way, you need to take down the old picture of "Dad" that you've hung on the wall of your heart and mind. Replace that faulty image a new picture—a picture of the heavenly Father who is perfect in His love and grace and mercy. The heavenly Father who longs for a relationship with you, His child.

Changing your understanding of God as Father doesn't happen overnight. It's a process, and it takes time. You will constantly take down old images and replace them with new, more accurate pictures. It may take a few months or years. Or it even might take a whole lifetime. That's okay. God is patient. The more you experience His love and grace, the more you'll be able to trust Him. Over time, you'll see in your own life the evidence of His concern for you.

Take a few minutes to climb into your Daddy's lap. Find a quiet place where you can be alone to read some passages from His Word. (They're written just for you!) Listen to His heart for you, His dearly loved child. Ask Him to help you trust Him as a little girl trusts her earthly father. Remember that God loves you more than you could ever imagine. In reality, your name is written on His hands. Isaiah 49:16 tells us, "Look, I have inscribed you on the palms of My hands; your walls are continually before Me."

That's the heart of the God who created you, who loves you, and who died for you. That's a heavenly Father you can trust. He is picture perfect.

For you did not receive a spirit of slavery to fall back into fear, but you received the spirit of adoption, by whom we cry out, "Abba, Father!" —Romans 8:15

"Look, I have inscribed you on the palms of My hands; your walls are continually before Me."—Isaiah 49:16

Help!

I have been a Christian since I was a little kid, and most of that time, I never did anything really wrong. But last month, I messed up big time. Like the police got involved. I've even prayed to God for forgiveness. But I still feel overwhelmed with guilt. What do I do?

Signed,
Wish I could have a do-over

Dear Do-Over,

I understand your struggle. I think every person who has ever done something wrong—especially "big" sins—wrestles with guilt. When you ask God for forgiveness, He grants it. He is faithful and just to forgive us and cleanse us (1 John 1:9). If that's the case (and it is), and you still feel guilty, then ask yourself the question, *Why do I still feel guilty?*

Here are some reasons you might discover.

1. You can't forgive yourself. Sometimes when we think God hasn't forgiveness us, it's because we haven't forgiven ourselves. Over the years, I've learned that forgiving other people is way easier than forgiving myself. It's a process, so keep at it.

2. You don't believe God really loves you. You may be wondering, *God couldn't love me after I've made such a big mistake. Why would Jesus die for me?* When you doubt God's forgiveness and love, in essence you're saying that your sin is too big for God. But no sin is too big for Him to forgive.

3. You are actually feeling shame, rather than guilt. There's a *huge* difference between guilt and shame. Guilt is from God, but shame is from Satan. Guilt leads to positive change, but shame leads to deeper despair. And although guilt is resolved after asking for forgiveness, shame gets worse after asking for forgiveness.

The truth is, once God forgives, He forgets. The truth is, Christ came to set you free, so don't let yourself be taken captive by an enemy who wants to keep you in prison. John 8:31–32 says, "So Jesus said to the Jews who had believed Him, 'If you continue in My word, you really are My disciples. You will know the truth, and the truth will set you free.'"

So hold tight to His teaching—you are His beloved, and you are forgiven.

SUBMITTING TO AUTHORITIES:
The Command Nobody Wants to Follow

by Pam Gibbs

Nobody likes to be told what to do. From the time you were little, you have rebelled against authority. As a toddler, you climbed on the coffee table when your parents told you not to. You refused to eat your peas even when told to do so. Your mom told you not to touch the cake. You touched it.

As you've become older, the more you've rebelled. And you've rebelled against more people. Your teacher tells you to turn off your cell phone. Nope. Still on. Your coach tells you to run a mile, and you skip out as soon as possible. Your parents tell you to be in by 11 p.m., and you come in at 11:05 p.m.—just to show them you don't like the rule.

The whole goal of adolescence is gaining independence. FREEDOM. When you turn eighteen, you can do what you want when you want. Nobody gets to order you around. You can get a tattoo if you want, stay out until 2 a.m. if you want. Go to R-rated movies. Eat junk food. Drink too much coffee. Ah, pure freedom.

Except that you can't do whatever you want.

Why? Because when you submit to God as the Sovereign Lord of your life, you agree to do His will. And His will is for you to submit to authority.

What God Says About Authority

God has placed people in authority over you. Some are government leaders. Others are church leaders. And then there's your parents. Each of these has been put into place for your good and His glory.

Parents. Early in the Bible, God commands children to submit to their parents' authority. Remember Exodus 20:12? "Honor your father and your mother, so that you may live long in the land the LORD your God is giving you." Oh yeah. That command. Did you notice the promise God gave to you if you follow this verse? Lengthened life. That tells me that submitting to your parents' authority can keep you (and me) out of situations that could actually harm us. That's why parents tell their kids not to jump off the roof like Superman. Not that I've tried. Really.

Government. Believe it or not, the leaders of your local, state, and national government have authority over you. Romans 13:1–2 says, "Everyone must submit to the governing authorities, for there is no authority except from God, and those that exist are instituted by God. So then, the one who resists the authority is opposing God's command, and those who oppose it will bring judgment on themselves."

Yikes. That's a pretty strong word of caution. To rebel against governing authorities is rebelling against God.

I know what you are thinking. What if the government is corrupt? What if the leaders make bad decisions? God didn't provide any escape clauses for obeying government. Even Jesus kept the civil law when He walked the earth, and the governors and emperors were as bad as it gets. As long as the laws don't contradict the commands of Scripture, God wants you to honor your leaders.

Employers. If you haven't yet, at some point you will have a job (I hope). You will be supervised by a manager, boss, or some other leader. Scripture commands submission to these authorities as well. First Peter 2:13 says, "Submit yourselves for the Lord's sake to every human authority" (NIV). Why would submitting to authorities be "for the Lord's sake"? Because you are His representative on this rock called earth. When you claim to follow Jesus, others will expect behavior that reflects Him. Coming in late and leaving early doesn't provide a good example of respecting others. Neither does being lazy or stealing money from the cash register. Christ's reputation is damaged (and so is yours) when you disrespect, dishonor, and disobey your employers.

Teachers, coaches, and other authorities. Remember 1 Peter 2:13? That Scripture applies to these authorities as well. Colossians 3:23–24 tells us, "Whatever you do, do it enthusiastically, as something done for the Lord and not for men, knowing that you will receive the reward of an inheritance from the Lord. You serve the Lord Christ." Ultimately, you are serving and submitting to God, not parents, teachers, bosses, or coaches. Your submitting to human authority is an act of obedience to God.

How to Submit to Authority

Submitting to authority is really, really practical. Here are some starting steps you can take:

1. *Pray that God will give you a submissive spirit.* I'm not saying that you should let people mistreat you and abuse your work or your skills. Rather, ask God to give you a willing heart to honor Him by honoring authorities.

2. *Pray for those in authority over you.* Let me ask you a really tough question: Do you pray for your parents as much as you complain about them? Do you pray for your teachers as much as you gripe about them with your friends? What about your coach? Your boss? What about the president, and other elected officials? Ask God to give them wisdom. Pray that they will seek God as they lead. And ask God how you can be a blessing to those in authority over you. Be careful, though, He may just give you some ideas!

3. *Show appreciation to those in authority.* Tell your teacher thank you when she helps you with an assignment. Send your pastor or youth pastor a handwritten note letting them know how much you appreciate them. Buy a gift card for your coach at the end of the season. Even if you can't spend a lot of money, a simple gesture to show appreciation matters to them. Most of the time, leaders only hear when they do something wrong.

4. *Set an example.* Respect your teachers by not talking in class. Arrive to work a few minutes early. Don't criticize the coach in front of other players. Vote when you turn eighteen (and after that too!). Set the example for those who look to you for authority—your siblings, classmates, younger students in the youth ministry, coworkers. You can change the dynamic and culture of your home, your school, and your workplace just by setting a positive example of submitting to authority.

You won't always agree with your parents. You'll disagree with your coaches too. That doesn't mean you get to stop submitting to them. The Bible is clear on that. But here's something to think about: How you treat those in authority over you will determine how much authority He gives to you to lead others.

Whatever you do, do it enthusiastically, as something done for the Lord and not for men, knowing that you will receive the reward of an inheritance from the Lord. You serve the Lord Christ.
—Colossians 3:23–24

A SOLDIER'S CALL TO DUTY

Share in suffering as a good soldier of Christ Jesus.

—2 Timothy 2:3

I'm part of the fellowship of the unashamed. I have Holy Spirit power. The die has been cast. I have stepped over the line. The decision has been made. I'm a disciple of His. I won't look back, let up, slow down, back away, or be still.

My past has been redeemed, my present makes sense, and my future is secure. I am finished and done with low living, sight walking, small planning, smooth knees, colorless dreams, tamed visions, mundane talking, cheap living, and dwarfed goals.

I no longer need preeminence, prosperity, position, promotions, plaudits, or popularity. I don't have to be right, first, tops, recognized, praised, regarded, or rewarded. I now live by faith, lean on His presence, walk by patience, lift by prayer, and labor by power.

My face is set, my gait is fast, my goal is heaven, my road is narrow, my way rough, my companions few, my guide reliable, my mission clear. I cannot be bought, compromised, detoured, lured away, turned back, deluded, or delayed. I will not flinch in the face of sacrifice, hesitate in the presence of the adversary, negotiate at the table of the enemy, ponder in the pool of popularity, or meander in the maze of mediocrity.

I won't give up, shut up, or let up, until I have stayed up, stored up, prayed up, paid up, and preached up for the cause of Christ. I am a disciple of Jesus. I must go till He comes, give till I drop, preach till all know, and work until He stops me. And when He comes for His own, He will have no problem recognizing me—my banner will be clear.

—Anonymous

HE IS ALIVE
Why You Can Believe in Jesus' Resurrection

It's one thing to believe that Jesus lived and died. Historical records tell us He did. Most historians will even admit that He existed.

However, believing that He rose from the dead is another matter.

As you face life after high school, you will likely encounter people who do not believe that Jesus rose from the dead. Some will be your college professors. Others will be classmates or coworkers. Someone might even engage you in a friendly debate about the possibility of such a remarkable declaration. What answer will you give? How would you explain *why* you believe in the resurrection of Jesus? Saying, "because the Bible tells me so" may be sufficient evidence for you, but people who don't know the power of the Bible might need different reasoning.

Fortunately, you don't have to check your brain at the door when you become a Christian. You *can* be a Christian *and* give intelligent, rational reasons for why you choose to believe. The two are not incompatible. Check out the following defenses for why the resurrection did in fact occur just like the Bible records.

But Can You Trust the Bible?

The first question you must ask yourself is whether or not the Bible is a reliable source for information. Can you trust what the New Testament says about the resurrection? Yes.

First, the biblical accounts were all written by eyewitnesses or people who knew the eyewitnesses personally; eyewitnesses make the best historians. Second, scholars collected and examined early handwritten copies of pieces of the New Testament and those copies all say the same thing, which means the story didn't change from person to person. Third, those early handwritten copies were written close to the time when the original books were written, so there was little time for errors to occur between copies. Lastly, early non-Christian writers like Josephus and Tacitus verify important details about Jesus' life, including His Jewish heritage, His rejection by the Jewish leaders, and His crucifixion under Pilate. If those details are true, then it is likely that all of the details recorded in Scripture are true too.

Evidence 1: The Empty Tomb Itself

Scripture records that Jesus' followers went to the tomb after the Sabbath to give Him a proper Jewish burial, only to find an empty tomb when they got there. In addition, Jewish and Roman traditions admit an empty tomb. First-century men including Josephs (a historian) and Gamaliel (a member of the Sanhedrin) both admitted to the empty tomb.[3]

Another piece of evidence of the empty tomb was the action of the disciples. They did not go off to Rome or another country to

BC and AD or BCE or CE

BC means "before Christ." AD is the abbreviation for the words *anno domini*, which is translated "in the year of our Lord" (not "after death"). In recent years, historians have pushed for using the abbreviations BCE and CE, or "before common era" and "common era" to avoid any religious connotations. Although the abbreviations may change, the dividing line in history is still the birth of Christ.

preach the resurrection. Instead, they stayed in the city where Jesus' tomb was. If He was still in the grave, the Jews could have made fools of the disciples by opening the tomb and producing the body. But that never happened.

Evidence 2: The Stone Removed

All four of the Gospel writers mention that the stone had been moved from in front of the grave. Keep in mind that the stone probably weighed between 1½ to 2 tons. How would it be possible for the disciples to sneak up on a bunch of Roman guards and remove that stone without waking them up and being discovered? It wouldn't have been possible. This refutes the theory that the disciples simply removed and hid His body.

Evidence 3: The Appearances of Jesus

After His resurrection, Jesus appeared to a bunch of people, including Mary Magdalene, the disciples, a guy named Cleopas (see Luke 24), Thomas and the other apostles (see John 20), and on one occasion more than 500 witnesses (see 1 Corinthians 15).

You can tell one person or a few people that they are just making up a story. Can you refute the eyewitness testimony of 500 people? Not so much.

Evidence 4: The Lives of the Disciples

History tells us that these early disciples spread the story of Jesus' death and resurrection at great cost. James (the son of Zebedee) was executed by Herod around AD 44 (Acts 12:2). Andrew went to modern-day Turkey and Greece, where tradition says he was crucified. Tradition also says Thomas was pierced through with a spear, and James the son of Alpheus was stoned and then clubbed to death. Peter was crucified. In fact, he asked to be crucified upside down because he didn't feel worthy to die the same way Jesus did.[4] Ask yourself: would these men have died to perpetuate a hoax? Would these men endure prison, beatings, whippings, and death for nothing? These men were absolutely convinced of the resurrection. Look at Peter's life. Before the resurrection, he was a coward, denying Jesus in order to save his own skin. After the resurrection, he was the leader of the early church. Proof positive.

Evidence 5: The Seal

In the original Greek of Matthew 27:63–64, the word *secure* indicates that a Roman seal was placed on the tomb to deter anyone from disturbing the grave.[5] People feared that seal. Punishment for messing with it and breaking into the tomb was huge—automatic crucifixion upside down.[6] That's a hefty fine to pay for a practical joke.

The Most Important Evidence: Your Life

You can use logical proofs and evidence to show why you believe the resurrection occurred. However, the most important evidence is your changed life. No one can deny the change that Christ has made in your life. When you talk with friends, share about what He has done for you—how He calms your fears, helps you control your temper, gives you purpose and hope. Share how reading the Bible gives you guidance in making decisions and how worship reminds you of God's control over your chaotic life.

In the end, that may be the best evidence of all.

Oops! Wrong Date

When scholars calculated the BC/AD system, they made a mistake in pinpointing the year Jesus was born. Later scholars discovered that Jesus was actually born around 6 to 4 BC, not AD 1.[7] This doesn't change anything about Jesus' death or resurrection, but it might help you win that trivia contest.

3. See http://www.leaderu.com/everystudent/easter/articles/josh2.html.
4. See http://www.christianity.com/church/church-history/timeline/1-300/whatever-happened-to-the-twelve-apostles-11629558.html.
5. See http://www.cbn.com/spirituallife/onlinediscipleship/easter/renner_buried.aspx.
6. See http://www.leaderu.com/everystudent/easter/articles/josh2.html.
7. See http://www.gotquestions.org/BC-AD.html#ixzz38n-W15Ije.

What happened to Jesus' body?

Most historians will agree that Jesus' tomb was empty. However, to refute Jesus' resurrection, many theories have been suggested to explain how a dead person walked out of a tomb.

The "swoon" theory. This alternative theory suggests that Jesus didn't really die. Rather, he merely passed out from exhaustion and blood loss. However, considering the beatings and whippings (many people died from this before even being crucified) and pierced side, this theory just doesn't hold up.

The stolen body theory. Some people claim that the disciples moved the body while the guards slept. Remember that 2-ton boulder over the grave? It's highly unlikely that the disciples could accomplish that feat without waking up the soldiers. Besides, remember the disciples' state of mind. All of them fled in fear of being arrested themselves. Later, they met together secretly, still afraid of the soldiers. Why would these timid cowards attempt such a daring plot?

The wrong tomb theory. This theory states that the women who first reported Jesus' missing body had actually gone to the wrong tomb. Then the disciples who went to verify the women's claims must have also gone to the wrong tomb. However, if the followers of Jesus had just made a geographical mistake, the Jewish authorities would have quickly pointed out the proper tomb, squelching any crazy rumors of a resurrection.

How Can I Talk to My Non-Christian Friends About Christ?

by Pam Gibbs

Most Christian teens *want* to talk about God with their non-Christian friends, but coming up with the words and actually speaking up feels like a ginormous task. You don't want to mess up. You want them to understand how much your relationship with Christ means to you. At the same time, you don't want to push them away from Christ or make them feel guilty.

And you don't want to come across as a jerk.

There are no rules to follow that will guarantee success or eliminate awkward moments. However, here are a few that can make the conversation more comfortable and perhaps more positive.

1. Be humble.
When talking with your friends about a relationship with Christ, don't approach them with a know-it-all attitude that says, "I'm right and you're wrong." People do not respond well to arrogance, especially when it comes to religion. If you act like you are superior to them because you know God, then they will probably not respect you enough to listen to what you have to say. Keep in mind that you are just a fellow sinner who is showing another sinner how to find mercy and grace.

2. Listen.
Listen to what your friends have to say. It doesn't mean you have to agree with their opinions, but listening will help you understand their religious background and biases. You might be able to determine why some people get angry when you talk about God. Many people who are defensive about Christianity have had a bad experience with a Christian at some point in their lives.

If a friend shares a story about being hurt or disappointed by a Christian, apologize for what happened (even if you didn't cause the hurt). Let them know that Christians are humans and humans are prone to sin. Tell them to look directly to Jesus for the sincerest example of Christianity.

3. Pray for opportunities.
Ask God to give you opportunities to talk about your faith in a natural way. For instance, perhaps you've just studied about the theory of evolution in one of your science classes. The following lunch period would be prime time to talk about what happened in class. Ask friends what they thought (see #2). Wait for them to ask what you thought.

4. Use your own personal experience.
One of the most valuable tools for sharing your faith is telling your own journey toward Christ. No one can take away that experience, and it can be the basis for

later conversation. Although others may disagree about God's existence or evolution or sin, others cannot tell you that your experience is invalid. When the opportunity presents itself, talk about answered prayers or how God has helped you through a tough challenge.

5. Invite them.
Let them know about events at church, Christian events, concerts, or Christian organizations at your school. It's hard to turn down the opportunity to have fun, so sometimes your friends just need an invitation. If your friends see other people their age who are following Christ, they may be more receptive to it.

6. Lay off the Christian lingo.
Using phrases like "sanctified," "born-again," and "saved" can be overwhelming to someone who doesn't know what you are talking about. Also, try not to use the word *lost* when referring to non-Christians. They don't see themselves as "lost" and may be insulted if someone calls them that.

7. Don't be afraid to say, "I don't know."
It's okay to admit that you don't have all the answers. If a friend asks you a tough question you can't answer, tell them you will talk to your pastor or youth minister and will come back with an answer. You may want to invite that friend to come along. Although a pastor or youth minister may not have an answer either, there is nothing wrong with explaining that some questions will not be explained this side of heaven.

8. Focus on your sins ... not theirs.
If your conversations about Christianity always center on your friend's sin and need for Christ, they may become defensive over the long haul. Instead, try focusing on your own shortcomings and how Christ's forgiveness has impacted your life. Don't be afraid to share your weaknesses and areas of your life in which you have asked Christ to help you change.

9. Don't give up.
Seldom does a person become a Christian after hearing the gospel one time. God is at work in your friends' lives, even if you can't see how. Never cease praying for them. Your words and your actions may have an impact on their coming to Christ years down the road.

10. Leave the results to God.
You never know what God is doing in the heart of another person. Only He can draw other people to Himself. Even if a friend becomes a Christian as a result of your example or encouraging words, God did the work—not you.

St. Francis of Assisi once said, "Preach the gospel at all times. Use words when necessary."[8] Wow. That's a tall order. Francis was a wise man to recognize that our actions and love toward others will have a greater impact than our words. Let your life speak as an example of what God has done in your heart. Even though you may feel like you are talking to a brick wall, keep praying and keep sharing. You never know what God may be doing in the lives of your friends.

8. http://en.thinkexist.com/quotes/st._francis_of_assisi

What About Those Who Have Never Heard About Christ?

by Pam Gibbs

How can a loving God send anyone to hell?

That question is one of the major objections to a person believing in God. After all, who would want to believe in a God who is so mean? If hell is as horrific as the Bible describes it, no loving deity would ever send anyone to that place. Either the Bible is wrong about hell, or it is wrong to describe God as loving. Seems like a logical conclusion, right? Well, let's take a closer look.

God's Heart Toward People

First, let's look at a verse about God's intentions toward all people. The question assumes that God wants to "send people to hell." However, Scripture is very clear that God doesn't want anyone to go to hell. His desire is for every person to receive forgiveness through Christ's sacrificial death. In the New Testament, 2 Peter 3:9 says, "The Lord isn't slow about keeping his promises, as some people think he is. In fact, God is patient, because *he wants everyone to turn from sin* and no one to be lost" (CEV). Did you catch that? God wants every person to choose Him.

Humans' Heart Toward God

However, from the very beginning (all the way back in Genesis), God has allowed people to make their own choices—even if those choices ultimately break His heart. When God gave human beings the freedom of choice, He knew that many people would use that freedom to reject Him. When people reject Jesus and His offer of forgiveness, they suffer the consequences of their choice: separation from God for all eternity. God doesn't *send* anyone to hell. People choose hell when they suppress the truth of God that is plainly all around them.

Being Humans Versus Robots

At this point, you might argue that God should *compel* us to choose heaven over hell. Since He knows what hell is like (that it was never intended for humans, but only for the devil and his angels), He should have forced people to follow Him. However, to compel a person to love God isn't really love at all. To force a person to choose God isn't really a choice at all. God didn't want robots with no emotion and no soul. He created free-will beings under a loving, sovereign Lord. A decision this side of eternity to follow Christ will result in an eternity with Christ in heaven. God wants us to choose to love Him. Only then is it real love.

What about the people who never hear the Gospel?

What about the native on an island far away from civilization, the one who has never heard the news about Jesus Christ? Why would God doom that person to hell without even having a shot at choosing God? Romans 1:19–20 provides the answer to this question. It says, "Since what can be known about God is evident among them, because God has shown it to them. For His invisible attributes, that is, His eternal power and divine nature, have been clearly seen since the creation of the world, being understood through what He has made. As a result, people are without excuse."

Have you ever seen the Rocky Mountains and wondered how God could create something so magnificent? Have you ever seen tropical fish swimming around coral and thought about how creative God was to come up with all those colors? Have you ever listened to a fierce thunderstorm, raw with power? The existence and reality of God is made known through creation. Nature reveals the power and evidence of God, and instinctively humans are drawn to Him. They are drawn to search for the Creator of the creation.

God is perfect and just and will act in keeping with His sovereign character, drawing people to Him from the entire earth. In fact, Revelation talks about people "from every tribe and language and people and nation" (Revelation 5:9). Although we may not know how God accomplishes it, He gives all people a choice to believe Him or not.

The Lord isn't slow about keeping his promises, as some people think he is. In fact, God is patient, because he wants everyone to turn from sin and no one to be lost. —2 Peter 3:9 CEV

Worthy are you to take the scroll and to open its seals, for you were slain, and by your blood you ransomed people for God from every tribe and language and people and nation, and you have made them a kingdom and priests to our God, and they shall reign on the earth. —Revelation 5:9–10 ESV

FACTS ABOUT THE AFTERLIFE

- Jesus talked about hell more than anyone else in the New Testament.[9]

- When polled, 92 percent of Americans believe in God, 85 percent believe in heaven, and 75 percent believe in hell.[10]

- Nowhere does the Bible affirm reincarnation.

- In the Bible, the word *hell* is translated from several different words with various meanings.[11] In the Old Testament, *Sheol* can be translated "grave," "hell," "death," "destruction," and "the pit." It identifies the general abode of the dead, where life no longer exists (see Psalm 49:13–14).

- In the New Testament, *Hades* can be translated as hell. It is described as a prison with gates, bars, and locks (see Acts 2:27–31). *Gehenna* means "the fires of hell" or "hell." It is usually associated with the final judgment (see Matthew 10:28). *Tartarus*, means "hell" or "the lower regions." It designates a place of eternal judgment (see 2 Peter 2:4).

9. See http://www.christianitytoday.com/ct/2011/marchweb-only/rob-bell-universalism.html?paging=off.
10. See http://www.statista.com/statistics/245496/belief-of-americans-in-god-heaven-and-hell.
11. See http://christianity.about.com/od/whatdoesthebiblesay/a/Hell-In-The-Bible.htm.

WHY ARE YOU HERE?
God's Purpose for Your Life

by Vicki Courtney

Don't you know that the runners in a stadium all race, but only one receives the prize? Run in such a way to win the prize. Now everyone who competes exercises self-control in everything. However, they do it to receive a crown that will fade away, but we a crown that will never fade away. —1 Corinthians 9:24–25

I've heard it said that you never see a U-Haul behind a hearse. That's because you can't take anything with you to the next life. No cars. No houseboat. No shoe collection. No jewelry. Scripture says that the "stuff" here on this earth will one day be consumed by fire (2 Peter 3:10). However, when you look at the lives of most people, it seems like they spend their lives pursuing the very things that have no eternal value. They are wasting their lives on what does not matter ultimately. Why gather prizes that we can't take with us when we can invest our time and energy in things with eternal value? If we are to run with purpose, as the verses above describe, we must understand our purpose for existence. If someone had asked me at your age what my purpose in life was, I would have stared back dumbfounded. I had no idea.

A Christian's purpose in life is clear: To know God and make Him known.

Know God

Our chief goal is to know God. God created us to experience Him and to worship Him. He sent His Son as His exact representation, so to see Jesus is to see God. He also sent the Holy Spirit to dwell within and guide us, so that we might know Him in that way. Finally, He provided the Bible as a means to know Him. It is a revelation of His character and a constant reminder of His love and mercy. If you do not regularly spend time reading your Bible, it will be hard to get to know Him. If your schedule is tight, find a devotional book that focuses on short passages of Scripture.

If you are not using a devotional book, read through the New Testament, starting with one of the Gospels (Matthew, Mark, Luke, and John). Take your time. Reflect on how God made Himself known through Jesus and what that means for you today. Also pay close attention to the book of Romans. It contains many important truths that can build your trust in God and prepare you for the future.

Another way to know is to talk to Him. In church terms, that's prayer. Prayer doesn't have to be saved for bedtime and emergencies, like that math test you forgot about. Get in the habit of talking to God throughout your day. The more you communicate with Him, the better you will know Him. Remember, though, that communication is a two-way street. We often talk to God, but rarely do we listen for His voice. Think about it: if you never call her or talk to your best friend, how can you really know her? She won't be your best friend for long. The same is true when it comes to our relationship with God. You won't know Him if you don't talk—and listen—to Him.

Scripture says that the "stuff" here on this earth will one day be consumed by fire (2 Peter 3:10).

Make Him Known

The sayings on bumper stickers crack me up. With all the worthy causes in the world, how do people determine where to invest their time and energy? With challenges like finding a cure for cancer, feeding the hungry, saving women from sex trafficking, and (most importantly) telling people about Jesus, it seems ridiculous to funnel time, money, and energy into causes and issues that won't matter for eternity.

For example, years ago, the development of a new mall in Austin was halted because an environmental group claimed that an endangered cave beetle *might* be hiding under rocks where the proposed mall was to be built. If these rare beetles indeed were there, the environmental group claimed that the mall development would kill off the cave beetle. The beetle was less than an eighth of an inch in length, had no eyes, and lived in total darkness under rocks. I had to drive ten extra miles to another mall so a cave beetle—that no one had actually even seen—could camp out under a rock in total darkness. My extra drive probably created more emissions from my car, probably angering a different environmental group. I can't win.

Christians have been given a cause far more important than saving the baby whales, the spotted owls, the rain forests, and yes, even the cave beetles. We have been given the purpose of spreading the gospel message of Christ's sacrificial death and glorious resurrection. See if you can find our job title in the passage on the next page.

Save the Baby Whales

Stop Global Warming

Have You Hugged A Tree Today?

Visualize World Peace

Everything is from God, who reconciled us to Himself through Christ and gave us the ministry of reconciliation: That is, in Christ, God was reconciling the world to Himself, not counting their trespasses against them, and He has committed the message of reconciliation to us. Therefore, we are ambassadors for Christ, certain that God is appealing through us. We plead on Christ's behalf, "Be reconciled to God." He made the One who did not know sin to be sin for us, so that we might become the righteousness of God in Him. —2 Corinthians 5:18–21

We are His ambassadors! An ambassador is an official messenger and representative, like the American ambassador to Russia. Being an ambassador can feel overwhelming when you consider that we work directly for God. It is our job to be His representatives—to reflect His character and His intentions toward humanity. The passage above spells out our duty: to share the message of reconciliation. Don't let the big words throw you off—it simply means that He has entrusted us with sharing the good message that Christ paid the price for our sins. He has called all of us—not just preachers, youth ministers, and missionaries—to tell others about how to know Him.

Your mission field is your school, neighborhood, job, and yes, even your church. As long as there are people who haven't heard about Jesus, your job is to tell them about Him. And believe me, lots of people don't know about Him—even in America.

Your purpose in life is to know God and make Him known. Anything less is like chasing after cave beetles.

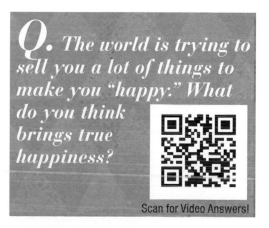

Q. *The world is trying to sell you a lot of things to make you "happy." What do you think brings true happiness?*

Scan for Video Answers!

FOLLOWING GOD'S WILL

by Pam Gibbs

Wouldn't it be great if God gave us a cheat sheet so we could make all the right decisions and never go wrong? That way, we'd always follow God's will and never veer off on our own. We'd never sin, never feel unsure of our decisions, never second-guess our choices.

The truth is that God *has* given us His instructions for following Him—the Bible. Scripture gives you the directions to take, although they're not as clear as a map. You won't flip open the Bible to find who you are supposed to date or marry. You won't open it and find what college you are supposed to attend or what to major in. And you probably already know that you won't find God's will about whether or not you should cut your hair!

However, God does tell us some things He does want for your life and mine. John 6:40 says, "For my Father's will is that everyone who looks to the Son and believes in him shall have eternal life" (NIV). And another piece of God's will is found in 1 Thessalonians 4:3, which says, "It is God's will that you should be sanctified" (NIV). We can know with certainty that God's will for you and me is to follow and grow in our faith. But you probably already knew that.

You are probably wondering about dating the wrong person. Or taking the wrong job. Or signing up for the wrong classes. Maybe you don't know whether or not to go a party or whether or not to go on a mission trip. Over your lifetime, you will make millions of everyday choices, and you want to make the choices that lead to your good and God's glory. Although the Bible does not tell you which car to buy or which book to write a report on, you can follow some basic guidelines that will help you make good choices.

What Does God's Word Say?

God gave us His Word to guide us in our daily lives. It tells us how to love Him and honor Him. Jeremiah 6:16 says, "Thus says the Lord: 'Stand in the ways and see, And ask for the old paths, where the good way is, And walk in it; Then you will find rest for your souls'" (NKJV).

This "good way" is found in the pages of the Bible. For example, Romans 12:2 says it like this, "Don't be like the people of this world, but let God change the way you think. Then you will know how to do everything that is good and pleasing to him" (CEV). If you're wondering whether to go to a party, ask yourself, *Do I want to go just so I'll fit in with everyone else?* This verse clearly teaches us to go against the crowd mentality. Sometimes the Bible gives clear instruction about our lives. Marry a godly man. Don't focus on material wealth. Don't worry about tomorrow. Don't be judgmental or show favoritism. But what do you do when the Bible isn't so clear?

What Does Godly Counsel Say?

In addition to Scripture, God has also given you the counsel and wisdom of older believers who have walked with God for a long time. When Scripture isn't very clear, ask that godly adult about it. You could ask your grandmother, parents, or even your pastor or Sunday School teacher. When you share with them, be honest and give them all of the facts. And be willing to accept their counsel, even if you may not like their answers. Remember, God has given them as gifts to guide you, not to make sure you're happy.

What Does the Holy Spirit Say?

You also need to ask God what He thinks. If you are a believer, the Holy Spirit lives in you. Scripture says that He will guide you into all truth (John 16:13). In other words, if you will listen to Him, He will nudge your heart in the right direction. This requires that you take the time to be still long enough for Him to speak. Unfortunately, God doesn't audibly speak out loud and say, "Go to _____ college" or "Don't go out with _____." However, He will make you uncomfortable and hesitant. If there's hesitation, wait. Haste makes mistakes.

The Three-Legged Stool

Think of God's Word, godly people, and God's Spirit as three legs on a stool. If all three legs of a stool are strong and in place, the stool is safe for you to sit on it. However, if one of the legs is missing, you certainly don't want to sit on it. You'll find yourself on the floor in a nanosecond. In much the same way, if God's Word, godly people, and God's Spirit all point to the same answer, you can pretty much trust your decision. However, if the three conflict with each other, there's a problem. God's Word will never contradict with His Spirit, and His people won't contradict His Word.

I'm pretty sure God will give you the freedom to choose what color of car to buy and what kind of haircut to choose. He wants you to develop your decision-making skills as you grow. For the big stuff, though, you can rely on the gifts He has given you. Follow those, and you won't head down the wrong path.

WHAT DOES IT MEAN TO BE A CHRISTIAN?

by Vicki Courtney

I didn't become a Christian until I went to college. However, I vividly remember friends asking me every so often, "Are you a Christian?" I recall feeling somewhat uncomfortable with the question and not quite sure how to answer. I was too embarrassed to confess that I didn't really know what "being a Christian" meant, so I always told them yes. Most didn't persist any further, and I breathed a sigh of relief.

If you are not sure about what it means to be a Christian, read carefully the rest of this article. If at the end you realize you have never responded to God's offer of forgiveness, would you consider doing so? God is chasing after you and actively drawing you to Himself. You will never face a more important decision in your life than the decision to accept or reject Jesus Christ.

How to Become a Christian

The central theme of the Bible is God's love. This love was revealed when Jesus Christ, God's Son, came into the world as a human being, lived a sinless life, died on the cross, and rose from the dead. Because Christ died, your sins can be forgiven, and because He conquered death, you can have eternal life. You can know what will happen to you after you die. But this gift of forgiveness and eternal life cannot be yours unless you accept it. God requires an individual response from you. The following outline tells the story.[12]

God Loves You

"For God loved the world in this way: He gave His One and Only Son, so that everyone who believes in Him will not perish but have eternal life."—John 3:16

God loves you. He wants a personal relationship with you. And He wants to give you a life that will last forever, even after you experience physical death.

We Are Sinful

*For all have sinned and fall short of the glory of God.
—Romans 3:23*

You may have heard someone say, "I'm only human—nobody's perfect." This verse says the same thing: We are *all* sinners. We *all* do things that we know are wrong. And that's why we feel separated from God. God is holy and good, and we are not. We are sinners.

Sin Has a Penalty

For the wages of sin is death.
—Romans 6:23

Just as criminals must pay the penalty for their crimes, sinners must pay the penalty for their sins. The penalty of sin is spiritual death. You will not only die physically, but you will also be separated from our holy God for all eternity. The Bible teaches that those who choose to reject God's forgiveness will spend eternity in hell.

Christ Has Paid Our Penalty!

But God proves His own love for us in that while we were still sinners Christ died for us!
—Romans 5:8

Jesus Christ has paid the penalty for all your sins. You don't have to lead a good life and do enough good deeds before God will love you. Christ loved you enough to die for you, even when you were rebelling against Him.

12. Source: Taken from "Your Christian Life" 1965, 1968, as "Aids to Christian Living," 1986 as "Practical Steps in Christian Living," 1995 as "Beginning Your Christian Life," 1997 as "Your Christian Life," Billy Graham Evangelistic Association.

Salvation Is a Free Gift

For you are saved by grace through faith, and this not from yourselves; it is God's gift—not from works, so that no one can boast.—Ephesians 2:8–9

The word *grace* means "undeserved favor." It means God is offering you something you could never provide for yourself: forgiveness of sins and eternal life with Him. God's gift to you is free. You do not have to work for it. All you have to do is joyfully receive it.

You Must Receive Him

But to all who did receive Him, He gave them the right to be children of God, to those who believe in His name.
—John 1:12

When you receive Christ into your heart, you become a child of God and have the privilege of a relationship with Him, like a daughter to her father. You can talk to Him in prayer and hear from Him through God's Word. To be a Christian means to have a personal relationship with God through Jesus Christ. And best of all, it is a relationship that will last for all eternity.

Therefore, if anyone is in Christ,
he is a new creation. The old has passed
away; behold, the new has come.
—2 Corinthians 5:17 ESV

The Last Word on God

The LORD your God is with you,

the Mighty Warrior who saves.

He will take great delight in you;

in his love he will no longer rebuke you,

but will rejoice over you with singing.

—Zephaniah 3:17 NIV

RAPIDES PARISH LIBRARY

P9-DEO-573

722

SLEDGEHAMMER

How Breaking

with the Past

Brought Peace to

the Middle East

SLEDGEHAMMER

DAVID FRIEDMAN

BROADSIDE BOOKS

WITHDRAWN FROM
RAPIDES PARISH LIBRARY

The opinions and characterizations in this piece are those of the author and do not necessarily represent those of the US government.

SLEDGEHAMMER. Copyright © 2022 by David Friedman. All rights reserved. Printed in the United States of America. No part of this book may be used or reproduced in any manner whatsoever without written permission except in the case of brief quotations embodied in critical articles and reviews. For information, address HarperCollins Publishers, 195 Broadway, New York, NY 10007.

HarperCollins books may be purchased for educational, business, or sales promotional use. For information, please email the Special Markets Department at SPsales@harpercollins.com.

Broadside Books™ and the Broadside logo are trademarks of HarperCollins Publishers.

FIRST EDITION

Designed by Elina Cohen

Library of Congress Cataloging-in-Publication Data

Names: Friedman, David Melech, author.
Title: Sledgehammer: how breaking with the past brought peace to the Middle East / David Friedman.
Description: First edition. | New York, NY: Broadside Books, 2022. | Includes index.
Identifiers: LCCN 2021036846 (print) | LCCN 2021036847 (ebook) | ISBN 9780063098114 (hardback) | ISBN 9780063098121 (ebook)
Subjects: LCSH: Friedman, David Melech. | Arab-Israeli conflict—1993—Peace. | Israel—Foreign relations—Arab countries. | Arab countries—Foreign relations—Israel. | Israel—Foreign relations—Islamic countries. | Islamic countries—Foreign relations—Israel. | United States—Foreign relations—2017–2021. | United States—Foreign relations—Israel. | Israel—Foreign relations—United States. | United States—Foreign relations—Arab countries. | Arab countries—Foreign relations—United States. | United States—Foreign relations—Islamic countries. | Islamic countries—Foreign relations—United States.
Classification: LCC DS119.8.A65 F75 2022 (print) | LCC DS119.8.A65 (ebook) | DDC 956.05/3—dc23
LC record available at https://lccn.loc.gov/2021036846
LC ebook record available at https://lccn.loc.gov/2021036847

22 23 24 25 26   LSC   10 9 8 7 6 5 4 3 2 1

I wrote this book for several reasons: to advocate for a strong US-Israel relationship, to provide historical context for the Abraham Accords, to move American foreign policy away from decades of wooden and mistaken theories, and to acknowledge the Divine force that I believe guided my path.

Far more important, I wrote this book for several people: my children, my grandchildren, and my incredible, devoted wife.

This book is for Daniel, Jana, Meira, Chaim Meir, Leora, Shmuel Moshe, Jacob, Danielle, Isla, Alex, Henry, Aliza, Eli, Olivia, Aiden, Julian, Talia, Sam, and Katie. It is for you and, God willing, the additional children and grandchildren that you will bring into the world. Especially for those yet to be born who may not get to know me very well, here is a glimpse of what I care about and what motivates me. But it is only a small glimpse. My love for all of you is a far greater motivation; it's just a lot harder to put into 250 pages.

To my beautiful wife, Tammy, I owe you everything. Our forty years of marriage have gone by in a blink, and I know and pray that the best is yet to come. You hold my heart and I never want it back. Thank you, thank you so very much.

Pray for the peace in Jerusalem, they shall prosper that love thee.

—Psalms 122:6

Contents

SLEDGEHAMMER

SLEDGEHAMMER

BIRTH OF A METAPHOR

The prophets Isaiah and Micah each use identical words to describe the ultimate in diplomacy: "They shall beat their swords into plowshares." Converting the equipment of war into tools of peace is the goal of every American member of the foreign service. But most overlook the fact that the prophets didn't use the phrase "convert their swords," they used the word "beat" (a more literal interpretation of the Hebrew would be "crush"). The prophets suggested a less-than-delicate approach to peacemaking might be necessary, something requiring more than a scalpel or a file. Perhaps even a sledgehammer.

As US ambassador to Israel, that was my approach. It led to a once-in-a-generation series of peace agreements between Israel and five Muslim countries. This book tells the story of how those peace agreements—the Abraham Accords—came to be.

I didn't choose this "sledgehammer" metaphor; it chose me. It began fifteen years ago with a burst sewage pipe in the City of David, an eleven-acre ridge just south of the Temple Mount in Jerusalem.

The City of David, one of the most archaeologically excavated sites in the world, is Jerusalem central—the very place where the kings of the Bible ruled and the prophets of the Bible preached.

Local plumbers were called in to determine the source of the water break. As they excavated the terrain, they realized that there was something unusual below street level. As often happens in Jerusalem, this prompted a call to the Jerusalem Municipality, which in turn resulted in a rushed visit from the Israel Antiquities Authority. As the experts examined the hole in the ground, they realized that they had stumbled upon a discovery of literally biblical proportions—they had uncovered the ancient steps leading to the Pool of Siloam.

The Pool of Siloam was originally built by Hezekiah, king of Judah, in the eighth century BCE, and fed by the Gihon Spring through the Siloam Tunnel. Hezekiah built the water tunnel to ensure an adequate water supply to the ancient City of Jerusalem, especially in the event of a threatened siege from Judah's enemies to the north. The Babylonians apparently destroyed the pool at the end of the sixth century BCE, but the Hasmoneans rebuilt it. King Herod enhanced it about two hundred years later.

Archaeologists and scientists concurred that this discovery was the Pool of Siloam. The pool was the public bath where Jewish pilgrims would purify themselves before ascending to the Temple. According to Christian tradition, the Pool of Siloam is where the New Testament records that Jesus cured a blind man.

Discovery of the Pool of Siloam prompted a follow-up inquiry as to how the pilgrims ascended to the Temple once they had cleansed themselves. Further excavation then revealed something even more amazing: an almost perfectly preserved flagstone road ascending directly from the Pool of Siloam to the southern entrance of the Temple Mount, its construction attributed to Pontius Pilate in the year 30—a few years before the crucifixion of Jesus and approximately forty years before the destruction of Jerusalem by the Romans and the subsequent expulsion of the Jews. It was indeed a significant archaeological find with great spiritual significance to Christians and Jews alike.

Palestinian opposition to this project, however, was intense. They protested that the archaeologists were weakening the foundations of homes in the City of David community, although little evidence supported this claim. What really agitated Palestinian leadership was the impending reality that their favorite narrative that Jews had no historical connection to ancient Jerusalem was about to be further discredited and exposed as a lie. Even though Jerusalem is mentioned more than six hundred times in the Old Testament and not once in the Koran, decades of Palestinian leadership successfully had espoused the argument that Jerusalem is holy only to Muslims and Christians but not to Jews. This was always a self-contradictory argument, since if Jerusalem was holy to Christians, it is because Jesus prayed there as a Jew. Although this falsehood was accepted by UNESCO and other international organizations, the City of David excavations, along with other projects throughout Jerusalem, were creating scientific proof that, to the contrary, ancient biblical Jerusalem was real, it was vibrant, it was Jewish, and sites mentioned in both the Old and New Testaments do exist.

By 2019, nearly half of the ancient street from the Pool of Siloam to the Temple had been excavated. I was given a rare opportunity to view this thoroughfare, dubbed the "Pilgrimage Road," early that year. What I saw was astounding: ancient flagstone steps matching exactly the steps at the southern entrance to the Temple Mount.

I've been to countless museums displaying Jerusalem antiquities. But to me, the Pilgrimage Road was very different from those displays behind glass cases. Those were merely a shard of glass, a piece of clay, or a shred of parchment. The Pilgrimage Road presented a unique opportunity to immerse oneself in a world destroyed some two thousand years ago and walk the steps of thousands of Jews who made the pilgrimage to Jerusalem three times a year for the major festivals—including the historical Jesus. Walking the Pilgrimage Road was an opportunity to feel the anticipation of the pilgrims as they prepared for a deeply spiritual experience. It was a way to step back in time into the world of the Bible.

The world of the Bible is not just significant to me because I am Jewish. I am an American deeply concerned that we as a nation have become untethered from our founding principles. This world of the Bible was the world drawn upon by our Founders in creating the great American Republic. The Declaration of Independence, perhaps the most profound document since the Bible, contained the guarantee to every person of "unalienable rights" endowed by our Creator. These "rights" weren't just a good idea that found their roots in the political discourse of Thomas Hobbes or John Locke or the Federalist Papers or the Magna Carta—or even the Code of Hammurabi. These unalienable rights endowed by God were his will as revealed in the Bible. And the word of God, as described by the prophet Isaiah, was first expressed in the City of David: "For out of Zion shall go forth the law and the word of the Lord from Jerusalem" (Isaiah 2:3).

The City of David—the center of Jewish life in the days of the Bible—thus meant as much to me as an American as it did as a Jew, and I was determined to make sure that American political leaders were exposed to this great monument to our Judeo-Christian heritage. On January 15, 2021, just days before I left office, I formally recognized the City of David as an American heritage site. It was a fitting final act.

But in early 2019, even after we moved the US embassy to Jerusalem and after the United States had withdrawn from UNESCO, the City of David remained off-limits within our State Department. It was considered "too controversial" then to celebrate Israel's ancient connection to Jerusalem.

I pushed back on this flawed thinking and ultimately prevailed. In conjunction with the City of David, the US embassy in Jerusalem scheduled a ceremony to observe the opening of the Pilgrimage Road for June 30, 2019. On that day, I hosted a delegation of US ambassadors from several European nations, along with US Special Representative for International Negotiations Jason Greenblatt and Senator Lindsey Graham. It was a peaceful, meaningful, and uplifting ceremony. Since that date, almost every visiting American dignitary has visited the City of David with great fascination, leaving the site with even greater inspiration.

Ceremonial "openings," of course, often involve some physical act to symbolize the achievement. At the City of David, a plasterboard ceremonial wall was constructed and I was given a sledgehammer to break through to the path of the Pilgrimage Road. After I took a few whacks, the remainder of the US delegation followed in kind until the wall was down, and we were clear to begin the march up the ancient road.

Needless to say, the plasterboard was not load-bearing and had no effect on the structural integrity of the houses some sixty feet to the surface.

Nevertheless, the picture of me wielding a sledgehammer was widely distributed throughout the worldwide media. One reporter after another saw this event as purposely designed, and highly likely, to provoke violence. I was assailed for my lack of diplomatic sensitivity. Reporters who should have known better adopted the false narrative that I had embarked upon a personal quest to destroy Palestinian homes. *The New York Times*, one of my fiercest critics well before I took office, published the headline, U.S. ENVOY SWINGS SLEDGEHAMMER IN EAST JERUSALEM, AND A METAPHOR IS BORN.

I had expected no violence and there was none.

Palestinian and American pundits feigned outrage, but no one on the ground really doubted the centrality of Jerusalem to the Jewish people. Asked by the media that day why I swung a sledgehammer, I replied, "It was the appropriate tool to open a ceremonial wall leading to an underground excavation. If we were opening a bridge, we probably would have used something else."

I was too glib in giving that answer. The truth is that a sledgehammer was exactly the tool needed that day in June 2019, and it was a metaphorical sledgehammer that was required, and that I wielded, throughout my four years as the US ambassador to Israel.

Sledgehammer is a book about what happens when the United States stops listening to the diplomatic elite and challenges the parties to look past the grievances of their grandparents in favor of the opportunities available to their grandchildren. We'll look at events big and small, from Fourth of July parties to wrangling over the embassy in Jerusalem, in order to explore two ideas.

The first is America's support for Israel. You have probably heard that if US support for Israel is not "balanced" with support for Palestinian interests, the entire region will destabilize. How the Muslim world views our support for Israel is something we consistently get wrong. We misread the signals they send. We make assumptions that don't turn out to be true. We ascribe motivations that don't exist.

The United States' special relationship with Israel appears to the elites as a diplomatic challenge, but it is actually a source of great strength. It's not an obstacle to be overcome; it's the fulcrum from which we can move the world. With Iran a greater concern for most Middle Eastern countries than Israel, we saw our diplomatic initiatives regarding Jerusalem, the Golan Heights, and elsewhere as providing assurances to Israel and the moderate Sunni nations that Israel could count on US support, which in turn would serve to curb Iranian adventurism. It is Iran, not Israel, that threatens the region.

The focus on the practical concerns about Iran hints at a second, deeper issue: Everyone wants tangible results, not empty promises. The essence of classical diplomacy is polite ambiguity. But the core of real diplomacy is trust. And trust is built with actions, not words.

For the Arab world, trust was created by restoring our support for moderate Islam, instead of radicals, and extracting enough movement from Israel toward the Palestinians such that the Arab countries could justify their actions and not be perceived as betraying the Palestinian cause. Putting out the president's vision for peace demonstrated that Israel was willing to make territorial compromises that gave cover to the Arab states and that Israel was willing to negotiate peace (even if the Palestinians rejected the deal). There also needed to be a deferral by Israel of its sovereignty declaration over parts of Judea and Samaria, again, to show that Palestinian interests were being given appropriate consideration.

For Israel, trust was created by finally recognizing many of its core principles—regarding Jerusalem, the Golan Heights, and the fact that communities in Judea and Samaria were not illegal and that plans for sovereignty over those communities would come in due course. There also was the need to convince the Israeli right that peace with Arab states was worth the delayed realization of territorial claims. There were lots of needles to thread, but I think we succeeded where others had failed. We did so because all the players trusted us.

What I saw when I first faced confirmation by the Senate in March 2017 was a US policy toward Israel that was fundamentally broken and devoid of trust. It was broken in its failure to recognize the existential risks confronting this tiny nation; it was broken in its ignorance of the deeply held beliefs of so many Israeli people regarding the sanctity of their biblical homeland; it was broken in its failure to comprehend the strategic interests that Israel serves and its vital assistance in protecting the American homeland; it was broken in its wooden and outdated interpretation of international law; and it was broken in its misreading of all the signals with regard to how to advance peace.

Just days after I was nominated, the Obama White House permitted the United Nations Security Council to adopt Resolution 2334, a resolution that held even the Western Wall, Judaism's holiest prayer site, to be illegally occupied territory. It was a stunning betrayal of Israel during the waning lame-duck period of an exiting administration. It had the predictable effect of leaving Israelis and Palestinians more apart than ever—and people like me angry and bewildered.

The US-Israel policy that existed when we took office was simply beyond repair. It was dominated by self-proclaimed experts with no real-world negotiating experience who were perfectly content to repeat the same failed approach time and time again in the futile hope of a different outcome.

We all know the adage that doing the same thing over and over again and expecting different results is the definition of insanity; the State Department calls it diplomacy.

I had a very different view of diplomacy. I had no interest in spending taxpayer money repeating failed strategies. Like a broken bone that had set without proper medical treatment, US-Israel policy could be fixed only by breaking it and allowing it to set properly. It required nothing less than that proverbial sledgehammer to get this right.

Make no mistake, I wasn't looking to be provocative or to cause confrontation. As I told my colleagues time and time again, this was the Middle East and things work differently here. To start a conflict, project weakness; to make peace, project strength. I had no doubt that taking a sledgehammer to old and failed US policies—policies that had only extended the violence and misery of people in the region—was the right path to peace.

My views were shared by my colleagues, Jared Kushner, Mike Pompeo, Steven Mnuchin, Nikki Haley, Robert O'Brien, Jason Greenblatt, Avi Berkowitz, and, of course, my boss, President Trump. "Peace through strength" was our mantra, and our foundational premise was that America would be an honest broker for peace only if it stood with its allies, adhered to its values, respected the truth, and honored its heritage.

IT TOOK A SLEDGEHAMMER TO IMPLEMENT THAT POLICY BUT, IN THE end, we were proven right: We created the Abraham Accords between Israel and four Muslim nations. We normalized relations as well between Israel and Kosovo, a Muslim nation in Europe.

The sledgehammer did not result in the predicted explosion of violence. Rather, it resulted in an explosion of peace.

1

DONALD AND ME

Donald Trump and I first met at his office in Trump Tower in 2004 to discuss his New Jersey casinos. I enjoyed our first meeting. He was funny, smart, and strategic. Atlantic City had already proven to be a great investment for Donald—he had raised hundreds of millions of dollars in debt against three casino properties and had used a good deal of those funds to invest personally in New York City real estate just before values took off. He was, as they say in the casino business, already playing with the house's money. But there were legal complexities that needed to be addressed.

Donald and I had been introduced by Howard Lorber, a close friend of Donald and part of a group of businessmen trying to save Western Union. I had handled the Chapter 11 case for Western Union, doing everything I could to keep at bay a group of aggressive creditors led by Carl Icahn and Leon Black, who had their sights on ownership of Western Union at a steep discount. I worked with Howard and his partner, Bennett LeBow, to keep Western Union in bankruptcy just long enough for the value of its new money-transfer business to replace its old telegram business, which had gone the way of the kerosene lamp. By 1994, they ended up selling the company, paying off all the creditors, and returning hundreds of millions to Mr. LeBow and Mr. Lorber.

Howard Lorber went on to become one of New York's leading real estate players and maintained a close friendship with Donald Trump. When the Trump casinos in Atlantic City began to experience reduced cash flow in the early 2000s, Howard enthusiastically recommended that Donald and I speak. If not for Howard, I don't know that I ever would have met Donald Trump and I certainly would not have taken the path that forms the subject of this book.

As we were chatting in his office in 2004, Donald told me that the best lawyer he ever used was Roy Cohn, the notorious sidekick to Senator McCarthy's Communist witch hunt in the 1950s, who had become a "fixer" for many high-profile clients. I told Donald that I was nothing like Roy Cohn. I didn't have a personal relationship with a single judge and I played by all the rules. What I brought to the table was simply a very smart guy who would outwork and outthink the opposition. I'm not sure if that resonated with him as much as the fact that just before we met, *The American Lawyer*, a magazine known for comparing the income levels of major law firms, had named my firm the most profitable in the country. Whatever the reason, I was hired on the spot.

Many have questioned Donald Trump's business acumen given the bankruptcies of his Atlantic City casinos. The evidence is otherwise. No one could have made money in Atlantic City in the last fifteen years. Morgan Stanley lost over $900 million on its Revel project; Carl Icahn and Caesars lost fortunes as well. Between intense competition arising from new casinos opening in New York and Philadelphia and cheap flights to the Caribbean, coupled with the failure of local officials to create a welcoming environment, Atlantic City had become the loss leader for the gaming industry. No lawyer could make Atlantic City profitable, but I would try to extricate Donald as cleanly as possible from a hornet's nest of angry creditors.

Before I even got started, I suffered a terrible loss. The greatest man I had ever known, my father, passed away. We were extremely close and I depended upon him for his wisdom and advice. A practicing rabbi for more than fifty years in one of the largest Conservative congregations in the United States, Rabbi Morris Friedman had the stature, the commanding presence, and the intelligence to be an outstanding trial lawyer and to command an income of ten to twenty times what he earned from the pulpit. But he dedicated his life to teaching and advancing the values of Judaism, and that calling gave him great satisfaction.

In the Jewish tradition, I observed seven days of shiva (literally translated as "seven") or mourning for my father. During that period, my house was packed with friends and family offering consolation to my mother, my sister, my brother, and me. The last day of mourning saw a blizzard come to our small Long Island community. The phone rang off the hook as friend after friend, many living just a few blocks away, called to apologize for waiting until the last day and not being able to navigate the weather for an in-person visit.

Late in the afternoon that day, the house was almost empty. Out of the corner of my eye I saw some commotion in the foyer and even a hint of flash photography. Seconds later, into the living room walked Donald Trump, having spent four hours in his limo driving the twenty-five miles from midtown Manhattan.

I was surprised to see him. I would have been surprised to have seen anyone brave the weather but especially someone whom I had known only briefly. He spent over an hour with me as we shared stories of our respective fathers. He clearly revered his father, especially his acumen as a builder. He recounted how difficult it was to break into the construction business when his father was getting started; how it required enormous fortitude to stand up to unions, politicians, and even organized criminals, who each controlled aspects of the job. And while his father was engaged in all this tumult, he nonetheless created a safe and comfortable environment for his family.

Both of us seemed to have a strong need for paternal approval. I told him how my father used to boast about my brother's score of 1570 (out of 1600) on the SATs and how my siblings (my sister also broke 1500) suggested that I must have been switched at birth when I barely broke 1300 (although, having skipped two grades, I took the test at fourteen and graduated from high school the next year). I didn't feel that I had come equal with my brother the doctor until I was almost forty and I gave my father $250,000 and asked him to select the charities to which to donate the money. He reacted far more joyously than if the money had been given to him personally. That's what it took to break even with Doctor Mark.

Donald had his own stories. He was one of five and his father, like mine, had high expectations for his kids. Donald wasn't taken seriously as a kid and, like me, lacked the self-discipline and seriousness of purpose that autocratic fathers admire. But then he pulled off a huge and improbable deal, his first in Manhattan, by converting the decrepit Commodore Hotel, a dangerous eyesore, into the gleaming Grand Hyatt. And from that moment forward, Fred Trump Sr. looked at his son Donald in a very different way.

It was quite a conversation that day as I observed my last day of shiva. Donald and I became friends and remain so to this day. Being his friend does not mean that I approve of everything he does. In fact, I have offered my dissent on occasion and as recently as December 2020, when I urged him to accept the election results and focus instead on amplifying his extraordinary four years in the White House. I told him that few presidents had done in two terms what he had done in one.

That was one of the rare occasions where he did not take my advice.

On almost all levels, Donald and I have nothing in common, except for our devotion to family: We both have great respect for our parents and a limitless commitment to our children. Otherwise, Donald led a public life of conspicuous consumption and promotion, and I tried to maintain a modest existence based upon faith and fidelity. So why would I maintain a friendship with someone so different from me? Simply put, because I always saw in Donald the potential for great things. In our discussions, there was always a better angel sitting on one of his shoulders and I was confident that I could draw it out, at least on occasion.

When it came to the kids, I saw in Donald what I see in the mirror: a father who defines his success first and foremost by the quality of the lives of his children. Only one other person that I've known over the years impressed me the same way: Charles Kushner. Charlie is a few years older than me and his children are a few years older than mine. We didn't know each other well when the kids were growing up, but we did overlap at the Wyndham Hotel in Miami Beach for several Passover holidays. I loved the way he treated his children with love and respect and how much pride he held in them. I felt exactly the same way about my family.

I got to know Charlie and Jared when I was representing them in restructuring their investment in 666 Fifth Avenue. When they bought it, the price paid set a record for a New York City office tower. It was after Charlie had suffered through his prison sentence for tax evasion and witness tampering. The crime he committed was the outgrowth of a family squabble that unfortunately was all too common among the second generation of prominent Jewish real estate families. I knew, without being told, how difficult the experience had been for the Kushner family, and I was impressed by Charlie and Jared's determination to build back their business in the face of daunting challenges. The experience undoubtedly was foundational for Jared when he began work in the White House.

Jared was quite an impressive kid in those days. He was running the restructuring of 666 Fifth and met frequently, one on one, with some of the biggest real estate lenders and investors in the world. As Manhattan office rents were plummeting, Jared needed to keep tenants in place, attract new ones, raise capital, and negotiate with some of the toughest vultures in the real estate business, many salivating at the prospect of owning a trophy New York property at a steep discount. Jared never got discouraged—at least he never showed it publicly—throughout this very difficult process. He kept his head down and his proverbial eye on the ball and drove the restructuring to a successful conclusion. It would have been an impressive outcome for anyone, let alone someone not yet thirty years old.

Once, in 2005 or 2006, Donald and I were riding in his limo having left a meeting of Atlantic City creditors. As we passed a magnificent office building, he lamented that he had been in litigation over the ownership of the building for several years and had spent $2 million in legal fees with nothing to show for it. I asked him what he would take to settle and he said he just wanted his fees back. I asked him if I could call someone I knew who was on the other side of the dispute and he agreed immediately. I made the call from the car and put my cell phone on speaker:

"Jeff, it's David Friedman. How are you?" We exchanged pleasantries and then I continued.

"Jeff, I'm thinking of representing Donald Trump on your fight with him. I think I've got a really good appeal."

"David, why would you do that? The case is a complete loser. You'll just spin your wheels and you won't even get paid."

"Possibly, Jeff, but Donald is giving me a huge piece of the upside if I win and I think I've come across a really creative strategy."

"Will Donald settle?"

"I sure hope not. I want to take this all the way."

"How about ten million dollars?" Donald's eyes were as wide as saucers. He began violently nodding his head up and down. I smiled back at him.

"No way, Jeff. I'm in this for a big score. Don't insult me."

"David, the case is dogshit. Fifteen million dollars." Donald was beginning to enter cardiac arrest. I smiled back at him again.

"Thirty million dollars, Jeff. And that's only because I like you." Donald was now looking at me like he was going to kill me. I put my finger up to my lips, warning my client not to make any noise.

"Done at twenty-five million dollars. Deal?"

"Deal."

I hung up the phone and looked across the vehicle. Donald was stunned. He thought I walked on water. He has repeated this story in my presence in the Oval Office at least ten times; I can only imagine how many more times in my absence.

The truth is that I didn't walk on water, and I had no delusions about the quality of the case. What I did know was that Jeff and his colleagues were about to make a fortune refinancing the property in one of the lowest interest-rate environments in history. My threatened appeal could potentially delay or disrupt that transaction at a cost that could be in the hundreds of millions. Buying off that risk made eminent sense to a group of hedge funds that were primed to earn an enormous profit. Why Donald's other lawyers didn't get this was beyond me.

When the call was over, Donald said he wanted to pay me a

"bonus" for that success. He asked me what was my hourly rate. I answered that my hourly rate was irrelevant; even if it was $10,000 an hour, that wouldn't compensate me for the value that I had provided him. He asked me what I wanted. I said, "Well, you wanted two million dollars and I got you twenty-three million dollars more, so give me a third of the excess."

"For a ten-minute call! Who gets over seven million dollars for a ten-minute call?"

"Donald," I said, "what would you like to pay?"

"Two hundred fifty thousand."

"Fine, pay that and let's always be on good terms."

Our fee discussion on the Atlantic City matter was even more interesting. Back in 2014 we finished our last of several restructurings. By then, all the casinos in Atlantic City were virtually worthless. Donald no longer wanted to control the properties; what he wanted was to reclaim his name, which was owned by the company for gaming worldwide, some free ownership in case things miraculously improved, and a release from numerous lawsuits that were threatened by creditors.

We teamed up with a group of the casinos' bondholders and filed a reorganization plan that achieved all of Donald's objectives. The mortgage on the casinos, meanwhile, had been acquired by Carl Icahn and he filed his own plan to foreclose on the properties and bring lawsuits against Donald. The litigation in the Bankruptcy Court in Camden, New Jersey, over which plan would be approved was dubbed "the battle of the billionaires." Preparing for the fight, I tried to get Donald's attention so that I could prepare his testimony. He told me he needed no preparation and that he understood the issues perfectly well.

I told him the following: "Donald, in everything else that you do, you can be in charge. But when I have you on the witness stand, you belong to me. You prepare as I say and you do what I tell you."

He prepared well, and we won the "battle of the billionaires." About a week later he got wind that I was charging him a fee of $5 million He got me on the phone.

"David, I need a discount. I'm not paying you $5 million!"

"Was there something unsatisfactory about our work?" I asked.

"No, the work was great. I just don't pay retail for legal fees, never."

"Well, Donald, there is a first time for everything. No discount, not one penny."

"Well, then I won't pay anything until you become more reasonable."

"Donald, I'm not worried. I delivered to you a huge victory and you're paying me in full."

"Why, David, are you so confident?"

"Because I was paid yesterday. When we closed the restructuring and there were wire transfers heading in all directions, one of those was mine."

"You got me. You are the best lawyer I ever met and I should have known I could never get the better of you. Keep the money and thanks!"

I had earned Donald's respect as a lawyer and as a person. I won for him time and time again, but I did so playing by the rules and being faithful to my principles. Apparently, I was somewhat unique among his many legal advisers.

MORE RECENTLY, DONALD WAS BUILDING THE TRUMP INTERNATIONAL Hotel in Washington, DC, as magnificent a renovation as any I've ever seen. The General Services Administration, which owned the property, wanted him to sign a "completion guarantee," in which he promised to finish the job and not leave the GSA with a partially built structure. Since his earlier difficulties in the 1990s, where he had guaranteed billions of debt, Donald had a rule that he would not sign another personal guarantee. But the GSA was not budging. Everyone in the Trump Organization was petrified of bringing the guarantee to him for signature and I was asked to get involved for this limited purpose.

I negotiated the guarantee with the GSA down to a negligible risk. I then called Donald and told him to sign the papers. He said he hates signing guarantees. I said I hate running on a treadmill but I do it because I have to. I told him to sign if he wanted to build the hotel and not to sign if he didn't. He signed and the hotel was completed.

I charged him nothing for that, but he and his entire team were grateful.

As a lawyer, I was pretty good, but nowhere near as good as Donald thought. Any lawyer who says he always wins his cases is either lying or only takes very easy cases. I was neither. In fact, I took lots of very hard cases and certainly lost occasionally. But when it came to Donald Trump, I never lost. Some of the wins were improbable and they contributed to the very high esteem in which I was held. Looking back on those days, I can't help but think that perhaps God was boosting my reputation with an individual who he knew would one day place me in a position of authority where I could perform God's will. I didn't consider that then, but I do now in retrospect.

Another improbability was getting to work with Ivanka while she was dating Jared. Ivanka was in charge of the day-to-day decisions on the Atlantic City casino restructuring. She was diligent and brilliant. Ivanka understood the challenges in getting to a good outcome. Her father was a high-profile "deep pocket" who could not restrain himself from boasting how much money he took out of the casinos—understandably infuriating the unpaid creditors. Ivanka made sure to project an entirely different image; in dealing with the lenders she was serious and professional, avoiding limos, private aircraft, and other trappings of privilege. Among the many seasoned hedge-fund managers who inhabited the capital structure of the Trump casinos, there wasn't a single one who didn't respect Ivanka. She was a significant factor in our legal success.

One day, while scouring some deal documents, Ivanka asked me why the papers provided that New York law would govern the rights of the parties. I'd never been asked that question in almost thirty years of practice. She wanted to know what the differences might be in, say, Delaware or New Jersey. She was entitled to an answer and, at no cost to her, we provided it. Absolutely no detail escaped her review.

While she was dating Jared, she was also converting to Judaism. Like everything else she did, Ivanka took her conversion very seriously and we had lots of interesting discussions about the Jewish faith. At the same time, and in keeping with my improbable run, I had achieved a great outcome for the Kushner family in restructuring their investment in 666 Fifth Avenue. When Jared and Ivanka married, I was given the high honor of signing their ketubah, the ancient Jewish marriage contract.

Just before the wedding ceremony took place, the officiating rabbi thought it would be a good idea to explain to Donald all the intricacies of the Aramaic ketubah that I had signed. Not terribly interested in the subject matter, Donald told the rabbi, "If David signed it, I'm sure it's fine."

There were times over the past four years when I wished that someone in the White House could have advised the president with the same authority as I did when he was my client. While he did listen to his advisers on many occasions, sometimes he didn't. Often he was right, occasionally I thought he was wrong. And sometimes he signaled a point of view and his advisers just weren't strong enough to push back. When that happened, there wasn't much I could do after the fact and six thousand miles away. But just a little bit more good advice taken to heart might have avoided a bunch of unforced errors.

When I advised Trump, he was just a real estate mogul, not unlike many of my other high-profile clients—challenging but manageable; when he was in the White House, he had almost single-handedly performed the impossible—winning the presidency with no prior political experience. That made him far less manageable. He had every reason to believe, with some justification, that he was the smartest one in the room, but everyone benefits from good, dispassionate advice.

Like many who preceded him in the Oval Office, sometimes he accepted those benefits, sometimes he didn't.

WHILE MY RELATIONSHIP WITH THE TRUMPS AND THE KUSHNERS had little to do with Israel, the subject did come up once and it made an impression. Back in 2004, I was with Donald in a conference room waiting for a meeting to start when I pulled out a set of blueprints. It was the proposed design for a 4,800-square-foot home I was building in central Jerusalem. Donald loves blueprints and he stood over my shoulder nodding approvingly as I explained the layout. When I finished, he asked how much this would cost and I told him. He was in shock.

"David, why are you spending so much money in Jerusalem? For that price, you could get yourself a place in East Hampton and relax by the beach on weekends."

In response, I first explained to Donald that every single inch of Jerusalem has been fought over for more than three thousand years; no one is fighting over East Hampton. Which did he think was the better long-term value? I then looked him straight in the eye and told him, "Just before I bought this apartment, my cousin's fiancée and her father were blown up by a Palestinian terrorist in a suicide bombing at a restaurant just a few blocks from my new home. It was the night before she was to be married to my cousin. The next morning, I went out and purchased the biggest home I could find. This home is more than just a piece of real estate. To me it is a symbol that the Jewish people will never be forced from their homeland and that these evil terrorists will fail."

From the look on his face, I could see that I had registered with him an important point. I did not know then how important, but Donald Trump certainly understood from that day forward that Israel was important to me.

2

ISRAEL AND ME

My parents weren't Holocaust survivors. Their parents managed to escape Europe in the 1920s, and my parents were born in America. Some of my grandparents' siblings were not as fortunate and they perished in Hitler's war against the Jews. Growing up, I didn't fully appreciate the intensity of my parents' feelings as they watched from a safe distance as one-third of world Jewry (including some of their relatives) were murdered. But the intensity was profound and those feelings—ranging from sadness to rage to guilt—undoubtedly remained with them throughout their lives. While my home was a very happy one, there was a tinge of sadness that I sensed from an early age. I came to understand that beneath-the-surface melancholy when I was in seventh grade and read the book *Night* by Elie Wiesel. The autobiography of a young boy's painful survival in Auschwitz completely changed my perspective. I was stunned that people could be so cruel, that governments could be so evil, and that Jews could be singled out for execution. It was simply unfathomable to me that a twentieth-century Western nation could systematically and viciously seek to exterminate an entire race. That my parents had survived simply by the random fact that they were born in America, while their less fortunate relatives perished, made the entire concept all the more personally unnerving.

My father was deeply committed to the survival of the Jewish people at a time when survival was far from assured. He became a rabbi to actualize that commitment. During the early days of his career, survival was seen in a physical sense. He fought for the creation of the State of Israel as a safe haven for Jewish refugees from Nazi-ravaged Europe. During the 1970s he would chain himself to the Russian Mission in Manhattan to demand freedom for Soviet Jewry. One day I accompanied him to a rally and watched as he was arrested for refusing to leave his sit-in. Fortunately, even though I was only about twelve years old at the time, I knew enough people in the crowd to get a ride back to Long Island while my father was being processed at the Manhattan police precinct.

In 1967, the Six-Day War changed everything. For the first time in two thousand years, Jews projected real power. For the many still struggling to process the murderous Nazi regime, this image of proud Jews successfully defending themselves against those who seek their destruction was profoundly moving. As a nine-year-old, I vividly recall my parents crying tears of joy on the third day of the war as the Old City of Jerusalem came under Israeli control for the first time since the Bar Kochba revolt in the year 132 CE. Within days they began planning for my bar mitzvah at the Western Wall, even though there were still four years before that event would be held.

Taking my first trip to Israel in 1971 at the age of thirteen was transformational. I saw a people swelling with pride in their Jewish nation, possessing a self-confidence and collective ambition unknown to the Jews of the Diaspora. At twelve I had won a New York

City-wide Bible contest and was pretty familiar by name with most of Israel's historical sites. But to see those sites, many within walking distance from my Jerusalem hotel, left a lasting impression.

But as I beamed with pride as a young teenager at the rebirth of the Jewish state—the ultimate rejoinder to anti-Semitism and guarantor of Jewish survival—I realized that the Jewish people were still not safe. I watched with horror as eleven Israelis were brutally murdered at the 1972 Munich Olympics while the German authorities permitted the terrorists to flee. The sports announcers, thrust into the midst of an emotionally charged news event, struggled unsuccessfully to find the right balance between the horror of the crime and the ongoing competition among the athletes who continued to play. Of course, there could be no balance. The games should have ended right then and there; a nation that permits terrorists to kill innocent athletes and get away has no right to host an international contest dedicated to peaceful coexistence.

My father often commented, bitterly, that the world loves dead Jews. He observed that the nations of the world will always coalesce to condemn the Holocaust or the Munich massacre, the pogroms of eastern Europe, or other calamities that resulted in dead Jews. What the world cannot accept, he lamented, were strong Jews, Jews who defended themselves, Jews who avenged the murders of their people, Jews who acted to protect themselves in the same manner as any other nation. That, he said, was too much for the world to bear.

Yom Kippur 1973 was yet another watershed event. We were in synagogue all day as my father led the services for some three thousand worshippers. Although we were disconnected from the television, word slowly filtered through that Israel had been attacked simultaneously on three borders by Egypt, Syria, and Jordan, with other Arab states joining the battle. The details were sketchy but the news generally wasn't good. We learned that Syria had descended the

Golan Heights into the Galilee and Egypt was heading steadily north in the Sinai. There wasn't much for my father to do as a rabbi some six thousand miles from the battle. But he did something I would not have imagined. As the fast ended, he ordered all the exits to the sanctuary shut. No one was permitted to leave. He then announced that he would be accepting pledges from the pulpit to the Israel Emergency Fund, to be paid in full the next day. Until he reached $250,000, no one would be able to exit to break their fast.

He raised the money, although from fewer than two hundred of the thousand families in attendance. But what resonated with me that day was not his fundraising prowess but rather his willingness to take a stand notwithstanding the moaning and groaning of many of the parishioners. We heard lots of murmurs from the crowd: "What right did he have to shut the doors?" "Did he violate the fire code?" "Doesn't he know that people might faint from lack of food?" "Can a rabbi do this to a congregation?" He didn't care. He stood up for his sacred principles just as he had in submitting to arrest to protest the plight of Soviet Jews. I learned a great deal from that event.

When I was at Columbia in the mid-1970s, I tried to understand the mentality of my parents' generation. As I studied modern Jewish history, I grew to appreciate my father's frustration and anger. American Jews of the early twentieth century were, in large part, the antithesis of the proud Jews of Israel. Most were concerned with being accepted as loyal Americans and saw support for Israel as an impediment to their assimilation into American society. Some proclaimed Judaism to be a religion only, not a nationality. And they saw no particular religious imperative to Jewish sovereignty over the land of Israel, even if it was the biblical homeland promised by God to the Jewish people in the Bible. The Pittsburgh Platform of 1885, the document by which the Reform rabbinate, the largest stream of American Jewry, expressed its foundational values, said the following:

"We consider ourselves no longer a nation but a religious community, and therefore expect neither a return to Palestine . . . nor the restoration of any laws concerning a Jewish state."

Other streams of Judaism were not much different in practice. While Orthodox Jews continued to pray daily for the return to Zion and the rebuilding of Jerusalem, few were willing to stand with the Zionist movement, which largely was secular and even hostile to religious observance.

That view changed in the run-up to the Holocaust, as Jewish leaders saw the need for a Jewish state as a place of refuge. Two Reform rabbis, Stephen Wise and Abba Hillel Silver, led the American Zionist movement as a means of rescuing the remnant of European Jewry. But this form of Zionism, in which Jewish nationalism was justified on the basis of anti-Semitism, was less than the full argument that could be made for a Jewish state and could be understood—unfairly—as a means by which the American Jewish community would avoid the burden of absorbing more needy Jews.

While the Holocaust was a basis to advance the argument for the immigration of Jewish refugees into Palestine between 1945 and 1948 and to challenge the restrictions imposed by the British, and undoubtedly it was a means to garner international sympathy for the Zionist movement, if the Holocaust alone was the raison d'être for the State of Israel, then the argument can be made—and some Jewish leaders made it—that a Jewish refuge could be established in Africa, or indeed anywhere, rather than the biblical homeland of the Jewish people.

Arab leaders have often complained that they weren't responsible for the Holocaust and shouldn't have to pay its price. They conveniently ignore the fact that Jews have been present, to greater or lesser extents, in the land of Israel for thousands of years. Some also ignore the fact that they were complicit in Hitler's evil plans.

During my four years as ambassador, I have heard well-meaning Americans refer to Israel as arising from the ashes of the Holocaust. Many Israelis hate this reference, especially those who can trace their Israeli lineage to a time well before Hitler rose to power. Modern Zionism preceded the Holocaust by half a century and Jews always have lived in Israel. The Holocaust obviously was a factor in the timing of the creation of modern Israel, but by no means was the Holocaust the originating force or the primary justification of the Jewish movement to restore their biblical homeland.

I think my father found Jewish American equivocation on a future State of Israel unbearable. He entered the rabbinate to activate the souls of his congregants to see Judaism unapologetically as a vibrant religious and national movement that had so much to offer the world. He made it his life's work to ensure the survival of an ancient faith whose adherents had suffered far too much and for far too long by restoring them to the land of their forefathers. To him, Zionism presented the entire package—religious fulfillment, prophetic realization, and social justice. In the words of the prophet Ezekiel, Israel brought back to life the "Valley of the Dry Bones."

My father also saw Jewish survival being threatened in a spiritual sense. He used to say that Jewish education was a mile wide and an inch deep. He ran classes all week long and encouraged his congregants to enroll their children in Jewish day schools. He made a dent in the problem but, if he were alive today, I think he would acknowledge that the problem has only grown worse. As I have said many times, Jewish illiteracy in America is an existential risk. The percentage of American Jews today who have a basic familiarity with Jewish texts and Jewish history is small and shrinking.

Although not political and always open-minded to Democrats and Republicans, my father was the only rabbi in history to host a sitting president in his synagogue and at his home for a meal—President

Ronald Reagan came for lunch in 1984. He received that honor as the president of the New York Board of Rabbis. I was there when Reagan arrived, with my wife, my mom, and my siblings. It gave me a thrill like none I've experienced since my first visit to the Oval Office in 2017.

Reagan's speech at Temple Hillel in October 1984 doesn't get the historical credit it deserves. I think it marks the turning point at which the Republican Party became the party of Israel. I will never forget the thunderous applause that Reagan received when he said, to a packed house, "If Israel is ever forced to leave the United Nations, the United States and Israel will walk out together."

I brought my father's perspectives into my adult life. With my work as a trial lawyer, there was not much time to engage in outside activities, but there was more than sufficient time to give away money. When I made money, I would give some to Israeli charities. I'd give some money to humanitarian organizations such as food banks, some to hospitals and health care providers, and some to educational institutions in Judea and Samaria. I became the president of the American Friends of Bet El Yeshiva Center, a position my critics would raise often as indicating a personal commitment to "West Bank settlement construction" that was allegedly antagonistic to bipartisan US policy and international law.

My critics were not entirely wrong. I was in favor of "West Bank settlement construction," although I used different phraseology—the biblical reference of Judea and Samaria. I always hated the term "West Bank," since it ignored the very term—Judea—that associated the land with the Jewish people, and the territory it referred to was much larger than just the western bank of the Jordan River. But what my critics assumed as fact was a position with which I strongly disagreed ever since I studied the issue at NYU Law School: Building Jewish communities in Judea and Samaria was neither illegal nor uniformly inconsistent with prior US policy.

Judea and Samaria are where the rubber meets the road in the Israeli-Palestinian conflict. It is home to more than two million Palestinian Arabs and half a million Israeli Jews. It is disputed territory; it is not, as almost the entire world maintains, illegally occupied territory.

Judea and Samaria are biblical Israel. When Abraham was called by God to leave his home and settle in the land of Canaan (future Israel), his first stop was in Elon Moreh, near the biblical city of Shechem (the Palestinians refer to Shechem as "Nablus," from the Roman name "Neopolis"—Palestinians do not pronounce the letter "p"). When Abraham sought to purchase a burial cave for his wife, Sarah, he chose Hebron and the Bible records in detail his negotiations for the property. When Jacob dreamed of the ladder ascending to heaven and angels climbing up and down, he was in Bet El. When the Ark of the Covenant came to rest in Israel and a temporary tabernacle was constructed, that was in Shiloh. When Joshua brought the Israelite nation across the Jordan River, he did so at Qasr al-Yahud (Arabic for the "Bridge of the Jews"), where John the Baptist also is said to have baptized Jesus. When King David sought to unite his monarchy in a central capital, he chose Jerusalem and paid the owner for the territory even though it was offered to him at no charge. All these places and so many more biblical sites are located in Judea and Samaria.

In the Six-Day War, Israel, acting in self-defense, captured Judea and Samaria from Jordan, as well as Gaza and the Sinai Peninsula from Egypt and the Golan Heights from Syria. Once a cease-fire was reached, the United Nations convened all the warring parties and reached an agreement among all but Syria (which later signed on after the Yom Kippur War in 1973) for the framework of a settlement of the conflict. The framework—UN Security Council Resolution 242—provided for Israel to withdraw from "territories" (Israel successfully rejected the term "all territories") in exchange for "secure and recognized boundaries free from threats or acts of force."

To date, UN Resolution 242 is the only agreement reached among all the parties to the Six-Day War (including Syria through Resolution 338). Since that resolution was passed, Israel has returned or relinquished more than 85 percent of the territory it captured, comprising the entire Sinai Peninsula and the Gaza Strip. The American negotiator of UN Resolution 242, former undersecretary of state and former dean of Yale Law School, Eugene Rostow, has opined that, in accordance with UN 242, the Jewish claim to settle in Judea and Samaria is "beyond dispute." While Rostow's view is rejected by some American scholars, there is no better authority on this issue. Rostow's firsthand input into drafting the resolution as well as his unquestioned legal scholarship make him singularly qualified to interpret this key UN provision.

But you don't need to be a legal scholar to understand this issue. The facts aren't complicated. Up until the end of World War I, the territory then known as Palestine included all of what is now Israel, Judea and Samaria. It also included what is now known as Jordan. Palestine was controlled by the Ottoman Empire and inhabited by Palestinian Arabs and Palestinian Jews. After the defeat of the Turks, Palestine was conveyed in trust to the British under a Mandate for Palestine. The Mandate incorporated the San Remo Resolution, which adopted the Balfour Declaration of 1917, which provided for "the establishment in Palestine of a national home for the Jewish people," without "prejudice to the civil and religious rights of existing non-Jewish communities in Palestine."

In 1946, all of Palestine east of the Jordan River (about 72 percent of the overall territory) was severed and became the Hashemite Kingdom of Trans-Jordan. That left the remaining portion of Palestine, including Judea and Samaria, or the West Bank, as the maximum remaining territory from which to create "the national home for the Jewish people."

But even that residual landmass of 28 percent of Palestine was considered too large for a Jewish homeland. In 1947, the United Nations adopted the "Partition Plan" for Palestine—UN Security Council Resolution 181—which gave Israel a state in about half the territory of what remained. The Israeli provisional government struggled mightily with this plan—on the one hand it created a Jewish state for the first time in two thousand years; on the other hand its dimensions were unworkable and indefensible. Ultimately, given the imperative of statehood to absorb the hundreds of thousands of Jews languishing in European displaced person camps, Israel accepted the plan. Every Arab nation rejected it.

In 1948, Israel declared its independence and all its Arab neighbors immediately attacked, determined to annihilate the fledgling Jewish nation. They failed, and Israel's largely successful defensive efforts expanded its boundaries well beyond the territory that was assigned to it under the Partition Plan. Jordan did succeed in capturing Judea and Samaria and East Jerusalem, which it held until the Six-Day War. During those nineteen years between 1948 and 1967, the Jews living in East Jerusalem, Judea, and Samaria either fled or were expelled. In 1950, the Hashemite Kingdom of Trans-Jordan annexed Judea and Samaria and changed its name to Jordan (now being on both sides of the river), an act considered illegal by almost the entire world, including the Arab League.

No nations other than the United Kingdom and Pakistan ever recognized Jordanian annexation or sovereignty over this territory west of the Jordan River—Judea and Samaria.

So let's sum up the basic facts: The territory that I call Judea and Samaria is part of the territory earmarked for a Jewish state by the San Remo Resolution adopted by the League of Nations, and is the biblical heartland of the Jewish people. Up until 1918 and for some four hundred years prior, the Ottoman Empire controlled Judea and

Samaria, but it relinquished its claim upon its surrender at the conclusion of World War I. Jordan had no right to annex it in 1948, and Israel captured back this territory—to which it had a valid claim independent of its conquest—in a defensive war in 1967. Moreover, Jordan renounced its claim to the territory in 1994, when it signed a peace treaty with Israel. One need not be a scholar to conclude that Israel has the best claim to the territory, and America's foremost authority on the subject of UN 242 agrees!

The "best claim," however, doesn't mean the only claim. The two million Palestinians living in Judea and Samaria may have limited legal or historical claims, but their very presence within the territory, as well as their right to live in peace and dignity, is compelling. Concluding that Israelis have a legal right to reside in Judea and Samaria thus doesn't resolve the conflict, it only puts it within the proper context—a territorial dispute by parties each with legitimate arguments. Israel cannot absorb two million Palestinians into its country; the security, demographic, and economic challenges are unmanageable. Jordan has refused to absorb these same Palestinians even though many hold Jordanian citizenship and were once part of Jordan. And Palestinian independence presents its own series of potentially existential risks to Israel, Jordan, and the Palestinians themselves.

We spent the entirety of our years in office trying to thread the needle on all these competing risks and claims and I think we came out in the right place. But in the days and years preceding my appointment I was convinced of one thing: *The increasingly progressive position developing within American political circles that Israel could and should surrender the entirety of Judea and Samaria in exchange for a naked promise of peace would lead to catastrophic results.*

Throughout my adult years, most liberal Americans, especially Jews, believed in the wisdom of Israel surrendering Judea and Samaria, notwithstanding its biblical, historical, and security significance, as a means of achieving a two-state solution with the Palestinians. They ignored the inconvenient truths of Palestinian terror and incitement, espousing the meaningless platitude that "one makes peace with enemies, not friends." Of course, the correct phrase should be "former enemies," not groups of terror organizations continuing to seek Israel's destruction, violating the human rights of even their own people and in a constant state of conflict with each other. Many on the left have attempted to co-opt the legacy of Prime Minister Yitzhak Rabin, who was assassinated in 1995 by a far-right Jewish terrorist, claiming that he would have agreed with their progressive goals. The moral authority of his legacy is significant, since he literally gave his life to the cause of peace in signing the Oslo Accords.

But Yitzhak Rabin was anything but an appeaser of terror. One of the most distinguished generals in Israel's history, Prime Minister Rabin explained to the Knesset where he thought the Oslo Accords would lead: The agreement, he predicted, would result in the creation of a "Palestinian entity" that would be "less than a state," with Israel retaining a substantial portion of Judea and Samaria.

That vision by one of Israel's greatest peacemakers did not differ materially from the Vision for Peace that we promoted in early 2020. But it differed dramatically from the vision of progressive Americans who steadily shifted the goalposts to the point where their agenda of surrender bore no resemblance to the vision of Yitzhak Rabin, their deceased mentor.

The American Jewish Left became more and more out of touch with the reality of terrorism in the post-Oslo era. In the year after Oslo, Palestinian terrorism increased fourfold, each suicide attack on a bus or a restaurant more lethal and horrific than the prior. But the Left continued to push for concessions, bearing absolutely none of the risks from their enclaves in Los Angeles or the Upper West Side.

Although Rabin was viewed as a martyr for peace, his view of peace became unrecognizable in the liberal salons in the decades that followed. I have no doubt that had Rabin lived to see the full range of Palestinian terror attacks post-Oslo, he either would have repudiated the agreements or reaffirmed his commitment to the Palestinians receiving "less than a state."

AS THE OBAMA ADMINISTRATION CAME TO POWER, I FELT THE NEED to do more than just donate to Israeli causes. I was furious that President Obama excluded Israel on his first trip to the Middle East and all but apologized in Cairo for American support of Israel. I started to write a column for *Israel National News*, a right-wing Internet publication, hoping to offer a pragmatic and principled means to support Israel and its quest for peace.

I wrote about negotiations in the Middle East. I argued that American liberals and the administration they served had no clue how to proceed. They were perceived by their interlocutors—from Iran to Syria to the Palestinians—as weak and stupid. While they accepted words and smiles as meaningful gestures of good faith, I pointed out the cheapness of that currency. I focused on the dispensation some clerics give under Sharia law to lie to nonbelievers to achieve one's goals. My views later were confirmed by a statement of Abdelsalam al-Majali, the former prime minister of Jordan, who signed the peace treaty with Israel: On local Jordanian television he explained that he signed the agreement because at the time Israel was strong and Jordan was weak; but he assured his listeners, "If we ever have military power will we let them keep Haifa? We'll take it."

My emphasis on the importance of strength was not born of an interest in seeing Israel oppress its enemies. It was, in my view, the only path to peace. Arabs instinctively gauged the strength of their opponents and acted accordingly. Being perceived as weak was a death knell to a successful negotiation. And it wasn't just physical strength, it was strength of principles and values as well.

When American Jews offer the Palestinians the prospect of dividing Jerusalem and controlling all of Hebron or Bet El, the Palestinians see their American friends as standing for absolutely nothing. And then a true peace becomes unattainable because the Palestinians will never make peace with someone they don't respect. And people who don't honor their religious traditions most certainly are not respected within the Arab world.

Among all my studies about the importance of the land of Israel to the Jewish people, none influenced me more than the very first commentary on the Torah, by Rabbi Shlomo ben Yitzchak, known by the acronym "Rashi." Rashi was the most prolific biblical commentator in Jewish history.

Rashi asks the question why the Torah begins with the story of Creation. After all, he suggests, Judaism is a practice of observing God's commandments, and the first commandment—observing the New Moon—doesn't appear until well into the book of Exodus, the second book of the Bible. Why not start there?

Rashi answers that the entire story of Creation is to reinforce the right of the Jewish people to the land of Israel. Because God created the world, he had the right to give out the land as he saw fit. And so God's promise of the land of Israel to the Jewish people was an assurance of perpetual title—a biblical title insurance policy, if you will. I was struck by the overwhelming significance that Rashi assigned to Jewish sovereignty over the land of Israel, all the more so given that his observation was made in the eleventh century! On this file, not much has changed in the last thousand years.

This was my background, and these were my points of view— some would say my baggage—that I brought with me to an improbable career in Middle East diplomacy. But while my emphasis on strength and sovereignty was unique in American diplomatic circles, my business background also helped me tackle sensitive issues. Strength and finesse go hand in hand.

I did have one more secret weapon—my wife of thirty-six years, Tammy. There is no greater advantage in life than marrying the right person the first time. Devoted, loyal, beautiful, smart, and fully aligned with me intellectually and emotionally in our views on Israel, Tammy provided me with immeasurable support and confidence in everything I chose to do. I needed every bit of that support in the years that followed.

3

THE TRUMP CAMPAIGN

When Donald and Melania took that famous escalator ride down to the lobby of Trump Tower, I was nowhere to be found. Early on, I didn't take the campaign that seriously. What were the chances that a real estate developer and TV star with no prior political experience could make a serious run at the presidency? But by the end of March 2016, he seemed to have the Republican nomination locked up.

In April 2016, we spoke about his chances and I offered to help him on issues relating to Israel and its neighbors. He suggested that I become his adviser on Israel matters along with Jason Greenblatt, his general counsel. Jason is a serious lawyer who cares deeply about the issues and I thought we would work well together. We did.

While my views on Israel were pure, from the heart and untethered to any partisanship, I now found myself, for the first time in my life, in the middle of a political campaign, and a presidential one to boot. Staying true to principles, Jason and I were tasked with looking for ways that our views would resonate with potential voters.

Jason was more disciplined than I was in doing outreach to faith groups and other supporters of Israel. He was a corporate lawyer, measured and reserved. I was a litigator by training and by nature, and saw the campaign as more than just appealing to potential supporters. There were false accusations directed at us and our policies and I was perfectly amenable to crushing the opposition if I could do so with intellectual honesty.

One vocal critic of the Trump campaign's Israel policy particularly drew my ire: an organization called J Street. It was created as the progressive answer to the American Israel Public Affairs Committee (AIPAC), the larger and more mainstream pro-Israel lobbying organization. J Street also was a self-proclaimed "pro-Israel" group, but to my point of view, its positions were anything but. J Street, which had no expertise in matters of national security, nonetheless supported the Joint Comprehensive Plan of Action (JCPOA)—the US-Iran deal of 2015—even though the deal was strongly opposed by the democratically elected Israeli government. The Iran Deal gave the mullahs in Iran—who were publicly vowing to destroy the "Zionist Entity"—a clear path to a nuclear weapon and did nothing to curb Iran's support for terrorist organizations or its acquisition of ballistic missiles. In the aftermath of the Iran Deal, it became evident just how bad the deal was, as Iran continued to be the world's most malign state sponsor of terror, proving beyond dispute just how naive and reckless were those who predicted that Iran would self-correct.

While I disagreed vehemently with J Street's advocacy, I was not angered by its left-wing views but rather its heavy-handed tactics. There are Israelis who share those views although they are a small minority within the country. But the left-wing Israelis have every right to express their views—they pay their taxes in Israel, send their children to the Israeli army, and bear the risks of being wrong. J Street does none of those things.

J Street is simply born of a fundamental hypocrisy—it professes a Zionist outlook but does not respect the democracy of Israel. The very core of Zionism is for the Jewish people to govern themselves in their national homeland—indeed those are the concluding words of Israel's national anthem, "Hatikvah." But J Street seeks to frustrate that self-governance by lobbying American leaders to impose their will upon Israel against the will of Israel's own democratically elected leaders. And, of course, J Street members bear none of the risk if, for example, their advocacy of Israeli surrender of territory to a Palestinian terror state backfires against the Israeli public.

I disagreed with the decision of the Israeli government to enter into the Oslo Accords. But I never even thought of lobbying the American government to restrain Israel from proceeding with those agreements, nor did any Jewish leader to my knowledge, because we respected Israel's democracy and its right to make its own decision to protect its citizens. J Street does not afford Israel that respect.

I made the dumb mistake of comparing J Street to kapos. In a May 2016 article in *Israel National News*, I used these words:

> Are J Street supporters really as bad as kapos? The answer, actually, is no. They are far worse than kapos—Jews who turned in their fellow Jews in the Nazi death camps. The kapos faced extraordinary cruelty and who knows what any of us would have done under the circumstances to save a loved one? But J Street? They are just smug advocates of Israel's destruction delivered from the comfort of their secure American sofas—it's hard to imagine anyone worse.

These intemperate words weren't a political mistake—most potential Trump supporters were thrilled by the criticism of an organization they abhorred. And they weren't a policy mistake—our emerging policy regarding Israel was diametrically opposite that of J Street. But my words were a huge tactical mistake because they shifted the discussion away from the substance of J Street's attacks on Israel and created instead a straw man of an issue that I could not win: *Are liberal Jews as bad as Nazis?* The answer is "Of course not."

By letting my rhetoric overwhelm the substance of my views, I gave J Street an easy opening. And I created a tagline, "worse than kapos," that has been repeated over and over by my critics to this day. J Street made all it could of my mistake, including using my words to mount a fundraising campaign. It never addressed the merits of my argument—it didn't need to. It just hid behind my regrettable language to gain sympathy.

It was a painful lesson. I learned the hard way that just three misplaced words—"worse than kapos"—could dominate the discourse and obfuscate an otherwise important message. I should have known better. I have long felt that Holocaust analogies are always inappropriate. The Holocaust was a singular event in human history and any comparison to anything else simply dilutes that singularity. I promised myself no more errors.

But I still made more mistakes. In September I was invited to a private dinner in New York with Yossi Dagan, the head of the Shomron Regional Council, an organization that supported Jewish communities in Samaria. We had a candid discussion about the Israeli-Palestinian conflict and I questioned the conventional wisdom that Israel would lose its Jewish majority by applying its sovereignty over Judea and Samaria. The discussion was premised on demographics, that is, how many Palestinians would be absorbed into Israel in that scenario. My point was largely about the absence of good data but, out of context, my comments could be seen as advocating for a full declaration of sovereignty.

This is a complicated issue and not one I intended to put into the public discourse at that time. But, unknown to me, my entire conversation was videotaped, with segments selectively leaked to the media. Another lesson learned: Don't be too trusting of people pushing a political agenda, even those with whom you largely agree. The video was an unpleasant distraction, but it passed quickly.

In contrast to the actions of J Street and the duplicity of some claiming to be friends, I also made some wonderful new acquaintances. The Christian Evangelical community embraced my unapologetic support for Israel as well as my appreciation for Israel's biblical heritage. Evangelicals, of course, are also a much larger voting constituency than pro-Israel Jews, and, this being a campaign season, I spent a lot of time getting to know them better.

Evangelical Christians are not any more monolithic than Jews. There are many streams and approaches. But what I found refreshing about the Evangelicals was their devotion to Scripture, to the word of God communicated through the Bible. And while I was on a completely different theological plane than them—I didn't accept Jesus as the son of God or the New Testament as the word of God—most Christian values derive from the Old Testament, where I found my religious home.

As an Orthodox Jew, I shared the Evangelical view of loyalty to the sacred texts. Often those texts require interpretation, and Orthodox Judaism accepts a tradition that incorporates many generations of rabbinic law amplifying the Torah. But we draw the line at violating express biblical prohibitions such as, for example, eating pork. No mental gymnastics enables the Orthodox to overcome a prohibition of this nature. Many in the non-Orthodox camp, however, argue that outlawing pork was unique to a period when pork was a health risk to humans, such that the prohibition would not continue today when science has eliminated the risk of diseases like trichinosis. The Orthodox are not receptive to that type of thinking: if God took the trouble to outlaw a particular act or conduct, we cannot rationalize it away.

As it relates to Israel, Evangelicals see their support as mandated in the Bible. They are well versed in God's words to Abraham, which they paraphrase as "I will bless those who bless Israel." Some of the key provisions of Scripture include the following:

> I will bless those who bless you [Abraham] and whoever curses you I will curse . . .
>
> (Genesis 12:3)

> You who call on the Lord, give yourselves no rest, and give him no rest till he establishes Jerusalem and makes her the praise of the earth.
>
> (Isaiah 62:6–7)

> And I shall put my spirit in you and you shall live, and I shall place you in your own land . . .
>
> (Ezekiel 37:14)

Other similar verses heralding the rebirth of a Jewish state abound. It was incredibly empowering to discover a very large community of faithful who shared my view that standing with Israel was a quintessential American value.

In any democracy, and America is no exception, one hopes that the values that one wishes to advocate are consonant with the political will. It's very hard to ask a candidate to go against his or her voters. I was always prepared to advocate for the US-Israel relationship as being decidedly in the best interests of America. But having a relationship with the leaders of some eighty million faithful who felt the same way was incredibly empowering. It gave me the confidence to know that what I felt was right morally was also right politically.

As the Republican Party Convention approached in July, Jason and I were tasked with developing the Israel plank of the party platform. Platforms generally are aspirational and don't matter that much to voters. But Israel had become an exception. In 2012, the Democratic Party dropped a provision from prior platforms that Jerusalem be recognized as Israel's capital. When pro-Israel members of the party expressed outrage, the party chairman awkwardly sought a voice vote from the floor reinstating the provision. While he claimed that "the ayes have it," the noise from the crowd was anything but supportive. The anti-Israel wing of the Democratic Party had been put on full display.

In light of that fiasco four years earlier, Jason and I had free rein to create a Republican Israel plank that contrasted favorably with the Democrats. And we did. Our plank supported recognition of Jerusalem and made no mention of a two-state solution, a break from the Republican Party platform of four years earlier. The change was picked up across the media and greeted with delight from activists within the party.

I was challenged by many about the omission. My response was consistent: A two-state solution presents a means to resolve the Israeli-Palestinian conflict, but not the only means and not under the current circumstances. The Palestinians have done nothing to assure Israel or the region that they have the capability of living side by side in peace in an independent state. Indeed, just the opposite is true. Everything we know about Palestinian government presents a significant threat to Israel, the region, and even the Palestinian people. In this context, insisting upon a two-state solution is to insist on no solution. It also gave the Palestinians a free pass on their malign behavior.

Getting the platform out was very important to both Jason and me. It was a way to commit Candidate Trump to certain policies that we saw as essential to our support. Donald's approach to Israel during the campaign had been inconsistent and at times confusing.

At one point he said he hoped to be "neutral" regarding the Israeli-Palestinian conflict, creating a massive opening for Hillary Clinton to respond that she would never be neutral with regard to an ally as important as Israel. I immediately called Donald and he okayed my response: "The Obama administration had been overly conciliatory to Israel's enemies. By saying he would be 'neutral,' Mr. Trump was promising to reverse those practices."

With the platform approved by the Republican Party, we now had a written set of policies on which we could hopefully run and ultimately govern. Jason and I followed that up by issuing, with Donald's approval, just two days before the election, a sixteen-point statement setting forth the Trump campaign's position on Israel, a recitation of pro-Israel policies never before articulated by any presidential campaign. Among other things, the statement recognized the 3,500-year connection of the Jewish people to the land of Israel; condemned BDS (the movement to boycott, divest from, and sanction Israel), UNESCO, and the Iran nuclear deal; criticized Palestinian leadership; and promised a move of the US embassy to Jerusalem. In the event that Donald Trump became President Trump, Jason and I were confident that we had outlined a policy of unprecedented support for the Jewish state.

I WOKE UP LATER THAN USUAL ON THE MORNING OF TUESDAY, November 8, 2016—Election Day. I had been before a packed house the night before making the closing argument to a local crowd of Israel supporters. The questions I got were excellent and they caused me to really refine and articulate the case for Trump. I stayed back after the crowd dispersed and chatted with the sponsors. I didn't want the evening to end, as I feared it would be my last in this rarefied space.

As I regained consciousness that Election Day morning, I was enveloped in sadness. The party was over, I thought. Beginning to-morrow, my views would be associated with a losing candidate and of no further value. I looked at the *New York Times* app on my iPhone and checked the gauge illustrating the election outcome probability. It had not moved all week, still pointing to a 95 percent probability of victory for Hillary Clinton.

I briefly contemplated ditching the election night festivities. I did not relish being surrounded by disappointment. But my wife was having none of it. She felt it was my obligation to support my friend Donald Trump at this difficult moment. She was right.

That night was unlike any other I had ever experienced. As the evening wore on, the race was far tighter than expected. By midnight, the *New York Times* gauge was at fifty-fifty. An hour later Trump was favored eighty-twenty. By three a.m. it was over: Hillary Clinton had conceded and Donald Trump addressed us as the president-elect.

As I left the event with my wife and a few of my kids at around five a.m., I had an overwhelming sense that my life was about to undergo a profound change. After dropping off the family at our home on Long Island, I quickly showered, changed, and headed back to Manhattan.

I arrived at Trump Tower just before eight a.m. Although the building was surrounded by Secret Service, I had enough contacts inside to find my way in. I took the elevator to the twenty-sixth floor and walked past Donald's office. I peeked my head in and there he was. "Congratulations, Mr. President," I said.

He motioned me in. "Can you believe it, David. I never ran for office in my life and I won the presidency with almost no help from even my own party!"

We talked for a few minutes about the incredible turn of events. Once there was a lull in the conversation, I injected, "Mr. President, as we talked about before, please make me ambassador to Israel."

"I will, David. But obviously I need to make some other nominations first." As he said that, his office started to fill up with most of his campaign team and I drifted into the back of the room. I left shortly after to chat with Jason Greenblatt and some others in the office, and then went home to get some sleep.

In politics, I learned, nothing is certain. Over the next few weeks there were rumors of numerous potential candidates for my job, each of whom had a sponsor who was close to the president. But in addition to support from Trump, I had the backing of Jared Kushner, who was intimately involved in personnel decisions. Jared was with me all the way. In early December, an article appeared in *The Jerusalem Post* that the job was going to Mike Huckabee. I got a bit agitated reading that, but a subsequent exchange of text messages with Jared reassured me. He said, "Don't worry." I worried anyway because that is my nature and because Huckabee would have been an excellent choice.

By December 8, most of the key cabinet posts had been selected and I decided to make another visit to Trump Tower. Once I got word that Donald's office was open, I walked in to remind him of my interest in the job. This time he agreed to make the nomination immediately and he began to dictate a press release to his assistant. I left the office thinking this was a done deal.

Apparently, my visit caused a bit of a ruckus. Minutes later, Reince Priebus, soon to become the first White House chief of staff in the Trump administration, demanded that my nomination be placed on hold and that no more prospective nominees waltz into the office unaccompanied by him. I had never met Reince and could understand how he might have wanted to be involved in a nomination of this magnitude. So it took a few days before he was assuaged and on December 15, 2016, President-elect Trump announced my nomination as US ambassador to Israel.

My nomination was the first of a series of firsts: It was the first time an ambassador to Israel was nominated before Inauguration Day. It also was the first time an ambassador to Israel was the first among the hundred or so ambassadors appointed by the president (and the first confirmed); it was the first time a nominated ambassador to Israel had no prior diplomatic or government experience. Most striking, it was the first time the nomination for ambassador to Israel was rejected by the opposing party and subject to a contested hearing before the Senate Foreign Relations Committee.

The press release issued by the Trump transition team on December 15 made quite a stir. It contained a typically flattering description of the nominee and a vote of confidence from the president-elect. But it also contained the following quote attributable to me:

"I intend to work tirelessly to strengthen the unbreakable bond between our two countries and advance the cause of peace within the region, and look forward to doing this from the U.S. Embassy in Israel's eternal capital, Jerusalem."

The press release ignited a five-alarm fire within the elite world of liberal foreign policy punditry. *The New York Times* led the charge. I was front-page news the next two days, and the subject of a lead editorial demanding that my nomination be withdrawn and an opinion piece by a former ambassador to Israel explaining why I was woefully unqualified for this extremely sensitive position. Two days later, *The Algemeiner Journal*, a moderate Jewish website, summed up the liberal paper's response with this headline: NEW YORK TIMES IN FULL-FLEDGED FROTHING FREAKOUT FRENZY OVER FRIEDMAN PICK.

Much to my chagrin, my nomination became the lightning rod that galvanized pent-up sentiments on both sides of the Jewish aisle. Left-wing organizations like Peace Now, Ameinu, Truah, the Reform movement, and especially J Street, came out against me with guns blazing. An equal number of right-wing groups, from the Zionist Organization of America to the Orthodox Union, National Council of Young Israel, and others, provided full-throated support. In the middle, organizations like the Conference of Presidents of Major American Jewish Organizations and the Jewish Federations of North America also came out to support my nomination, generating a fair amount of internal criticism within each organization. At this challenging time, I drew enormous comfort from my rabbi, Zalman Wolowick, from the Chabad movement, perhaps the most dynamic and influential Jewish force in modern times. I was privileged to honor Rabbi Wolowick with the opening prayer at the dedication of our embassy in Jerusalem some seventeen months later.

Among those most enthusiastic about my nomination were leaders of the Evangelical community. They saw real divine providence in my selection. On the day of my hearing before the Senate Foreign Relations Committee, a very large group called Christians United for Israel—led by Pastor John Hagee, who became a dear friend and supporter—took out a full-page ad in *The Washington Post* that read in large bold letters, CONFIRM DAVID FRIEDMAN!

J Street made it their number one priority to defeat my nomination. They began a media campaign and encouraged correspondence and phone calls to all the members of the Senate, whose consent was required for my nomination to go through. They made a lot of people mad, some at me and some at them. They made sure that every member of the Senate knew that I had compared J Street members to Nazis, arguing that my temperament made me ill suited to a diplomatic position in the Middle East.

But for every J Street attack there was an equal and opposite statement of support. Never had an ambassador's appointment to any country been this controversial. By contrast, my predecessor, Dan Shapiro, whose left-wing views on Israel were every bit as unacceptable to right-wing Republicans as mine were to left-wing Democrats, was approved unanimously by the Senate.

I had come along just as the Left-Right partisanship divide with regard to Israel had reached its peak, and I was the spark that ignited this intramural explosion.

THROUGH ALL THE CONTROVERSY, OCCASIONALLY I DID SEE SOMEthing that made me smile or at least appreciate the humor in how bizarre things had become. The comic strip *Dry Bones,* by the artist Yaakov Kirschen in *The Jerusalem Post,* was one item that gave me a lift. It showed the main protagonist, a European-born Israeli, observing: "After years of trying to convince the US that undivided Jerusalem is our eternal capital city . . . Israel is now faced with an ambassador who wants to convince us!"

Nonetheless, I wasn't happy with all this attention, even when it was favorable. While the ideological rift within American Jewry had been around and getting worse for decades, I found no comfort standing on the fault line. At one point in late December, I called the president-elect to apologize for all the noise I was causing. He found it all pretty amusing.

I wish I could say the same.

4
CONFIRMATION CONTROVERSY

Right after Inauguration Day, the fun began. As the only ambassador on the docket, I was assigned my own adviser/handler, called a "Sherpa," and coached through what was expected to be an unprecedented confirmation battle. My preparation leading up to the hearing was threefold:

1. Filling out lots of paperwork and other disclosures about the most minute aspects of my personal and professional life and going through various security clearance procedures,

2. Preparing for the hearing before the Senate Foreign Relations Committee through mock sessions called "murder boards," in which a panel of people playing the role of specific senators would grill me on various aspects of my life, and

3. Paying courtesy calls on all the members of the SFRC and other key leaders of the Senate.

I did four murder boards in total. In the first, I made everyone crazy by giving long-winded answers in which I explained the complexities and nuances of policy questions and provided extensive defenses and justifications when accused of misconduct. Essentially, I tried to show how smart I was (or at least thought I was). When I was asked the sure-to-be-raised question of why I referred to J Street as "worse than kapos," my initial response was, "I overreacted because I felt that J Street had betrayed the Jewish people by fraudulently representing itself to be pro-Israel." That caused a firestorm of reaction from the advisers. They told me I can't speak that way. After some discussion we agreed that the following answer was both appropriate and truthful: "In the heat of a political campaign I allowed my rhetoric to get the best of me. I regret those comments and assure you that if confirmed, my remarks will be measured and diplomatic."

Over and over again, I was told to keep the answers short, not to lecture the senators, and not to provoke follow-up questions. As a trial lawyer for more than thirty years, I got the drift. The second and third murder boards went fine. The fourth time around was just too much preparation and so I intentionally reverted to long-winded, controversial answers just to have some fun. I was the only one who thought it was funny.

MEETING THE SENATORS RANGED FROM PLEASANT AND UNEVENTFUL to interesting and engaging to absolutely bizarre. I met with more than sixty of them, but a few were unforgettable.

When I met with Bernie Sanders I could see that he was angry even before we started. The first thing he did was hand me a letter and ask that I respond in writing within the week. From a quick glance, I saw that he was asking me to respond to his thesis that financial aid to

Gaza was more important than aid to Israel. I asked him if he wanted our conversation to be limited to an exchange of letters or whether we were going to have a discussion as well. He said he had just one question for me: "Why does Israel use disproportionate force against the people of Gaza?"

I responded to his question with my question: "What is disproportionate force?"

He responded, "Israel kills many more people in Gaza than Gazans kill Israelis."

I couldn't believe the insanity of that response. "So your point," I said, "is that when a nation is attacked it should trade life for life with its enemy rather than try to defeat it. About how many dead Israeli soldiers would you prefer, Senator?"

"This isn't a war," he said. "It's an occupation."

At this point I completely gave up on any chance of getting his vote. "How many Israelis live in Gaza, Senator? How many Israeli soldiers are on the ground in Gaza, Senator? The answer is zero. And, in case you haven't noticed, Gaza is run by a brutal, anti-Semitic, misogynistic, homophobic regime called Hamas. Do you feel they are a good partner for peace?"

Now Sanders was even angrier. "The people of Gaza are suffering and Israel is making them suffer more. They are blowing up hospitals."

Now I was angry too. "Senator, when Hamas fires a rocket into a civilian population center, does Israel have a right to respond?"

"Well, Israel has Iron Dome, which we paid for."

"But Iron Dome doesn't always work. And once a rocket goes off, a siren sounds and parents have to wake up their sleeping children in the middle of the night and carry them to small, dank bomb shelters. Do you think any civilians should have to go through that?"

"No," he answered.

"So does Israel have the right, under those circumstances, to fire back at the rocket launcher?"

"Yes," he answered.

"Good. Now, if the rocket launcher happens to be in a building that looks like a hospital, what does Israel do? And be careful about your answer because if you say Israel has no right to fire back in that case, you are validating Hamas's strategy of using civilians as human shields. So what say you?"

"This meeting is over," Sanders replied. "Please send me your response to my letter in writing this week." I sent my letter the next day. As advised by my Sherpa, I ignored our heated exchange and focused dryly on the importance of US military aid to Israel and the challenges of dealing with Hamas.

That was frightening. An individual who almost became the Democratic candidate for president was siding with terrorists over one of America's strongest allies.

Fortunately, I didn't hear anything like that from any other senator, but I did hear other disturbing things.

One of the senators on my list was Benjamin Cardin, the ranking member of the Foreign Relations Committee with a strong record of support for Israel. He was considered one of the keys to getting bipartisan support for my nomination. When I walked into his office, he greeted me with a large entourage of staffers.

Senator Cardin shared with me his love of Israel and long history of support. He mentioned that he was troubled by my past rhetoric but allowed that many people get overheated in a political campaign. But then he got to his key point of criticism—I was not committed to a two-state solution for Israel and the Palestinians. The senator said the following: "Mr. Friedman, you must know better than anyone the issue of demographics. The territory from the Jordan River to the Mediterranean Sea is basically 50 percent Jewish and 50 percent Arab.

I desperately want to preserve Israel's Jewish character but we are fast approaching a condition where Israel will have to choose between being Jewish or Democratic, and that's an impossible choice. That's why two states are so important, one for Jews and one for Palestinians."

Senator Cardin had articulated the classic well-intentioned argument of many American Jews and even some Israelis. But I believed he was wrong, at least in his approach, and I answered him carefully.

"Senator, I would say first that the demographics are not fifty-fifty since Israel will never absorb any portion of Gaza. So that takes two million Palestinians out of the equation. But the more important point is your assumption that without two states, Israel will have to choose between being Jewish or democratic. With all due respect, that's a secondary issue. You only get to that issue after you've solved the primary issue of being alive or dead. And, right now, Israel would be on the wrong side of that calculus if it permits a Palestinian state in the center of its country."

He responded: "I'm not saying conditions are ripe today for a Palestinian state, but that must be the stated policy goal of the United States."

And I concluded: "And I'm not saying a two-state solution wouldn't be a good outcome under the right circumstances, but signaling to the Palestinians that they are entitled to statehood notwithstanding their malign activity, including compensating and inciting terrorists, rejecting religious freedom, widespread corruption, and violating the human rights of their own people, will just ensure that they will never modulate their behavior to achieve the solution you seek."

I thought it was a good meeting and that we understood each other. Our differences were more nuanced and tactical than substantive. We also had a good conversation at the hearing itself. But shortly after the hearing, Senator Cardin issued a press release that he was voting against me. I wasn't sufficiently committed to a Palestinian state.

Kirsten Gillibrand was a bad joke. I had many friends from New York who had given her lots of money and even sponsored fundraisers for her. They called to assure me that she would be supportive. We met in her office and she dispensed immediately with any pleasantries. "Why should the United States provide so much humanitarian aid to Israel, when by all accounts its people live well, and so little money to Gaza?" she asked.

"We don't provide one penny of humanitarian aid to Israel," I responded. "It's all military assistance and it was put in place by a Democratic administration in recognition of the fact that it is essential to both US and Israeli national security."

She quickly changed the subject and showed no sign of being "supportive" (she wasn't).

Cory Booker was delightful when we met. He had a write-up on me and commented that the controversial things that I had said were not nearly as bad as some of the things he said in the past. He told me about his love for Israel and the Jewish people and, as we left, said "*Yihiyeh b'seder*"—Hebrew for "it will be all right."

It was all right, until the hearing. Then he turned into another person entirely. Showing none of his jovial self from our meeting, he looked me in the eye and said, with great fervor, "Do you understand how much pain you have caused with your ugly words?" Huh? What happened to "*Yihiyeh b'seder*?" I thought. This whole world of politics where you say one thing in private and another in public was all new to me. I didn't like it.

And then there was Chuck Schumer. He was the Senate minority leader at the time and had significant influence over his party on matters affecting Israel. Senator Schumer, when speaking to Jewish crowds, often referred to himself as a "*shomer*," meaning a "guardian" of Israel, making a slight modification to his last name for dramatic effect. I went to my meeting with him with some degree of optimism: He was a supporter of settlements in Judea and Samaria, he had a rocky relationship with J Street at the time (although he subsequently began attending their events in 2019), he was the senator from my home state, and I had even made numerous contributions to his campaigns.

We talked for a while about Israel and about New York. He told me that I was a pretty good guy, better than he had been led to believe, and that I had the votes, so not to worry.

I said in response: "Respectfully, Senator, I know I have the votes. I don't want your vote in order to be confirmed. I want it because you will be sending a strong message of bipartisanship on Israel, which you have advocated on numerous occasions. You will demonstrate that those on the left can deal respectfully with right-wing supporters of Israel just like the Republicans supported my predecessor, Dan Shapiro, a lefty."

He thought about it and just smiled at me. "I'm not giving Trump the win. Sorry."

I also paid a courtesy visit to Nita Lowey of Westchester, New York, even though as a House member she would not be voting on my nomination. Congresswoman Lowey had a long and distinguished record of support for Israel. We had a very pleasant meeting. But as I got up to leave, she stood up, looked me in the eye, and said, "Promise me you won't move the embassy to Jerusalem."

I was stunned. I asked her, "Didn't you support the Jerusalem Embassy Act in 1995?"

She said of course she did, but the embassy should be moved only if there's a peace deal.

"But that's not what the law says," I protested. "The act doesn't require Palestinian consent to the move! The Jerusalem Embassy Act recognizes Jerusalem as Israel's capital and requires the move of the embassy absent a waiver granted by the president on the grounds of national security."

"Don't do it," she said. "We don't need the violence."

I left that meeting terribly disheartened. Here was a lifelong supporter of Israel and its right to have its capital in Jerusalem all but admitting to me that she, and presumably her colleagues, saw this commitment as aspirational only and subject to a Palestinian veto. To her, the Jerusalem Embassy Act was just a collection of empty words devoid of meaning.

Two Democratic senators, a minuscule but welcome minority, did show some spine on my nomination: Senator Robert Menendez of New Jersey, whose support for Israel has been resolute throughout his career, and Senator Joe Manchin of West Virginia, an independent thinker and a strong supporter of Israel as well, who thought the president was entitled to his representative on the ground. I had long meetings with both and they approached my nomination professionally and apolitically.

But they were voices in the wilderness.

MY CONFIRMATION HEARING WAS DESCRIBED BY SENATOR MARCO Rubio as "unreal." He was offended by much of the grandstanding by the Democrats and so was I. One, Senator Tom Udall of New Mexico, was perfectly pleasant when we met. He even included his wife in the meeting who had worked on a kibbutz in her youth. But when it was his turn at the hearing, he made a five-minute speech filled with anger and vitriolic criticism, and then left the hearing so I couldn't respond. Another senator, Jeanne Shaheen from New Hampshire, shared with me a message from one of her constituents who felt that I had "devalued" her support for Israel. "What should I tell this woman?" she asked me.

"Give her my number," I responded.

At a short break in the hearing, my lawyer and a good friend, Eric Herschmann, pulled me aside with some late-breaking news. J Street had compiled a "dossier" on me at a cost of almost $100,000 and given it out to each Democratic senator. One of them passed it to Eric. I didn't have time to read it as it appeared several inches thick. "David," he said, "this says you are delinquent in your taxes!"

I knew that wasn't true so we pulled out that section and I started to quickly peruse it. The headline indeed read FRIEDMAN IS DELIN-QUENT ON HIS TAXES. The section recited that the property taxes on my condo in Florida were due on January 31 each year. However, there was an opportunity to pay as early as November of the prior year and receive a small discount. Even though I had indeed paid the taxes in January before they were due, because I missed the discount period (I was pretty busy then!), the dossier referred to me as delinquent. I scanned the remainder of the document as well and saw references to my children, friends, and others. I was pretty shocked by all this but didn't have time to process it. The hearing was about to reconvene.

The dossier never came up at the hearing, undoubtedly because it was worthless, but Rubio made an important point that guided me forward. He warned me, on the public record, that I was being confronted by an orthodoxy within the State Department and the "so-called smart people within the American foreign policy establishment," who seek an evenhanded approach to Israel and the Palestinians even though Israel was our most important ally in the region and the Palestinians remained engaged in terror. As I moved forward, I realized how right he was.

Not all the opposition at the hearing came from Democratic senators. Five former ambassadors to Israel wrote a letter to the committee explaining how incredibly important the post of ambassador to Israel was and how demonstrably unqualified I was for the job. I thought that was just a cheap shot. None of them knew me and none of them had a particularly successful tour of duty that would have entitled them to pass judgment on someone else. The litigator in me wanted to call them as witnesses and cross-examine them, but that wasn't how this game was played.

There was also much hostility from the back of the room. As I made my opening statement, I was interrupted five separate times by protesters who accused me of everything from being a war criminal to a mass murderer. With each outbreak, the hearing was halted and the interloper was arrested.

We were tipped off in advance that there would be some ugly interruptions. Knowing that, Eric gave me some good advice. All the photographers sitting on the floor between the senators and me wanted nothing more than a good shot of me contorting my face with anger or frustration at the protesters. They would be looking for the same from my wife and kids. So we all practiced looking forward emotionless as Eric simulated the shouting. We followed that advice scrupulously and gave the press absolutely nothing.

The hearing lasted about five hours, unprecedented for a hearing on the nomination of an ambassador. I had enough preparation both in the murder board sessions and in thirty years in and out of courtrooms to deal with this process. The bottom line was that I knew more about the subject matter than many of my adversaries and they were not going to engage with me in a public debate. What they were likely to do, they did: make speeches and then leave before a response.

One subject I prepared for on my own was defending a statement I had made previously that the State Department had a history of anti-Semitism. My handlers at State wanted nothing to do with that issue—they saw their careers ending if they helped me respond in any manner other than to apologize. But I was ready to defend that accusation on my own, if it came up. I carried few papers in the folder I brought to the hearing, but I included the first page of Treasury

Secretary Henry Morgenthau's report to Roosevelt in 1943. In that report, he stated:

> *You are probably not as familiar as I with the utter failure of certain officials in our State Department, who are charged with actually carrying out this policy, to take any effective action to prevent the extermination of the Jews in German-controlled Europe.*

Unbeknownst to my Sherpa and others preparing me, I was hoping this would come up and I was most ready to respond. But it didn't.

The press reluctantly concluded that I showed sufficient composure, regret for past mistakes, and command of the subject matter, such that no Republican would vote no. Two weeks later, the committee approved my nomination by a vote of 12 to 9. Two weeks after that, the entire Senate voted to confirm my nomination, with Manchin and Menendez joining the Republicans. All the remaining Dems voted no—suggesting at least to me that their mantra of bipartisan support for Israel was far less than met the eye.

I was disappointed by the Senate vote. Many supporters congratulated me and pointed out that one becomes an ambassador, "extraordinary and plenipotentiary" as the title reads, whether with a majority of one or with unanimous consent. But I remained discouraged that almost half of the Senate had been driven by such petty politics. I read a survey done by *The New York Times* during this period where Democrats and Republicans each were asked to rank other countries in order of their importance to the United States. The Republicans had Israel at 5; the Democrats had it at 28. All of this reinforced my view that whatever we could do to make the US-Israel relationship stronger, we needed to do within what I hoped would be the first of the president's two terms.

Once we gave up power, I saw real risk on the Democratic side.

ON THE LIGHTER SIDE, DURING MY OPENING STATEMENT AT THE hearing, one protester stood up and blew a shofar, the ceremonial ram's horn blown in the synagogue on Rosh Hashanah. As the police came to arrest the blower, he threw the shofar to the rear of the room to conceal the evidence.

After I had been confirmed by the Senate, a few friends of ours, the Smalls and the Maidenbaums, who had attended the hearing to provide moral support, presented me with that shofar—they apparently had retrieved the discarded ram's horn. The Lucite case holding the contraband shofar now had a silver plaque on which the following words were engraved: CONGRATULATIONS AMBASSADOR, YOU DID NOT BLOW IT!

At least not yet.

BATTLING THE STATE DEPARTMENT

The Indian Treaty Room is a spectacular setting in the Executive Office Building. No one is quite sure exactly what treaty the room refers to, but that's what they call it. On March 29, 2017, I stood at the front of the room with my hand on a family Hebrew Bible held by my wife, Tammy, put on a kippah (skullcap), and "affirmed" rather than swore as Vice President Mike Pence administered the oath of office. The Orthodox Jewish tradition does not permit swearing except in a rare case in a judicial proceeding. This was the first time, as far as anyone knew, that this practice was followed by a political appointee wearing a head covering, and many took notice for better or worse.

Normally, right after taking office, a new appointee goes to "Ambassador School." I was scheduled to do a month of consultations with various officials in DC, followed by a month to get my personal life in order, followed by a month in school. Following that, I would make my way over to the embassy in Tel Aviv and assume my post.

But those plans abruptly changed once the ceremony ended and

I caught up with Jared and Jason. The president had decided to make his first trip abroad to the Middle East and would be arriving in Israel on May 21. So all the preparations would need to be accelerated in order for me to be on the ground before his arrival.

I did have time for a few consultations within the State Department and I'm glad for that. But not for the reason you might expect. The most valuable thing I learned was not about Israel or the Middle East, but about the hidebound, self-satisfied American bureaucracy. It gave me great insight into the "Deep State" and the entrenched thinking that drove the process without regard to which administration was in power. From then on, I would have to fight against this establishment for every big win we had: moving the embassy, resetting policy, and moving forward toward peace.

My most important meeting was with "L"—the Office of the Legal Adviser (each division within the State Department is assigned a letter). When I arrived, I got the distinct feeling that I was taken about as seriously as a summer intern—someone who didn't really get it and who would be gone in due course.

I sat with five lawyers within the office and began by asking this question: "Why doesn't the United States recognize Jerusalem as the capital of Israel, as required by the Jerusalem Embassy Act of 1995?"

They looked at each other, each with a smug smile as if they were about to school me. The lead attorney responded: "Because that law is subject to a presidential waiver and it has been waived twice a year by both Democratic and Republican presidents since the law was enacted."

"Well, that's just not true," I said, as the looks changed from smugness to concern. "The Jerusalem Embassy Act permits the *move* of the embassy to be delayed by presidential waiver. But the *recognition* of Jerusalem is not waivable it simply is declared in the statute."

There was an awkward silence as the lawyers looked at each other, at the ceiling, and even the floor. And then the lead attorney offered the following: "That law is unenforceable."

I was stunned by the remark. "Who said it's unenforceable? Have you challenged the law in court? Has a judge agreed with you? This law was approved by more than ninety percent of Congress. It reflects the will of the American people! How can you just ignore it?"

"Ambassador, it encroaches upon the role of the president and the State Department to make foreign policy. It's not a valid law."

"So let me just understand your thinking," I said with some exasperation. "If I don't think the Internal Revenue Code is constitutional, I don't need to pay my taxes or challenge the law in court. I can just ignore it?"

We were done. They dismissed my hypothetical as nonsense and invited me to leave.

I was so incensed by that meeting that I immediately put in a call to Rex Tillerson, the secretary of state. I wanted him to know the imperiousness of his legal staff and how they were likely to impede presidential policy. While I had no trouble calling the president, the secretary was a different story. He had multiple screeners who wanted to know exactly why I was calling. I informed them.

In the end, he didn't take my call.

Later that day I mentioned to someone I trusted at State that I couldn't get through to the secretary. He shared with me the gossip that apparently already was circulating the immense halls of Foggy Bottom. When an assistant reported to the secretary that Ambassador Friedman was calling, Tillerson's response was, "He's not my ambassador!"

I processed that information fairly quickly. It looked like the State Department considered me a lightweight, easy enough to ignore. I would have to find a way to change that and work around Tillerson. But with that challenge, I had to make sure what I was doing was good with the president. I was glad to have had this insight into Tillerson and given time to recalibrate my approach.

We were off to Israel on May 14, 2017. Unlike all my predecessors, I insisted that my wife and I be taken straight from the airport to the Western Wall to offer a prayer for America and Israel. The press coverage of our arrival at the Wall was massive. I was met at the Wall by Rabbi Shmuel Rabinovitch, the rabbi in charge. I had hoped to meet President Reuven Rivlin or Prime Minister Benjamin Netanyahu there, but in those days it was forbidden for an Israeli official to meet an American official at such a controversial location.

Nonetheless, I felt that I had gotten off on the right foot.

While I was at the Wall, there was a smaller crowd surrounding someone else. We both wondered who the other VIP might be. One of my guards told me it was Steven Tyler of Aerosmith, who was scheduled to perform the next night. I asked him to arrange for us to meet.

My wife, our daughter Talia, and I met with Steven and his entourage at the Kotel plaza. I thanked him for performing in Israel, especially when there were performers, like Roger Waters of Pink Floyd, who insisted that Israel be boycotted. We hit it off and he invited us to hang out with the band backstage the following night.

And we did. As a guitarist I was blown away by the chance to play a few licks on Joe Perry's guitar and spend some time with Joey Kramer, the Jewish drummer who loved Israel. This was just an incredible way to begin the job.

I knew, however, that a lot of serious work lay ahead.

JUST THREE DAYS BEFORE THE PRESIDENT'S SCHEDULED ARRIVAL, I was invited by the prime minister to attend the opening ceremony, at the Jaffa Gate entrance to the Old City of Jerusalem, commemorating the fiftieth anniversary of the reunification of Jerusalem—a high point of the Six-Day War in 1967. I was to sit between him and President Rivlin for the entire event. Of course, Tammy and I accepted.

About two hours before we were to take the five-minute drive from the King David Hotel to the Jaffa Gate, my phone rang. It was a senior member of Tillerson's staff. "Ambassador Friedman, I'm calling from the State Department. We're calling to advise you not—not—to attend the Jerusalem Day event that you were planning to go to."

That was one of the big disadvantages of being an ambassador. Your whereabouts, present and planned, were always known to a large number of embassy staff, many of whom were only too happy to tattle on their boss. "Why shouldn't I go? I already accepted an invitation by the prime minister."

"Well, we'll just chalk that up to your inexperience. Jerusalem Day is very controversial and no ambassador to Israel has ever attended a ceremony in fifty years."

"I don't think its controversial," I responded. "Before 1967, the Western Wall was a Jordanian parking lot for camels and donkeys. Now it's a beautiful plaza open to all worshippers. Why wouldn't I want to celebrate that?"

"It's not done, Ambassador. The Palestinians feel differently. If you attend, you could cause controversy that could tarnish the president's upcoming visit."

I couldn't believe what I was hearing. While aggravated, I saw this as a good opportunity to show them I was not under their control. "I'll tell you what," I said, "since you are so concerned about the president's trip, take down this number." I proceeded to recite nine digits. Then I suggested, "Call this number and tell the guy on the other end that you really think I shouldn't go to the ceremony. I'm sure he will be really interested in what you have to say. If he calls me within the next two hours and tells me not to go, I won't. Otherwise, I'm going."

"Whose number is this?"

"It's the president's private cell. Have a great day."

I never heard about this again. I attended the Jerusalem Day ceremony and it was terrific. I received a great introduction by the prime minister to the people of Israel and was deeply moved to have played a prominent role at such a historic event.

There was absolutely no backlash from the Palestinians and no impact whatsoever on the president's upcoming visit.

THAT'S NOT TO SAY THERE WEREN'T OTHER SCREWUPS IN GETTING ready for the visit. As we were actively engaged in the extensive logistical preparations for the president's trip, a major diplomatic incident ensued. It was all because of the Jerusalem consulate.

The Jerusalem consulate had been a thorn in the side of the American embassy long before I arrived. In the simplest of terms, it was an anachronism, an irritant, and an unguided missile. The consulate was founded in 1844, 104 years before the creation of the State of Israel, when Jerusalem was controlled by the Ottoman Empire. It was the brainchild of American Christian Zionists who saw the return of the Jews to Jerusalem as essential to America's spiritual health. When Israel became an independent state, the consulate remained on the theory that Jerusalem would remain a *corpus separatum*—a separate body. Of course, in those days, Jerusalem was divided between Israel and Jordan.

After the Oslo Accords in 1993, someone in the State Department had the idea of turning the Jerusalem consulate into a de facto mission to the Palestinians.

It was a terrible idea.

The United States did not recognize a state of Palestine (and still doesn't), Jerusalem was the capital of Israel whether or not formally recognized as such, and the consulate was located in the heart of Jewish Western Jerusalem far from Palestinian communities. To make matters worse, the Jerusalem consul general, the chief of that mission, was selected by the State Department, not the president, was not subject to Senate confirmation, and did not report to the ambassador to Israel. The State Department had created their own agent in charge of Jerusalem, Israel's most important city, who operated independently of the ambassador and even the president.

I learned that this absurd dynamic had blown up many times in the past. But a couple of days before the president arrived, it was blowing up in my face.

As embassy and consulate personnel interfaced with the Shin Bet, Israel's equivalent to the FBI, to address the video feed that would enable a broadcast around the world of the president's visit to the Western Wall, the consulate representative was growing frustrated with Israel's security demands. He thought it appropriate to complain to the Shin Bet as follows: "You should listen to me because you don't even have a right to be here since this is illegally occupied territory."

That incredibly stupid comment led the headlines in all the Israeli papers the day before the president arrived. I was absolutely livid and demanded to know who said what. The consulate folks all denied the statement and covered for each other. I spoke to all the reporters and did as much damage control as I could.

I also made a note to myself to have the consulate shut down.

WORD OF MY STUBBORN INSISTENCE ON STANDING WITH OUR ALLY Israel had now circulated widely within the State Department. Another senior staffer decided to call me and offer the following advice: "Mr. Ambassador, don't be so Jewish."

"What?"

"Don't be so Jewish. You represent the United States of America. Tone down the Judaism in your work."

Don't be so Jewish.

I was furious. "Do you think I am under any disillusion as to who I represent? I'm not a politically correct person but I have to ask you, why do the laws of political correctness not apply to Jews?"

"Just a free word of advice." Worth the price.

6

TRUMP IN JERUSALEM

Having been on the ground only a few momentous days, I was now facing a presidential visit. Most ambassadors go a full term without such a visit, but not here. Although most of the preparations revolved around the president's schedule, including who was attending what and what the president would say, I became aware of a more unusual but equally pressing issue.

The Palestinians had pulled off a brilliant move. They had a surrogate inform one of the president's supporters—a respected businessman, major philanthropist, and active player in the region—that they were prepared to make peace with Israel on very favorable terms, even to include conceding all of Jerusalem to Israeli sovereignty and giving up the return of refugees, but the problem was that Bibi Netanyahu was unwilling to negotiate peace. They were betting that the president would focus less on the details—which any seasoned diplomat knew the Palestinians never would accept at that time—and instead form a view that it was Bibi and not Palestinian president Mahmoud Abbas who was at fault. The surrogate informed the president that he needed to pressure Netanyahu and embrace Abbas in order to make a deal.

Trump bought it. Before heading to the Middle East, he let it be known to those within earshot that he understood on good authority that Abbas was desperate to make a deal and Bibi didn't want to make peace. He was going to put the screws to Netanyahu to force a deal.

Jason Greenblatt called me in a panic. He had started his work on Inauguration Day and was far ahead of me in his engagement with the Palestinians. He knew that Abbas was not only not "desperate" for a deal but would never even consider making the types of concessions that were attributed to him. This was shaping up to be a diplomatic nightmare.

Jason asked me if I thought he should warn Netanyahu. I told him that given the manipulation by Palestinian leadership, Bibi should know what to expect. Jason made the call.

In response, the prime minister called me in for a meeting. He was very agitated that the president was coming to Israel with the impression that Abbas wanted peace and he didn't. I suggested to him that he prepare a short video of Abbas's comments of recent vintage where he shows his true colors. I emphasized that this needed to be completely honest—nothing out of context and nothing subject to multiple interpretations. He wondered what he would do with the video once it was prepared. I told him that he could play it if the opportunity presented itself.

A less serious problem was raised just before the president's arrival. Jason called me from Saudi Arabia concerned that the Saudis had put on a reception of unimaginable pomp and circumstance. They had tons of horses, magicians, musicians, and sword dancers. They even built a magnificent edifice in the president's honor. Jason wanted to know what Israel had planned.

I told him there was no way Israel could match the Saudis. At best

I would expect a red carpet and a guy with a trumpet. I suggested he manage all the expectations.

Nonetheless, greeting the president on the tarmac in Israel as he debarked from Air Force One was a majestic experience that I was not emotionally prepared for. At that moment, it sank in that I was the representative of the United States of America to the State of Israel. The moment was incredibly inspiring.

After the president and his wife descended the stairs, they greeted President Rivlin and Prime Minister Netanyahu and their respective wives, and then Tammy and me. He took Tammy's hand and said to her, "This is the only job David wanted. I'm so happy he has it."

After the leaders took their paces and were escorted to the reviewing stand for their opening remarks, I was escorted to the front row of the audience and seated next to Rex Tillerson, who had exited the rear of the plane along with Jared and National Security Advisor H. R. McMaster. I gave Rex a big hello and shook his hand warmly.

After the opening session we loaded into a few military helicopters and followed Marine One to Jerusalem. First stop: President Rivlin's office.

We had hoped to skip this visit in favor of a longer stay at Yad Vashem, Israel's incredible Holocaust Museum. We had offered to meet Rivlin at that site, but Rivlin insisted that Trump come to his office. We entered a private meeting, about seven of us on each side. Rivlin, a nice but stubborn man, spoke for far too long and with little coherence. He thanked Trump for bombing Mosul (an attack on Iraq in March that killed many civilians), although from the context it was clear that he was referring to Trump's attack on Syria's Shayrat Airbase in April with fifty-nine Tomahawk missiles in response to Bashar al-Assad's use of chemical weapons. By the time he was finished, you could tell that the president was tired and unlikely to stay on message.

After a few perfunctory words of thanks, Trump regaled Rivlin with stories about Saudi hospitality and how lucky Rivlin was to have me as an ambassador. He emphasized that I had given up a massive income to take this job because of my love for Israel. Then he quickly got serious. He looked Rivlin in the eye and told him that while he understood that Abbas was desperate to do a peace deal, the prime minister of Israel was unwilling. He implored Rivlin to tell Bibi to make peace.

That last comment knocked everyone off their chairs. Although the meeting was private and off the record, we all envisioned a headline tomorrow that Trump had praised Abbas and criticized Netanyahu—the worst possible dynamic for the president's popularity or for the prospects of the peace process. Fortunately, and incredibly, the event wasn't leaked.

We went straight from Rivlin to the King David Hotel, where the president was staying. The first event was a one-on-one meeting between Trump and Netanyahu. As that meeting was being held, the advisers on both sides were kept in separate rooms. After about forty-five minutes, we got the word that the president wanted "Jared, Jason, Rex, and David." We entered the room and were joined by four of Netanyahu's guys.

The conversation was cordial and productive. Bibi and Trump were hitting it off well and seemed to have a common view on Israel's security risks. Bibi made the point that Israel's "narrow waist" in the middle of the country was the distance of Trump Tower to the George Washington Bridge. After a lull in the chat, I noticed a TV screen off to the side and asked the president if he had seen the tape. He asked, "What tape?" I told him that at my suggestion Bibi had prepared a two-minute collection of Abbas's speeches that I thought was worth watching. "Sure, let's see it," the president said.

With that we watched two minutes of Abbas honoring terrorists, extolling violence, and vowing to never accept anything less than Israel's total defeat. Abbas ranted that the blood of every *shaheed*—literally a martyr but also a terrorist—was holy and would be avenged.

After the tape ended, the president said, "Wow, is that the same guy I met in Washington last month? He seemed like such a sweet, peaceful guy." The tape clearly had made an impact.

When I was back in DC about a month later, Tillerson and Mc-Master asked to see me. They were livid that I had encouraged Netanyahu to make a video and show it to the president without first clearing it with them. They thought it was a cheap propaganda trick. I asked them if they were aware of the misinformation that had been given to the president before he embarked. Their blank look said it all. "Look, guys," I said, "I work for the president, nobody else. He had been given bad information. Frankly, I'm surprised you didn't know about it. I am going to make sure that he is well informed so that he gets Israel policy right. And I will keep doing that as long as I have this job, and even after I don't."

It was important for the president to have seen the tape. The following day he was in Bethlehem to meet with the Palestinian Authority. He had expected me to join the meeting but Abbas refused, claiming that the US ambassador to Israel had no business being in Palestinian territory. When Trump arrived and didn't see me, he asked why and was irritated by the answer. He then laced into Abbas over the tape, demanding to know who he really was, a peacemaker as he claimed in Washington or a terrorist as he proclaimed on the tape. Abbas was stunned by the president's tone, apparently confident that he had positioned himself perfectly to emerge as the good guy. The meeting ended with words of reconciliation, but Abbas learned then and there that he wasn't going to pull the wool over the American administration as he had done successfully so many times before.

WE DODGED THAT BULLET AND OTHERWISE THE VISIT WAS UNPRECE-dented and deeply moving. From his words at Yad Vashem to a stirring speech at the Israel Museum, the president seemed to bring the US-Israel relationship all the way back from the dark days of the prior administration. Here are some of his words:

> *Jerusalem is a sacred city. Its beauty, splendor, and heritage are like no other place on earth. The ties of the Jewish people to this Holy Land are ancient and eternal. They date back thousands of years, including the reign of King David whose star now flies proudly on Israel's white and blue flag. . . . I stand in awe of the accomplishments of the Jewish People, and I make this promise to you: My Administration will always stand with Israel.*

The highlight was a trip to the Western Wall, the first such visit in history by a sitting president of the United States. President Trump was met there by Rabbi Rabinovitch—we had not yet overcome the long-standing State Department prohibition against an Israeli government official hosting an American leader at Judaism's most holy prayer site.

From my bar mitzvah in 1971 forward, I had been to the Western Wall hundreds of times. But nothing was like the experience of accompanying the most powerful man in the free world to those ancient stones, touching the seemingly lifeless rocks that were anything but, and saying a prayer.

As we returned to the helicopters for a brief flight back to Air Force One, now a full week into my ambassadorship, I felt that we were finally on the right track. My feelings later were confirmed by the thank-you note I received from the president, which began:

> *Dear David:*
>
> *Thank you for the tremendous job you and your Embassy team did in executing my trip to Israel. . . . Seeing you on the ground—in*

your element—reaffirmed my decision to appoint you as the Ambassador to Israel. There is no one better to serve the United States in this important role. You will do a fantastic job and I think you will be able to help us negotiate the ultimate deal. It will be a blessing to Israel and to the world!

7

THE DAUNTING CHALLENGES OF DAILY LIFE

Although I tried to remain focused on the commitment I made in the press release announcing my nomination—moving the US embassy to Jerusalem—the competing tasks and emergent crises were abundant. I also had to work to reform embassy rules and to build trust in my office. And I had to contend with the continued bad-faith actions of the Palestinian Authority.

After the president's departure I began to settle into daily life as a chief of mission with some eight hundred employees. When the president was in town, there had been some rumors that, while here, he would recognize Jerusalem as Israel's capital. That rumor, much to my disappointment, was nothing more. But I was determined to push this issue as best I could from six thousand miles away from the Oval Office.

As May 2017 came to an end, we were up against the six-month deadline under the Jerusalem Embassy Act for the president to either move the embassy or issue a waiver. Almost every official in DC had advised him to waive and I learned that the president was going to accept that advice. I didn't see an opening to change that outcome, so I focused on the language of the press release. I wanted a strong presidential commitment to move the embassy with words that the move of the embassy to Jerusalem was "not if but when." With that language, I felt I could start moving the governmental scrum in the right direction. I got all the necessary sign-offs for that language.

On June 1, 2017, just hours before the press release was due, I got a frantic message from Michael Anton, head of communications at the National Security Council. The president on his own had struck the language I wanted. There was no one willing to try to change his direction. I called the president directly.

"Mr. President, I strongly advise that we keep the language I wrote."

"David, why should I tip my hand? I hate binding myself to future actions. Who knows what will be in the future?"

"Mr. President, you promised to do this and I promised to do this, but there are many forces out there that will try to get in our way. I need to start plowing this field and this language gets me started."

We went back and forth a bit and I wouldn't give up. Finally, the president said, "David, if I put back the language, will you stop yelling at me?" (I wasn't yelling.) I answered, "Of course," and he authorized me to put the words back.

I hung up the phone and sent an email to about ten people to add back the words, "The question is not if that move [of the embassy] happens but when." Michael Anton responded, "You saved us on this." With "not if but when" now our foreign policy, I was eager to close the deal on Jerusalem. But waiting for the right moment required more patience than I would have imagined. From June until November 2017, Jerusalem was aflame with controversy, violence, and diplomatic challenges. Every time I tried to focus on its political status, I was overtaken by events.

On June 21, 2017, Jared, Jason, and I started our shuttle diplomacy in the region, perhaps better characterized as a listening tour. While Jared was in the air, Hadas Malka, a beautiful Israeli police officer, was stabbed to death by a Palestinian terrorist at the Damascus Gate to the Old City of Jerusalem. Once on the ground, Jared agreed with me to go two hours out of our way and to delay meetings with Israeli government officials, in order to pay a condolence call. Apart from the moral imperative of consoling a family in a time of their grief, the visit sent exactly the right message throughout the country. While ambassadors had made shiva calls before to terrorist victims, there had never before been a visit of this nature by a close relative of the president.

Some of the diplomats in our camp were concerned that if we came down too hard on the Palestinians, we would jeopardize the prospects for diplomatic advancement. I pushed for a brutally hard message: *Terrorism will kill all chances of US support for the Palestinian cause.*

I delivered that with the seriousness of a heart attack.

AFTER JARED AND JASON LEFT, I GOT SIDETRACKED A SECOND TIME BY the blowup of the ecumenical deal for the Western Wall. The Wall is administered by the Orthodox rabbinate and the main plaza requires strict adherence to Orthodox practice, including the separation of men and women. The non-Orthodox streams of Judaism, based primarily in the United States, had been given a small section of the terrain, referred to as Robinson's Arch, from which to engage in ecumenical prayer. That area was not as accessible or impressive in appearance as the main plaza, and for years there had been negotiations to upgrade the non-Orthodox section. A deal was reached in 2017 but after the liberal politicians and clergy publicly declared victory, the Israeli Orthodox establishment felt humiliated and the deal quickly blew up.

Rabbi Rick Jacobs, the head of the Reform movement, was in Jerusalem at the time the deal fell apart and demanded to see me. Just before he arrived at my suite at the King David Hotel (the US ambassador's quarters in Jerusalem at the time), I saw a report in *The Jerusalem Post* that Rick was advocating that American Jews stop supporting Israel.

Rick arrived quite distraught. He felt betrayed by Netanyahu and the religious parties and argued that it was my role to intercede on behalf of American Jewry. I told him that regardless of how upset he was, he could not advocate for a boycott of Israel—that would be a reckless and even suicidal position for his movement and the American Jewish community. He claimed that he never even suggested such a thing and I offered to get him on the phone immediately with the reporter so he could correct the record. He refused that overture.

He was angry and I understood his anger. He felt betrayed by the Israeli government and by having his Jewishness invalidated. Even though this was someone who protested my nomination, it was painful to me to see another Jew feel rejected by the Jewish state. I wanted to help but I also wanted him to see the other side of the issue.

"Rick," I offered, "you cannot expect to export American legal principles into Israel. There is no First Amendment here. The USA does not have a national religion, but Israel does, just like lots of other countries in the region and even in places like the UK. Israel has no separation of church and state."

"I understand, David, but Israel has an obligation to the Jews of the Diaspora, the vast majority of whom are not Orthodox."

"Well, I could argue that the Jews in the Diaspora owe even more to Israel, since the Jews in Israel make great sacrifices to maintain a Jewish state, sacrifices not required in America."

"We need Israel to be more appealing to American Jews, David."

And here we were back to the progressive Jewish mistake—a demand that Israel adopt liberal American sensibilities so that liberal American Jews will like Israel more. But there is never even a suggestion that perhaps liberal American Jews need to try harder to understand Israel. Perhaps a good start would be for them to visit Israel, but more than two-thirds of liberal American Jews never have.

"Rick, Israel is a democracy. If your side wants to change Israel, move here! There are almost no Reform Jews in Israel. The Jews who pray at the Western Wall are overwhelmingly Orthodox and, for better or worse, religion and politics are not separate here. I'd love to see things worked out, but after the Reform movement spiked the football by proclaiming victory in the Western Wall dispute, what did you think would happen?"

He didn't see it that way and reiterated that it was my job to heal the rift. I took his anguish to heart, regardless of his anger and his politics, I could see that he was in pain.

I SPENT WEEKS TRYING TO BROKER SOME PROGRESS. IT WAS FRUS-trating and disheartening seeing such rifts between Jewish groups. In the end, the government of Israel agreed to make significant improvements to Robinson's Arch, but not enough to satisfy the other side. The negotiations continue sporadically to this day.

In between crises, there also was time for some fun. I didn't realize that the American embassy's Fourth of July celebration in Israel was the social event of the year. All the planning had already been done before we arrived, and Tammy and I were shocked that not only was the food not kosher, but hamburgers from McDonald's and ice cream from Ben and Jerry's were being served alongside each other. We quickly rearranged the buffet tables with red carpets leading to meat products and blue carpets to dairy products. At least that would shield to some extent against the prohibited mixing of meat and dairy products and make the observant more comfortable.

The event took place in our massive backyard in Herzliya with a stunning view of the Mediterranean Sea. The temperature was well above ninety degrees and the crowd was more than twenty-five hundred people. The budget was a paltry $65,000—not nearly enough for a crowd that size. There was a receiving line to meet Tammy and me that extended for a quarter mile out the door. By the time the last person got through, we were exhausted from standing and the crowd was drenched in sweat and dehydrated. Nonetheless, the crowd seemed thrilled to be there and the Netanyahus and the Friedmans drank a toast from the stage and Bibi and I addressed the crowd. President Rivlin came separately and left early. In my four years, rarely did he and Netanyahu share the stage at an event.

After the first Fourth of July party, we decided to treat our guests a bit better. We moved to air-conditioned venues with on-site parking and all the food was strictly kosher. In 2019, the embassy had its first-ever Fourth of July celebration in Jerusalem at the International Convention Center. By then we had increased the budget tenfold. Most importantly, after that first party we ended the receiving line—an old-fashioned custom that fostered more resentment than goodwill. Never again did I force anyone to wait in line to shake my hand. Going forward we just joined the crowd and circulated among them.

On July 4, I also picked up an interesting insight into the differences between the United States and Israel. Before the party began, I flew on a helicopter to the USS *George W. Bush*, a massive aircraft carrier that was anchored off the coast of Haifa. I had already been many times on Israeli helicopters and was used to the boarding procedure—you just get on, muffle your ears, and try to fasten your seat belt before takeoff. On this day, because we were landing on a

US military ship, only a US helicopter would do. Before boarding, an American pilot handed us life vests and helmets and offered a safety briefing. He made sure to tell us that we were flying over water and that in the event of engine failure they would need to ditch. In that event, the pilot explained that the helicopter would flip over because of the weight imbalance. When that happened, he suggested that we might be disoriented but we should make sure to follow the bubbles on exit and be careful not to kick our feet! I looked at Air Force Brigadier General Corey Martin, my defense attaché sitting next to me, and said with as much severity as I could muster: "If this bird ditches, you better get me the hell out or I promise you will never get another star." Fortunately, we never needed to test that threat. The contrast between the US and Israeli flight procedures is a good proxy for many of the differences between our two countries.

On other occasions, I was more serious in my efforts to make an impression on my staff. For the Maccabiah Games that first July, a quadrennial competition among Jewish athletes from around the world, I was invited to throw out the first pitch at the final baseball game between the United States and Canada. As I arrived to the field, I was taken aside by a member of the staff from our public diplomacy section whom I was meeting for the first time. He said to me, "Sir, this is being carried live on local TV. The pitcher's mound is farther away from home plate than it looks. I recommend that you stand a few feet in front of the mound."

He could tell by my look that I thought he was nuts. "You obviously don't know me because if you did, you would know that I would never ever accept a handicap in an athletic competition. I'd rather roll the ball to home plate than stand in front of the mound. I haven't thrown a baseball in twenty years, but I guarantee you I will not embarrass myself."

I didn't. I hummed it straight to the catcher. He did not have to move his glove to catch the ball. I turned to my staffer and said, "Never look at me again with low expectations. And tell that to all your friends in the embassy."

I think that did me some good.

GETTING BUY-IN FROM THE EMBASSY STAFF WAS A MATTER OF IMPOR-tance to me. I had already begun to observe the stunning disloyalty within the Oval Office that was reflected in many inappropriate leaks of confidential discussions. I had always valued employee morale when I was in the private sector and I wanted my embassy staff to feel valued and operate cohesively. In the private sector, if you wanted to make someone happy you had the option to pay them more money. That didn't exist in the government. But I quickly realized you could deliver nonmonetary benefits if you knew how.

That summer one member of my press staff came to me nearly in tears. She told me that as a foreign service officer she had changed locations every three years, much to the chagrin of her teenage son. Now, in Tel Aviv, her son finally was thriving but she was scheduled to depart as her son began his senior year in high school. She could not bear to tell him that he would not graduate with his class.

I asked her what she had done to try to get a one-year extension of her tour in Tel Aviv. She said she had tried everything but was told repeatedly that this is the life she signed up for. She did not know where to turn. I asked her who the ultimate decision maker was and she said it was the undersecretary for management. I called him right then and there with her in the room—itself an astonishing move since most calls at our level were pre-coordinated by a whole group of phone call "arrangers." After he picked up the phone, I made a "personal re-quest" to keep her another year and he said "sure." Problem solved.

What a world! So many dedicated people with so little control of their lives. I did everything I could to help my people advance, including getting my deputy chief of mission an ambassadorship. I treated everyone the way I would have wanted to be treated and that had an extremely important impact in the execution of my mission.

Things were leaking like a sieve in the Oval Office and Foggy Bottom, but we were a well-tuned machine at Embassy Tel Aviv.

UNFORTUNATELY, OUR INTERNAL CONTROLS DID NOT EXTEND BE-yond our guarded embassy walls. The second half of July 2017 brought one disaster after another. July 19 brought my biggest challenge to date as two Israeli policemen of Druze heritage guarding the Temple Mount were killed by terrorists who had stored their weapons in the Al Aqsa Mosque. Never before had the mosque been used as a weapons depot. Israeli police were compelled to shut Al Aqsa for a day and fully search it.

The police moved quickly. After a thorough search they concluded that the mosque was safe and it was reopened. However, they determined that it was necessary to install magnetometers—metal detectors—to screen the worshippers before they enter.

Some context here. There are eleven entrances to the Temple Mount upon which Al Aqsa stands. Ten of them are for Muslims only. The eleventh—the Mugrabi Gate—is for non-Muslims who already go through metal detectors and, upon arrival, are prohibited from offering any words of prayer. Only Muslims may pray on the Temple Mount under a long-standing protocol reached between Israel and Jordan, even though the Temple Mount is the holiest site in Judaism and perhaps equally holy to Christians.

So in response to an unprecedented terror attack, Israel installed the same security screening devices that already apply to non-Muslims; the same devices used around the world at airports, museums, sporting events, government facilities, and houses of worship. In response, Abbas threatened another intifada and falsely accused Israel of plotting a takeover of the Temple Mount. I can attest to the word "falsely," as I was actively engaged with the Israeli Security Administration (the Shin Bet) and saw firsthand how hard they were trying to find a solution acceptable to all. They took down the metal detectors and replaced them with less obtrusive CCTV cameras that would not slow down the entry. These types of cameras are prevalent at the Great Mosque in Mecca, Islam's holiest site. Nonetheless, the Palestinian leadership continued to object and continued to incite worshippers to boycott the mosque.

The incitement worked. Soon after I returned home from a visit to the mourning tents of the Druze families who had lost their sons, a Palestinian terrorist massacred a family in the town of Halamish.

July 21, 2017, was a Friday night and the Salomon family were at the Shabbat table preparing to celebrate the birth of a son and grandson. A terrorist jumped a security fence encircling the town and burst into their home clutching a knife. It was later revealed that his motivation was to avenge his perception of an Israeli assault on Al Aqsa. He stabbed to death the grandfather, his daughter, and his son, and injured the grandfather's wife. During the attack, his son's wife, Michal Salomon, ran upstairs, barricaded herself and her five children in the bedroom, and kept them silent until the screams below had subsided. The attack was so heinous that, in contrast to the reporting on past attacks, the papers all ran a picture of the blood-soaked living room caused by the terrorist.

The entire nation of Israel was deeply moved by this attack, as well as many throughout the world. There was strong condemnation from the Trump administration and many other good people, although the sentiments were more muted among those claiming that Halamish is occupied illegally by Israelis (as if those lives were any less precious). Not a word, however, from Abbas or his spokesman. Needless to say, I was furious.

And it got even worse. Abbas's incessant vilification of Israel over an alleged but nonexistent threat to Al-Aqsa led to an attack on an Israeli working in the Israeli embassy in Amman, Jordan. In response, the Israeli shot dead the attacker and his colleague. The Israelis in Amman understood the potential for this to spin out of control and immediately took steps to extract their people from a potentially volatile situation. But Jordan would not permit the extraction. Meanwhile, Jordanians began to assemble in the streets to protest. This was heading to another potential Benghazi and a rupture of Israel-Jordan peace, and King Abdullah was nowhere to be found.

I called Jared frantically, knowing that he had a good relationship with the king. He tracked him down in California and worked things out. The Israeli was released along with most of the Israeli embassy staff. On July 31, I returned to DC to explain to President Trump just how dysfunctional and malign the Palestinian leadership had been during this past terrible month. I told the president that I did not believe Abbas will ever be a peace partner and that progress will only come, in the long run, from holding the Palestinians accountable for terror and incitement.

"So what do you want to do now, David, throw parties like all the other ambassadors?" the president asked.

"No," I responded. "I want to move the goalposts back to where they belong with regard to the conflict and work with Jared to perhaps make peace from the outside in—beginning with Israel's natural allies. While the Palestinians are dysfunctional, there are Arab neighbors that may be ready to normalize with Israel."

"Okay, go for it then. Good luck."

I returned to Israel in August to much better news as our daughter Talia made aliyah and became a dual citizen of Israel and the United States. Tammy and I were so moved and proud to be given access to the tarmac to greet her as she descended from the plane. It's a striking example of the press's attitude about Israelis that in a State Department press briefing that day, Said Arikat, a reporter for the *Al Quds* newspaper, asked spokesperson Heather Nauert if it was a good idea for the ambassador's daughter to be joining what "is perceived as an occupation army." (She didn't even join the army.)

IN SEPTEMBER I BEGAN TO PUSH THE ENVELOPE ON POLITICAL ISSUES. In a press interview on September 7, I referred to Israeli control of Judea and Samaria as an "alleged occupation." The Palestinian leadership freaked out and the State Department issued an immediate clarification: "There has been no policy shift regarding the West Bank." The left-wing newspaper *Haaretz* gleefully reported that I had received a "rebuke." Little did they know that this State Department language was my own. Heather called me to ask how she should respond and I gave her this language. I was plowing the field but we were not yet changing policy. A few days later the Supreme Sharia Judge of the Palestinian Authority said I was motivated by a "Satanic urge."

With that I was off to my first (and only) United Nations General Assembly.

I was very put off by the whole thing: 190 countries all treated the same. Erdoğan and Khamenei walking the halls with their entourages receiving great respect while the United States sits in alphabetical order all the way in the back. I went out to get some fresh air and had a very hard time getting back, even with good credentials. I broke through the masses to walk up a driveway just as Nikki Haley was waiting for Trump to arrive. When Trump saw me, he invited me to accompany him to several bilateral meetings not related to my area of responsibility. The looks on the State Department diplomats when they saw my attendance were not pleasant.

Trump delivered a great speech at the General Assembly. He laced into Iran and North Korea like no one before him. I sat in the lead US chair when Bibi spoke and then had the privilege to hear Abbas attack me personally and by name in his speech. He also threatened to prosecute Israelis at the International Criminal Court.

This only renewed my resolve not to let the Palestinians stand in the way of regional progress. I did another interview when I returned to Israel and was asked what I thought of the West Bank settlements. I said that they are part of Israel—the residents serve in the army, have Israeli citizenship, and are considered Israeli by the government. While I knew the answer would draw controversy, I also knew the facts were not debatable. Nonetheless, the Palestinian Authority responded with even more vitriol than before. An organization called Americans for Peace Now did a big media blitz demanding that I be fired. As the Palestinians fumed, the Israeli and American Right were ecstatic—they had never heard a US official speak in these terms. I was slowly moving the pile on these issues. Serious journalists like Eli Lake weighed in to voice their agreement with me.

And while the State Department, again, rejected my statement, I managed the response so as to maintain ambiguity on our official position.

OCTOBER 2017 WAS FULL OF JEWISH HOLIDAYS. SUKKOT, THE ANCIENT festival celebrating the harvest, was especially meaningful as I was given the opportunity as a Kohen, a descendant of Aaron the High Priest (and Moooo's brother), to bless over one hundred thousand people at the Western Wall with my son and grandson.

And then the United States surprised the world by pulling out of UNESCO—a great call by Nikki Haley after UNESCO rejected any Jewish connection to the Cave of the Patriarchs in Hebron. Just a few days later, for the first time in fifteen years and with my encouragement, Israel proposed a new building in Hebron. It was in a building lot right between two Jewish homes and had no impact whatsoever on local or broader issues. Prior administrations sadly would have opposed this minor zoning matter. We didn't. The timing was exquisite.

On October 15, 2017, President Trump decertified the Iran nuclear deal. It was a massive act of courage and strength. The United States was now on the path to restore and increase economic sanctions on Iran. It was in a position to hold Iran accountable for its regional support of terrorists, its efforts to destabilize Yemen, Iraq, Syria, and Lebanon, and its stockpiling of dangerous missiles. I was elated.

With the wind at our back, I felt it was time to restore the push for Jerusalem. The question of "not if but when" had arrived.

Even my "challenge coin" reflected the subliminal quest for US recognition of Jerusalem. These coins are allotted to high-ranking civilian and military personnel as a token of thanks to be offered to counterparts. Everyone is free to design their own coin. Mine had an image of the Liberty Bell on the reverse side, with the biblical words, found on the bell, "Proclaim Liberty Throughout the Land" inscribed in their original Hebrew. What many receiving the coin did not know was that the biblical phrase was a reference to the Jubilee Year that occurs every fifty years and mandates that all debts be forgiven and property returned. I had prayed for a second Jubilee for modern Israel in 2017—the first Jubilee, or fifty years, spanned the Balfour Declaration in 1917 to the Six-Day War in 1967. The second, I hoped, would span the Six-Day War to the president's recognition of Jerusalem as Israel's capital in 2017. But 2017 was fast coming to a close.

BUT, OF COURSE, NOTHING IS EASY AND CURVEBALLS ABOUNDED. IN late October, I was asked by the State Department to clear the semiannual certification required by Congress that the Palestinian Liberation Organization satisfied the requirements of eligibility to maintain its mission in Washington, DC. Some people in DC must have suspected I didn't want to do it. A bunch of really smart people at State and NSC cleverly alerted me that the fact that the PLO had just joined Interpol, the international police agency, did not present a statutory basis to deny certification. I marveled at their strategy to have me focus on a straw man in the hopes that I would miss the real issue. No chance. I agreed with them about Interpol but pointed out that Abbas's speech at the UN regarding prosecuting Israelis at the International Criminal Court was expressly a disqualifying fact to maintaining the mission. The law was clear that any attempt by Abbas to encourage ICC prosecution of Israelis was antithetical to the diplomacy in which the PLO mission was supposed to engage and necessitated closing the mission.

They asked to regroup and respond in a few days. When the response came, I was underwhelmed: They responded that there's no evidence that Abbas really meant what he said. I said yes there is: He said it loud and clear on the biggest stage in the world—the UN General Assembly! And his intent isn't even relevant under the statute.

Now here was the problem. While I am no fan of the PLO and have no doubt that Abbas's speech should have resulted in its disqualification to maintain a mission in DC, I did not want to waste even a penny of political capital on this issue at this time. I wanted recognition of Jerusalem and I was petrified that if the PLO mission were shuttered, there would be less of an appetite to deliver what might be considered a second blow. It was an odd conundrum.

I sent a note to Rex, who would make the final call on this, that I believed the PLO's eligibility was uncertifiable based upon Abbas's statements at the UN. But I also extended an olive branch and said that if he felt compelled to certify and intended to rely on the justifications offered by the lower-ranking officials, I wouldn't make a fuss.

Rex made the right decision. Indeed, it was the only decision he could have made. He refused to certify eligibility and set the PLO mission on a path to closure. The PLO's secretary-general, Saeb Erekat, responded with a letter of outrage, declaring, "This decision means to us that the US is fully withdrawing from sponsoring the peace process and will lead to severe consequences." I was struck by how tone-deaf the letter read—the closure was entirely a problem of the Palestinians' own making by failing to abide by US law. Their reaction gave rise to little sympathy and I was relieved that it did not appear to create an impediment to the Jerusalem initiative.

BEFORE OCTOBER CAME TO AN END, SECRETARY OF THE TREASURY Steven Mnuchin came to Jerusalem with his wife. This was his first time in Israel. He was deeply moved by what he saw and ended up making more trips to Israel than any other cabinet secretary. I stood with him at the Western Wall after we had a private tour of the Church of the Holy Sepulchre, where Jesus is said to have arisen after his crucifixion. Mnuchin said to me: "Let's see if I got this right. Anyone can pray at the Church and anyone can pray at the Wall. But on the Temple Mount, only Muslims can pray and they get ten entrances without metal detectors and everyone else gets one with a detector, even though the Temple Mount is holy to all?"

I said, "Correct."

He responded, "So what in the world is the beef with Israel controlling Jerusalem?"

Those words gave me that last push of encouragement to reset our policy on Jerusalem. I made arrangements to visit the president in early November.

8

"IF I FORGET THEE, O JERUSALEM"

I arrived in Washington on the morning of November 14, 2017, to make the case for Jerusalem. The prior weekend I attended the annual dinner of the Zionist Organization of America where I received an award. I gave a speech that echoed the president's words that the embassy would definitely move; the only issue was when. But just before I began to speak, I was sent a picture that became the focal point of my speech.

Our youngest daughter, Katie, was on a trip with her class to Eastern Europe. As I was ascending the stage, I heard my phone ping, and up popped a picture of Katie and a friend with a flag of Israel draped around their shoulders standing on the train tracks to Birkenau, the murder factory within Auschwitz. In just one haunting picture I saw the past and the future and the moral imperative that the Jewish people, and the Jewish state, are never again subject to an existential threat.

That picture gave me all the motivation I needed to start the push for the embassy move, and it propelled me forward with a great sense of purpose.

I spent the fourteenth getting ready. I met with Ted Cruz and several other senators to sensitize them to the push that was coming and to encourage them to weigh in with the president as the opportunity arose. I checked in with Jared and Jason to get the latest sense of the president's thinking and, most important, I steadied my own thoughts, fully cognizant of the importance of what awaited.

I was well aware that the president's institutional establishment hated this idea. They were going to predict a massive calamity with many lives lost. I searched for a way to address this issue and concluded that my best chance lay with a phased approach.

On November 15, I was in the Oval Office. Sitting alongside me was National Security Advisor H. R. McMaster (no longer mad at me), Chief of Staff John Kelly, Jared Kushner, and Jason Greenblatt. The president knew why I was there. He acknowledged, matter-of-factly, that I was there to move the embassy. I sought to downplay the magnitude of the decision, given what I perceived as a partially hostile crowd. I highlighted that it was premature to actually move the embassy inasmuch as we didn't yet have a building that we were ready to move into. What I advocated for instead was just the recognition of Jerusalem as Israel's capital and a direction to begin the process of moving the embassy.

The president asked whether this two-step process was in keeping with his campaign pledge. I responded in the affirmative, both because it was well known that the actual move was impossible to do immediately and because I thought the pronouncement, without more, would allay the fears of a security issue, as there would be no immediate change in the facts on the ground. I had seen the Palestinians react to speeches—they usually don't, except with more speeches. I've said plenty of controversial things and they never led to violence. What matters is what people see on the ground, at least in the immediate aftermath of the announcement, and they wouldn't see anything different.

The president continued to express concern that the recognition of Jerusalem without a simultaneous move of the embassy might not be enough. I was concerned that my colleagues might jump on that comment to advocate for a delay of years until an embassy was ready, effectively burying this historic initiative. I told the president that US recognition of Jerusalem as the capital of Israel, even independent of the embassy move, would be celebrated far and wide by his base and by many others. They understood that moving an embassy takes some more time and would accept that.

The president looked at McMaster, noted his approval of my approach, and sought his reaction. McMaster offered that I had presented a creative approach that merited further study and committed to run an "interagency process" on the subject.

To me, that sounded good and bad, slightly more to the bad. I feared an "interagency process" would be a burial ground for my "creative approach."

The president endorsed this course of action, and everyone stood up to leave. But before the room emptied, I requested of the president that I be closely involved in every aspect of the "interagency process." With that comment, I saw some disapproving looks around the room. But the president wholeheartedly agreed, and I was off and running.

With that, the meeting broke up but we lingered in the hallway. McMaster offered to oversee a "pros and cons" memo that would be presented to the president. He assured me that I could see it before it was finalized. We agreed to meet again the next day in the late afternoon.

As I was walking back to Jared's office for a "postgame" meeting, Kelly pulled me aside for a private conversation.

"David, where will you be for the next two weeks?" he asked.

"I was planning to head back to Israel in two days."

"Well, don't. I know how much you want to get this done, and here's a secret: So do I. But it won't get done unless you are physically here. Now I am not going to advocate for recognition, that's your job. But I will make sure that you are in attendance at every meeting where this is discussed."

"What about Jared and Jason?" I asked.

"I don't want the history books to record that the decision was made at the behest of three Orthodox Jews. David, you have the president's ear on this and you are not intimidated by Rex or HR or Mattis. This is on you."

"General, I'll be here until this is done."

With that, I walked back to Jared's office and updated him on where things were. I would have an eventful two weeks, no question about that.

The next day I again worked the Senate in the morning and stopped by late in the day at the office of H. R. McMaster. He was with three or four members of his senior staff. We sat down and he handed me a piece of paper that purported to list the risks and then the opportunities of recognizing Jerusalem as Israel's capital. There were about ten enumerated risks, each one described in its own paragraph. I scanned these items, more interested in seeing the listed opportunities. After flipping through the risks section, I got to the last page, with the heading "Opportunities." Beyond the heading, the page was blank.

"So this is what we have so far, David. What do you think?" HR asked.

"What do I think?" I said incredulously. "I think that in a hundred out of a hundred cases, if a decision memo presents the action being considered as having only risks and no opportunities, the action will not advance. You know that as well. So I think you don't want to do this!"

"No, David, that's unfair. We just didn't see this proposed action presenting any opportunities."

"HR, I'll tell you what. I will write the entire 'opportunities' section. I just want it included as written and unedited. If you want to footnote that this came exclusively from me and you disagree with all or some of my points, that's fine."

"That is acceptable," he responded.

I walked out, a bit stunned. I was being played here by the president's foreign policy guys, but it just made me more determined to push forward. I went back to Jason's office and used his computer to write the "opportunities" section.

The opportunities here were enormous and I could not believe that they had eluded the intellectual grasp of so many otherwise smart people. At the very least, I thought it would be appropriate to highlight these factors:

- Recognition will strengthen the presidency and will highlight the president keeping a promise, fulfilling the will of the
  American people, demonstrating that America stands with its
  allies, and inspiring the tens of millions of Americans who love
  Jerusalem.

- Recognition will demonstrate that America doesn't flinch when
  threatened by rogue regimes or terrorists.

- Recognition will advance the cause of peace by signaling that
  the Palestinians no longer hold a veto on significant issues and
  that America is no longer wedded to failed practices of the past.

- Risks have been mitigated by the bifurcation of recognition and
  the actual embassy move, and by an announcement that will
  leave open the prospects of a two-state solution.

- In this region, unforeseen events can overtake policy. The timing now is good; it may not last.

I wrote an extensive list of "opportunities." To his credit, McMaster included my points as written and acknowledged that they were reasonable. I think he was pressured significantly by Mattis and Tillerson. I got to know him better over the years and I see him, in his own right, as a very good friend of Israel.

But the "interagency process" didn't end with the memo; that's where it started. The memo was then circulated to all parties that had "equities" in the issue, a fancy term for other agencies that cared. Because Jerusalem was such a controversial topic (needlessly, in my opinion), with security and diplomatic ramifications worldwide, there were countless agencies that wanted to participate, including Homeland Security, numerous intelligence agencies, and US embassies from Morocco to Pakistan. I participated in daily secure video calls with the screen divided into twenty-four or more boxes, one for each participant. It began before a decision was made and continued for weeks thereafter.

A massive amount of diligence was done in evaluating possible Jerusalem recognition. It took many days, but it can be summed up in a nutshell: Everyone thought it was risky because it had always been thought to be risky but no one could identify any specific threat to the proposed action. That didn't mean people did not speak excessively about what might, could, or should happen in any number of remote locations around the globe. But the risks were hypothetical and speculative.

There were frequent follow-up meetings throughout November. True to his word, General Kelly made sure I attended all of them. Some were a bit pointed. Rex said to me, "Apart from all your arguments about politics, messaging, atmospherics, and putting pressure on the Palestinians, how in the world does this make the United States or even Israel any safer or more secure? Our relationship with Israel is fine; we don't need to make it any better. Why are we pouring gasoline on a fire?"

Kelly was right that I was not intimidated by Rex. I responded, "Mr. Secretary, America will be stronger and safer because it will be led by a president who can be trusted to stand with an ally and keep a promise. And that alone will resonate throughout American foreign policy."

We weren't changing each other's minds and the president had gotten wind, in part from me, that there was a lot of squabbling going on. He announced that we would have a final meeting on November 27 in the White House Situation Room to resolve the matter.

I spent the morning of November 27 nearly overcome by the sense of responsibility that the future of American policy on Jerusalem was on my shoulders. I would have appreciated one of the murder boards that helped me through my Senate confirmation hearing, but I was essentially on my own. The meeting wasn't until three p.m. so I had plenty of time to run through my head all the land mines that might arise. I felt well prepared.

To my surprise, I saw that all the Israeli headlines that day led with a story that I had bowed out from attending a memorial service in Gush Etzion for Ezra Schwartz, a Sharon, Massachusetts, teenager who was murdered there a year ago by a Palestinian terrorist. The articles all claimed that I had gotten cold feet about visiting Judea and Samaria and that I was more talk than action. Had I been in Israel I most certainly would have attended. But, unbeknownst to the press, I was in Washington, DC, fighting for the recognition of Jerusalem. One of my many encounters with fake news.

We gathered in the Situation Room precisely at three p.m. At the head of the table sat the president, and the table included Vice

President Pence, Secretary of State Tillerson, Defense Secretary Mattis, National Security Advisor McMaster, Chief of Staff Kelly, and me. On the video screen was UN Ambassador Nikki Haley—Rex had objected to her attending in person.

The president opened the meeting. "Let's get Jerusalem resolved now. I want to hear the objections one at a time, and David will respond after each one. Rex, why don't you start?"

He opened a loose-leaf binder and began to read verbatim a prepared statement. "Jerusalem, since its capture by Israel in 1996, has been viewed as a *corpus separatum*—a separate body, by the United States because of its sensitivity within the Middle East and the competing claims. The United States has never taken a side on Jerusalem."

"David," the president said, "how do you respond?"

I was stunned that Tillerson's staff had given him a talking point that contained such a glaring mistake. I quietly thanked God for the opening. "Mr. Secretary, I will concede that you know 99 percent of the world better than me, but not this part of the world. Do you really want to have a debate? You're just reading from prepared text, which, by the way, is wrong. Jerusalem was captured in 1967, not 1996, and the United States passed a law in 1995 by an overwhelming bipartisan majority deeming Jerusalem the undivided capital of Israel. How much deeper do you want to go into this?"

Tillerson looked me in the eye, slammed his loose-leaf closed, and slowly said in a great Texas drawl, "I've said my piece."

Mattis then chimed in that he'd been to Israel many times and almost never went to Jerusalem. He said the defense establishment was in Tel Aviv and most of his counterparts were based there.

"What about that, David?" the president asked.

"General Mattis," I asked, "why isn't the capital of the United States in Virginia?"

"I don't understand your question?"

"Well," I continued, "if you are right and the seat of government is where the military is based, then America's capital should be in Virginia where the Pentagon is located. Alternatively, if a capital is where the legislature, the Supreme Court, and the chief executive reside, then Israel's capital is in Jerusalem just like ours is in Washington, DC."

"That's a fair point," Mattis replied.

We continued to discuss the issue with Pence and Haley, noting how they favored the recognition of Jerusalem. Seeking to conclude, the president asked me to sum up with the single best reason to go forward.

"Mr. President, the world is watching. What they are watching for is whether you are truly the courageous leader you claim to be, or just another politician who gets cold feet and breaks a promise. The choice here couldn't be more stark: stand with an ally and fulfill the will of the American people, or cower in fear to rogue actors and Islamic terrorists. How you decide this issue will reverberate in Iran, North Korea, and anywhere else that America is challenged, and your message of peace through strength is all on the line, right here."

No one responded. There were a few seconds of awkward silence and the president said, "Of course that's right. Let's do it." He left the room.

The rest of us stayed behind and Rex, seemingly exasperated, lamented, "How am I going to keep my embassies safe all around the region?"

General Mattis, to his great credit, said the following: "Mr. Secretary, I don't agree with the president's decision, but it's been made and we need to execute on that policy. We know exactly how to protect our embassies and our people abroad. No one will be at risk."

I left the Situation Room feeling like I had won a round, an important round but just a round. I knew there would be multiple attempts by others to have a private audience with the president and change his mind.

I stayed in town three more days working on the announcement with countless officials in communications, diplomacy, and security. I wrote a first draft of the announcement and worked on edits. I checked in with General Kelly twice a day to make sure we were on track. On November 30, with a likely announcement just after the weekend, I told Kelly I was returning to Israel.

He asked me why. He assumed I would want to stand next to the president during the announcement. I told him, "General, I don't expect any violence. But if there is any, God forbid, I need to be there on the ground, not hiding in DC."

He understood.

The news that a possible Jerusalem announcement was imminent had started to leak out. The president was starting to get calls from leaders around the world begging him not to recognize Jerusalem. Thankfully, after a few he got tired of hearing the same thing and stopped taking them. On December 1, Senator Dianne Feinstein wrote a letter to the president, telling him several times that recognition would "spark violence." The tone of many other pundits and leaders was apocalyptic and gloomy. That same day, *Haaretz*, the Far Left Israeli news site, ran an opinion headline by the head of Peace Now that read: DAVID FRIEDMAN IS UNFIT TO BE AMBASSADOR TO ISRAEL. FIRE HIM. John Kerry had already predicted "an absolute explosion" if the plan went forward. CNN said it "was expected to roil the region" and ABC consulted experts who opined that the move "could be dangerous." Vox damned the historic announcement as "an explosive move that will break from 50 years of US foreign policy, potentially derail US hopes of restarting the Israeli-Palestinian peace process, and threaten to spark violence across the region."

Before I returned to Israel, I sat with Mike Pence. "Mr. Vice President," I said, "I'm going back to Israel and I fear that once I leave, the efforts will intensify to stop the recognition. You outrank every one of these critics and they're all wrong. Promise me you'll hold the line and bring this home."

He shook my hand and thanked me with a look of determination that assuaged my fears. I learned that he was resolute in the last couple of days in keeping the opposition at bay. Jared or Jason kept me informed of various attempts to get the president to reconsider and then called back with relief that Pence had held the line.

I got back on December 1, 2017, only to learn that the announcement was delayed until December 6. Those were the most tension-filled five days of my life. We kept working the speech and checking signals on all fronts.

We remained a go although the resistance hadn't let up.

ON DECEMBER 5, TAMMY AND I HOSTED THEN FLORIDA GOVERNOR Rick Scott. I shared with him and his security detail the fact that the president likely would be recognizing Jerusalem the next day. An hour later, Governor Scott told me that, for security reasons, he was being advised to leave before the announcement. I said to him, "Rick, you have the opportunity to be the only American governor on the ground in Jerusalem when this historic announcement is made. Don't give that up. Stay and celebrate—you will be completely safe."

He took my advice and I believe he is grateful to this day.

On the evening of December 6, 2017, I was sitting in my home office in Herzliya with the TV on and making the final edits to the president's speech. I sat there with Tammy, my chief of staff, Aryeh Lightstone, and his wife, Estee, and my daughter Talia. At about seven p.m., noon in Washington, I watched as President Trump recognized Jerusalem as the capital of Israel.

The small room broke into applause. Tammy, Estee, Talia, and perhaps even Aryeh were crying as the TV showed American and Israeli flags projected onto the walls of Jerusalem's Old City.

I was stone-cold serious, relieved that we had come this far but knowing that there was still much more to do. I felt very privileged to perform what I believed was God's will and I silently said a prayer that there would be no violence. Thank God, there was little, and nothing like the apocalypse foretold by the left-wing press.

9

HOW TO BUILD AN EMBASSY IN THREE MONTHS FOR HALF A MILLION BUCKS

The first step had been taken, but now came the actual physical move of the embassy, a process that was complicated by further State Department obstruction, complaints from Democrats, and shoddy journalism. Rex Tillerson was smarting from his defeat in the Situation Room but still clever and powerful enough to frustrate further advancement, including the move of the embassy. The reaction to the president's recognition of Jerusalem was overwhelmingly positive and virtually free of backlash. But to many Americans, it was the move of the embassy that really counted. After all, the watershed law was called the Jerusalem Embassy Act, not the Jerusalem Recognition Act.

Although the president spoke clearly, in his December 6 announcement, that he was directing the move of the embassy, he gave no time line. Rex saw that as an opportunity to deep-six the project in bureaucratic purgatory. He issued a memo shortly after the announcement that he wanted a full study done on the embassy move, including environmental, security, functionality, and aesthetic assessments at all potential locations with hundreds of related byzantine requirements. The undeniable, albeit unspoken, message was that the embassy was not leaving Tel Aviv for at least ten years, if that soon. The press team at State reinforced this message at every opportunity.

And that wasn't the only thing that the State Department did to slow me down.

Shortly after the president's recognition of Jerusalem, I messaged back to Washington that it now was appropriate for the State Department to permit American citizens born in Jerusalem to have their place of birth designated on their passports as "Israel." Prior to the announcement and for the prior seventy years, US citizens born in Jerusalem could only have their birthplace designated as Jerusalem—they literally were not acknowledged to have any nation of birth!

I was assured by the NSC that this issue was under review yet again and that I would receive a draft of a memo from State proposing a resolution of the issue, on which I was free to comment. It never happened. Some weeks later the State Department announced that there would be no change to the "place of birth" designation notwithstanding the Jerusalem recognition. It took me by surprise and I was furious. The reasoning behind the decision was completely spurious. Because the United States did not recognize the specific boundaries of Jerusalem (not something we do with regard to any other city), the State Department contended that one could not determine precisely whether an American was born in Israel or not. That's precisely why, under my proposal that State refused to even consider, Americans could opt out of the "Israel" designation in favor of just "Jerusalem." But to deprive *every* American born in Jerusalem from being recognized as being born in Israel just perpetuated the insult that the president had corrected—it suggested that Jerusalem was not a part of Israel. This slight was picked up by many of the president's supporters and it detracted from the goodwill created by the Jerusalem recognition.

State was completely locked in on this view, not because it was correct but because this was an opportunity to regain control over US policy toward Israel, an issue on which many diplomats considered it their right to override the president. It took me another three years to fix this. It wasn't until October 2020 that the State Department finally allowed Americans born in Jerusalem to have a nation of birth—Israel.

I thus had plenty of reasons to suspect that even if I was lucky enough to serve two terms, given the current State Department orientation, I would never serve a day in the United States embassy in Jerusalem.

I began to canvass the local options with some trusted embassy colleagues in Tel Aviv. Given the security requirements and other bureaucratic hurdles, the only way we could open an embassy in Jerusalem within a year or two was if we retrofitted an existing American diplomatic facility. In Jerusalem, the only two eligible buildings both belonged to the Jerusalem consulate, one on Agron Street in the center of town, which housed the consul general's residence and the diplomatic offices, and one in a suburb called Arnona, which housed a modern consular facility that issued passports to Americans and visas to those seeking to visit the United States.

I went on several unannounced tours of the Arnona facility and realized that the embassy could take it over and be in business in Jerusalem immediately by continuing its consular functions. This would not impair the functioning of the consulate—it could continue to engage in its diplomatic activity on Agron Street as the de facto mission to the Palestinians. But instead of the consulate issuing visas and passports, that role would be transferred to the embassy, one of its traditional functions. All I needed was about $150,000 at Arnona to build some extra office space for me and a few staff and replace some plaques. I liked the idea but realized that if word got out, the State Department would shut down this idea before it even received a fair hearing. So I kept working on this under a "close hold," as they say in government.

In January 2018, Vice President Pence visited Jerusalem and delivered a powerful speech at the Knesset, Israel's parliament, in which he spoke about the story of Israel being the story that motivated and inspired the founding of America. I met with him at the King David Hotel to go over the details of his speech and he was most interested in what he could say about when the embassy in Jerusalem would open. I told him that I hoped we'd open within the year, although the State Department would not support that. He told me he would check with the president. I said to him that as long as he was having the discussion, could he request that the president put me in charge of the embassy opening. Otherwise, I feared it would never get done.

After his speech at the Knesset, I accompanied the vice president to Yad Vashem, Israel's memorial to the Holocaust. Joining us on the tour were Prime Minister Netanyahu and Rabbi Yisrael Meir Lau, the former chief rabbi of Israel, who survived the Buchenwald concentration camp as a young boy under the protection of his older brother. Rabbi Lau is a prolific author and a brilliant spiritual leader. He is widely adored in Israel and considered something of a national treasure.

At one point along the tour, we arrived at a picture of about two hundred young boys and girls, all emaciated concentration camp survivors, flanked by American soldiers in uniform who came to their rescue. It was difficult to make out the face of any one child, there were so many in the picture. Nonetheless, the prime minister pointed to a single dot on the canvas and asked Rabbi Lau to tell the vice president who that was. Rabbi Lau responded that it was him. The prime minister then asked Rabbi Lau how many descendants he had. He replied that the number was in almost constant flux but it was well over one hundred.

Prime Minister Netanyahu then looked at Vice President Pence and said, "Never underestimate the importance of saving even a single life."

I'd been to Yad Vashem many times before, including as the ambassador. But I will never forget that moment. It left both Pence and me wiping away the tears from our eyes.

I accompanied the vice president to the airport upon his departure. We stood on the tarmac in the cold January rain and he shook my hand, looked me in the eye, and said, "Thank you for everything. I spoke again to the president. You are in charge of moving the embassy." With that he ascended the stairs to his plane.

I didn't have the time or the composure to follow up with Pence about what it meant to be "in charge." Does that mean I should convene an interagency process, or does it mean I can act unilaterally or something in between? I decided not to dwell on the procedures I might have to observe in the future. Rather, I began to drill down on whether opening an embassy in Arnona—the only option that seemed feasible within a reasonable amount of time—was really possible.

To do this, I needed to greatly expand my circle of trust. I had no doubt that word of my inquiries would make its way back to the State Department. But I simply couldn't be "in charge" of this process without fully understanding what was involved.

I arranged conferences with foreign service officers who were experts in security, logistics, real estate, land use, management, and law. I posed the same scenario to each—repositioning the Arnona campus of the Jerusalem consulate as the Jerusalem embassy. After countless conversations, in many cases subject to repeat follow-up calls, by early February 2018 I was satisfied that the Arnona option was feasible and the optimal means of moving the embassy in the near term.

I then arranged a call with the president. With Kelly as chief of staff, this was far more complicated than it had been under Priebus.

I cleared the subject matter with Kelly, including exactly what I was proposing, and the call was placed. I opened as follows:

"Mr. President, I need to know when you would like to move the embassy? I assume as soon as possible, but I wanted to confirm."

"David," he answered, "I would do it tomorrow but Rex says it will take many years with the land acquisition, zoning, design, security protocols, etc. He thinks it will take at least ten years and cost a billion dollars."

"Mr. President, I can open an embassy in three months for $150,000. We already have a great site. It meets all the security requirements and it is already performing some embassy functions. I just need some money to build a few offices and some new plaques. I suspect that State will insist that more money be spent down the line, but after going through this with my staff, I really don't think that more than $150,000 is needed to support the opening."

"David, that's incredible. When do you want to open it?"

"I would recommend May 14, 2018. It happens to be the seventieth anniversary of Israel's independence."

"That sounds great. Listen, spend up to $500,000. Let's make it really nice."

"Mr. President, will you let Rex know that I am moving ahead in this manner?"

"David, just let him know yourself. Send an email to anyone you think necessary—you have my authorization."

I hung up the phone and took a deep breath. We were on the verge of a truly historical and wonderful development. While I did not relish sending an email that undoubtedly would ruffle some feathers, I was not going to shy away from the authority I had been given.

On February 9, 2018, I sent the following email to David Satterfield and Joan Polaschik, who led Near Eastern Affairs at the State Department, along with William Todd, who was in charge of State

Department Management, and Donald Blome, who was the consul general in Jerusalem, copying Kelly, McMaster, Kushner, and Pence's chief of staff:

> I just spoke at some length with the President and he has directed me to oversee the opening of the Jerusalem Embassy . . . with a ribbon-cutting ceremony on May 14, 2018. Can you please . . . make sure that we are keeping to the President's directive?

I sensed some significant dislocation in Foggy Bottom when the email was received, but no one confronted me directly with any opposition. Two weeks later, to much fanfare, we announced that the Jerusalem embassy would open on May 14, 2018, in Arnona.

I put more than two hundred members of my staff to work in plowing through the legalities, constructing the additional office space, and planning the ceremony. It was a huge amount to do in less than three months and we devoted almost all of our time to this task. Among the staff, there was a palpable sense that they were involved in something truly historic and that feeling motivated everyone to work tirelessly and brilliantly. I couldn't help but notice the dedication and loyalty that were displayed by the team, in stark contrast to the early days when I was considered a passing curiosity.

Getting a construction crew to do the work wasn't easy. The State Department had rigorous eligibility requirements for construction of embassies including that the construction company must have performed a certain minimum amount of work for the State Department in the past. The only eligible company in the region that could meet our deadline was of Turkish origin. I watched as a Turkish crew worked every day on the job, and I fervently hoped that the Turkish president, Recep Tayyip Erdoğan, would never learn of their involvement and call them back. Erdoğan was a vocal critic of the embassy move. Fortunately, this never hit his desk, and to this day I remain surprised that the left-wing Israeli media, who would have loved to drop a wrench in this process, missed the story, notwithstanding the fact that all signs at the construction site included warnings written in Turkish.

When it came to the embassy plaque, President Trump initially had suggested to me that it be in dark bronze with gold letters. I told him no, that's the wrong look for Jerusalem. I recommended that we carve the words and the seal on a slab of Jerusalem stone with perhaps some gold accents on the lettering. He liked the idea very much.

I drafted the text for the plaque. The top lines, which read UNITED STATES EMBASSY, JERUSALEM, ISRAEL, created a great deal of heartburn back at Foggy Bottom. The staff at NEA—Near Eastern Affairs—felt strongly that because the president had not determined the "final boundaries" of Jerusalem, we could not be certain that the embassy was in Israel and hence the plaque should not read "Israel."

I blew my stack in conversations with mid-level bureaucrats who offered us nothing but resistance. "Are you telling me that the president has moved our embassy in Israel to a location that may not be in Israel? Is that what you are saying?" I got so fed up that after an hour of this insanity I told them, "The guy making the plaque is including 'Israel' in the text; he works for me and no one here will tell you who he is. So I guess you are just out of luck."

When I calmed down, my chief of staff, Aryeh Lightstone, correctly suggested that this issue was too important to be resolved on the basis of who knew the plaque maker. I agreed and proceeded to clear the text with the president, the vice president, and the national security advisor—by this time, John Bolton. I spoke with each of them and made the obvious point that our embassy to Israel must be in Israel. There was no pushback.

I looked around at other embassy openings to see whose names appeared on the dedication plaque. In almost all cases, the plaque named the president, the secretary of state, and the ambassador. At the time I was designing the plaque, Secretary Tillerson had been relieved and Pompeo was not yet confirmed. So instead of naming the secretary, I included Vice President Pence. His staff later told me how moved he was to be on the plaque and that it was his greatest honor in office.

I had a few extra embassy plaques fabricated and paid for them myself. I sent one to the president, who enjoyed it very much and kept it in the Oval Office leaning on a table against the wall. One day, Larry Kudlow, the president's economic adviser, wasn't paying attention as he entered the Oval and knocked into the plaque. It teetered back and forth and then fell to the floor, breaking into pieces. The president wasn't happy. In short order, Jared was calling me to order another plaque. This was becoming an expensive proposition. Nonetheless, I sent the president a replacement with a note that if Moses had broken the first set of the Ten Commandments and then replaced them, we should do no less with the embassy plaque.

The embassy's opening ceremony was a very big deal. Our team did an incredible job creating seating for eight hundred guests, spectacular staging, and a means to broadcast the event live around the world. I emceed the event and designed the program: speeches by American and Israeli leaders as well as Jewish and Christian clergy, followed by an uplifting musical interlude by an incredible singer whose parents had escaped from Ethiopia and been smuggled into Israel through the Sudan, followed by the unveiling of the embassy plaque by Steven Mnuchin and Ivanka Trump. The ceremony was breathtaking and viewed live by hundreds of millions of people.

Jared Kushner, in keeping with his general preference for working behind the scenes, initially was reluctant to speak at the opening. I wouldn't hear of it. Jared had enormous influence with his father-in-law on many issues, including the Middle East. Jared's support for the embassy opening was essential to its success. Jared said something in his speech that sounded good at the time but proved prescient in the years to come: "When there is peace in this region, we will look back upon this day and remember that the journey to peace started with a strong America recognizing the truth."

Amen.

While there were many moving pieces at the embassy dedication ceremony, the one that worried me the most was the unveiling of the plaque. That task was assigned to the leader of the US delegation, Treasury Secretary Steven Mnuchin. During the rehearsal the day before, I tugged and tugged on the canvas that covered the plaque, but it would not release. I imagined this fiasco happening in real time and all the pundits cackling that perhaps opening an embassy in Jerusalem was not meant to be. To avoid this potential catastrophe, I put two guys on the roof of the embassy from which the canvas was hung to make sure we would have a clean unveiling. Thank God, we did.

I wish I could say the opening went off without a hitch, but it didn't. As expected, there was no violence in Jerusalem—just one small peaceful rally attended primarily by Jews. Nor was there violence in any other place in the world, except for one: Gaza. For several weeks, Hamas militants had been protesting and terrorizing at the border between Gaza and Israel. Their primary beef was not with Israel but with the Palestinian Authority, which had cut off their financial assistance. They had been sending kites rigged with explosives and firing rockets toward Israeli civilian neighborhoods, doing great damage to property and psychological damage to people who had to constantly run into shelters. The mob was active and ready for violence on almost any given day and easy enough for Hamas to incite.

On May 14, 2018, as we opened the embassy, Hamas sent the mob off into full battle, burning tires, throwing explosives, and rushing the border, hoping to infiltrate and murder Israelis. Approximately sixty Gazans were killed that day, more than fifty of whom were Hamas members. A Hamas official openly acknowledged this fact in an interview with the Palestinian news outlet Baladna TV.

It was unavoidable and it might have happened even without the embassy opening, but it was a bad look having the split-screen TV coverage of the embassy opening and Gaza burning, even though the two were separated in distance by more than sixty miles. Many in the press criticized Israel for killing terrorists rushing its border. The criticism diminished fairly quickly, however, as no one succeeded in identifying a less lethal means for Israel to defend itself.

A second hitch involved complaints from Democrats that they weren't invited to attend the opening ceremony. I read in several papers that six members of Congress—Eliot Engel, Ted Deutch, Brad Sherman, Brad Schneider, Albio Sires, and Tom Suozzi—wrote me a letter demanding to know why ten Republican House members and four Republican senators attended, while no Democrats were present.

While they leaked the letter to the press, I never received it.

I called Ted Deutch directly. I had met him previously and was convinced that he was a strong supporter of Israel. But I saw this letter as a political stunt. "You are messing with the wrong guy," I said. "This is complete bullshit. I invited many Democrats and I even have responses from some. One couldn't come because he had a wedding, another had his daughter's graduation. The Republican congressmen came on a government aircraft which was available to Democrats as well. You want to start this fight, go right ahead. But I will finish it."

Ted responded that he was not made aware of the plane and more could have been done to create a more bipartisan environment.

I was having none of it. "Here's why Democrats didn't come: As speaker after speaker at the ceremony thanked Donald Trump, he was going to get a thunderous ovation. Democrats in attendance could either be filmed joining in and appearing not to sufficiently hate Trump for their base, or sitting on their hands and looking ridiculous. That's why you didn't come, and that's why your colleagues didn't come. Your plea for bipartisanship is complete BS and if I hear one more word about not being invited, I'm going to defend myself and you and your friends will come off very poorly."

That was the end of that.

One more hitch. While my experience with the press until that point had been mixed, I learned the day before the embassy opening just how venal some reporters could be. To my shock, I saw a headline falsely proclaiming that I was a supporter of Jewish terrorists. It was by a reporter I had never met (some guy named Ron Kampeas) who confused the name of an organization I supported with a similar-sounding but entirely different far-right group. He never checked with me, never called the embassy, and just vomited out a false headline at the worst possible time. And it was spread by all those seeking to detract from the embassy opening. I didn't have time to deal with this defamatory and reckless story, but fortunately my staff had all the facts at their disposal and handled it. The article was corrected, but, much to my disappointment, the reporter never even apologized, even when proven completely wrong.

All these challenges aside, on May 14, 2018—the 364th day since I arrived at my post—the United States embassy in Jerusalem finally was open and operating. General Kelly wrote me that day from DC to say, "This Irish Catholic was so proud, long live Israel!"

From that day forward, whenever and wherever the president spoke at a rally, he regaled his audience with how he opened the Jerusalem embassy far ahead of time and way under budget, bestowing accolades upon me that got better and more flattering with each succeeding version.

It gave me enormous gratification that even among crowds with few if any Jews in attendance, the move of the embassy was always the president's loudest applause line.

SEVERAL MONTHS LATER I WAS LEAVING MY OFFICE WHEN I SAW A tour bus parked alongside the road. About fifty people were gathered around the embassy plaque, taking pictures. I got out of the car and walked up to the group to say hello, whereupon one of the tourists informed me that there was a line.

"I'm not looking to cut the line, I just thought I'd say hello. You seem to like this plaque. Well, so do I."

Someone asked me what connection I had to the embassy. "Well," I said, pointing to the names engraved on the stone, "I'm not Donald Trump and I'm not Mike Pence, but I am David Friedman."

The crowd, an Evangelical Christian group from north Florida, burst into Hallelujahs. I took a picture with each visitor and I marveled at the joy they shared in visiting the embassy.

Sometime later I shared this story with a reporter from National Public Radio. He reported that we had created a "shrine" in Jerusalem for the first time in over a thousand years! It sure felt that way.

About a year later, Rick Perry, the former governor of Texas and the secretary of energy, came to visit the embassy. Taking a look at the plaque, he said he couldn't think of anything more meaningful in public service than having one's name on the Jerusalem embassy. I had to agree.

I felt truly blessed and humbled that God had chosen me for this place and time.

10

COUNTERING FALSE NARRATIVES

With the United States embassy to Israel standing proudly in Jerusa-lem, I thought momentarily that a short respite from all the politics might be in order. I was wrong. I had created far too much of an up-heaval in State Department orthodoxy for the move of the embassy to stand without a response. Because the move itself was very popular among American citizens, the attack shifted to me personally.

There were two controversial aspects of the embassy move—the violence in Gaza and the absence of Democrats in attendance. The opposition saw both as an opportunity to at least vilify the messenger if not the message.

I was bombarded with press inquiries about how I could celebrate an event that included the death—some said the murder—of sixty Palestinians. I responded primarily with two points: first, that the responsibility lay with Hamas, which cynically sent impressionable youth to rush the border with battle cries about killing Jews, and sec-ond, that Israel had responded with legitimate means of self-defense.

"But sixty people died," responded many reporters.

"I know. That's terrible," I responded. "What should Israel have done differently? Those who were killed overwhelmingly were Hamas terrorists. If anyone got through, it would have led to many civilian deaths."

"But sixty people died," they responded again.

"Again, how could Israel have defended itself in a less lethal manner?"

"Israel could have used water cannons."

"Aha," I responded. "Water cannons. What do you know about water cannons?"

"They are not lethal."

"Neither is a nerf gun. But would water cannons work in this situation?"

No one had any idea. No one bothered to ask anyone in the IDF or even a military expert from another country. Had they inquired, as I did, they would have learned that water cannons would have been ineffective on the Gaza border. Apart from the problem of accessing sufficient water in the desert, by the time a terrorist was in range of a water cannon, Israel was in range of that terrorist throwing a grenade or an improvised explosive device. Israel needed to maintain a buffer on its border to protect its citizens that a water cannon could not achieve. But that was far too dry and technical a point than just lamenting the body count.

I was so outraged by the media coverage that I penned an op-ed for Fox News: LIBERAL MEDIA SIDES WITH HAMAS OVER TRUMP. While the death toll in Gaza was absolutely an appropriate subject for serious inquiry and review, something the Israel Defense Forces already had begun, the media's reflexive alignment with misogynistic, homophobic, and anti-Semitic terrorists just to fuel their hatred of Trump was too much for me to accept.

As the left-wing media in Israel and the United States focused obsessively on the deaths in Gaza, something they would undoubtedly have ignored had those deaths occurred on any day other than the day we opened the embassy, I was invited to address a conference sponsored by the Media Line, a local news service, on the state of media in Israel. It was a great opportunity for me to get a few things off my chest. The conference definitely got more than they bargained for.

As I addressed the crowd, I lectured on the importance of a free press and an accurate press. I chastised them for the willingness of every news service to republish the reporting of a different service, even if the plagiarizing news agency made no effort to investigate or validate the facts. This amplification was exactly the path to the "big lie" that responsible media should be particularly careful to avoid. I reminded them how so many of them had amplified a story accusing me of funding terrorists, which had dropped right before the embassy opened. How many of them considered before running with the story whether it was true or, if it wasn't, whether it was appropriate to drop a bombshell like that at such a time? I asked them why they felt no need to apologize to me when they realized the story was false.

I shared with the audience a conversation I once had with the *Times of Israel* editor, David Horovitz. I had called him to offer my criticism of an article that I had shown him to be demonstrably wrong. His response, not unique to his publication, was, "We are always balancing the competing goals of getting it right and getting it fast." I then said to the crowd, "Imagine any other profession whose consumers would tolerate shoddy work performed in the interest of speed. Imagine a surgeon who says, 'I only have the operating room for forty minutes, so I'll do as well as I can in the allotted time.' No one but the press operates under this 'balance' and it is wrong. Get it right. Period. If you don't, you will present a great risk to democracy."

Then I turned to Gaza. "How many of you," I asked, "conducted a serious inquiry into how to contest an armed angry mob rushing the southern border?"

I knew the answer. "Not one of you," I castigated, "has suggested any less lethal means for Israel to defend its citizens." Then I concluded with a line that would be repeated many times since: I admonished them to do some serious work and "keep your mouths shut until you figure it out."

With this intemperate language, for which I have no regrets, I gave a platform to some on the left to continue their demagoguery. Not surprisingly, the charge was led by Cory Booker, who saw an opportunity to accuse us of stifling a free press. Referring to my "keep your mouths shut" comment, he made this statement to Secretary Pompeo in writing at the conclusion of a Foreign Relations Committee hearing: "More than a degradation of the free press by a sitting US ambassador, Ambassador Friedman's egregious attack dangerously echoes efforts to discredit and intimidate the press in the United States, Israel and around the world."

I doubt that Booker saw more than the offending words. I can't imagine he understood the issue of the faulty reporting I was criticizing. Someone in the State Department undoubtedly saw this as an easy attempt to placate the left by piling on a right-wing ambassador, and he was only too happy to oblige. Morgan Ortagus, the State Department spokesperson who did an excellent job advancing my efforts, explained the context of the comment and that ended the inquiry.

But the press perceived other vulnerabilities that they thought worth exploiting. I did a long interview with *The Times of Israel*, a center-left website, about a host of issues. They were particularly interested in the now-debunked theory that Democrats were not invited to the embassy opening. I explained, again, that Democrats were more than welcome. We talked about the challenges to bipartisan support for Israel. I referred the reporters to a recent Pew Research poll that Americans identifying as Republican were overwhelmingly more likely to support Israel than those identifying as Democrats. I was not making the case that the Republican Party's policies are more pro-Israel than the Democrat policies, just that the poll results reflected a very disparate view among the constituencies.

The headline of the article read, AMBASSADOR DAVID FRIEDMAN: REPUBLICANS SUPPORT ISRAEL MORE THAN DEMOCRATS. That put the "pro-Israel Democrats" on the defensive even more than usual. Many accused me of stoking the flames of conflict and destroying bipartisanship. I didn't buy it. Again, I was talking about poll numbers, not policies. And, in any event, while bipartisanship is important, it is not worth the price of sinking to the lowest common point of consensus. I'm not aware of any other issue in which either party suggests that the other should abandon heartfelt principles solely to achieve agreement. The reality is that when *The New York Times* asked Republicans and Democrats to list America's allies in order of importance, the Republicans had Israel at 5 and the Democrats at 28. Many Democrats claiming to be pro-Israel prefer to ignore this data, but it's not going away.

As the embassy news began to fade, including the Gaza violence and the Democrats' claims of not being invited, other efforts were made to undercut my influence, which plainly had grown too large for many in government to accept. A particularly offensive effort was reflected in a headline in *Politico*: TRUMP AMBASSADOR BLOCKS SCRUTINY OF ISRAEL. The subtitle added that I "resisted an effort to apply stricter human rights tests to US military aid to the country."

This was a dishonest hit piece unscrupulously leaked by someone at State. The issue related to what's referred to as the Leahy Law, a law that prohibits the United States from funding foreign military operations in which the applicable military unit engages in gross violations of human rights, unless the military has an effective system in place for bringing such violators to justice. The United States vets Israel and many other nations that receive military aid to confirm that each relevant nation complies with the law.

There was a growing feeling at this time among Congress and some State officials that the Leahy Law vetting procedures were inadequate for Egypt, which had been accused of numerous human rights violations. I was not involved in revamping these procedures until someone at State, unknown to me, argued that if changes were made for Egypt, then they should be made for Israel as well. There was a complete disconnect in this reasoning: Israel's democracy, its human rights record, and its military bore almost no resemblance to Egypt's. I repeatedly pressed the State Department, without knowing who was behind this, to explain to me why Egypt's defective practices were relevant to Israel and why Israel's existing robust system of preventing, and punishing if necessary, gross violations of human rights was not adequate. Some unknown person at State obviously was looking to restrict our military support for Israel.

In the end, the folks I dealt with at State, all career foreign service officers, agreed that changes for Egypt did not require corresponding changes for Israel. We all agreed that Israel properly was subject to Leahy Law vetting and that the procedures put in place by the IDF were adequate to comply with the law. Unfortunately, some unknown malcontent in Foggy Bottom was sufficiently aggrieved by my reasoning to hand over all my emails on the subject to a reporter and mischaracterize the issues.

This went all the way to Senator Patrick Leahy, the original sponsor of the law. Shortly after the *Politico* article came out, Leahy had a chance to question Secretary Pompeo at a public hearing:

LEAHY: Have all our ambassadors been told they have to support [the Leahy Law]?

POMPEO: Yes sir, they are. It's part of their formal onboarding, training, processing.

LEAHY: One U.S. Ambassador said the law does not apply in the country where he's posted so he doesn't have to look at it if there's any violations of it, even though we spend a great deal of money to help the police and military forces in that country. Is he correct?

POMPEO: Senator, I'm not familiar with the situation. If you'll identify it for me, I will look into it. That does not sound remotely consistent with what I described to you.

LEAHY: I appreciate that, and as we leave here, I'll tell you exactly who the ambassador is.

Of course, that ambassador was me. Not once, not ever, did I say or imply that the Leahy Law did not apply to Israel, but rather that there was no reason to create special additional regulations for Israel based on the misconduct of an entirely different country. But someone within the State Department who violated federal law by leaking out sensitive communications, a reporter who stretched the truth beyond recognition, and a grandstanding senator who was only too happy to embarrass the pro-Israel community all came together to create another big lie. After a review of the record, it was clear that Leahy's accusation was flat-out false and neither State nor Congress took any further action on this matter.

I wish I could say that was the worst display by a member of Congress in the aftermath of the embassy move. But it wasn't.

A month later I was paid a visit by a group sponsored by J Street. Many were surprised that I met with them given the outrageous conduct they displayed in opposition to my Senate confirmation as well as their anti-Israel advocacy. But I decided, nonetheless, to give them an audience. I was optimistic that there might be some common ground with an organization that claims to be pro-Israel. There turned out to be no basis for my optimism.

J Street brought to the meeting Congresswoman Pramila Jayapal, a progressive Democrat from the state of Washington who was making her first visit to Israel. Jeremy Ben-Ami, J Street's president, introduced Jayapal and invited her to speak.

"Mr. Ambassador," she began. "This is my first visit to Israel and it's an incredible country. I just visited Yad Vashem, so I certainly have a good sense of the tragedies that have befallen the Jewish People. But I also just visited Khan al-Ahmar, and I must say that there Israel is committing a war crime."

The conditions in Khan al Ahmar are the object of misguided activism within Western Europe and progressive America. If you drive down from Jerusalem to the Dead Sea on Highway 1, you see the "village" on the right alongside the road—a scattering of tents and tin-roof huts with an occasional camel or motorcycle interrupting the desert landscape. Khan al-Ahmar is inhabited today by about 150 Bedouins, a significant increase from the past before left-wing NGOs made it a cause célèbre.

It is illegal and unsafe housing, pure and simple. But Israel's government has been attempting to change that for years. Israel and the Bedouin community have been in litigation for more than a decade about the village's future. The Israeli Supreme Court has made numerous rulings that the community is illegal but has delayed its demolition order to encourage a consensual resolution. Israel constructed a completely new community for the Bedouins with concrete housing that even included a new school building. But the Bedouins refused it. The court's demolition order remains in effect although Israel has yet to enforce it.

This was one of the most cynical manipulations of innocent civilians that I had seen by the Far Left.

The Bedouins in Khan al-Ahmar were bit players in the Israeli-Palestinian conflict, interested primarily in maintaining their nomadic lifestyle. Had no one intervened, they probably would have moved voluntarily and set up camp a mile or so down the road or accepted Israel's generous offer. But millions of dollars poured in from the Left to fund attorneys and public relations specialists.

I turned to Congresswoman Jayapal and began, "If, after visiting Yad Vashem, you consider Khan al-Ahmar a war crime, then you didn't pay sufficient attention at Yad Vashem.

"In your vast study of the Holocaust, did you happen to notice whether Hitler gave the Jewish people ten years to litigate their rights to remain in their homes? And was there a judicial system in Nazi Germany that bent over backward to find a means for Jews to live safely and with dignity? And did Hitler claim the Jews had violated the zoning laws or did he claim they were a subhuman plague that required eradication? And did you notice whether Hitler built for the Jews alternative housing which was of a far superior standard than what they had?

"Congresswoman," I continued, "this is your first trip to Israel. It is a very complicated place. I must have come here close to one hundred times before my appointment and each time I came, I learned something. One trip curated by J Street does not make you an expert and my advice to you is to practice a bit of humility."

I went on. "You may be right that there is a better way to resolve the Khan al-Ahmar dispute, although none has been presented, and I would be happy to have that discussion. But accusing Israel of committing a war crime tells me you know nothing about Israel and nothing about war crimes." I turned to J Street's leader and then back to the congresswoman: "You have been ill served by your tour guides." And I walked out.

I left that meeting with deep concern that a false narrative was gathering steam in Washington. Jayapal was very popular among the progressives. She was smart and shrewd and politically astute. She obviously had concluded that there were enough anti-Israel voters out here for her to try to own that space. And in J Street, she had a willing accomplice.

More than anyone else, Congresswoman Pramila Jayapal convinced me that we needed to advance the pro-Israel agenda with all dispatch while the White House was in Republican hands.

BUT NOT ALL OF THE INCOMING POLITICAL MISCHIEF CAME FROM America. Mahmoud Abbas, the president of the Palestinian Authority who was now in office more than twelve years beyond the term for which he was elected—or as we say, in the sixteenth year of a four-year term—had begun attacking me and my colleagues since the president's recognition of Jerusalem. He had extended his wishes that Trump's "house be destroyed," threatened to throw a shoe at Nikki Haley, and called me a "son of a dog." Asked by a reporter what I thought of my new nickname, I said that as we approach the holiday of Passover, dogs are held in high regard because they did not bark and wake up the Egyptians when the Jews were escaping Egypt. So I assumed it was intended as a compliment.

Now, in the post-embassy environment, Abbas ramped up the attacks. It began with the murder of Yotam Ovadia in July 2018 in the town of Adam, perhaps the most liberal community in all of Judea and Samaria. The killer was a Palestinian man whose wife had left him with five children. By all accounts, he was suicidal. But there are different ways to take one's life—this terrorist chose the most profitable. He was killed in the act of murdering Mr. Ovadia. In this manner, his children were guaranteed a stipend in perpetuity from the Palestinian Authority.

I visited the Ovadia family during shiva and called out the barbarism of the PA's "pay for slay" program. The PA never condemned the murder or expressed any sympathy for the victim, instead condemning me for the visit into "Palestinian territory." Then, they ramped up the anger another notch: Several ceremonies were held in Ramallah burning my picture. In response, I was given one of the largest security details of any ambassador in the world. In Israel, only Netanyahu had more personal protection than I did.

In addition to resistance from American liberals and Palestinians, I also took some heat as a result of unforced errors by my own staff. Following a visit to an excellent "special needs" educational center in the Jewish ultra-Orthodox city of Bnei Brak, one of the sponsors handed me a large framed picture of Jerusalem and we stood for a photo. Five minutes later, I got a call in my car from one of my staff.

"Ambassador, what have you done?"

"I don't know. What have I done?"

"You took a picture with a rendering of Jerusalem with Al Aqsa and the Dome of the Rock missing and the Third Temple in its place."

"Oh shit. Is that what was in the picture?"

The rules are very clear that no one gives me any gift or picture unless it's been screened by our public diplomacy team. Here, the picture was screened but the sensitivity eluded the screener. Now I was at the center of a storm that quickly was escalating. Many among the Palestinian leaders were calling for a violent uprising on Al Aqsa.

"Get me on every major news station tonight," I told my staffer. I needed to nip this in the bud.

I did the major Israeli news stations that evening and made sure that I would be picked up in all of the Arab-language press. I apologized profusely and maintained, truthfully, that I had no idea what was in the picture. I had the person who pulled this bonehead stunt informed that he would not be welcome at any other embassy events.

There is no issue more sensitive in Israel than the Al Aqsa Mosque. Going back to 1929 and the massacre of almost one hundred Jews in Hebron, perceived threats to the mosque have been the rallying cry for Muslim terror. There are legitimate discussions that are appropriate, and will be held one day, about religious freedom on the Temple Mount. But those require the utmost sensitivity and I was absolutely mortified to be an apparent supporter of such an obnoxious display.

THE POST-OPENING ENVIRONMENT IN THE SUMMER OF 2018 THUS had the usual array of challenges, amplified by those who opposed our policies, but I got through it intact, mindful of the need to keep my foot on the gas.

My chief of staff, Aryeh Lightstone, shared with me at this time a Torah passage that I found very inspiring. In the two Jewish Temples (the real ones, not the mock-up from Bnei Brak), one ascends from one level to another by stairs. But there is one exception: With the holy altar, one ascends by a ramp. What is the meaning? With stairs, wherever one stops, the surface is flat and one can remain with no effort. But with a ramp, once you stop, you start sliding back. With a ramp, if you're not going forward, you're going backward. That message resonated deeply with me.

I was on a mission that, like the altar, was holy. I needed to keep moving forward.

11

SAVING UNKNOWN LIVES

Not everything is politics or policy.

On July 13, 2018, I received an email from the National Security Council. Earlier that day President Trump was in London meeting with Prime Minister Theresa May. She made a request of the president that he convey to the government of Israel an appeal that Israel assist in rescuing a Syrian humanitarian group called the White Helmets, some of whom were facing imminent massacre by the brutal Syrian Army. Trump, I was told, then assured May that "David Friedman will handle it." In the words of the cable, "The President would like you to work with Israel to plan to stage them in Israel while we work onward movement. We have a commitment from Canada to take the bulk of them."

The White Helmets were doing incredible work in Syria assisting civilians in the face of unspeakable suffering. But they were not immune from controversy. Syria, Russia, and Turkey had all falsely accused them of being affiliated with al-Qaeda, and they were not on good terms with many of the Kurds, notwithstanding their common enmity toward Bashar al-Assad, Syria's dictator. Like so many other relationships in the Middle East, there were ambiguities about the White Helmets' allegiances, and they certainly had no fondness for Israel. But it was only Israel that could save them now.

Initially, I saw this assignment as involving a phone call or two to my friend Yoav Horowitz, Netanyahu's chief of staff. He was a former elite commando as well as a successful business executive and we worked very well together. But before I even got started, it became clear to me that we were heading in the wrong direction.

Britain's ambassador to Israel already had reached out to Israel's Ministry of Foreign Affairs. So had Canada's ambassador. Each diplomat had spoken with another diplomat who then spoke with some of my colleagues back in Washington. They discussed operations, planning, staging, and forward movements, all with no authority to commit their own governments to anything. After I received an unrealistically optimistic note from the State Department's Bureau of Near East Affairs (NEA), I responded: "Seems to me there are a lot of well-meaning folks scurrying around and perhaps over their skis. I think we need fewer people with better contacts and detailed info on the plan."

I followed up with a phone call to David Satterfield, a very experienced and talented diplomat who now was running NEA: "David, there's very little time here and this is a big ask of Israel. We are asking them to enter Syria in the middle of a war in which they want no involvement and to extract hundreds of people that may be security risks, while otherwise keeping their northern border intact. I will get this done as Trump's representative working with Bibi's guy. Any more people involved and this will fall apart." He agreed and we shut down all the other diplomats.

I was glad to have cut through the fog but now struck by the responsibility on my shoulders alone to work with Israel to save lives that were in imminent danger. This became my obsession for the next week.

On July 16, I worked through the deliverables that Israel would need in order to proceed with what was looking like an increasingly risky operation—the extraction of seven hundred White Helmets, including family members, from Syria into the Israeli Golan Heights, and their transfer into Jordan. Jordan would then hold them pending their immigration to Canada. Israel needed, among other things, the names of the people being rescued, contact information of the officials in charge in both Syria and Jordan, a commitment from Jordan that they would accept the refugees immediately, a full operating plan timed to the minute, and a commitment by all to maintain complete silence so as to avoid compromising the operation or a civilian rush to the border.

There was an additional component as well. This operation was certain to anger the Russians, with whom Israel maintained a delicate balance of power in Syria. After checking with DC and with the UK ambassador in Israel, I assured the Israelis that both America and the UK would inform the Russians, once the operation was completed, that Israel was acting at the request of those nations.

The operational issues began to center around Jordan. Jordan had been assured that its hosting of these seven hundred refugees would be very short term, just long enough to process the onboarding to Canada or another host nation. By July 18, Canada had gone soft on the magnitude of its intended absorption, which infuriated me since it was Canada's commitment that got this started. I pushed my colleagues in Washington and the UK ambassador to Israel, David Quarrey, to fill the gap. Over the eighteenth and the nineteenth, the gap was closed as the UK, France, Germany, and Sweden stepped up.

There was then a new issue with Jordan. Elements within the Jordanian government didn't want the White Helmets to suffer the "taint" of being rescued by Israel. They preferred that the rescue operation be conducted under the cover of the United Nations to minimize Israel's perceived involvement. It was a ridiculous request. In the first place, the request was practically impossible. The United Nations did not have the ability or authority to conduct this type of operation and, even if it did, it could not have met the time line. In forty-eight more hours, the White Helmets likely would be dead.

I got Henry Wooster, our chargé d'affaires (acting ambassador) to Jordan, on the phone. I was furious. "Henry, you tell those racists in Jordan that they drop this UN bullshit or my next call is to the president, who will call the king with very critical comments about his foreign ministry. Do they think the White Helmets would prefer death to the 'taint' of Israel? We don't have time for this!" By July 20, I learned that Jordan had dropped its demand.

From July 19 to 21, I barely slept as issues kept popping up, some logistical, some political, some just ridiculous. I needed to keep an even keel while at the same time making it abundantly clear that problems needed to be solved, not debated.

On July 21, the Israel Defense Forces began the rescue operation, at all times coordinating with me and my defense attaché. I was keeping the National Security Council updated and received this email from Robert Greenway, a distinguished retired senior intelligence officer and combat veteran of the United States Army Special Forces who ran the Middle East Desk:

Thank you sir, I pray this goes off without a hitch. We are all very grateful for all you've done, it would not have occurred without you and while they may never know it they are in your debt.

At about midnight, Israel crossed into Syria with an armed convoy of buses and rescued about 430 White Helmet refugees and their families. Sadly, another 300 who were identified for rescue were held in curfewed towns and could not get to the meeting point.

The videos of the rescue were stirring: young Israeli female soldiers bringing blankets and infant formula to terrified mothers and their babies; families being bused out of hell to a brighter future. I was overwhelmed and relieved that the operation was a success.

This wasn't Israel's first humanitarian effort in favor of Syrians suffering the dire conditions of their civil war. Since 2016, as part of a program known as Operation Good Neighbor, Israel has accepted Syrian children into its northern hospitals, provided treatment, and returned them to their families. Israel has also sent many tons of supplies across the border. But this was the first time Israel intervened by sending its troops across the border to avert a massacre. It was a surreal experience to be the point guy coordinating this rescue. There were far more qualified and experienced personnel to tackle this, but I was the only one who could cut through the morass by threatening the wrath of Trump. It turned out to be the most effective tool in the box.

As the news got out of the successful rescue, numerous countries took credit for the outcome. Some gave themselves too much credit but at least included Israel among those worthy of praise. Except France. It heralded its relatively minor role in the absorption of the refugees and expressed its thanks to many other nations. But not a word of thanks was offered by France to Israel, the only nation to risk its own citizens. I found that very disturbing.

Rescuing the White Helmets was not my only opportunity to save strangers from Arab extremists. There also was the incident of Issam Akel.

Akel was a Palestinian American dual citizen living in Jerusalem. He was a real estate broker. One transaction he handled was the sale of a home in the Old City of Jerusalem from an Arab to a Jew in October 2018. Under the law of the Palestinian Authority, this is a capital offense punishable by death. Late one evening, Palestinian police entered Akel's home and took him away in handcuffs as his wife and two young daughters cried hysterically.

Because Akel was an American, I learned quickly of the incident and had my staff follow up. After two weeks of pressing the PA, we received a note from the "Attorney General of the State of Palestine" explaining that Akel "is being investigated for the charge of seizing/tearing away part of the Palestinian Territories to a hostile State." I was incensed that this was even a crime, let alone one that could result in such harsh treatment. I was determined to get Akel freed.

My colleagues at the embassy who dealt with the PA urged caution. They advised that if I got involved publicly it would elevate the situation and make it politically more difficult for the Palestinian Authority to grant leniency. I certainly didn't want to make things any more difficult for Akel and his family and so I had my staff visit him and inquire of his status as often as possible.

Not surprisingly, as usual, the velvet hand didn't work with these thugs. The PA provided no assurances of releasing Akel and, on October 29, a PA court extended his detention for another fifteen days. I had a contact of mine reach out to his wife and she relayed that he was being tortured and asked whether a US embassy official could discreetly demand his release.

We had several meetings with the Palestinian leadership. My staff, many fluent in Arabic, explained to the Palestinians why it was in their interests to release their prisoner. They reported back to me that the Palestinians were sorry they arrested him and that this was more trouble than it was worth, but they needed to find a politically palatable way to end this saga. They felt there would need to be a trial first and then perhaps some form of clemency. Unfortunately, my folks couldn't advance this much further. Our consular affairs people—nice and well-intentioned—were clueless and powerless about how to exert pressure.

We watched this carefully throughout November with multiple starts and stops of the "judicial" process. By the end of the month, Akel's wife had lost hope. Her husband continued to be tortured and there was no hard commitment for his release. She asked that I increase the pressure, even at the risk of creating a political impasse. She saw no other option.

On November 28, 2018, I issued this tweet:

The Pal Authority has been holding US citizen Issam Akel for 2 months. His suspected "crime"? Selling land to a Jew. Akel's incarceration is antithetical to the values of the US & to all who advocate the cause of peaceful coexistence. We demand his immediate release.

That made some news. Headlines regarding Akel's incarceration, a subject previously not covered by the media, now ran in Reuters, Breitbart, and almost everywhere else. Senator Ted Cruz and others in Congress echoed my demand. The Palestinians were feeling the heat from abroad, but, as usual, they cared more about the heat from within. As they were struggling to find a solution, Akel continued to suffer.

Toward the end of December, we received word that the PA was going to convict Akel and then release him. I had my team begin to work on the logistics of meeting Akel and extracting him from PA-controlled territory, and then getting him and his family travel documents to leave the country. But I had no confidence that the PA would keep this commitment. Just to keep them honest, I had my staff deliver a message that if Akel was not freed in the first week of 2019, I would recommend to the president that the United States free him by any and all necessary means.

On December 31, Akel was sentenced by a Palestinian court to life in prison. While the Israeli public shuddered at this news, we were advised that this was a necessary "formality" to his release. Sure enough, two days later, Akel was released to the custody of our consular officers and brought to a safe house pending his departure to the United States.

He was in bad shape when he was released, including broken ribs and damaged eyesight from hours of bright lights beamed at his eyes. Just before he left for the United States, he came to see me with his wife and two beautiful daughters to say thank you. We spent a half hour together and I could see that he was still in severe discomfort when he moved. Nonetheless he was happy and grateful. He wrote me a note:

> Thank you very much for all your effort and dedication . . . for all of what you have done for me and my family. You raised me from down [under] earth to happiness and life.

I was deeply moved by our meeting. As with the White Helmets, my position had given me the chance to save a life. In contrast to the Syrian refugees, in this case I had the chance to experience a brief thirty minutes of gratitude and receive a kind note. But the feeling was similar: Being blessed with the opportunity to intervene in a dire circumstance to save one or more individuals held for me intense meaning the likes of which I had never before experienced.

THE LESSON HERE WAS BOTH UPLIFTING AND DISHEARTENING. THE United States can be an incredible force for good anywhere and everywhere in the world. But how many of those opportunities must have been squandered over the years because no one had the authority, the will, or the competency to act?

I could only lament how much more the US government could do in leading the world.

12

UNDIVIDING JERUSALEM

My relationship with the State Department improved dramatically when Mike Pompeo became the secretary of state. In contrast to Rex, Mike was fearless. He was also brilliant, strategic, principled, and a man of faith.

Over the summer of 2018, I made a brief visit to DC to see Jared and the president on our fledgling peace plan and stopped by with Jared to see Pompeo.

"Mike," I said, "you're killing me!"

"What?" he responded, very unsure about what I meant.

"For over a year," I went on, "Rex wanted nothing to do with me and I wasn't a big fan of his. So if I wanted to get something done, I went straight to the president. You, my friend, are different. I have too much respect for you to go around you. So I've been trying to get some buy-in from you on some big things, but you've been too busy."

He started to laugh. "David, there's a lot going on around the world. I'm really sorry to slow you down. What interests you?"

"The short answer is the Six-Day War. Notwithstanding fifty years of effort, Israel has been unable to resolve the key lingering issues and we can help. Jerusalem is mostly done, the Golan Heights is wide open for resolution, and the West Bank—or Judea and Samaria as I prefer to call it—is very complicated but subject to some really interesting work that Jared and I have been advancing that we'll talk about now."

Pompeo was very receptive to a longer discussion on all these things, but we only had a few more minutes to spend right then.

"David, what do you want to start with?"

"Mike, the president's Vision for Peace, that Jared and I will brief you on, comes first. But the viability of the Jerusalem consulate is something that can be addressed in parallel and is entirely an internal State Department issue. In a nutshell, I think the consulate is an anachronism that serves no purpose other than to divide Jerusalem, which our laws say must remain undivided. And its merger into the embassy would serve many salutary purposes. Can I get you a write-up on this for your consideration?"

He was agreeable.

The Jerusalem consulate was established in 1844 at the behest of Warder Cresson, a Christian Zionist who beseeched President John Tyler to authorize him to establish the post. Upon authorization, he made the lengthy trip by sea to Turkey and then by land to Jerusalem. Upon arrival at the Jaffa Gate to the Old City, he reportedly made the following ceremonious declaration: "I hereby extend the protection of the United States to the Jews of Jerusalem."

The consulate remained within the Ottoman Empire as a mission to a city rather than a country. In 1912, it moved to Agron Street, named after Gershon Agron, the founder of *The Palestine Post*, later renamed *The Jerusalem Post*. In 1948, the consulate found itself within the sovereign borders of the State of Israel in Western Jerusalem. The eastern part of Jerusalem was held by Jordan until 1967.

The consulate never made any sense once Israel was established. From 1948 until 2018, the United States embassy, responsible for managing the relationship between the United States and Israel, was located in Tel Aviv. But Israel's seat of government was in Jerusalem and the US ambassador would travel there often to meet with Israeli officials. Upon arrival, he would be reminded that he was beyond his area of jurisdiction—Jerusalem being a city administered by the consulate even though the consulate had absolutely no responsibility for the US-Israel relationship. And the consul general, who was appointed by the secretary of state without Senate oversight, was indifferent to the views of the ambassador.

Not surprisingly, conflicts arose often between the embassy and the consulate, whether on cables back to Washington, protocols for visits by American dignitaries, or statutory reports to Congress. The embassy would engage with the Israeli government and attempt to report the facts, while the consulate, with no official lines of communication, would promote largely anti-Israel ideology. But the State Department loved the consulate and deflected all the criticism because it gave State its own private megaphone in one of the world's most important and sensitive cities.

In 1995, the Oslo II Accords were signed and the State Department jumped on the opportunity to treat the Jerusalem consulate as the de facto diplomatic mission to the Palestinians. It was a big mistake. In the first instance, the consulate was in Western Jerusalem in a neighborhood that was almost 100 percent Jewish—designating that location a mission for Palestinians just sowed resentment and confusion. Second, the Oslo Accords did not establish a Palestinian state and the consulate's designation sent exactly the wrong message: that the United States would not require more from the Palestinians for diplomatic recognition. Finally, the seat of government of the Palestinian Authority was in Ramallah. If a mission was appropriate, that's where it should have been located.

I once asked a colleague who was a fervent advocate of Palestinian statehood why we didn't have a mission in Ramallah. He told me that it posed a security risk for Americans. I was shocked. I responded to him: "You are advocating that the United States recognize a Palestinian state but you think that even its seat of government is so dangerous that the US Marines can't protect American citizens stationed there?" He had no answer.

Just to summarize how ridiculous our diplomatic footprint was before we arrived, our embassy to Israel was in Tel Aviv, even though Israel's seat of government was in Jerusalem, and our mission to the Palestinian Authority was in Jerusalem, even though its seat of government was in Ramallah. American tax dollars at work!

I wondered why no one had ever tried to fix this before. But as I dug deeper into the history of the State Department and its leaders, I understood. The entire Mideast foreign policy establishment at State was a close-knit fraternity that revolved in and out of posts throughout the region, including in Tel Aviv and Jerusalem. Never—never—before was the US ambassador to Israel a true outsider to this cozy crew. Like so many other pockets within State, this was a self-promoting and self-sustaining echo chamber that hadn't had a new thought in generations.

Case in point was the current Jerusalem consul general, Karen Sasahara. She was a seasoned State Department official who spoke Arabic fluently but not a word of Hebrew. Her husband, Michael Ratney, served as the Jerusalem consul general in years past. Both served in posts throughout the Arab world. And they were friends with lots of others who gathered periodically to reinforce each other's views.

I was asked to speak with Karen to get her views on merging the consulate into the embassy. She did not mince words in her response.

"You are a freakin' bulldozer!"

"What?" I replied.

"A bulldozer. Just take a deep breath and slow down. I just got here. I get three years at this post and you just want to shut me down. Give me at least a couple of years before wrecking my life."

"Karen," I said as calmly as she was irate, "this has nothing to do with you, and you are free to argue to State why this is a bad idea. But I think this is a good idea and I will push for this right away. I am not a careerist like you. I don't know how long my job will last and to me every day that I don't advance the principles that I believe in is a wasted day. I don't have the luxury of wasting time."

The conversation turned to more mundane issues. She was so certain that I would prevail that she didn't even venture an argument against the move. She was more interested in personnel management, which we discussed. In keeping with State protocols, Karen ultimately was transferred to the position of chargé d'affaires in the US embassy in Amman, Jordan.

I wrote a lengthy memo outlining the advantages of merging the consulate into the embassy and placing all of Jerusalem, West Bank, and Gaza under a single chief of mission authority. This would give all my analysts, who reported almost weekly on political, social, security, and economic issues relative to Israel and the West Bank, the opportunity to actually visit the places they were writing on. It would give consulate staff, with deep contacts in Palestinian society, the ability to share those perspectives with their colleagues. It made everyone, including me, smarter, more open-minded, and more efficient.

And it would take politics out of security. Before the merger, the consulate gave security directives over travel within Judea and Samaria. They prohibited all embassy personnel from traveling anywhere but Bethlehem and Jericho without specific authorization. That seemed nuts to me. A place like Ma'ale Adumim, a Jewish bedroom suburb of Jerusalem in Judea, was far safer to visit than either of the two Palestinian cities. I would not tolerate political views influencing security decisions. Once the merger occurred, this and other bad policies were corrected.

There was another logistical advantage to merging the consulate with the embassy. The Jerusalem Embassy Act of 1995 required not only that the American embassy be moved to Jerusalem but that the ambassador's residence be moved as well. So even after we moved the embassy, the president was required to continue signing waivers delaying the full implementation of the law because until the residence shifted to Jerusalem, we were not in compliance.

The only residence in Jerusalem that would qualify as an ambassador's residence without many years of remodeling was the consul general's residence on Agron Street. So in merging, we had the opportunity, in all likelihood the only one, to be fully compliant with a law that had been on the books but largely ignored for almost twenty-five years. The merger thus made eminent sense from a practical perspective as well.

Throughout August and September, I worked the merger issues, from a policy perspective at State to a logistics perspective on the ground in Israel. I met with the staff at the soon-to-be-disbanded consulate to assure them of continued employment and to explain the benefits of a new Palestinian Affairs Unit that will have its voice amplified and elevated by reporting directly through the embassy. These were respectful and fascinating conversations. Many of our Palestinian staff were extremely candid and forthcoming about the kinds of things they believed Israel needed to do to improve their quality of life, like modernizing checkpoints and deploying more civilians in administering shared facilities. A great deal of professionalism was shown by the consulate's staff.

On October 18, 2018, Secretary Pompeo issued the following statement:

I am pleased to announce that following the May 14 opening of the US Embassy to Israel in Jerusalem, we plan to achieve significant efficiencies and increase our effectiveness in merging US Embassy Jerusalem and US Consulate General Jerusalem into a single diplomatic mission. I have asked our Ambassador to Israel David Friedman to guide the merger.

The secretary went on to make clear that we would continue our outreach to Palestinians and work toward a just and lasting peace.

A month and a half later, on December 6, 2018, the one-year anniversary of the president's recognition of Jerusalem as Israel's capital, we broke new ground. Prime Minister Netanyahu and I jointly lit the Chanukah candles at the Western Wall—the first time an Israeli prime minister and an American official appeared together at this holy site. In celebration, I put out this tweet:

More than 2000 years ago, Jewish patriots (Maccabees) captured Jerusalem, purified the Holy Temple and rededicated it as a house of Jewish worship. The UN can't vote away the facts: Jerusalem is the ancient and modern capital of Israel. Happy Chanukah from this blessed city!

The tweet got lots of "likes" but one notable objection: Simon Coveney, the foreign minister of Ireland, responded by calling my comments "provocative and biased." It was a nasty thing to say but it put in high relief exactly the choice in approaching peace: to stand with the truth or to run from it. We would choose the former.

The merger was complicated. It required combining two completely independent operations into a single mission, each with its own leadership, management, accounting practices, and security professionals. But in the end, we saved taxpayer dollars, rationalized our real estate footprint, created a platform for the free and open exchange of information and viewpoints, and, most important, enabled the mission to communicate with one voice the values and priorities of the American government. On March 4, 2019, we installed the embassy plaque on the Agron Street facility, this time with the added name of Secretary Michael Pompeo.

It was a thrill for both of us.

ON MAY 8, 2019, JUST AS WE REACHED, ONCE AGAIN, THE SEMIANNUAL requirement for the presidential waiver under the Jerusalem Embassy Act—a waiver needed to avoid crippling penalties upon State Department activities—Secretary Pompeo issued a statement: "I am pleased to report that I have provided my determination to Congress that the relevant elements of the Jerusalem Embassy Act of 1995 have been addressed. Accordingly, no further Presidential waiver of the funding restriction under the Act is necessary."

After twenty-five years, the Jerusalem Embassy Act, which recognized Jerusalem as Israel's undivided capital and required our embassy and ambassador's residence to be located there, was finally subject to full compliance by the United States. With God's help, Jerusalem would never be divided again.

13

PEACE: FROM THE OUTSIDE IN

When the president signed the proclamation recognizing Jerusalem as the capital of Israel on December 6, 2017, he sent me a duplicate original, which he signed with the admonition "We want only peace!" I had no doubt from my first day on the job that the president wanted to achieve peace in the Middle East. But while the goal was clearly expressed, the methodology, the strategy, and the tactics were subject to fierce debate.

It was considered almost a foregone conclusion by the experts that moving the embassy and consolidating it with the Jerusalem consulate would imperil any chances of peace. I don't know what the experts were seeing but it wasn't what we were seeing. Our support for Israel had made it a very attractive partner among the nations in the region and opened up a new way of thinking. We were hoping to cultivate those sentiments much further.

The book of Matthew has a famous saying: "Blessed are the peacemakers for they will be called the children of God." The book of

Psalms famously says, "The Lord will give strength unto his Nation, the Lord will bless his people with peace." The world of the faithful is a world desirous of peace, but it also is a world that believes the land of Israel was given by God to the Jewish people and it is not for humankind to undermine that gift. That view was shared by me as well as tens of millions of American Christians and Jews who supported the president.

How in the world does one make peace between Israel and the Palestinians without going to war with God? That was the question I wrestled with from the day I affirmed my oath to the Constitution. That affirmation itself symbolized the dilemma: upholding a commitment to the Constitution—which recognized no religion—with my hand firmly on top of the Old Testament!

There were some basic facts, however, that made the question academic during the early days of the administration: One, the Palestinians were not ready for peace, and two, given the preponderance of malign behavior by the Palestinians, Israel was not in a position to make any concessions.

Initially, my preference was to leave well enough alone. Our bilateral relationship with Israel was booming on all fronts and a peace process was likely to lead only to yet another failure. Any engagement with the Palestinians undoubtedly would require a commitment that we hold off on the recognition of Jerusalem, which I saw as a disaster. Jared Kushner and Jason Greenblatt were far more optimistic than I was that there was a deal that could be done, but to their credit, they fully supported the embassy move even though they recognized, accurately, that it would jeopardize their contacts with Palestinian leadership.

The three of us had robust debates about how to move forward after the embassy move. I thought the existing Palestinian leadership was a lost cause and doubted anyone or anything could change that.

They saw things a bit differently, having the benefit of extensive exposure to the leadership within the Gulf nations. They saw several nations that had no particular animus toward Israel, other than the fact that Israel was universally portrayed in their world as hostile and oppressive to the Palestinians. They had no doubt that normalization with Israel was possible if the Palestinian issue could be resolved.

Could peace be built from the outside in? Given the relationships that were developing between my colleagues and the Gulf states, was there a needle to be threaded that might open up the region to peace? Jared was optimistic and I pressed him on his optimism almost every day. He didn't relent.

Jared saw a real desire among the Gulf states to be further aligned with Israel, but they needed something that would give them diplomatic and political cover. We hypothesized that a "reasonable" peace plan might provide that cover, even if the Palestinians opposed it. Of course that begged the question of what was reasonable. We had no doubt that the Gulf states would be sympathetic to Israel's security needs since they faced similar threats. What we needed was to demonstrate that the condition of the Palestinians could be materially advanced within that protective framework for Israel.

We all decided to write a peace plan so it would be ready if the opportunity ever arose. The contents were initially to be negotiated among ourselves, based upon conversations we had with all the experts we had contacted over the prior years. Perhaps because of where we sat in our jobs or where we held our priorities, the negotiations were not far from arm's length, although all three of us were rock solid in our commitment to Israel's security.

Jared's wish list was the most practical. He wanted to see details of roads, infrastructure, free movement of goods and people, better health care, and transportation contiguity among all Palestinian cities and villages. In his travels to the Gulf, Jared learned that when the leaders in the region referred to Jerusalem, they didn't necessarily mean the city but more specifically the Al Aqsa Mosque. So he was particularly focused on making sure that our plan provided for a robust protocol for Muslim tourism, including hotels and restaurants, so that Muslims from around the world could pray at the mosque. It was a creative and well-received notion in the Arab world, and the Israeli government was very receptive to encouraging that tourism.

My issues were more conceptual. I was adamant that we could not demand that Israel concede territory to another sovereign state. There needed to be a far more nuanced structure whereby Palestinians maintained civilian control over their communities and even additional territory earmarked for growth, so long as Israel maintained overall security control. This solved two problems: First, it removed the security risk from Palestinian autonomy, and, second, it removed the religious and ideological complication of Israel conceding land. If Israel retained military and security control, it had not technically relinquished any territory, even if the Palestinians were given a "state."

I had other conceptual requirements as well: no evacuation of settlements, no "return" to Israel of alleged refugees, the disarming of Hamas, the creation by the PA of legitimate institutions of government, human rights, and religious freedom, dismantling the existing corrupt enterprises, and ending the barbaric practice of "pay for slay." Each of these undoubtedly would be a hurdle for the Palestinians to traverse, but the first one was absolutely the toughest: The Palestinians made it abundantly clear that they would not tolerate a single Israeli soldier on land they claimed as their own.

I thought this Palestinian demand was a straw man, a means to avoid a deal based upon a well-sounding but utterly unworkable principle. On this point, the Palestinians had strong supporters on the American Left who trumpeted the "indignity" of a continued Israeli military presence. I saw it differently: America maintained a military presence in almost all the locations where it had defeated its enemies, including Germany, Japan, and Korea. It wasn't an unprecedented practice and it did not impede friendly and productive relations. In any event, the issue was academic—Israel was not going to pull its troops. Whether in Lebanon, Gaza, or Sinai, Israeli withdrawal has led to a power vacuum that quickly ended up being filled by terrorists—Hezbollah took over Lebanon, Hamas took over Gaza, and ISIS built enclaves in Sinai.

This issue came up when the president visited Abbas in Bethlehem in 2017. Abbas complained that Israel was insisting on controlling Palestinian security. Trump asked him how much Israel was charging the PA for those security services. Abbas looked stunned. He replied that Israel was performing those services at no cost to the Palestinians.

The president jumped on this admission. He observed that the Palestinians live in a very dangerous part of the world and have virtually no ability to defend themselves. ISIS, Hezbollah, Hamas, al-Qaeda, Iran—any of them could take over the Palestinian territories in a day. He was incredulous that Abbas was rejecting free Israeli security support when Israel was the only player in the region that knew how to fight these implacable foes. Abbas looked at Trump as if he had two heads—no one had ever spoken to him before with this brutal clarity.

With the Palestinians dead set against Israeli security control and the president seeing their position as unreasonable, there was little likelihood that we would make a deal with the Palestinians in the near term. That then prompted the question, "Should we keep working on a peace plan?"

Jared not surprisingly remained a yes, but as time passed, so was I. Even if the Palestinians didn't come to the table, this no longer was a hypothetical exercise. We had engaged sufficiently with Prime

Minister Netanyahu and his team to know that there was a "realistic two-state solution" that Israel could endorse—not a "state" in a traditional sense, but a means for the Palestinians to live with dignity, autonomy, and prosperity.

I went back and looked at the expectations surrounding the Oslo Accords in 1995 and discovered just how far the goalposts had moved against Israel in the past twenty-three years. I studied the words of Yitzhak Rabin, the Israeli general, war hero, and architect of Oslo, who gave his life for the cause of peace and is considered, even today, the father of the pro-peace camp in Israel and around the world. When Rabin spoke to the Knesset seeking ratification of the Oslo Accords, this is part of what he said:

> We would like this to be an entity which is less than a state, and which will independently run the lives of the Palestinians under its authority. The borders of the State of Israel, during the permanent solution, will be beyond the lines that existed before the Six Day War. We will not return to the 4 June 1967 lines.

Bingo! We were exactly with Rabin—Palestinian autonomy without the full attributes of statehood, on territory that was less than the entirety of Judea and Samaria. That left room for Israel to retain all its settlements and maintain security control, just as we had intended to provide.

Given that Rabin was so revered among the Left, how did his vision slip so dramatically that the Left, in Rabin's name, came to advocate a fully sovereign Palestinian state along the pre-1967 borders? It's far from clear how the position evolved, although it is clear that both the Israeli and the American Left took enormous liberties in describing Rabin's views after Rabin passed away. We do know that in March 2014, President Obama welcomed President Abbas to the

Oval Office and offered a very different view from that of the revered Yitzhak Rabin:

> *And I think everyone understands the outlines of what a peace deal would look like, involving a territorial compromise on both sides based on '67 lines with mutually agreed upon swaps, that would ensure Israel was secure but would also ensure that the Palestinians have a sovereign state . . .*

Rabin would have choked on that speech, as did Netanyahu at the time.

The value of a well-conceived and constructed "Vision for Peace"— not a plan that would contemplate immediate execution but rather a "vision" that was more illustrative and aspirational—made great sense to me with or without Palestinian engagement. It was an opportunity to show what was possible for the Palestinians; it was an opportunity to show that Israel was willing to make concessions for peace; and it was an opportunity to give cover to the neighbors in the region who wished to engage further with Israel.

The Vision also gave me a chance to address the issue of refugees. The twentieth century created millions of them. The UNHCR, the United Nations refugee relief agency dedicated to all refugees other than Palestinian refugees, did its best to get the refugees settled somewhere, not letting perfection get in the way of the possible. In contrast, UNRWA, a refugee relief agency formed exclusively for the Palestinians, perpetuated hatred of Israel and weaponized a demand for Palestinian refugees to return only to Israel as a means of destroying the Jewish state.

There are countless heartbreaking stories of people forced to leave their homes during barbaric conflicts. Sadly, they continue today in Syria and elsewhere. But there is simply nothing unique about

Palestinian refugees from Israel's 1948 War of Independence, other than (1) they are now very old if still alive, (2) many left Israel voluntarily to get out of the line of fire of attacking Arab nations, and (3) they are among the few who are used cynically as political pawns, rather than beneficiaries of humanitarian relief. Palestinian refugees are certainly no more worthy than the equal number of Jewish refugees expelled from Arab countries after Israel became a state.

I thought it important to make abundantly clear that peace needed to be forward looking. No one would be expected to repatriate hostile segments of a population to vindicate a grievance of more than seventy years. We created some compensation funds to provide modest relief to those who could prove economic loss, but our view was that the best way to help anyone who still considered himself a refugee after all this time was to improve his prospects in the future, not redress his alleged grievances of the past.

This theme was explicated in our plan and I believe it makes an important contribution to future peace efforts.

There were a few collateral issues that were best addressed before the plan came out. Most important among them was the Golan Heights. Tackling the status of Judea and Samaria while leaving the Golan open made no sense. The entirety of the Golan was essential to Israel's security, there were virtually no non-Israelis living in the Golan who demanded independence, and the only competing claim to the Golan was held by Bashar al-Assad, Syria's ruthless dictator.

Netanyahu had been seeking US recognition of Israeli sovereignty over the Golan for decades, and with increased earnestness once we took office. I was highly supportive of the move for a host of reasons, but one of particular importance to our peace strategy: Recognizing Israeli sovereignty over the Golan presented an ideal opportunity to frame UN Security Council Resolution 242 in terms that could be scaled to the Israeli-Palestinian conflict. Because Resolution

242 entitled Israel to "secure and recognized boundaries," and because, by any fair assessment, there existed no such boundary on Israel's border with Syria other than the existing boundary that incorporated the Golan, recognition of sovereignty moved us forward on a rational and intellectually honest path that could extend to recognition of Israeli sovereignty over some portion of Judea and Samaria as well.

In March 2019, everyone in my world was talking about the Golan Heights. I think the primary instigator was Netanyahu himself, along with Ron Dermer, Israel's ambassador in Washington. The timing was important for Bibi as he had an election coming up and was traveling to Washington for the AIPAC conference on March 24. For the prime minister to speak at AIPAC, attend a Golan recognition ceremony at the White House, and then return to Jerusalem a conquering hero just two weeks before the elections scheduled for April 9 would have been a home run.

Contrary to reports at the time in the Israeli media, there was never a stated White House objective to help Netanyahu get reelected. At the same time, our discussions with the prime minister had advanced significantly and there was sufficient trust established such that we believed that we could advance a peace deal that Israel would accept. Certainly, everyone in my sphere would be happy with a Netanyahu victory so that our work could continue apace.

On March 21, Mike Pompeo was with me in Jerusalem. His visit was primarily Iran-related and the Golan was not on his agenda. While we were traveling back from the Western Wall in his car—a first in and of itself as he was accompanied by the prime minister (the first time a secretary of state joined the prime minister of Israel at this holy site)—John Bolton, then the national security advisor, called me. He said that he thought it was a good time for the president to recognize Israeli sovereignty over the Golan, but that he could not get traction with the president on the subject. Almost immediately after I hung up the phone, I got a call from Jared saying almost the same thing. He suggested that I give the president a call. I shared these conversations with Pompeo and asked him if he had any objection to me taking a run at Trump. He didn't.

When we got to our destination, I went off to a secure location to call the president. He took the call. He already knew I was calling about the Golan.

I reminded the president of our prior conversations on the subject and offered that I thought this was a good time to recognize Israeli sovereignty. I suggested that this would be a perfect place setter for the president's Vision for Peace that I thought we could get out within the next couple of months.

The president fully understood the security and geopolitical benefits of recognition but he was concerned that this would be perceived as a pre-election gift to Netanyahu.

I responded that this decision was not being recommended as a political gift for Bibi. Rather, it should be viewed as being in our national interest. It would correctly resolve some of the thorniest issues in the region, many loyal Americans support it, and the only aggrieved party would be a ruthless butcher, Bashar al-Assad, whom the president already had fired at with fifty-nine Tomahawk missiles in response to poisoning his own people. Recognizing Israel's Golan Heights sovereignty fell squarely within our new diplomatic perspective of peace through strength.

We continued to discuss the matter, and the president became convinced that US recognition of Israeli sovereignty over the Golan Heights was the right decision at the right time. I asked the president when he would like to make the announcement.

The president was not of a view to delay. He suggested that the announcement be made right away, and I concurred. With that he called in Dan Scavino, his director of social media, and asked that I dictate the tweet. Minutes later, the president tweeted the following:

> After 52 years it is time for the United States to fully recognize Israel's Sovereignty over the Golan Heights, which is of critical strategic and security importance to the State of Israel and Regional Stability.

As soon as the tweet was out, I called Bibi and told him I had good news and bad news. He was in no mood to play games and anxious to understand the president's position on the Golan Heights. I played the game anyway, informing him that unfortunately there would be no recognition ceremony in Washington as Bibi had hoped for. As he began to express his disappointment, I quickly interjected with the good news—that the president already had tweeted that the United States would recognize Israeli sovereignty. His excitement was palpable.

With that, he hung up the phone to jump on the good news.

About two hours later, I was at the prime minister's house for dinner with Secretary Pompeo. Before we sat down, the PM and the secretary made public remarks. Each was required to improvise as the notion that the Golan Heights would be talked about had not previously been considered.

Notwithstanding the absence of preparation, Pompeo's speech about the Golan was extraordinary. It turned out that when he was a cadet at West Point, he studied and wrote about the Battle of the Valley of Tears, the battle by which Israel held on to stop the Syrian army from advancing during the Yom Kippur War. Pompeo expressed his thanks that the efforts of the brave Israeli soldiers lost in that battle had been recognized as meaningful and worthy. I was seriously choked up.

That night was Purim and by the time dinner was over I needed to rush to catch a flight back to New York. I also needed to hear the reading of the Megillah, the book of Esther. I prevailed upon my friend Rabbi Peles of Chabad to read the text to me as I prepared to depart. My staff called ahead to hold the plane and I managed to board just before takeoff. As I eased back in my chair looking forward to eleven hours of solitude, I couldn't help but reflect on the tumultuous events earlier in the day. The book of Esther contains a famous passage where Esther's uncle, Mordechai, seeks to inspire her to use her new position of royalty to protect the Jewish people: "Who knows if perhaps it is for this purpose that you arose to leadership?" It was hard not to see some similarities with my own extraordinary personal experience.

We all regrouped in the West Wing on March 25. I was sitting in Jared's office about two hours before Bibi arrived, recounting the events of the prior week. I mentioned how Bibi really wanted a ceremony. Jared called some protocol people to see if we could cobble together a brief ceremony when Bibi arrived and there was no objection. We scurried around drafting a presidential proclamation and some talking points for the president and called ahead to Ron Dermer that his boss should expect a short ceremony.

As we walked over to the Diplomatic Room, where Netanyahu would be greeted by Trump, one of the protocol heads informed Jared, Jason, Pompeo, and me that we would have to wait outside. Since Bibi would be alone on his side, there could only be the president on the American side. There were at least ten photographers lined up to capture the historic moment of the president signing a proclamation declaring US recognition of Israeli sovereignty over the Golan Heights, and I wanted to be in the picture. Fortunately, as the president walked into the room, he caught my eye and said, "Come on in, guys." We all followed and were featured prominently on the front page of *The New York Times* the following day.

BY NOW WE HAD A GOOD WORKING DRAFT OF THE PRESIDENT'S VI-sion for Peace. Our plan was to move forward with the rollout once Israel's elections and government formation had concluded. There was only one problem: They didn't.

On April 9, 2019, Israelis went to the polls. The results, at first blush, indicated a stunning victory for Netanyahu—a broad right-wing government consisting of his party, Likud, along with the Orthodox, Kulanu, Religious Zionist, and Avigdor Lieberman's right-wing secular party. The coalition would total 65 seats within the 120-seat Knesset, with Netanyahu at the helm. Once the government was formed, we would launch the Vision for Peace.

Then came a stunning turnaround. Avigdor Lieberman refused to join the coalition. Without the 5 seats of Lieberman's Yisrael Beit-einu Party, Netanyahu would be stuck at 60, one shy of the majority needed to proceed. Lieberman claimed his reason was the presence of the ultra-Orthodox parties in the coalition, who generally did not serve in the army and who he felt did not otherwise adequately par-ticipate in civic responsibilities. It was not a believable position as Lie-berman had been in such coalitions before.

I met with Lieberman to see if I could break the logjam. I told him that we were prepared to launch a Vision for Peace, which I believed he would support. But we wanted Israeli buy-in and that just couldn't be achieved while the government remained this unstable. He didn't care. He wanted Netanyahu out. In a heavy Russian accent, he said it was a "mission impossible." It was clear to me from the conversation that it was his strong anti-Bibi sentiment that was the real impedi-ment to his joining the coalition.

Netanyahu was the longest-serving prime minister in Israel's his-tory and considered a political genius. Notwithstanding Lieberman's abandonment, everyone assumed he would peel off at least one more member of the Knesset to form a 61-seat majority. But he couldn't make it happen and Israel was forced to return to elections for a second time, now scheduled for September 17, 2019.

The elections essentially put the rollout of our Vision for Peace on hold. While our plan would, for the first time in the history of the conflict, afford Israel full sovereignty over all Jewish communities in Judea, Samaria, and the Jordan Valley with ample room to grow and expand, it also would present the reality—a harsh reality to many—that the majority of the territory would be transferred to a Palestinian entity called a "state," even though it had only civilian authority.

The devil was in the details but, during a campaign season, objective analysis of the details gave way to mischaracterization and demagoguery. Bibi understood this all too well. He asked us not to roll out the plan in the middle of a campaign—it would not get the attention and support it deserved. We reluctantly agreed, even though it cost us a lot of time, even more than we could have imagined when the September 2019 elections resulted in yet another deadlock!

While Israel's dysfunctionality continued, we tried to spend the time productively. An important piece of the puzzle was realigning America's position on the legality of Jewish settlements in Judea and Samaria.

Up to that point I had made some significant dents in the State Department's nomenclature regarding Judea and Samaria. The biggest was my elimination of the phrase "occupied territory" from all State Department reports that mentioned the area. I was willing to go along with "disputed territory" or even "West Bank," but I wanted the nomenclature changed to eliminate the term "occupied." I argued that territory is "occupied" only when the party in control has no rights to the land except by reason of military conquest—and that was not the case here. While Israel had accepted upon itself the humanitarian obligations held by an "occupier," it did so as a practical means of defining its role rather than as an acknowledgment that it did not have a valid legal claim to the land.

Since 1967, the US view of settlements has been a morass of confusing and self-contradictory statements. In the aftermath of the Six-Day War, settlement construction hadn't yet begun but the territory was viewed generally as disputed, with Israel thought to have the best claim. By 1978, President Carter had a diametrically different view—he saw the settlements as antithetical to peace and he had the legal adviser to the State Department, Herbert Hansell, issue an opinion that they were illegal. Known for decades as the "Hansell Memo," the document had never been revisited by subsequent administrations and generally evaded comment. That was unfortunate insofar as the work, only three pages in length, was shoddy and appeared reverse-engineered to achieve Carter's political objective.

There were some basic errors in the Hansell Memo that required correction. For one, the memo never acknowledged that Israel's legal right to the "West Bank" (the term Hansell uses) was confirmed by the Balfour Declaration and the San Remo Resolution, incorporated into the League of Nations resolutions that became the legal basis for reconstituting the Middle East after the fall of the Ottoman Empire; second, while referring to Israel as a belligerent occupant relative to Jordan, it fails to explain how that condition is relevant under circumstances where, as here, Jordan had no legal claim to the territory; third, it wrongly considered the settlements to constitute an illegal "forced transfer" by Israel of its population into occupied territory without any evidence that Israel had compelled anyone to move, and when, in fact, Israeli settlements resulted in no displacement of indigenous people. The memo also did not account for the fact that Israel recaptured its territory in a defensive war.

Even if correct, the Hansell Memo had been overtaken by events. Hansell rested his entire theory of illegality on his view that Israel was maintaining a state of belligerent occupancy relative to Jordan, from whom Israel captured the West Bank. But he acknowledged, "the laws of belligerent occupancy generally would continue to apply . . . until Israel leaves it or the war ends between Israel and its neighbors concerned with the particular territory." In 1994, Israel and Jordan signed a peace treaty that ended their state of war and included Jordan relinquishing all of its claims to the West Bank. The treaty ended the single pillar of Hansell's argument.

While the legal consequence of the Israel-Jordan Peace Treaty was to end the case that Israel was an illegal occupier, that didn't resolve the reality of two million Palestinians on the ground without a country. And we thought, and continue to think, that the Palestinians deserve better, assuming violence and terrorism can come to an end. The legal result doesn't diminish the Palestinian cause, but it puts it in the realm of a territorial and humanitarian dispute rather than a case of reclaiming stolen property. The difference matters.

With a proposed Vision for Peace that provided for Israeli sovereignty over Jewish settlements in Judea and Samaria, I was very concerned that the State Department, notwithstanding Pompeo as its secretary, would leak out a view that the vision was contrary to American law. While admittedly the legal views were all over the lot, with President Reagan saying that settlements were not illegal, Carter and Obama saying or acting otherwise, and most others just finessing the issue, the Hansell Memo stood unrebutted for two generations. If it was wrong, and I certainly thought it was, it behooved us to change it.

I raised this issue with Pompeo in some detail. He told me he wanted to get this right and invited me to work with the new legal adviser. We spent much of 2019 on the subject.

Within the Office of the Legal Adviser, there were some who strongly agreed with Hansell, some who did not, and some who saw the issue as complex and nuanced. We had numerous meetings and calls sorting out all the views. The views of the State of Israel also mattered as Israel had often taken public positions on these issues that we needed to reconcile. We spent three full days in Jerusalem in which I chaired meetings of American and Israeli government lawyers, many of whom had known each other for years, poring over precedent, drafts, and theories. Before the American delegation left for the airport, I pulled them aside to speak privately.

"Where are we on this?" I asked.

"I think we can get to a place where we are comfortable saying that there are good-faith arguments that settlements are not illegal."

"Will you support a conclusion that settlements aren't illegal and drop all the hedging?"

"The problem, Ambassador," one attorney responded, "is that there also exist arguments that they are illegal."

"But we all know that. That's true in any legal dispute. But let me ask you this: Who is your client?"

"What do you mean? Why is that relevant?"

"Well," I explained, "you are lawyers. If you are giving legal advice, then by definition you have a client. I'm asking the question because in the circumstances you have outlined, where legitimate arguments can be made on either side of an issue, I would think you would want to act at the direction of your client."

"But we think the issue can go either way," another lawyer stressed.

"Guys, when Jimmy Carter wanted an opinion from his State Department legal adviser that settlements were illegal, he got it from Hansell. Not a dissertation on the various positions or an acknowledgment that things could go either way. He got a full-throated finding of illegality. Why isn't Mike Pompeo entitled to the same courtesy, assuming what he's asking for is intellectually honest?"

Marik String, then the acting legal adviser, jumped in: "Well, we probably could say that settlements are not per se illegal, meaning not all settlements are illegal, but individual ones may be subject to local competing claims."

"Well, that's constructive," I said. "Obviously we are not delving into the specifics of individual zoning disputes or land claims. But if you are comfortable that settlements in Judea and Samaria are not per se illegal, I think that is a fair outcome."

And that's where we ended up. On November 19, 2019, Secretary Pompeo reversed the Hansell Memo and stated:

> *After carefully studying all sides of the legal debate, this ad-ministration agrees with President Reagan. The establishment of Israeli civilian settlements in the West Bank is not per se inconsis-tent with international law.*

The reaction to Pompeo's pronouncement garnered the usual re-sponses from the usual suspects: anger from the Left, praise from the Right, and some surprisingly nuanced reactions from the center. The one reaction that puzzled me the most was from the Union of Reform Judaism, which condemned the decision. I could not fathom a Jewish theological (as opposed to political) position that Jewish settlement in biblically significant places like Shiloh or Hebron, promised by God to the Jewish people, was illegal.

I was deeply grateful that 106 members of the House, led by Con-gressman Andy Levin of Michigan, wrote to Pompeo to condemn his decision. Without that letter, the record supporting the decision might have been incomplete insofar as some members of the Legal Department at State were reluctant participants. But the letter created a platform for a more fulsome response.

In response to the letter, the State Department's Legislative Af-fairs Office advocated for a typical muted response, something like

"Thank you for your interest and we are seriously considering your views." No way. I called Pompeo and told him this was a golden opportunity for him to make his case conclusively. He accepted my offer to draft a responsive letter.

The response from Pompeo blew away the Left. Congressman Levin, in his letter, made several specious assertions. He claimed that Pompeo's decision reversed well-established policy that enjoyed bipartisan support. Pompeo responded that his decision reversed John Kerry's mistaken view articulated in defense of UN Security Council Resolution 2334, passed in the waning days of the Obama administration, *which view was met with bipartisan condemnation.* Levin stated that settlements were a barrier to peace. Pompeo responded with a quote from then Senate minority leader Chuck Schumer: "It's sure not the settlements that are the blockage to peace." Levin recited what he claimed was the "accepted view" that settlements violated the Fourth Geneva Convention. Pompeo responded that this view not only was not "accepted," but it was rejected by Yale Law School dean and Undersecretary of State Eugene Rostow, who represented the United States in negotiating the framework for a resolution of the conflict in 1967.

The House's "hanging curveball" was hit out of the park by Pompeo. We finally had put this issue on solid footing.

The last predicate for the president's Vision for Peace was now in place. All we needed was for Israel's electoral mayhem to end.

There was still plenty of time to wait.

14

THE STORMS BEFORE
THE STORM

By the early summer of 2019, we had a plan to roll out the president's Vision for Peace. At the end of June, Jared hosted the Peace to Prosperity Conference in Bahrain, which brought together government and business leaders in the United States, Israel, and the Gulf. Although the sole topic of the conference was bringing financial and economic advancement to the Palestinians, the Palestinian Authority boycotted the event. Nonetheless, the conference was attended by some Palestinian business leaders—themselves boycotted and threatened upon their return—and demonstrated that the world's public and private sectors were standing by ready to assist if a political solution could be found.

All that was left to get started was political stability in Israel. As soon as Israel formed a governing coalition, we would get the buy-in of the new government and then socialize the plan with the Gulf nations and other allies who had agreed to be helpful. Unfortunately, the September election in Israel led to another draw and on December 11, 2019, the Knesset again voted to dissolve and scheduled a third round of elections, for March 2, 2020. It was a significant setback in timing and momentum, but it wasn't the only speed bump on the path to peace.

In August 2019, two of America's most controversial congress-women announced a visit to Israel. Ilhan Omar and Rashida Tlaib, in their short careers, had displayed disturbing hostility to Israel and the Jewish people, supporting the boycott of Israel and its products, accusing Jewish Americans of using their money to buy political influence, and advocating a reversal of America's long-standing bipartisan support for the Jewish state.

Israel had passed a law a year earlier barring entry to tourists who sought to advocate boycotts or sanctions against it. The concept was pretty straightforward: Israel was facing significant political and economic pressure from abroad. While it might not be able to stop that pressure, it was not going to facilitate activists coming into Israel to advertise their cause, especially to create video clips and interviews that were misleading. Nothing prevented Israelis or Palestinians from engaging in this activity—the law simply prohibited foreigners from advocating boycotts of Israel on Israeli soil.

Many liberal Americans were opposed to this law. They argued that principles of free speech were paramount in balancing the issues. This argument missed the point. Israelis and Palestinians had free speech. But Israel had the right to control its borders and had no moral obligation to facilitate visits for those who sought Israel's destruction.

I had no problem with the law. The question was whether Israel would enforce it against two members of Congress. Just a few weeks earlier, a bipartisan delegation of seventy members of the House of Representatives visited Israel and were shown all sides of the Israel-Palestinian conflict. Omar and Tlaib refused to attend that session, deciding instead to grandstand on their own.

Ambassador Dermer initially had informed congressional leadership that Israel would make an exception to its anti-boycott law because the visitors were members of the United States Congress. When Trump learned of that decision, he thought Israel was crazy. He could not understand why Israel would open its borders to people he considered anti-Semites.

The issue percolated for a week or so until the proposed itinerary of the trip made its way to me. The visit was entitled "U.S. Congressional Delegation to Palestine," and, apart from the flight landing in Tel Aviv, the entirety of the visit was in "Palestine," or Judea and Samaria as I would say. And no meetings with Jewish residents of Judea and Samaria were on the agenda.

For me, this was a bridge too far. Not because it's my business who Israel lets into its borders, but because here were two isolated members of Congress seeking to establish a new foreign policy of the United States. The United States did not recognize a state or even a place called Palestine, and this end run around our policies and our values should not be tolerated.

I passed the itinerary on to Dermer, who shared it with Netanyahu and Israel's interior minister, Aryeh Deri. We talked through the issues and it was left to Israel to decide. Upon seeing the itinerary and recognizing that this was an agenda designed solely to damage Israel—there was not a single opportunity for Israel to present its side of the story—they recognized that the proposed visit was squarely prohibited under Israeli law.

Deri asked me what America's position would be if Omar and Tlaib were denied entry. I said we would support the decision as a proper exercise by Israel of its internal laws. They then made the decision to bar their entry, and all hell broke loose.

I put out a statement that said the following:

> *The Boycott, Divestment and Sanctions (BDS) movement against Israel is not free speech. Rather, it is no less than economic*

warfare designed to delegitimize and ultimately destroy the Jew-ish State. Israel properly has enacted laws to bar entry of BDS activists under the circumstances present here. . . . This trip, pure and simple, is nothing more than an effort to fuel the BDS engine that Congresswomen Tlaib and Omar so vigorously support. Like the United States, Israel is a nation of laws. We support Israel's application of its laws in this case.

In response, Congressman Ted Lieu sent me the following message on Twitter that he subsequently deleted: "You are an American. Your allegiance should be to America, not a foreign power. You should be defending the right of Americans to travel to other countries. If you don't understand that then you need to resign."

And with that, we had come full circle to the ugliness of my confirmation hearing two and a half years earlier. The progressive Left saw this as a golden opportunity to attack Israel and the anti-Israel NGOs piled on. Calls were made inside Congress for me to be "investigated" and for Ambassador Dermer to be sent home. None of those went anywhere.

I watched in shock as organizations like J Street and Peace Now accused me not just of dual loyalty—almost a monthly occurrence—but of doing more to "undermine loyal American Jews working in public service than anyone since Jonathan Pollard." Because I supported Israel's application of its anti-BDS law against two anti-Semitic individuals who happened to be members of Congress, I was now on par with an American spy convicted of selling highly classified information to another country!

I had wrestled with this issue in the days leading up to the decision. I knew that by supporting it, I would be on the receiving end of a massive backlash. Many suggested to me that the best approach was to encourage Israel to let them in and to use the opportunity to educate the congresswomen on the true state of Israeli-Palestinian affairs. But after seeing their itinerary, it was obvious that this was a setup—a means for these two to film carefully scripted, edited, and manipulated video to spout their anti-Israel venom. The sponsor of the trip, an organization called Miftah, had in the past accused the Jews of drinking the blood of Christians on Passover. Miftah ultimately was forced to apologize.

Israel had every right not to be a punching bag. It had no obligation to virtue signal its openness to all points of view. But the blowback was intense nonetheless.

Tlaib complained loudly and emotionally that Israel was preventing her from visiting her grandmother who lived in the West Bank. After seeing her in tears, I called Netanyahu to suggest that she be allowed to enter Israel on humanitarian grounds. The approval was issued almost immediately. Hours later, Tlaib declined the visit anyway.

From the Omar/Tlaib debacle, I remained on the defensive. While Congress never launched its threatened "investigation," in September 2019, the US Office of Special Counsel did open an investigation based upon complaints it received that I violated the Hatch Act.

The Hatch Act is a complicated piece of legislation that, in simple terms, prohibits executive branch employees from engaging in political activity. I was not allowed to say "vote for X" although I was allowed to defend X's policies. Where the line gets drawn is complicated, but the investigation conducted against me related to activity that didn't even approach prohibited conduct. It was just meant to intimidate me.

In April 2019, my oldest son arranged for me to join him in meeting Rabbi Beryl Povarsky, the head of the Ponevitch Yeshiva in the Israeli town of Bnei Brak. Rabbi Povarsky is a Torah scholar and I enjoyed the meeting. We spoke in Hebrew, and he mentioned to me how unusual it was that a president of the United States would be so supportive of Israel. I told him it was indeed special but we had less than two years left in our term and I asked him to bless us for another four years because "what we see on the other side is very frightening."

"Everything comes from heaven," Rabbi Povarsky responded.

"So help us out. You're closer," I quipped.

Unbeknownst to me, one of the rabbi's students had videotaped the meeting and released it to the religious Jewish media. From there, it was translated into English and received widespread attention. The *Forward*, a left-wing Jewish publication, published a headline, AMBASSADOR TO ISRAEL URGED TOP ORTHODOX RABBIS TO PRAY FOR TRUMP'S REELECTION.

Well, that was a first for the Hatch Act police—an ambassador seeking divine intervention on behalf of a candidate. They asked me a series of questions about the event: Who attended? What was the purpose of the meeting? Why was the conversation recorded? Why was it disseminated to the media? What government purpose was served? etc. I was flabbergasted by the inquiry but responded seriously. I explained that this was a private meeting organized by my son with no governmental purpose, no one else attended except my bodyguards, and I was unaware of the recording or its release to the media.

There were more follow-up questions and answers. At one point I asked how it possibly could be illegal for a government employee to ask anything of a priest, rabbi, or minister in a private meeting. On October 7, 2019, justice prevailed and the Office of Special Counsel informed me that I did nothing wrong and that it was closing the investigation. Much to the dismay of those who filed the complaints, it was concluded that my meeting was solely personal in nature rather than in an official capacity.

The storm grew far more ominous on November 12, 2019, when

the Israel Defense Forces conducted a targeted killing of Islamic Jihad leader Abu al-Ata along with members of his family in the Gaza Strip. Islamic Jihad is a terrorist group committed to Israel's destruction and al-Ata was reported to have been planning imminent attacks against Israel.

That same day, I was attending the annual Marine Ball at which United States Central Commander, General Frank McKenzie, and I were the guests of honor. After a long celebratory evening, I was pulled aside by my defense attaché and informed that Islamic Jihad had launched hundreds of rockets into Israel and there was a rumor that an Israeli soldier had been kidnapped. The latter news was devastating—if Islamic Jihad was in fact holding an Israeli soldier, I had no doubt that Israel would go to war.

I sent my family home and had my security detail bring me to the prime minister's residence where he had agreed to see me. He was fully engaged with his defense team but allowed me to chat with him from time to time. The good news was that all soldiers had been accounted for and none were missing. At the same time, the barrage of rockets was massive and causing significant damage.

I was not in the inner sanctum of the prime minister's "situation room" but I had enough contact with him to see him in action. He was rational, strategic, and fully in control. The question that evening was whether Hamas would join the attacks with Islamic Jihad. They were rivals and Hamas was not considered to be anxious for a battle. Israel sent a very clear message to Hamas: *Stay out of the battle and Israel will leave you alone; join with Islamic Jihad and there will be an overwhelming response.*

I asked the prime minister if he thought it would be helpful if the United States made clear that it would not rein in Israel's response. He nodded in agreement. I then immediately put out the following tweet:

Palestinian Islamic Jihad, an Islamist terrorist organization backed by Iran, is again attacking Israel with hundreds of missiles aimed at civilians. We stand with our friend and ally Israel at this critical moment and support Israel's right to defend itself and bring an end to these barbaric attacks.

Hamas did not enter the war and Islamic Jihad ended the barrage, recognizing that its alternative was to be bombed back to the Stone Age.

IN MY FOUR YEARS IN OFFICE, ISRAEL DID NOT HAVE A PROLONGED battle either with Hamas in Gaza or Hezbollah on the Lebanese border. The reason is simple and a good lesson for my successors: Unlike some prior administrations, we made it abundantly clear that if Israel were attacked, the United States would place no limitations on its right of self-defense. None of this "proportionate force" nonsense that creates no disincentive for the enemy to attack. As a result, Israel's enemies, while prone to the occasional attack, itself barbaric and evil, nonetheless calibrated their violence to avoid an all-out war. They knew they would have been obliterated.

Because of their alliance on so many policy fronts, many people compare Trump with Netanyahu. In reality they don't have very much in common. Like concentric circles, they overlap only with regard to their populism and "America First" or "Israel First" perspectives. But while Trump is instinctive and very close with his staff, engendering enormous loyalty, Netanyahu is far more cerebral and cautious, willing to review data and more data exhaustively before making a decision. Most of the high-ranking members of his former staff have formed their own parties and have competed with him, presumably because they didn't see the opportunity for the advancement that they craved under his leadership.

If I needed someone to make the right call without the benefit of much study or review, I'd choose Trump. He was very quick and capable on his feet. If I wanted the right answer without regard to time, Bibi was in a class by himself. On numerous occasions I would accompany him and American officials like John Bolton or Mike Pompeo on helicopter trips to the north or south. It's too noisy to speak on a helicopter. With the twenty minutes that Bibi would have to himself on the chopper, instead of closing his eyes or gazing out the window, his staff always had on hand a massive tome of historical nonfiction that he pored over studiously until landing. He is that cerebral.

Bibi never took his eye off the ball. On one occasion we were at a public event and he asked to speak with me privately. Our host ushered us to an elevator and offered us a private office four floors up. After we entered the elevator, we were followed by two of Bibi's bodyguards, one of mine, and his paramedic. The elevator was overloaded and after rising about two floors, we got stuck. As a serious claustrophobe, I tried my best to avoid panicking as Bibi continued to speak with me as if nothing had changed. In the excruciating ten minutes that we were trapped, I barely processed a word he was saying while I doubt he even noticed our predicament.

What made Bibi different from every politician, however, was the weight he carried on his shoulders. In countless conversations I had with him, he raised the burden of standing in the shoes of his older brother Yoni, who lost his life in the heroic rescue operation of the Israeli aircraft hijacked to Entebbe Airport in Uganda. Bibi, who also was shot but survived in another rescue operation, saw his survival as a mandate to protect and defend the Jewish people. I had no doubt how seriously he took that responsibility, notwithstanding all the political, legal, and ethical accusations that followed him wherever he went.

It was because of the extremely candid, respectful, and trusting relationship that Jared, Bibi, and I shared that we all felt that a unique opportunity might exist one day to really advance the cause of peace. If we could just get past all the land mines.

A completely unnecessary irritant was the planned ceremony in Israel to commemorate the seventy-fifth anniversary of the liberation of Auschwitz. The event was under the supervision of President Rivlin in coordination with Yad Vashem. The event was set to welcome forty-seven leaders from around the globe, including Prince Charles, Vladimir Putin, and Emmanuel Macron.

Rivlin had planned an extravagant affair with a state dinner the evening before the main event and a ceremony that would include speeches by all the key dignitaries. But there were massive problems.

The first was the effort to obtain the attendance of either President Trump or Vice President Pence. The timing was very disadvantageous for both but I was pressed over and over again to convince one to attend. I focused on Pence and after several conversations he was gracious enough to confirm to me his attendance, which I passed back to Rivlin. The very next day, I was advised—not by Rivlin but by my own staff—that Nancy Pelosi had accepted an invitation to attend as well.

I called Rivlin's office to ask about that undisclosed invitation. I mentioned that I was told that there would be only one attendee per nation, either a president, a prime minister, or a vice president. Why was the Speaker of the House included? Their response was this was none of my business.

I was furious. "You beg me to bring Pence as the representative of your most important ally, who is only doing this out of his love for Israel, and you don't have the decency to inform me that you are going around my back to invite the person responsible for Trump's impeachment! Someone whose status would not merit an invitation if from another country."

Mike Pence, to his great credit, was too much of a gentleman to let this slight affect his decision to attend. But a second issue arose, and this was a matter of principle. Pence learned that Putin would be a featured speaker and would direct his remarks to a false revision of history whereby the Soviet Union was portrayed as a victim of the Holocaust in contrast to Poland, which would be cast as the aggressor.

This issue is the third rail of Holocaust history, perhaps its most controversial and debated subject. On the one hand, the Poles committed unspeakable atrocities against the Jews during World War II. On the other hand, Poland was one of the few nations in Europe that did not surrender to the Nazis, it formed a courageous resistance movement, and it lost more than six million of its citizens (three million of whom were Jewish). In contrast, the Soviets had agreed with the Nazis to split up Poland between them and the Soviets only became allies after the Nazis turned on them. And, of course, after the Holocaust, the Soviet Union became as lethal a killer of innocent lives as the Nazis themselves.

Pence was furious that the conference, which was being sponsored by a Russian oligarch, was being used to present this one-sided and erroneous view of history. He made the request that Poland's president, Andrzej Duda, be given a short opportunity to speak about Poland's experience in the war to balance out the perspectives. He said it was appropriate because of the increasingly important role of Poland as an ally of both Israel and the United States. His request was denied.

Pence arrived the morning of the ceremony and we met to discuss his speech. While very disappointed in Rivlin, his commitment to Israel prevented him from being too critical. He simply added the words to his speech, "This is not the time to alter or revise the history of the Holocaust." He delivered his speech beautifully and flawlessly and had only one request from the sponsors: The upcoming wreath-laying ceremony involved forty-seven nations and would take several hours. Because he was exhausted from a long trip, he asked to go first. The response was that the wreaths would be laid in alphabetical order: The United States would follow Thailand. With that news, Pence left in frustration and I hung around to lay the wreath for the United States.

The speech by Putin went as advertised and the next day the academic community within Yad Vashem disassociated itself from the entire event. I then received a call from Rivlin's office demanding a one-on-one "courtesy" meeting between Rivlin and Pence. All I could do was express my disgust. "I didn't think it was possible to politicize the seventy-fifth anniversary of the liberation of Auschwitz but you succeeded in doing so." I also expressed my view that with all the incredible things Israel has to offer, why convene the leaders of the world around a Holocaust event? Why not something more positive?

It only validated my father's view that "the world loves dead Jews."

AT ONE POINT, AND IN THE FACE OF TRULY UNWARRANTED ACCUSA-tions of anti-Semitism against Trump, I challenged my staff to come up with a demonstrable action—not a speech—against anti-Semitism even though that task probably exceeded my responsibility. Aryeh Lightstone had a brilliant idea: We would create a US delegation that would lead the "March of the Living."

The March of the Living has been around for more than thirty years. It is an outstanding program that joins tens of thousands of people, mostly students, for a visit to the Nazi death camps followed by a visit to Israel. The "march" is the death march from Auschwitz to Birkenau, the murder facility that housed the gas chambers that so efficiently almost eliminated an entire race.

We assembled a group of US ambassadors from Europe—Ric Grenell from Germany, Duke Buchan from Spain, Ed McMullen from

Switzerland, Callista Gingrich from the Vatican, and Georgette Mos-
bacher from Poland—along with Special Envoy to Monitor and Combat Anti-Semitism Elan Carr and the chairman of the US Commission
for the Preservation of America's Heritage Abroad, Paul Packer, and
all met in Kraków, Poland, where we received a tour of a once thriving
Jewish community that is beginning to be reconstructed. We then
went to Auschwitz and walked the mile to Birkenau with thousands
of others. I led the march along with Rabbi Lau, who carried a Torah
that had been hidden in, and saved from, a concentration camp, and
our entire US delegation. We then flew late that night back to Israel to
reconvene at the Western Wall. It was the first US government delegation to Auschwitz-Birkenau and a trip that I hope becomes institu-
tionalized within future US administrations.

THERE WERE MORE DISTRACTIONS AS 2019 CAME TO A CLOSE. TEXAS-
based Noble Energy was trying its hardest to get Israeli approval to
turn on the Leviathan pipeline off the coast of Haifa, one of the largest deposits of natural gas in the world. With its discovery and development, Israel had achieved the miracle of energy independence. But
the Israeli bureaucracy made it exceedingly difficult for the facility to
become operational. We were not in a position, nor were we qualified,
to impose our views on this complicated situation, but we did engage
aggressively to facilitate the discussions and make sure all the deliverables were clearly articulated.

It was exhausting, but it bore fruit, and Leviathan went online
just before 2020 began.

AND THEN THE UNITED STATES ELIMINATED THE WORLD'S MOST LE-
thal terrorist, Qasem Soleimani, commander of the Iranian Quds

Force. Celebrations erupted in Israel and in parts of the United States just as vows of revenge were shouted by Iran's Supreme Leader. For the next few days all eyes were on Iran and its possible response. The counterattack came several days later with missiles fired by Iran against American positions in Iraq. Fortunately, there was no loss of life.

With all these events occurring in sequence and at times simultaneously, and with Israel headed for its third consecutive election, it was awfully hard to focus on a peace plan. But I did my best to move the ball forward in small increments. I gave several addresses on the elements of peace and Israel's right to retain at least some of Judea and Samaria; I attended the opening of the Ariel University Medical School, the first institution of its kind in that region; I presided at the groundbreaking of a fully fortified school on the Gaza periphery, which could withstand rocket attacks from Hamas and Islamic Jihad; and I prayed at the Western Wall at every opportunity, seeking God's help in advancing peace in this troubled region.

The Hebrew word for peace, *shalom*, appears in many Jewish prayers, in my case most notably in the priestly benediction that I, as a Kohen, recited daily: "May God lift his divine presence unto you and grant you peace." As I turned the corner into what might be my last year in office, I tried to give those words greater focus and concentration.

The challenges were daunting. My popularity among the Palestinian leadership was continuing to decline, with my likeness being burned in Ramallah from time to time and my security detail ever increasing.

One day in early 2020, Jared, Steven Mnuchin, and I were in Jerusalem discussing the prospects for peace while being given a tour of ancient Jewish coins and other artifacts. With the presentation of a two-thousand-year-old coin minted by Jews during the Second

Temple revolt, Mnuchin looked at me and said: "Here's how I know we will prevail. Two thousand years have passed since this coin and I, a Jew, as secretary of the Treasury, sign the currency of the most powerful nation on earth. We've come a long way."

Indeed we have. That gave me some renewed optimism.

15

A VISION FOR PEACE

In the world of finance, the term "arbitrage" is used to refer to an investment strategy where the investor makes money, or at least minimizes losses, regardless of the direction in which the market moves. In that sense, the Vision for Peace that Jared Kushner and I were advancing was becoming an arbitrage—we wanted to create a positive advancement regardless of how the "market" reacted.

Long before our peace plan came out, it was predicted to be far too skewed in favor of Israel. What else could be expected from an administration that had recognized Jerusalem as Israel's capital, validated Israel's sovereignty over the Golan Heights, and legitimized Israeli settlements in Judea and Samaria? In truth, the plan was constructed with a maximalist view toward the Palestinians: creating the maximum amount of Palestinian autonomy that Israeli security requirements could bear (statehood with full civilian autonomy, subject to Israeli overriding security control), creating the maximum amount of Palestinian territorial expansion that Israel's political, security, and historical considerations could tolerate (more than doubling the existing Palestinian geographic footprint), and creating the maximum package of capital investment to jump-start the Palestinian economy (more than $5 billion in seed capital that could support many more billions of loans). But there were limits to which Palestinian aspirations could be maximized.

The evacuation by Israel of eight thousand Jews living in the Gaza Strip in 2006 was a painful lesson that no Israeli has forgotten. It almost brought a civil war upon the country. If removing eight thousand Jews from Gaza was that controversial, the notion that Israel could ever evacuate one hundred thousand or more Jews from Judea and Samaria, Israel's biblical heartland and territorial center, was just out of the question. It could destroy Israel and deeply injure the interests of the United States, which depends so heavily upon Israel within the region. A US-sponsored plan that recognized this reality was essential to a fact-based approach.

We therefore believed, for multiple reasons, that notwithstanding the certain initial rejection of the plan by the Palestinians, there was a clear strategic purpose in moving forward. The plan could be given life by implementing much of the proposed territorial allocation, or at least keeping Israelis and Palestinians on their respective sides of the lines long enough for those lines to become the new terms of reference. And the plan, assuming endorsement by the government of Israel, would demonstrate Israel's willingness to set forth publicly, for the first time in its history, the terms, conditions, and boundaries by which it was willing to live side by side with a Palestinian state in peace and harmony. This demonstration, in turn, was likely to create significant space for other moderate nations in the region to move closer to Israel.

Very few nations in history have returned to their enemy land conquered in a defensive war. We thought Israel's demonstrated willingness to do that, in a clear and specific document, could move the region dramatically. Even if not, the plan would still advance the Israeli-Palestinian conflict, even if only theoretically at first. But either way, we were comfortable setting the arbitrage in motion.

The first component of the arbitrage was to hedge the outcome of the Israeli elections. When neither party could form a coalition after the September 2019 elections, I decided that we needed to lock down Israeli support regardless of who became the next prime minister. That prompted my outreach to both the Netanyahu camp and the camp of his political rival, Benny Gantz. Gantz was a former commander of the Israel Defense Forces, deeply patriotic, and, at six foot four and ruggedly handsome, an unusual look for an Israeli politician.

It was less complicated to garner Netanyahu's support. We had been in discussions for almost three years and had an excellent understanding of his views on what was negotiable and what wasn't. We understood his views on Israel's security needs, the corresponding limits on Palestinian autonomy, and Israel's minimum territorial requirements in any deal. During those discussions, we understood that while any sovereignty declaration over territory in Judea and Samaria earmarked for Israel would be deferred pending an agreement, at least the friction of Israeli settlement building would end—if Israel endorsed the plan it was free to build on its side of the boundary. When we shared with him and Israeli ambassador to the United States Ron Dermer the contours of the proposed deal, they were supportive. They did not, however, think releasing the plan made sense during the election season, even though the season showed no sign of ending.

Gantz was a relative newcomer to the political stage and I had not discussed the plan with him prior to the September elections. When I finally did, he was generally supportive but wanted to know much more about the proposed security protocols. He appointed Amir Eshel, a distinguished pilot and former head of the Israeli Air Force, to work with me to become familiar with the plan.

I spent hours with Eshel. He asked many thoughtful and detailed questions and I was completely candid with him about our approach. When we finished, he told me that this was the first plan ever proposed to resolve the Israeli-Palestinian conflict that Israel's security establishment could endorse. In particular, he enthusiastically endorsed Israel's overriding security supervision, its permanent presence in the Jordan Valley alongside Israel's border with the Kingdom of Jordan, and its control of Palestinian airspace. I was elated to hear that.

It was self-evident, however, that Gantz was not comfortable with the process. He knew that Bibi had a lengthy and accomplished track record with the Trump administration while he was a newcomer. Bibi also was a master politician who had forgotten more about election strategy than Gantz would ever know. Gantz understood that the Israeli electorate loved Donald Trump and he was not going to be any less pro-Trump than his rival. But he openly acknowledged his fear that he was being played by Netanyahu.

Gantz thus supported our plan as a political matter as well as on its merits, but he thought it would be perceived as another Bibi victory and he asked us not to release it until after the next election, scheduled for March 2, 2020. Bibi, somewhat surprisingly to us, thought that releasing the plan was fraught with electoral peril for himself as well—while it was undoubtedly good for the State of Israel, his rivals would focus only on the "gives" and none of the "gets." He thought that could hurt him and so he joined in the request not to release the plan until after March 2.

And so, as Jared and I and the rest of the team reconvened at the beginning of 2020, we saw our Vision for Peace slipping away.

THERE WAS NO REASON TO THINK THAT THE THIRD ROUND OF ELECtions on March 2 would be any more conclusive than the first two.

Even if coalition negotiations were successful, government formation wouldn't occur until late April. And a fourth election would push this out to the fall. By that time, President Trump would be deep into a campaign for his second term, and we would not have the bandwidth to get this done. The last thing we wanted to saddle upon the president was the uncertainty of a Middle East peace plan—with all its complexities and nuances—just as he was making the case to the American people to be reelected.

Jared and I realized it was now or never to launch the Vision for Peace. We first approached Netanyahu. He fully understood the timing and the risk that this opportunity would slip away. He also understood the political risk. As we were exploring alternatives, he asked whether the United States would approve Israeli sovereignty over the territory within Judea and Samaria that was earmarked for Israel under the plan—an expanse of about 30 percent of Judea and Samaria including all the existing Jewish communities, some territory for expansion, and the Jordan Valley. Jared asked what he would commit to in exchange. Bibi initially wasn't sure. I suggested that in exchange for the United States recognizing Israeli sovereignty, the prime minister would need to commit to negotiating the plan with the Palestinians in good faith for a period of, say, four years, and to refrain from any building construction during that period on the land earmarked for the Palestinians.

I thought this building moratorium, not within Jewish communities but elsewhere within the territory, was the essential piece to the puzzle—it enabled us to say to the Palestinians that they had four years to negotiate this deal without fear that their position would erode further; in essence, that they weren't being jammed. We kicked it around for a while and Bibi agreed that he would support the plan, even prior to elections, based upon the revised terms.

I then went to Gantz and explained to him that we were frustrated.

The Israeli candidates had taken almost an entire year to get through their internal politics but nothing had been resolved. I told him that Bibi had agreed to support the plan with the new provision that the United States would recognize Israeli sovereignty in exchange for Bibi's commitment to engage with the Palestinians on the plan's terms and not build any new settlements during a four-year period of engagement. Gantz saw that this was moving forward and he did not want this to be seen as Trump siding with Netanyahu over him. He immediately got on board, issuing a statement, reversing himself, that he "hopes President Trump releases his peace plan as soon as possible."

We had now solved the timing issue caused by Israel's elections, but more challenges lay ahead. In particular, we needed to guarantee that the plan would be endorsed by a large majority of the Israeli people and that it would be received favorably by our allies in the region.

I dealt with the Israeli side of the equation. I needed to protect the president against the risk that after he made a deal with Bibi, Bibi might lose the election in March and the Israeli vote would be viewed as a repudiation of the Trump Plan. I also needed to expand the buy-in from Israeli leaders so that the plan wasn't trivialized as a preelection gift to Netanyahu. I concluded that the only way to do that was to have Benny Gantz attend the rollout ceremony and express his support for the plan.

His participation would be a classic arbitrage hedge against the election outcome—one of the two would be the next prime minister, so if both publicly supported the plan, there was no downside for us; there was no way that the plan could be seen as rejected by Israel.

This, however, created a massive issue for Netanyahu. He was outraged by the suggested breach of protocol; he was the prime minister and Gantz was barely a member of the Knesset. He viewed it entirely inappropriate for Gantz to share the stage at this momentous ceremony. I told Bibi that we needed this for our own politics and to create the right perception. Ultimately, I convinced Bibi to let Gantz sit in the first row and simply be acknowledged by President Trump without Gantz speaking.

Bibi remained concerned that the president would call up Gantz for a picture. I candidly acknowledged to the prime minister that once the cameras started rolling, I could not guarantee what Donald would do. He goes off script and follows his gut. I didn't pretend to control that. I told him he would have to take that risk.

I then went back to Gantz and tried to sell him on sitting in the first row and being thanked by the president. He wasn't happy about being relegated to the audience but reluctantly agreed. It seemed a better alternative than staying home.

MEANWHILE, WHILE I WAS NEGOTIATING THE STAGECRAFT OF A rollout ceremony with Israel's two political rivals, Jared Kushner was out selling our plan to the Gulf and the broader Arab world. Jared's issues were entirely different. There were no political rivals in any of those nations, but there was a great deal of hesitancy to support a plan that the Palestinians undoubtedly would trash. After working the region with Robert O'Brien and Avi Berkowitz, who had succeeded Jason Greenblatt as the special envoy, they were surprisingly optimistic about at least a few favorable responses.

On January 14, 2020, I joined a call with the president, Jared, Secretary Pompeo, NSA O'Brien, and CIA Director Gina Haspel to get the go-ahead to roll out the peace plan, its full name being the president's "Vision for Peace, Prosperity and a Brighter Future." Subject to his approval, we were shooting for a ceremony at the White House in two weeks—January 28, 2020.

The president got right to the point. "David, why are we doing this? The Palestinians are going to say no and we won't have peace."

"Mr. President," I responded, "there's nothing I could put on a piece of paper today that Israel and the Palestinians would agree to. But there is still something that can be done to move down the playing field, probably into the red zone. For the first time in history, because of the trust we have developed with Israel, we have a right-wing prime minister agreeing to the territorial dimensions and other terms by which we would live side by side with a Palestinian state. We have sign-off by Israel on a conceptual map—unprecedented and unheard of in the history of the conflict. And with this, we think we will move several key Arab nations toward Israel like never before."

The president was pleased with this answer. Jared added his view that he thought our Arab allies would surprise us positively. I added the point about bringing Gantz to the White House to hedge against Israel's election outcome. We were cleared for January 28.

After the call, Jared and I regrouped. I wanted to go over with him some of the downside risks. The first, in my mind, was a disconnect between the president's objective of promoting peace and Bibi's political needs of motivating his right-wing base. I thought it quite possible that there would be a fair amount of confusion as to whether this was a peace plan or a sovereignty plan (also called an annexation plan). I was very concerned that the Israeli right would embrace the sovereignty but reject the concessions for peace.

Jared was less concerned. He saw a second arbitrage opportunity here, not between Netanyahu and Gantz but rather between Israel and its neighbors. He had no doubt that the recognition of sovereignty the United States was offering Israel as an inducement to proceed would garner massive international resistance. But he saw that commotion ultimately landing in one of two places, either of which was acceptable to him: a historic recognition of Israeli sovereignty over its biblical heartland in conformity with a peace plan endorsed by the Israeli government, or a deferral of that sovereignty in exchange for a diplomatic achievement of greater value to Israel, the United States, and the region. In other words, either we would give life to the plan and render it all but irrevocable, or we would give life to potential normalization between Israel and other nations. Although I was a strong advocate for Israeli sovereignty over Jewish communities in Judea and Samaria, and believed that we could accomplish that recognition and still make peace in the future, I also understood that making peace first was a massive opportunity that we must pursue if it arose. I looked forward to driving all the vectors to the right conclusion.

And then it all blew up.

ON JANUARY 23, JUST FIVE DAYS BEFORE THE ROLLOUT AT THE WHITE House, Mike Pence was with me in my newly constructed office in the Jerusalem embassy along with Netanyahu. In front of a spray of cameras, Pence expressed how much he was looking forward to greeting the prime minister next week to discuss the peace plan. He also said, using words that had been cleared by the prime minister's office, that he was grateful that the prime minister had recommended that General Gantz be invited as well.

I didn't make anything of the last comment when it was made but it would occupy the next five hours of my life that felt like five hundred.

An hour later Benny Gantz was on the phone and he was furious. He was outraged by the appearance that it was Netanyahu rather than the president who was inviting him to the White House. He felt he was being set up by Bibi and would be humiliated.

I offered to clarify that the invitation was coming directly from Trump, but that didn't seem to matter. Although Gantz and I already had gone through the stagecraft and he had confirmed that he was on board, he now seemed to realize, perhaps with input from his political team, that the optics of him sitting in the audience while Bibi took a bow was not a good look for him. I tried to hold Gantz to our prior agreement but he was locked in and ready to blow off the entire event.

I wasn't going to tell Benny Gantz how important his attendance was to us—it made the rollout of the peace plan so much more credible and apolitical. It would just cause him to demand a higher-profile visit—which would then flip Bibi against the visit.

I had only a few days to put this back together.

I had an idea and called Gantz back. I suggested that he come the day before the rollout, meet with Trump in the Oval Office, tell him how much he liked the deal, and then go home before the ceremony. He and Bibi never would have to see each other.

Gantz responded that such a scenario was acceptable, and I committed to try to get it done.

I next called Jared to see if we could get Gantz into the Oval Office on the twenty-seventh. He said we could. I then informed Bibi of the change of plans.

But Bibi wasn't happy at all. He felt that this would elevate Gantz from a nonspeaking, non-visible role to a one-on-one in the Oval Office. I told him that he would have the room to himself on the day of the ceremony—along with a private reception in the White House. And besides, I said, we both knew that if Trump saw Gantz in the front row, he might very well call him up for a picture. I told Bibi this was the deal and that I couldn't change it, and finally he agreed that it probably was the best outcome for him anyway.

This is the insanity that apparently happens to competing candidates in their third round of Israeli elections! Here we were, talking about a game-changing approach to the Israeli-Palestinian conflict that, for the first time, met Israel's security needs. But what was important, at that moment, was who gets to sit where!

As we got closer to January 28, I could see that we were heading for yet another massive meltdown. Gantz and Bibi had very different views on sovereignty; Bibi wanted it immediately, Gantz wanted it only "in consultation with the international community," which to my mind meant "Never."

I was strongly in favor of sovereignty. I thought it crucial for Israel, after fifty years of confusion, to begin concrete steps to determine its eastern border. I also understood that if regional peace could be achieved on terms that did not cancel out sovereignty in the future, that would certainly take precedence. No outcome was as good as peace. My expectation was that we had at least a month to go through the mapping of territory and the legal process and see what might develop before a sovereignty declaration would occur. Jared hoped it might take longer so that he could maximize his time to trade a deferral of sovereignty for a peace deal. And Bibi thought it could happen the next day.

I got a sinking feeling when I saw that Bibi had invited to Washington the most strident supporters of the sovereignty movement. I wasn't sure what they were expecting but I doubted it matched up with Jared's or even my views. These guys were overtly rejecting the Vision for Peace but willing to accept the parts that they liked. They were absolutely the wrong people to represent the face of the Israeli reaction.

On the twenty-seventh, the day before the announcement ceremony, we had the Oval Office meeting with Gantz. It was great—cordial, friendly, and substantive. Gantz told the president that he totally supported the plan and that if he was elected prime minister, he would use it to make peace. He added one thing that caught me by surprise. He asked the president not to let Bibi declare sovereignty before the March 2 election. The president nodded in agreement.

On the twenty-eighth, we had the ceremony, and it was spectacular. A full house of Israel supporters rose to their feet to applaud with almost every sentence uttered by the president and the prime minister. Before the event, I had asked Israeli ambassador Ron Dermer to make sure that Netanyahu's speech was appropriately targeted toward peace rather than to a declaration of sovereignty. He said he'd help, but the speech was being aired in Israeli prime time and Bibi's electorate wanted to hear about the sovereignty—that was what would deliver the election.

I liked Bibi's speech, but then again, I was a strong advocate for sovereignty. President Trump, however, standing next to Bibi as he spoke for far too long, didn't hear enough about peace to his liking. I went straight to do media after the event and didn't catch the president's reaction, but I was told he was not happy with Netanyahu's performance.

Three attendees at the ceremony were called out by the president and received standing ovations: the ambassadors to the United States from the United Arab Emirates, Bahrain, and Oman. But even more important were some of the public reactions to the plan from other countries.

As it turned out, Jared Kushner had more than delivered on his effort to garner support from some key neighbors. The Kingdom of Saudi Arabia came through with the following statement:

> *The Kingdom appreciates the efforts of President Trump's administration to develop a comprehensive peace plan between the Palestinian and Israeli sides, and encourages the start of direct peace negotiations . . . under the auspices of the United States.*

In diplomatic speak, this was a ringing and completely unexpected endorsement. A similar statement came out of Morocco that noted how the plan converged with many of their own principles and how the treatment of Jerusalem properly provided for freedom of worship of all three monotheistic faiths.

The expectation among the foreign-policy elite had been that the Vision for Peace would die a fast and furious death, but the reaction ended up stunning everyone. In addition to Saudi Arabia, Morocco, UAE, and Bahrain, the following countries expressed support, to varying extents, for proceeding with the Vision: Egypt, Qatar, United Kingdom, Austria, Australia, India, France, Italy, Brazil, Colombia, Poland, Paraguay, Denmark, Chile, Czech Republic, Japan, Hungary, South Korea, North Macedonia, and Kosovo.

It was not the embarrassment or disaster that had been predicted, but a diplomatic home run!

The only people who came out against the plan—and we all took pleasure in repeating this—were the Palestinians, Iran, Turkey, every one of the 2020 Democratic candidates, my friends at J Street, and Jeremy Corbyn, the UK opposition leader frequently accused of anti-Semitism.

STILL, THE PENDING POLITICAL CAMPAIGN IN ISRAEL MADE THESE advancements less important to the Netanyahu government than sovereignty. That's where his votes were to be found. And we didn't understand at the time that while most of the territory subject to a sovereignty declaration under the Vision for Peace required much more detailed mapping before sovereignty could be effectuated by Israel, that was not true of the Jordan Valley, a large swath of land along the border with Jordan, which apparently had already been fully mapped out by the Israelis. An immediate declaration of sovereignty over the Jordan Valley gave us no room whatsoever for diplomacy. We would strike out before ever coming up to bat.

As I was speaking to about forty faith leaders right after the ceremony, explaining to them the general contours of the deal, I saw my phone vibrating repeatedly. Jared was trying to reach me.

I took a break from my presentation to see what was so urgent. As soon as I said hello, Jared jumped down my throat: "Did you know that Bibi is annexing the freaking Jordan Valley today?" I answered "No" and tried to maintain my composure and finished up.

Jared and I then met the Israeli contingent at Blair House.

It was a difficult and unpleasant meeting, the first of its kind in more than three years. And that tension would last for another two weeks.

Netanyahu said emphatically that we had a deal for immediate sovereignty. Jared responded that he thought the mapping process was a first step, which would take some time. He added that the president said he would recognize sovereignty "after the completion of the mapping process." To which Netanyahu responded that no mapping was necessary for the Jordan Valley. To which Jared responded, "We never discussed that." Sadly, everyone was telling the truth.

Jared was not budging. He wanted time. He saw in the unexpectedly positive reaction from the Arab nations in the region the possibility that something transformative might be possible. I was in agreement with Jared with one proviso: I thought we needed to have a well-defined process for the recognition of sovereignty firmly in place so that we could address the confusion that had emerged in our plan. Not only did we owe that to Israel, but by having this process in place with a tight time line, we would have a clear path toward sovereignty if we continued on that path, and we would also draw out any diplomatic alternatives that might be available. Jared agreed.

I now had to work this through the Israeli government. There were some hard feelings. Netanyahu felt that he was entitled to immediate relief. I assured him that we intended to move forward on the path to sovereignty but it needed to be a more deliberative process.

The pressure of the third election was getting to him and he was embarrassed that he had raised expectations on sovereignty without delivering. He thought that could be a fatal blow to his campaign.

I spent a few days working with him and his team on how to proceed. To relieve some of the pressure on him, I took some on myself—I tweeted that the United States would not support sovereignty on a piecemeal basis; it would get done right and it would take some time. If there weren't an election in four weeks, this would be easy to solve. But there was. At some points Netanyahu was ready to declare sovereignty unilaterally; at others he was more flexible.

I made several appearances before the Israeli media responding to the unfair and untrue accusations that Bibi had misled his followers on sovereignty. I explained, patiently, that the United States would support Israel's declaration of sovereignty as provided in the Vision for Peace, but the process would require a good deal of careful deliberation by a mapping committee to address the numerous highly detailed and technical issues. All of that was demonstrably true, as evidenced by the many experts who met with me and proposed creative but different ways to draw the final map.

When a task is assigned to a "committee," a common perception is that the intent of the assignor is to bury the proposed action in bureaucracy. The "mapping committee" was so perceived in Israel, again creating a backlash that Bibi was never going to follow through on his sovereignty pledge. To fix that issue, and to create the movement that we all wanted, I became the chairman of the committee and I added Aryeh Lightstone to the mix. That succeeded in giving the committee some credibility, although the campaign being what it was, the nastiness continued. The committee got to work right away, and I was enthusiastic that we would facilitate Israeli sovereignty in accordance with the Vision.

To this day, some accuse our sovereignty efforts as a "bluff"—a means to draw out the Palestinians and/or the moderate Arab nations. No way. We weren't bluffing, and I have no doubt we would have recognized sovereignty if the Abraham Accords hadn't come along. We were moving forward, but with a clear understanding that a real opportunity for peace was the gold standard.

BY MID-FEBRUARY, JUST TWO WEEKS AFTER WE LAUNCHED, WE WERE in a good place. The Vision for Peace was now well understood by the conservative, Evangelical, and Jewish communities, and we had received significant accolades. Others, mostly Democrat politicians and progressive Jewish groups, panned our effort, but we expected that. Prime Minister Netanyahu had reached an acceptable resolution with us—the sovereignty process was alive and well and he could still campaign that he was the one to bring it home. Gantz, as well, was bullish on the plan although less so on sovereignty. The political sides had been drawn with rare clarity.

The Gulf states were politely wondering if sovereignty could be delayed, but we were making no commitments. The table was set either for the historic declaration of sovereignty that I was pushing, or for an equally historic substitute whereby one or more Arab nations established ties with Israel.

We were content to let the elections play out and see what developed. All alternatives were good with Jared and with me.

We had our arbitrage in place.

16

THE ABRAHAM ACCORDS

Yuval Steinitz was a senior member of the Likud and the minister of energy. Observing the reaction to the Vision for Peace of the Israeli Far Right and Far Left, both of whom were in fierce opposition, he couldn't help but note the irony: The Israeli Left opposed the plan because we were killing the two-state solution, while the Israeli Right opposed it because we were creating a Palestinian state.

On that basis alone, Steinitz concluded, we must have drafted the correct plan.

Opposition to the plan was not limited to Israel's domestic audience. No collection of countries was more supportive of the Palestinian cause than the European Union. Through November 2019, the EU's foreign minister, Federica Mogherini, had been nothing but hostile to Israel's interests and completely exculpatory toward Palestinian misconduct. Her replacement, Josep Borrell, jumped right into her shoes and moved quickly to have the EU pass a resolution condemning the Trump peace plan.

Given the EU's track record, we knew this would pass unless we undertook significant engagement.

Jared Kushner and Avi Berkowitz mobilized our foreign policy team to push back, with most calls made by Jared directly. Jared made the case that preemptive rejection of the peace plan would just push the parties further apart and was thus antithetical to the interests of those seeking a peaceful resolution to the Israeli-Palestinian conflict. The results of that diplomatic blitz were incredibly encouraging: Six of the twenty-seven EU nations opposed the resolution, including Italy, Hungary, Austria, and the Czech Republic. It was a shocking blow to our opponents, but it did not deter PA president Mahmoud Abbas.

Abbas had a "go to" move that had never failed him before: the United Nations. He called for and obtained an emergency meeting of the Security Council to condemn the Vision for Peace. He addressed the Council with the Vision's map in hand and spoke of the deal in the most critical terms.

Abbas knew that no resolution could overcome a certain US veto. But he fully expected a 14–1 vote on condemnation, with the United States isolated from the rest of the world.

He severely miscalculated.

Abbas convinced a nonpermanent member, Tunisia, to sponsor the UN resolution. When we found out, Jared caused a high-level call to be placed to Tunisia's leadership expressing the frustration of the United States in Tunisia's misplaced condemnation of our efforts.

In short order, Tunisia's ambassador to the United Nations was fired and the resolution withdrawn.

Abbas pressed forward with other traditional allies on the Council, as Jared pushed back, defending the Vision for Peace in closed-door meetings. As a result, the Palestinian resolution could not even garner a majority vote on the Council, and the effort was abandoned.

Bitter disappointment was attributed to the Palestinian leadership. A senior Palestinian official was quoted as saying, "We are coming back with our tails between our legs. We were caught unprepared, and we didn't properly assess the American pressure on the members of the Security Council."

Although it was very important that the Palestinians not succeed in turning the world against our plan, I wasn't happy that the Palestinians had failed so miserably. It just reinforced the fact that the Palestinian leadership continued to live in a bubble untouched by and unaccountable to its people or the emerging realities. It saddened me that Abbas would not even consider a proposal that doubled the Palestinian geographic footprint, presented massive economic and educational opportunity to the Palestinian people, and provided for meaningful autonomy and dignity.

Palestinian failure was sad to watch but still an important component of our strategy. From the day we took office, two intractable Palestinian positions kept us and all our predecessors at a standstill: First, the Palestinians outrageously insisted on two states comprised of a Jewish/Arab binational state (Israel) and a Palestinian-only state (Palestine); and second, the Palestinians were confident that they had a veto on all issues—that until their impossible demands were met, the world would prevent Israel from moving forward in its own interests.

The Palestinians were now seeing, for the first time, that their neighbors and allies had other more important issues than them, and that the vilification of Israel was unfounded.

With the diplomatic wind at our back, we continued to sell our plan at every opportunity. On March 2, 2020, as Israel began counting its votes from the election going on the same day, I addressed the AIPAC Policy Conference before eighteen thousand people—my third time on the big stage. I explained the plan as follows:

The Far Left won't say this but the truth is that the Vision is massively pro-Palestinian. It represents the first time since the beginning of the conflict that the State of Israel has agreed to live side by side with a Palestinian state under precise terms, conditions, and territorial dimensions. It allocates the territory in Judea and Samaria in proportion to the respective sizes of the Israeli and Palestinian populations living there. It creates a platform for massive investment—not the handouts that the Palestinian leadership has embraced for so long with nothing to show for it other than the personal enrichment of the leaders themselves. And it provides a four-year runway for the Palestinians to achieve the necessary conditions of statehood, secure in the knowledge that during that period the territorial integrity of their state will be preserved.

When you students on college campuses hear Israel castigated as a nation intent on subjugating its oppressed minority, this plan, which has been overwhelmingly endorsed by the Israeli population, conclusively proves just the opposite!

I also took a stand for Judea and Samaria:

Now, some have challenged the president's Vision as leaving too much land to Israel. Imagine that! A demand that the Jewish state should surrender Hebron, the burial place of Abraham, Isaac, Jacob, Sarah, Rebecca, and Leah; Bet El, where Jacob dreamed of a ladder with angels ascending to the heavens and descending back to earth and where he received the word of God; Shiloh, where the ark of the covenant rested for hundreds of years before being moved to the Temple in Jerusalem; or Qasr al-Yahud, the "bridge of the Jews" where Joshua led the Israelite nation across the Jordan River and where John the Baptist baptized Jesus.

We are all familiar with the ugly term "Judenrein"—it was a term used by the Nazis for a place where Jews were not allowed. Well let me make something abundantly clear. Under the Trump administration, the biblical heartland of Israel in Judea and Samaria will never be Judenrein!

Those were the political bookends of our plan—a huge improvement in the quality of life of Palestinians, while remaining true to the ancient biblical heritage of the Jewish people. That was a plan many people could get behind, and I received thunderous applause when these themes were delivered.

Later that evening, I received word that Bibi had won the election. His Likud Party had won the most seats in the Knesset and his right-wing coalition had a narrow 61-seat majority. It looked like we were finally ready to begin the second arbitrage.

But a few hours later, Likud's number fell by two seats and no group looked like it could form a government.

There was soon to be more uncertainty in Israeli politics and, indeed, all over the world.

THERE WAS OTHER NEWS AT THAT MARCH 2020 AIPAC CONFERENCE that dwarfed even the Israeli elections. A highly contagious virus was circulating that looked invincible and already had put some attendees in the hospital in critical condition. As Tammy and I left the conference, I assumed that I had been infected. I had shaken thousands of hands and only occasionally disinfected with Purell.

Miraculously, Tammy and I were spared and we raced back to Israel, arriving just hours before the scheduled closing of Ben Gurion Airport. As I sat on the plane planning the next steps, I wondered how we could proceed in the face of the COVID pandemic. With limitations on travel, our diplomatic efforts would be slowed dramatically. We were thrust into further uncertainty, perhaps even more severe than Israel's dysfunctional politics.

Back in Israel, Bibi's coalition group was stuck at about 58 seats, with the elusive 3 nowhere in sight. Gantz could have mobilized the remaining 62 seats to form a government, but that would have forced him to absorb into his coalition the 13 members of the Arab Joint List as well as an additional Far Left party. He made clear, perhaps committing a rookie error, that he would not take that path. That left Netanyahu and Gantz with two options: Proceed to a fourth election at a massive cost to an already beleaguered economy, or join forces in a unity government.

On March 26, 2020, a unity government was announced to address the COVID pandemic and its effects. A rotation would be established whereby Netanyahu would be the prime minister for the first eighteen months with Gantz serving as alternative prime minister and defense minister, and Gantz would assume the leading role beginning in the nineteenth month until the thirty-sixth month. Most of Gantz's fellow members of the Blue and White Party were outraged at what they saw as Gantz capitulating to Bibi, and the party splintered. This left Gantz in a precarious position if the details of the announced deal could not be worked out.

Almost immediately after the announcement, there was friction. Gantz was demanding a veto on whether Bibi could declare sovereignty over territory in Judea and Samaria. Bibi asked me to call Gantz to see if it could be ironed out. I asked Gantz why he was raising this now, when he told Trump that he supported the plan as long as no sovereignty was declared before election day on March 2. He answered that as the defense minister he had an independent obligation to pass on any action that could create a security risk for Israel. I asked him to work with us discreetly on this issue instead of politicizing it. If there was a public perception that sovereignty was not happening, we would lose both sovereignty as well as our leverage to drive a peace deal.

On April 7, Netanyahu and Gantz agreed that sovereignty would not be declared before July 1. That created a bit of space for us to get to the right place, whichever place that might be. But there remained open issues between the sides.

With Gantz falling in the polls, I was approached by some on the right about the prospects of them breaking off and forming a narrow 61-seat right-wing government without Gantz. They would then move directly on sovereignty. I told them not to bet on Trump in those circumstances, especially when this group did not endorse the Vision for Peace. He was preoccupied with COVID and would not see as appropriate such a move by a narrow right-wing government under the current circumstances with the pandemic. Moreover, he would not see a precipitous sovereignty declaration as consistent with a commitment to peace. I made the point again and again to my friends on the right that the president had sponsored a peace plan with a sovereignty option, not a sovereignty plan without a peace option. The 61-seat coalition turned out to be illusory anyway.

On April 20, the unity government was formed. All of us on the American side working on the file expressed our congratulations.

With the parties having agreed that there would be no declaration of sovereignty before July 1, we now had at least eighty-one days to sort out the issues and to see what opportunities might arise from the tension that was being created.

And within a month, the Palestinians made a series of blunders that would have ramifications beyond what they might have imagined.

The State Department had embarked on a program to provide humanitarian aid around the world to ease the suffering caused by the pandemic. I tried to get $5 million—a small but still meaningful amount—earmarked for Palestinian health care organizations. After we funded the amount, the Palestinian Authority denied having received it and could not have been less gracious. Then, a PA spokesman announced that it was filing "war crime" charges against me at the International Criminal Court—even though I had immunity as a diplomat. Finally, and worst of all, Abu Dhabi sent an unmarked jumbo jet directly to Ben Gurion Airport with humanitarian supplies for the Palestinian people, the first time an Emirati commercial flight had flown directly to Israel. The Palestinian Authority saw this as a huge insult and refused to accept the supplies.

The supplies from Abu Dhabi were rerouted to Hamas in the Gaza Strip.

These events, in the aggregate, caused many within the United States and the United Arab Emirates to just scratch their heads in disbelief at the stubborn recklessness of Palestinian leadership.

This view of the PA as reckless was a view that only grew and expanded over the following months.

BY EARLY MAY 2020, WE HAD ENTERED A THICKET OF COMPLEXITY ALL revolving around the potential declaration and US recognition of Israeli sovereignty over Judea and Samaria. The right-wing parties in Israel were not part of the new government. Rather, they had been relegated to the opposition and began to lash out at the Trump peace plan. Two of their leaders, Yossi Dagan and David Elhayani, even went so far as to denounce the plan as creating "a Palestinian terror state." Naftali Bennett, a more moderate member of the Israeli right, called the plan "a disaster." Statements were leaked to the press that the Trump plan would only recognize Israeli sovereignty over parts of Judea and Samaria if a Palestinian state were created simultaneously, and that Israel's borders could never expand beyond the conceptual map even if the Palestinians continued to reject talks after four years. Both statements were false—no Palestinian state was to be created under the Vision for Peace unless and until the Palestinian leadership had met the conditions of the plan, something years away at best, and the Vision did not protect Palestinian territorial rights if they refused to negotiate. Some on the Israeli right went even further: Those on the right who had relationships with Evangelical leaders in the United States made requests that they inform the president of their opposition to the plan.

I met with some leaders within the Israeli Right to calm them down and try to stem their self-defeating actions. Two of them, I knew, neither spoke nor read English. I asked them who provided them with a Hebrew translation of the plan. They responded that none existed. And then I blew up. "You are feeding the press outright lies about the plan, misleading our voters, and making vile accusations about the best friend you have ever had in the White House. And you have never even read the plan. What in the world is wrong with you?"

The more moderate among the right wing immediately walked back the accusations. Naftali Bennett, Israel Ganz, and Ayelet Shaked all posted tweets that Trump was Israel's greatest friend. But the others held their ground. The actions by the Israeli Right, although perhaps well intended, were unhelpful and created confusion and mistrust that reached Washington, DC. At a time when few were willing to focus on anything other than COVID, their stridency and false accusations made it much more difficult for us to gain traction on sovereignty.

In mid-May, Jared sent me a picture of a headline from *The Washington Post* that Trump had circled and dropped on Jared's desk. It read, WILL TRUMP SAVE ISRAEL FROM NETANYAHU'S RECKLESS LAND GRAB? That was not a pleasant sight but it got even worse. Jared emailed me to warn that I was far away from the Oval Office and not current on the president's thinking. He thought I might be getting ahead of where the president was willing to go.

Plainly, sovereignty had lost favor with the president.

Even in Israel, sovereignty also had lost its luster. Polls indicated that the Israeli public now opposed it 42 percent to 32 percent, although I believed that this poll was temporal, reflecting the nation's overwhelming interest in defeating COVID. In America, most Jewish organizations also were opposed and AIPAC let it be known that members of Congress were free to express negative views about sovereignty. Letters poured in from House and Senate members on the American Right and Left, advocating all sides of the issue. But COVID-19 not only had become the dominant issue, it had become the only issue, and very few seemed to be in the mood for more turmoil. I'm not sure any of those letters were read by anyone in the White House with COVID going on.

On May 31, I had a heart-to-heart with Prime Minister Netanyahu and Speaker of the Knesset Yariv Levin. I explained that unlike moving the embassy to Jerusalem and recognizing the Golan Heights, which were done without advance notice, the sovereignty issue had become a *balagan* (Hebrew for a big mess). Even worse, it had been peeled off as an isolated issue untethered to the peace plan. In that context, it had no chance of advancement.

I told Bibi, "You haven't said a word about peace in two months, you haven't offered any initiatives to improve Palestinian life, and you've formed a government with people who are not with you on this issue. How do we proceed with sovereignty when it is opposed by your defense minister [Gantz] and your foreign minister [Gabi Ashkenazi]? No one seems to care about this right now in your country or mine and even Mark Meadows, the president's chief of staff who is very close to the Evangelical community, thinks that the Israeli right wing has sown so much confusion that even many Evangelicals are not on board."

I continued. "I know you want to get this done and so do I. But we have to do it right. We need a consensus on how to proceed within the unity government. I think we should phase in the sovereignty so there is a chance to engage in some diplomacy and we need a big package of practical initiatives for the Palestinians. Give me something I can sell to the president."

Bibi was amenable to that approach but he doubted that Gantz would play ball. Gantz knew that any sovereignty declaration would propel Bibi to enormous popularity, notwithstanding the current COVID-deflated polls, and that would leave him exposed to Bibi not delivering on the leadership rotation.

At the invitation of both Netanyahu and Gantz, I then embarked upon a week of shuttle diplomacy to try to develop a consensus. While I told Bibi that we wanted Gantz on board, I made sure that Gantz understood that he didn't have a veto. What I told him was that if he could get comfortable with a more modest approach, we would give that approach serious weight.

We talked all together, we talked separately. One day I walked into a scheduled meeting and I found them so furious with each other on a different issue that I just canceled the session. On another day I asked Gantz and Ashkenazi to just give me the minimal territorial dimensions of sovereignty in phase one that were acceptable, even if that was just one percent of the territory. I couldn't get an answer. What I did get was this response: "I'll give you an answer when I get from Bibi the guarantees that he'll keep our deal." Hearing that, I could see that the level of mistrust was insurmountable and the relationship was broken. It saddened me greatly.

I reported all of this to Jared. I told him that Gantz would not come on board. To keep the process moving we would need to go with Bibi alone. He was the prime minister and he had the votes to declare sovereignty. If we didn't, our efforts would come to a swift ending.

And then something unexpected happened, and our efforts took an interesting twist. Yousef Al Otaiba, the UAE ambassador to the United States, penned an op-ed published in Hebrew in *Yedioth Ahronoth*, an Israeli daily paper. He urged the Israeli people to resist a declaration of sovereignty over parts of Judea and Samaria, dangling possibilities of improved relations between the two countries. It was something that had been talked about behind the scenes for years, but the public statement in Hebrew in Israel made a lot of news.

The article reinforced my view as well as Jared's that sovereignty could be delayed in exchange for something of perhaps greater value. But the probability of sovereignty had to be real in order for it to be traded, and I personally remained anxious for it to occur. I arranged for Jared to speak with Bibi directly. He told the prime minister that the president was dealing with a massive pandemic, a crippled economy, and riots in the streets. He was far from sold on sovereignty and we would need help making the case for it. He needed to roll up his sleeves and do something big and bold on the Palestinian infrastructure and humanitarian side to give this some balance. He got the message.

His team got to work on the Palestinian deliverables—all non-security related improvements to infrastructure, education, and health care. Word leaked out that there was no deal with Gantz but that his consent would not be required for a sovereignty declaration. The press then reported, truthfully, that I had been summoned back to Washington to meet with the president on the issue.

And then the Palestinians committed yet another blunder. Seeing that I was meeting with the president and that a declaration of sovereignty might be imminent, the Palestinian Authority reached out to the State Department to arrange a call between Abbas and Pompeo. Jared and I spoke with Mike and we all thought it would be a good idea for him to hear Abbas out. An hour before the call was set to take place, the PA called again to say that Abbas would speak with Pompeo only if the United States agreed to cancel all consideration of sovereignty.

Pompeo was furious that Abbas was playing games, and the call never happened.

ON JUNE 24, 2020, I SAT IN THE OVAL OFFICE WITH JARED KUSHNER, Mike Pompeo, Mark Meadows, Mike Pence, Robert O'Brien, and Avi Berkowitz. The president came in and it was obvious immediately that the issue of sovereignty was not foremost on his mind. He was frustrated by COVID, and he was angered by what he saw as the double standard applied against him and his staff by the FBI, the Special Counsel, and the Justice Department compared to the seeming lack of interest in prosecuting those who spied on his campaign. When the conversation came back around to the peace plan, he said he understood how a phased declaration of sovereignty could give life to the peace plan but that he didn't think the plan was likely to garner much traction in the near term.

Alarmingly, he was content to make this a "second-term issue," but I pushed back and said that we needed to keep it alive for at least the summer to see what it would bring. Mike Pompeo was very supportive of sovereignty and, given the president's high opinion of his secretary of state, Trump ended the meeting by giving Mike authority to "do what you think is right."

I returned to Israel the next day. The readout of our meeting with the president was that no decision had yet been made. Throughout the succeeding three weeks, I worked with Israeli government officials to move forward on a phased-sovereignty approach with simultaneous infrastructure enhancements for the Palestinians. We worked on plans for a north-south highway that would link Palestinian communities within Judea and Samaria, improving the quality and efficiency of checkpoints from Palestinian communities into Israel, and even legalizing certain Palestinian home construction that had been undertaken without building permits. We were making good progress.

And then, on July 17, Ambassador Al Otaiba spoke with Avi Berkowitz to see if improved relations between the UAE and Israel might forestall the sovereignty declaration. Jared and I got on the phone to discuss this development.

Jared clearly thought peace with the UAE was a much bigger prize than sovereignty, and I couldn't disagree.

"Jared," I said, "if we can delay rather than cancel sovereignty, and get full—FULL—diplomatic relations between Israel and UAE, it is clearly better for America, Israel, and the world, and a massive win for the president. I'm fully on board."

It would be a big win all around. Getting sovereignty on the table and keeping it there, subject only to delay, meant that the issue was no longer toxic. Given the state of Israeli politics, this was as good as it got. And peace between Israel and the UAE was, well, Mideast peace.

And so the situation began to evolve from peace with the Palestinians to peace with other Arabs.

Hundreds of conversations ensued, including with Pompeo and O'Brien as well as General Miguel Correa, who worked at the NSC and had outstanding relationships with the UAE's royal family. The discussions dragged a bit and at times I thought the sovereignty train might get back on track. But on August 3, we got an email from General Correa quoting a message from UAE Crown Prince Mohammed bin Zayed: "Please pass to the President I will deliver."

I kept Prime Minister Netanyahu and Ambassador Ron Dermer abreast of all these developments. The prime minister saw sovereignty being delayed, perhaps for years, and I shared his disappointment. But I also knew that peace between Israel and the UAE was far bigger, and it was something that Netanyahu had worked for all his career. He was justifiably satisfied and proud of the outcome.

I flew back to Washington to get this wrapped up, with only a handful of people from each country aware of what was about to break. We worked on a joint trilateral statement and I paid careful attention to the verb chosen to put off the sovereignty declaration. "Israel will suspend declaring sovereignty" was the phrase we agreed upon. Suspension, by definition, is temporary.

I drafted and added to the joint statement a plug for our peace plan: "The United States and Israel recall with gratitude the appearance of the United Arab Emirates at the White House reception held on January 28, 2020, at which President Trump presented his Vision for Peace, and express their appreciation for the United Arab Emirates' related supportive statements. The parties will continue their efforts in this regard to achieve a just, comprehensive and enduring resolution to the Israeli-Palestinian conflict."

And there it was.

The Vision for Peace was about to achieve peace, not the peace the Vision provided, but certainly one at least as significant.

ON AUGUST 13, 2020, JARED KUSHNER, AVI BERKOWITZ, AND I GATHered in the West Wing. In one hour, we were to enter the Oval Office and stand next to the president as he hosted Prime Minister Netanyahu and Crown Prince bin Zayed on a call confirming their historic agreement. Following that call, we would invite in the press and make statements.

Less than thirty minutes before we were about to start, General Correa blurted out nervously, "We need a name." I asked him what he meant. He said all agreements like these have names, from the Oslo Accords to the Camp David Accords. I asked him if he had any ideas. He suggested the Abraham Accords, and I loved it immediately.

"Quick," I said, "let's let Otaiba and Dermer know and let's revise the president's talking points."

A few minutes later we stood around the Resolute Desk as the call was made. When it ended, the ten or so of us in attendance broke into simultaneous applause that must have lasted for at least five minutes. It was a truly heartfelt outpouring of emotion at having achieved something truly historic.

At the press briefing, the president gave Jared, Avi, a few others, and me a chance to speak. First up was me. "David," the president said, "explain why we are using the term 'Abraham Accords.'"

I suppose I could have said that this was what Miguel Correa came up with an hour ago, but instead I explained: "Abraham, as many of you know, was the father of all three great faiths: He is referred to as Abraham in the Christian faith, Ibrahim in the Muslim faith, and Avraham in the Jewish faith. No person better symbolizes the potential for unity among all these great faiths than Abraham, and that's why this accord has been given that name."

After the briefing, Jared, Avi, and I hugged and went off to appear on various media outlets. The reaction was overwhelmingly positive. Congratulations poured in from Evangelical groups, from AIPAC, and from Jewish groups of all religious and political stripes. David Ignatius of *The Washington Post*, a fierce critic of Trump's foreign policy, was effusive in his praise. And Tom Friedman of *The New York Times*, as vocal a Trump hater as I have read, called the Abraham Accords a "geopolitical earthquake."

Jared and I caught up later in the day. There wasn't much to say— just a deep sigh of relief, some mutual admiration, and much thanks to God.

I couldn't help but hearken back to the original rivalry between Jews and Arabs—the conflict between Abraham's two sons, Isaac and Ishmael. So intense was that conflict that Abraham, at the urging of his wife, Sarah, banished Ishmael and his mother, Hagar, from the family home. This upset Abraham greatly, but God promised Abraham that he would protect Ishmael and that both Isaac and Ishmael would give rise to great nations—the Jewish nation from Isaac and the Arab nation from Ishmael. When Abraham died, we learn that Isaac and Ishmael reconciled and together buried their father in the Cave of Machpelah in Hebron.

That reconciliation of some thirty-eight hundred years ago is now being re-created—by the descendants of Isaac and Ishmael— before our very eyes.

17

PEACE PROGRESSES

Following the UAE announcement on August 13, I was shuttled around "Pebble Beach," the term used for the multiple news network booths on the White House grounds, to be interviewed on the stunning news of peace in the Middle East. I received the same question from every reporter: "Will more Arab nations make peace, and if so, which ones?"

I answered each question identically. The UAE deal was an "icebreaker," and while I would not get ahead of the president in his efforts, I had no doubt that this would lead to more agreements. I was right in my prediction but far from clairvoyant; based upon our engagement we were sure that more peace was on the way.

The UAE deal was not without its controversy. The UAE had been attempting for years to purchase advanced weaponry from the United States and it was rumored that the deal was premised on an agreement by the United States to sell it F-35 joint strike fighter jets, the most advanced military aircraft in the world and used only by Israel within the Middle East. The entire issue was a red herring. The United States could only sell such aircraft to the UAE once the US administration had concluded, and demonstrated to Congress, that the sale would not disturb Israel's "qualitative military edge" within the region. That process was highly technical and relegated to the world of military experts, not politicians. Would peace between Israel and the UAE make it easier for the UAE to purchase better weapons? Almost certainly, as the threat assessment would change in favor of the transaction. But the legally required process for Israel to maintain its qualitative military edge would run its course professionally nonetheless.

Almost immediately after Israel and the UAE made peace, things started to change on the ground in each country. Even with the COVID pandemic, travel began in earnest. Soon the Abu Dhabi Department of Culture and Tourism issued an Emirate-wide announcement that "all hotel establishments are advised to include Kosher food options on room service menus and at all food and beverage outlets in their establishments." The warmth of the people-to-people engagement was truly inspiring.

On August 30, 2020, the first direct commercial flight from Tel Aviv to Abu Dhabi—El Al Flight 971 (UAE's country code)—took off, carrying a senior delegation of Israelis along with Jared Kushner, Avi Berkowitz, Aryeh Lightstone, and other senior American officials. It returned the next day on El Al 972, Israel's country code. Both flights were noteworthy as they were the first Israeli commercial aircraft ever to fly over Saudi Arabian airspace. During the years that John Kerry was secretary of state, he floated the idea of Saudi overflights for Israeli aircraft in exchange for an Israeli settlement freeze. Neither that condition nor any other was required for Israel's use of Saudi airspace.

As Netanyahu described it, this is what Israel had always aspired to: "peace for peace rather than land for peace."

Speculation was abuzz about which nation would follow the UAE on the peace train. On August 25, 2020, after some logistical negotiations by Aryeh and me, Mike Pompeo flew directly from Tel Aviv to the Sudan, the first direct flight of its kind in history. While many expected Sudan to go next, the winner was the Kingdom of Bahrain, which announced on September 3 that it would open its airspace to Israeli flights and pursue normalization. The official announcement among Israel, Bahrain, and the United States would be held within a week.

With everyone looking to the east, a surprise announcement then came from Europe. From the Oval Office, the news came out that Kosovo, a Muslim nation, would normalize with Israel and move its embassy to Jerusalem. This was Robert O'Brien's project, and with this success he assumed a prominent role within the peace team.

Meanwhile, the Palestinians continued to flail. On September 9, they attempted to pass a resolution of the Arab League condemning the Israel-UAE deal. Even though Abbas was reportedly the chair of the meeting, he could not even get it raised for consideration. An Emirati professor of political science was quoted in the Israeli press saying, "The Palestinian delegation found itself rejected at the Arab League . . . this is happening for the first time in history due to the stupidity of the corrupt Palestinian leadership."

On September 11, a day known for the horrors of radical Islamist terrorism, we returned to the Oval Office to formally achieve peace between Israel and Bahrain. I couldn't think of a better way to observe that tragic day. After the parties confirmed on the phone their agreement to make peace, we invited in the press and the president spoke. He thanked me, invited me to speak, and said something that summarized the mission to which I had been assigned:

Our wonderful ambassador to Israel, David Friedman, who has been really something. He's a great lawyer, he's a great talent and a great deal maker and I put him there for a reason, I put him there to get it done . . . just get it done, see if you can bring peace to the Middle East.

I listened to those comments with great emotion. They rang true—not the part about my skills as a lawyer, but the mission that was assigned to me and the hope and expectations of the commander in chief. It was deeply moving to have succeeded in that mission.

I tweeted out later that day that from Israel's treaty with Jordan to the UAE deal took twenty-six years while from the UAE deal to the Bahrain deal took only twenty-nine days. This was heady stuff!

We then announced that a signing ceremony among Israel, UAE, and Bahrain, overseen by the president, would take place on the South Lawn of the White House on September 15.

The ceremony was perfect, from the sunny late summer weather to the soaring emotions. Our team, including the president, had separate bilateral meetings with the delegations from Israel, the UAE, and Bahrain, and then we took our seats on the South Lawn as the four leaders spoke and sat down to sign. The crowd was overwhelmed with joy at the iconic sight of the Abraham Accords being signed. Afterward, a few of us on each side retired for a private lunch at the White House and then I was off to do media interviews the rest of the day.

THAT NIGHT, EXHAUSTED, TAMMY AND I CAUGHT A RIDE BACK TO Israel aboard Prime Minister Netanyahu's chartered plane. I slept for about eight hours and woke to get some coffee. Aryeh Lightstone then approached me and asked if I could give a quick interview with Ariel Kahana, a reporter for *Israel Today*. I agreed to a few questions, having no reason to anticipate the upheaval I was about to cause.

Ariel asked me if, given the rejection by the Palestinians of all that we were doing, I was considering bringing back to the Palestinian leadership Mohammed Dahlan, a former leader now living in UAE. I had never met Dahlan and had never given him a second thought with regard to the Palestinian leadership. I answered the reporter truthfully with, "We're not thinking about it."

The discussion was taped and there was no doubt what I said. But my quote was transcribed in error to read, "We're thinking about it." And with that a grand conspiracy theory was born. Fortunately, I wasn't aware of the error as we pulled into the gate at Ben Gurion and I was able to enjoy the water-cannon salute in honor of the Abraham Accords.

Abbas has always considered Mohammed Dahlan his main rival and he has never liked me, so of course he believed immediately that I was engineering a coup to replace him with Dahlan. My misquote was reported widely in the local press and, even after the correction was noted, some didn't believe it. The Peace Now organization accused me of dropping a trial balloon for regime change. Even Mohammed Dahlan himself felt the need to enter the picture to announce that he would only return to power if the Palestinian people willed it.

That only added fuel to the fire, although few outside Palestinian society were paying attention.

A FEW DAYS LATER, STEVE MNUCHIN, AVI BERKOWITZ, AND I LAUNCHED the first Israeli delegation to Bahrain, this flight denominated El Al 973 for Bahrain's country code. Mnuchin and Berkowitz then flew to Abu Dhabi and returned to Israel on the first Emirati delegation to Israel flown on Etihad Airways. This time the flight had the airline's full insignia and colors, in contrast to the prior flight with humanitarian supplies that had been rejected by the PA. Our meetings with

Israeli and Emirati leaders were inspiring, and Secretary Mnuchin led several advanced discussions with regard to how to really elevate these nascent relationships. The nations had so much in common and such enthusiasm to move forward in peaceful coexistence.

Flush with success over the UAE, Bahrain, and Kosovo, we turned our sights to Sudan. Normalization between Israel and Sudan would create enormous benefits for both countries, both commercially and in terms of security. Unlike with the UAE and Bahrain, Sudan required some give-and-take to move forward. Sudan had two leaders, a military general who was close to Israel and a prime minister who interacted with the Americans. The general was on board early, but the prime minister, like many leaders in the region, apparently thought that America has a bottomless wallet with an insatiable appetite for political gain. In several meetings in Khartoum, Sudan's capital, he overplayed his hand, asking for things that we would never provide. On October 18, 2020, I sat in a lounge in Ben Gurion Airport with Secretary Mnuchin, Avi Berkowitz, and General Correa on a call with Sudanese leadership. Correa made it very clear what the deal was and told the Sudanese the only answer was yes or no. We got a yes. Sudan would exit the notorious list of terrorist states and receive significant humanitarian aid. Other items on its wish list would not be guaranteed. And normalization with Israel would occur immediately. Normalization between Israel and Sudan was announced from the Oval Office on October 23.

Khartoum is known in diplomatic circles for the famous "Khartoum Nos"—the resolution reached at a meeting of the Arab League in Khartoum on September 1, 1967, just eight weeks after the Six-Day War, where the league resolved, "No peace with Israel, no recognition of Israel, and no negotiations with Israel."

Needless to say, it was enormously gratifying that we had converted the three "Khartoum Nos" into a single "Khartoum Yes."

We had also come a long way from the "Kerry Nos"—the spectacularly wrong assertion by John Kerry in 2016 that it was absolutely impossible for Israel to normalize with Arab nations without first making peace with the Palestinians. In Kerry's words, "No, no, no and no!"

I tweeted out the video of his speech, commenting, "Thank God we did not follow this stale, misguided, and conventional wisdom."

One more nation still eluded us: Morocco.

We had been pushing for normalization between Morocco and Israel for more than a year, but Morocco was looking for the United States to recognize its claim to the Western Sahara. There were many students of the issue who agreed that the region would best be served by Moroccan sovereignty, while others, fewer in number, advocated for the rights of the Polisario Front, who claimed the Western Sahara for its people. On December 10, 2020, the president decided to recognize Morocco's claim to the Western Sahara; Morocco, in turn, agreed to normalize with Israel.

It was the right thing to do for all nations.

The Jewish community in Morocco is more than a thousand years old. Approximately one million Israeli Jews are of Moroccan descent. During World War II, King Mohammed V of Morocco went to great effort to save the Jews of his country from the Nazis. Morocco's treatment of Jews soured after Israel declared its independence, causing many Moroccan Jews to emigrate to Israel in the 1950s. Nonetheless, many Israelis maintain warm feelings toward Morocco and have returned to visit and tour.

The reaction within both Israel and Morocco to normalization has been overwhelmingly positive.

The advancement of peace and coexistence between Israel and its neighbors is just beginning. The Saudis—the leaders of the Muslim world—are undoubtedly on a path to normalization. By allowing

Israeli overflights, and by publishing polls showing nearly 80 percent of the Saudi people are ready for peace, the signals are unmistakable, and the opportunity is there for the taking. But it will require careful US engagement and support, which does not appear to be a priority for the Biden administration.

The same is true of other countries in the Gulf, of Indonesia, and even Pakistan. And the Lebanese people, held hostage by Hezbollah, if adequately informed of what could be gained, would gladly resolve their border issues with Israel and be free of Hezbollah's malevolence. Peace between Israel and Lebanon would free up large deposits of natural gas off the Lebanese coast and bring desperately needed currency to the Lebanese people. Of course, that result remains unattainable for as long as Hezbollah has a sponsor in Iran.

THE WORDS "PEACE IN THE MIDDLE EAST" ARE OFTEN USED TO DE-scribe something impossible or at least highly unlikely to occur—as rare as a royal flush in poker or a total eclipse of the sun. But we took the opportunity—the icebreaker—handed us by the UAE and Israel, and scaled it across the region. It is an enormous point of pride.

We did not achieve what we did with a sledgehammer, despite the accusations and condescension of many. Once we firmly broke with the past, we were able to move forward with negotiation and diplomacy. The only thing we took a sledgehammer to was the stale notions of how to achieve peace, and the fatalistic conclusion that peace was unachievable.

For a diplomat, even an untraditional one, there could be no more gratifying achievement.

18

CLEANING UP

By the second week of October, notwithstanding all the successes we had with the Abraham Accords, I felt that we might be coming to the end of our rope. President Trump was in the hospital with COVID-19 and trailing by 10 points in many polls. The lifers in the State Department were just as adept in detecting weakness as in detecting strength. When I was on a roll, they did what I said or at least got out of the way. Now, they weren't returning my calls and were moving at a snail's pace on matters of importance to me.

I decided then to get reenergized for a sprint to the finish. We would leave nothing for a second term and go all out until Inauguration Day. If Trump won, we'd breathe a sigh of relief. If he lost, we'd at least know that we left it all on the field.

The main thing that I was accused of trying to push through before leaving office was actually the one thing over which I had no control—the sale of the ambassador's residence in Herzliya. The conspiracy theorists, and there were many, claimed that I had accelerated the transfer of the house to deprive my successor of the opportunity of moving the embassy back to Tel Aviv.

The theory didn't even make sense. The Jerusalem Embassy Act precluded the return of the embassy to Tel Aviv. The reality was that we were required by law to move the ambassador's residence to Jerusalem, and we accomplished that task with the merger of the Jerusalem consulate into the embassy. Once the residence was in Jerusalem, there was no basis to retain the Herzliya mansion, as beautiful as it was.

The sale was overseen by the State Department's Bureau of Overseas Buildings Operations. They hired brokers, appraisers, and lawyers and ran an open process designed to maximize the value. The sale ended up setting a record for the highest price ever paid for an Israeli residence, yielding a good outcome for the United States Treasury.

One thing that I was committed to get done was the recognition by the State Department that American citizens born in Jerusalem were born in Israel, with their nation of birth reflected on their passports. When the president recognized Jerusalem as Israel's capital in December 2017, I had attempted to right this wrong. But I was boxed out by Secretary Tillerson and never given the opportunity to weigh in on the issue. Tillerson made clear that the past practice of not associating Jerusalem with Israel would remain—not as a matter of principle but, in my view, as a passive-aggressive means of restoring his control over the issue.

I pushed the issue with Mike Pompeo and he supported the change but asked that I work through the issues with the Legal Adviser. It was a heavy lift. The Legal Adviser's office included several of the lawyers responsible for drafting the memo endorsed by Tillerson. Now they were being asked to reverse course. I wrote a lengthy analysis of how the president's recognition created a legal certainty that

Jerusalem was now in Israel; otherwise Jerusalem could not be Israel's capital. That reasoning seemed more than obvious. But a response came that because Jerusalem remained a final status issue with no determination of final boundaries, what if an American citizen about to give birth raced up to the Temple Mount and gave birth alongside the mosque? Would the parents claim the newborn was "born in Israel," thus reflecting a recognition by the United States of Israeli sovereignty over the Temple Mount?

No, I am not making this up!

I pointed out that there are numerous locations around the world where American citizens have choices about how their place of birth appears on their passports. An easy fix here would be to allow American citizens born in Jerusalem to choose Israel as their place of birth, while retaining the option to list Jerusalem instead. It should make almost everyone happy and give life to the reality that Jerusalem was within the State of Israel. With a big steer from Pompeo, we got it done.

But this change called for a very special ceremony. Sixteen years ago, the parents of Menachem Zivotofsky, an American citizen born two years earlier in Jerusalem, applied for a passport for their young son. They listed his place of birth as "Israel." The application was denied. The local consular office would only recognize Menachem's place of birth as "Jerusalem." Menachem had no nation of birth according to the laws of the United States.

The Zivotofsky family brought a lawsuit to enforce the 2002 Foreign Relations Authorization Act, which provided that "for purposes of . . . issuance of a passport of a United States citizen born in the city of Jerusalem, the Secretary shall . . . record the place of birth as Israel." While it seemed like an open-and-shut case, it was anything but. The Zivotofskys argued their case twice before the United States Supreme Court and, after ten years of litigation, walked away empty-handed. The court held that the law they relied upon was unconstitutional as it infringed upon the right of the executive branch to make foreign policy.

After the president's recognition of Jerusalem, counsel for the Zivotofskys contacted me and told me they were going to renew their lawsuit. I told them that they should wait and see if this could be fixed by the State Department. They were skeptical, justifiably, based upon their past experience, but they held their fire. And their patience was rewarded.

On October 30, at a small ceremony in front of the US embassy in Jerusalem, I presented to Menachem Zivotofsky the very first US passport given to an American citizen born in Jerusalem with the place of birth designated as "Israel." I said to Menachem at the ceremony, "After all these years, the United States finally recognizes that you have a nation of birth—the State of Israel."

Another item on my diplomatic "bucket list" was to address a significant defect in three bilateral agreements between Israel and the United States: The Binational Science Foundation, the Binational Industrial Research and Development Foundation, and the Binational Agricultural Research and Development Fund. These three foundations have been around for about fifty years and have produced exceptional collaboration between Israel and the United States in the fields of science, agriculture, and related research. More than $1.5 billion has been spent in these joint endeavors. But there was a limitation that each agreement contained: "Projects financed by the Fund may not be conducted in geographic areas which came under the Administration of the Government of Israel after June 5, 1967, and may not relate to subjects primarily pertinent to such areas."

This was a dirty little secret in the State Department: The United States officially boycotted research and development projects with Israel in Judea and Samaria. I was shocked to find out that this even existed, especially given the bipartisan support in the government against the BDS movement. These agreements were supposed to be entirely apolitical; they were designed to advance science and technology, not to penalize institutions because of where they were located.

It turned out that the bureaucratic challenges to deleting the single offending sentence within the three agreements were daunting. Lawyers appeared out of the ether with byzantine requirements that seemed overly complicated and devoid of purpose. Several different government agencies were said to be implicated, including the Office of the United States Trade Representative, who had the right to insist that no amendment to the agreements be made without a renegotiation between the two nations of an acceptable protocol for the protection of intellectual property. I kept saying, "We just want to delete one sentence." And the response was long, wooden, and with no sense of urgency.

I felt a great deal of passive resistance and sensed that the deep state was counting the days to my dismissal.

I did not take this well. I got in touch with the Prime Minister's Office and scheduled a signing ceremony to amend the agreements with the prime minister for October 27. I reached out to Ariel University, the only fully accredited university in Judea and Samaria and the primary beneficiary of the amendments, to reserve its campus for the ceremony. And I informed everyone involved that the necessary, and only the necessary, approvals must be obtained prior to October 27 or I would inform the secretary of state of all those who stood in the way of the ceremony and contributed to a diplomatic embarrassment.

It turned out that I still had some juice, even with my boss behind in the polls.

The ceremony took place, the amendments were signed by Netanyahu and me, and the United States no longer boycotts academic and research institutions in Judea and Samaria.

Most Israeli papers ran the signing picture of Netanyahu and me on the front pages. They misinterpreted the event completely by referring to the event as a last-ditch attempt to legitimize settlements. There was no need for that—Pompeo already had determined that settlements were legitimate. This event, rather, was designed to protect institutions from the vagaries of politics and to promote cooperation among peoples of diverse backgrounds, regardless of where they resided. Senator James Lankford of Oklahoma got it right in his congratulatory tweet:

> Congrats on moving to allow diverse investment in economic development in the West Bank. This brings Israelis, Palestinians and others together, allowing them to engage in business and forge relationships that are essential to bringing lasting peace.

Signing these amendments was a subtle but significant advancement in not treating Israelis differently based upon their postal code.

There was still some cleanup work to do. The United States required products made in Judea and Samaria to be labeled MADE IN WEST BANK, even where the products were manufactured in Area C, which is under Israeli military and civilian control. This made it far too easy for Israeli products to be subject to boycotts from the BDS movement. Before the Oslo Accords, the entirety of products sold in Judea and Samaria could be labeled MADE IN ISRAEL under US law. Since then, the required labeling changed to WEST BANK. The labeling issues were hypertechnical, but thankfully I was able to enlist my assistant, David Milstein, who had an encyclopedic command of this and so many other policy issues.

The issue was elevated in mid-November when the Court of Justice of the European Union ruled against the Psagot Winery in Samaria and required it to label its wine bottles as originating in an

"Israeli settlement." The State Department noted its disagreement with that ruling as "suggestive of anti-Israel bias" and facilitating "boycotts, divestments and sanctions (BDS) against Israel."

On November 18, 2020, Secretary Pompeo and his wife, Susan, made their last official visit to Israel. We planned a comprehensive agenda for the secretary that tied up the loose ends of his groundbreaking service. Prior to his arrival, I negotiated a fix to the labeling issue with the head of Customs and Border Protection. CBP doesn't engage in geopolitical policy in approving labeling changes; it focuses instead on avoiding confusion for the consumer. I explained to them that the term "West Bank" was itself misleading, as a product emanating from that area could be made under the authority of the Palestinian Authority, Hamas, or the State of Israel. You can't get more confusing than that!

We agreed that products would best be labeled on the basis of who controlled the civil laws within the territory. That would result in "Gaza" for the Gaza Strip, "West Bank" for the territory in Judea and Samaria controlled by the Palestinian Authority (denoted in the Oslo Accords as Areas A, B, and H1 [part of Hebron]), and "Israel" for Areas C and H2 (the other part of Hebron). With CBP's approval, Secretary Pompeo announced the change while he was in Israel.

We then went to the Psagot Winery to celebrate—the first visit by a secretary of state to a Jewish community in Judea and Samaria. Psagot, the victim of an adverse labeling decision by the EU, was at least now able to put MADE IN ISRAEL on its bottles sold in the United States. Grateful for the change in policy, the winery put out a run of wine labeled POMPEO and another labeled FRIEDMAN. Pompeo Wine was a big hit and sold out immediately; I believe that Friedman Wine is still available (probably at a discount). Neither of us is getting any royalties.

The Pompeos and I broke additional ground on that trip. Our

helicopter landed at Qasr al-Yahud in the Jordan Valley where they stood along the banks of the Jordan River at the spot where John the Baptist was said to have baptized Jesus. From there we flew up to Mount Bental in the Golan Heights, another first for a secretary of state.

Before he began his visit, Mike mentioned to me that he had been inspired while he was at West Point by the account of an Israeli soldier, Avigdor Kahalani, who almost single-handedly held off the Syrian Army until reinforcements arrived in the famous "Battle of Tears" during the Yom Kippur War. He asked me if Kahalani was still alive. When we arrived at Bental, Kahalani was there to greet Pompeo. Together, they looked down from the mountain to where the battle took place and Kahalani told his story. Both were deeply moved.

As we were leaving, Kahalani, an Israeli hero, distinguished author, and recipient of the Israeli military's highest honor, the Medal of Valor, came over to me and said in Hebrew, "I like you. You have big balls!"

That may have been the greatest compliment I received in four years of service.

I HAD ONE MORE THING TO GET DONE BEFORE RELINQUISHING MY position. The City of David had greatly moved me as the geographic source for so many of the values that motivated our founding fathers to create the great American Republic. I feared that without some recognition of its special role, the connection of ancient Jerusalem to modern America might be lost. To reinforce this bond, my colleague Paul Packer, the chairman of the US Commission for the Preservation of America's Heritage Abroad, and I jointly recognized the City of David as an American heritage site. A stone plaque reflecting this recognition has been installed at the City of David's entrance.

On January 11, 2021, nine days before leaving office, I was invited to address the Knesset and received their thanks and an award. I spoke at some length but left my colleagues with a particular thought that I felt was important: Israel is now the center of Jewish life in the world, both qualitatively and quantitatively. Israel now is responsible for the survival of Jews in the Diaspora, not the reverse, as was the case in generations past. It is a tremendous responsibility and I wished them luck in discharging it.

On January 17, 2021, I was invited to attend a cabinet meeting of the government of Israel, at which time many of the ministers bade me farewell. Prime Minister Netanyahu was very generous in his praise, offering a lengthy review of what he described as significant and unprecedented accomplishments on behalf of the US-Israel relationship. He also said this:

> I must say that over the years I have met many ambassadors from many countries, including from the US, our great ally, but I can say that there was never a better ambassador than David Friedman in establishing the deep ties between Israel and the US; in correcting the diplomatic injustices that were created over the years in global diplomacy regarding Israel, and in establishing the status of Jerusalem as the capital of Israel, and many other things some of which have yet to be told.

We had the luxury of a full day on the job on January 20, 2021. My posting ended at noon Washington time but that gave me until seven p.m. local time. In a tear-filled moment, I said goodbye to my house staff, who took care of our every need for four years, and then to the many members of my protective detail who literally risked their lives to keep me and my family safe. After hugs all around, it was onward to Jerusalem.

I finished off my tour of duty as it began, with Tammy at my side at the Western Wall. We separated briefly to pray at the men's and women's sections and then joined in the office of the Kotel rabbi, who had greeted us so warmly four years earlier.

Standing at the Wall contemplating the conclusion of my mission, I was overwhelmed by the presence of God in my life. Not prone to tears, I actually focused on mathematics and one of my favorite subjects as a student—probability.

We've all played games with dice and occasionally have rolled the same number multiple times. But the probability of rolling the same number with a single die ten times in a row is 1 in 60,466,176! I considered the fact that my career as ambassador was about as probable as rolling the same number ten times in a row—from meeting Donald Trump, to having outsized success as his lawyer, to his getting through to visit me in a snowstorm, to his running for president and winning, to his selecting me as ambassador, to getting Senate approval given the controversy of my appointment, to having the vision and the influence to move forward with our agenda, to being able to do so without provoking violence, to being able to bring peace, again and again.

This journey was not just improbable. It was so improbable that it was functionally impossible! And yet it happened. And when the impossible happens, the only explanation that I know is the will of God.

And so standing there, at the Western Wall, just minutes before my term expired, I did the single thing that the moment required—I thanked God.

PEACE IS POSSIBLE

On January 10, 2021, *The New York Times*, a harsh critic of mine, profiled my four years in office. The article began, "Love him or hate him, and most people who have paid attention fall into one camp or the other, David M. Friedman will complete his tour of duty in Israel this month having etched his name in history as one of America's most influential envoys."

I didn't set out to be loved or hated or even influential. I set out to strengthen the relationship between the nation of my birth, my home, and my citizenship, and the nation of my faith and my history. I acted out of principle alone, convinced, as I said many times, that support for Israel is a quintessential American value.

Accusations of "dual loyalty" were directed at me from the beginning, often by my coreligionists. It saddened and surprised me but never deterred me. I always felt that I was serving America's best interests and I would never have done anything except serve those interests.

One of America's greatest strengths is its diversity. I have rejoiced on many occasions as American ethnic groups celebrated their backgrounds and heritages, but this occurs all too infrequently among my friends of the Jewish faith. I hope I have made at least a small advancement in the expression of Jewish pride.

The divisions within the American Jewish community are deeply troubling. There are stark divisions within Israeli society as well, but in Israel Jews do not suffer an identity crisis, they just yell at each other. In America, the division doesn't lead to conflict—it leads to assimilation and abandonment of Jewish identity.

The numbers are striking and depressing: In 1941 there were eighteen million Jews in the world. In 1945, after the Holocaust decimated a third of world Jewry, there were twelve million. Today, seventy-six years later, there are only about fifteen million Jews—the Jewish people have only recovered half their loss from the Holocaust in a time period when the world's population has more than doubled!

But the numbers are even worse than that. In 1948, when the State of Israel came into existence, there were five million Jews in America and six hundred thousand Jews in Israel. Today, there remain five million Jews in America but there are seven million Jews in Israel! The entirety of the growth of the Jewish people over the past three generations has been in Israel alone.

What does that tell us about the Jewish communities in Israel and the Diaspora? A lot. Primarily, that they are heading in very different directions. In America, the trend line is very disturbing as the only growing demographic among Jews is the Orthodox. Many predict that the Jewish community in the United States will soon resemble that of Europe—pockets of highly observant Jews among a rapidly shrinking group largely unaffiliated with religious observance or identity. I sincerely hope this trend can be reversed.

Jews have a magnificent four-thousand-year-old history. Many of us pray today in the same language, at the same place, and with the same words that we used two thousand years ago. It gives me great inspiration to be a part of this grand continuum and I truly hope that this will matter to enough people that we will gain sufficient critical mass to pass our traditions to our children and generations yet unborn.

My advice below is free, and it may not be worth more than its cost, but having served four years in this incredible position, I have six final observations that I want to share:

First, one cannot discount the risks that Israel confronts almost daily. Israel has not been at peace with its neighbors for a single day in its seventy-two-year history. It is not situated between the Atlantic, the Pacific, Mexico, and Canada. Rather, it lies between terrorist states or territories controlled by terrorist groups who attack frequently. Very few other nations, and no other democracy, face these risks.

Second, one also cannot discount the very real and deeply perceived existential threats to Israel. Iran has said repeatedly that it will annihilate Israel. In the near future, it could have the means to do so. Israel will not let that happen. As chairman of the Joint Chiefs of Staff, General Mark Milley, an Irish Catholic from Boston, has told me and many others in summing up the Israel Defense Forces, "They will never go back to the ovens, they will fight standing up but never again die kneeling."

Third, the shadow of the Holocaust still informs the Israeli psyche and properly so. Fewer than eighty years ago, a seemingly civilized nation, lovers of art and music, Wagner and Nietzsche, decided to exterminate an entire race of people. While the Nazis are gone, hatred is not. The famous term "Never Again" is repeated often, but to the Jewish people, *it has little meaning disconnected from Israel*. Without Israel, what is the basis to conclude that Jews around the world are safe? Who else is protecting them? Who protected the Cambodians from the Khmer Rouge, who protected the Tutsis in Rwanda, and, even today, who is protecting Uyghurs from the concentration camps maintained by the Chinese Communist Party? While it is hoped that Jews flourish wherever they may reside, more and more, especially outside the United States, they are hedging their bets by applying for Israeli citizenship. Understandably so.

Fourth, America needs Israel every bit as much as Israel needs America. We need Israel's intelligence cooperation, its technological advancements, and its military alliance. This is especially true as America's military footprint in the Middle East shrinks without a corresponding reduction in the threat level. Israel keeps Americans safe at home just as America helps to protect Israel. But even more than the physical manifestations of mutual support, America needs Israel as a means of remaining tethered to its roots, its core values, and its basic freedoms. We are all aware of attempts by the Far Left to cancel America's history because of the imperfections of our predecessors. Israel is our ultimate history and if, God forbid, that history is canceled, our national foundation will be nothing but sand.

Fifth, it's time for Israel to grow up. More than half the nations in the General Assembly are younger than Israel. What are the territorial limits of Israel's borders? How should Israel balance its democratic and religious priorities? What is the right relationship to be achieved with non-Jewish minorities? These are issues for Israel to decide by itself for itself. Israel needs to worry less about what the world thinks and more about what it collectively thinks. I believe that with courage and determination in its self-governance, Israel will get to the right outcome and the world will respect Israel's decisions.

And, finally, peace with the Palestinians is possible. If we learned one thing about the Abraham Accords, it is that the historic conflict between Jews and Muslims is neither religious nor racial nor inevitable. Indeed, many do not even remember why the conflict ever existed. The Israeli-Palestinian conflict can be resolved with bold new Palestinian leadership who place the interest of their people above their own Swiss bank accounts. Inshallah!

The Bible tells us that God will bless those who bless Israel. I can't disagree. As one who worked hard to bring blessings to this Holy Land, I most certainly feel blessed in return.

THE ABRAHAM ACCORDS DECLARATION

We, the undersigned, recognize the importance of maintaining and strengthening peace in the Middle East and around the world based on mutual understanding and coexistence, as well as respect for human dignity and freedom, including religious freedom.

We encourage efforts to promote interfaith and intercultural dialogue to advance a culture of peace among the three Abrahamic religions and all humanity.

We believe that the best way to address challenges is through cooperation and dialogue and that developing friendly relations among States advances the interests of lasting peace in the Middle East and around the world.

We seek tolerance and respect for every person in order to make this world a place where all can enjoy a life of dignity and hope, no matter their race, faith, or ethnicity.

We support science, art, medicine, and commerce to inspire humankind, maximize human potential, and bring nations closer together.

We seek to end radicalization and conflict to provide all children a better future.

We pursue a vision of peace, security, and prosperity in the Middle East and around the world.

In this spirit, we warmly welcome and are encouraged by the progress already made in establishing diplomatic relations between Israel and its neighbors in the region under the principles of the Abraham Accords. We are encouraged by the ongoing efforts to consolidate and expand such friendly relations based on shared interests and a shared commitment to a better future.

Acknowledgments

This is my first book. I hope it is not my last. Perhaps the main reason I hope to write another book is the collaboration I had with Mitchell Ivers. Mitchell is an unabashed liberal and a lover of Israel. He proved to me something that I already knew: When it comes to Israel, what matters is not whether you are on the Right or the Left but rather what is in your heart. Mitchell's heart is in the right place, and his comments always reflected a love for the subject matter, never an attempt to substitute his views for mine. Our discussions were substantive, and when he challenged my thinking, he caused me to refine my writing in a way that contributed significantly to this work.

This is a memoir of my time in public office, and I had the privilege to work with some incredible people, both in the United States and in Israel. On the domestic side, my deepest appreciation goes to Vice President Mike Pence, Secretary of State Mike Pompeo, Secretary of the Treasury Steven Mnuchin, General John Kelly, Jared Kushner, Robert O'Brien, Ambassador Nikki Haley, Jason Greenblatt, Avi Berkowitz, Robert Greenway, Victoria Coates, and General Miguel Correa. Special thanks to my chief of staff, Aryeh Lightstone. And, of course, my sincerest gratitude to my old client and friend who, with no prior political experience, managed to get himself elected president of the United States: Donald Trump.

Israel is an extraordinary country, made so by its incredible people. I was welcomed and embraced by an entire nation, and those gestures will always remain with me. I am grateful for the relationships I forged with Prime Minister Benjamin Netanyahu, Isaac Herzog (now president), General Benny Gantz, General Gabi Ashkenazi, Mossad Director Yossi Cohen, National Security Director Meir Ben Shabbat, Ambassador Ron Dermer, Yoav Horowitz, Naftali Bennett (now prime minister), Rabbi Shmuel Rabinovitch from the Western Wall, the City of David team, and so many others. I wish all of you and your successors *mazal*, *bracha*, *v'hatzlacha* (luck, blessings, and success) in guiding the State of Israel, always with God's help.

As a newcomer to public life, I didn't know what to expect when I was placed in charge of the embassy to Israel. But I did know how to treat people with respect and to encourage and empower talent. I think I did that reasonably well, and the response was enormously gratifying. From my first DCM (deputy chief of mission), Leslie Tsou (now the US ambassador to Oman), to her successor, Jonathan Schrier, to so many skilled and committed diplomats, my thanks for getting on board and helping make history. I could not have done this without your support.

In the ambassador's residence, there was always something going on. Whatever events we held, they were planned and executed flawlessly, thanks to Galit, Chef Daniel, Nomi, Dido, Josephine, Zorayda, Joanne, and Mark. Thank you.

With the second-highest threat profile in the country, it was good to know I had the best bodyguards in the business. Thank you, Moshe, Assaf, Alex, Micky, Roi, Sergey, Sergey, Shlomi, Mony, Yariv, Yossi, Pierre, and so many others for your selfless efforts 24/7!

Finally, if you don't look good, what's the point? Matty, Ziv, David, and the rest of the team, thanks for the thousands of pictures providing a lifetime of memories.

I am indebted to all of you.

Index

About the Author

DAVID FRIEDMAN served as the United States ambassador to Israel from 2017 to 2021. Under his leadership, the United States made unprecedented diplomatic advances, including moving its embassy to Jerusalem, recognizing Israel's sovereignty over the Golan Heights, and, of course, brokering the Abraham Accords. For his efforts, Friedman was nominated for a Nobel Peace Prize and received the National Security Medal. He lives with his wife, Tammy, in Jerusalem.